TENTH EDITION

STRATEGIC MARKET MANAGEMENT

David A. Aaker

Vice-Chairman, Prophet
Professor Emeritus, University of California, Berkeley

WILEY

There is a tide in the affairs of men,
Which, taken at the flood, leads on to fortune;
Omitted, all the voyage of their life
Is bound in shallows and in miseries.
On such a full sea are we now afloat,
And we must take the current when it serves,
Or lose our ventures.
—*William Shakespeare, from Julius Caesar*

VICE PRESIDENT & EXECUTIVE PUBLISHER	George Hoffman
SENIOR EDITOR	Franny Kelly
PROJECT EDITOR	Brian Baker
EDITORIAL ASSISTANT	Jacqueline Hughes
DIRECTOR OF MARKETING	Amy Scholz
SENIOR MARKETING MANAGER	Kelly Simmons
MARKETING ASSISTANT	Marissa Carroll
DESIGN DIRECTOR	Harry Nolan
SENIOR DESIGNER	Maureen Eide
PRODUCT DESIGNER	Allison Morris
SENIOR PRODUCTION MANAGER	Janis Soo
ASSOCIATE PRODUCTION MANAGER	Joel Balbin
PRODUCTION EDITOR	Eugenia Lee
COVER DESIGNER	Kenji Ngieng
COVER PHOTO	© Mimo Khair Photography/Getty Images

This book was set in 10/12 New Caledonia by Thomson Digital and printed and bound by Edwards Brothers Malloy. The cover was printed by Edwards Brothers Malloy.

This book is printed on acid-free paper.

Founded in 1807, John Wiley & Sons, Inc. has been a valued source of knowledge and understanding for more than 200 years, helping people around the world meet their needs and fulfill their aspirations. Our company is built on a foundation of principles that include responsibility to the communities we serve and where we live and work. In 2008, we launched a Corporate Citizenship Initiative, a global effort to address the environmental, social, economic, and ethical challenges we face in our business. Among the issues we are addressing are carbon impact, paper specifications and procurement, ethical conduct within our business and among our vendors, and community and charitable support. For more information, please visit our website: www.wiley.com/go/citizenship.

Library of Congress Cataloging-in-Publication Data

Aaker, David A.
    Strategic market management / David A. Aaker, Vice-Chairman, Prophet Professor Emeritus, University of California, at Berkeley. – Tenth edition.
       pages cm
    Includes index.
      ISBN 978-1-118-58286-2 (pbk.)
1.   Marketing—Management.   2.   Strategic planning.   I. Title.
    HF5415.13.A23 2014
    658.8–dc23

                                                                    2013028806

Printed in the United States of America
10 9 8 7 6 5 4 3 2 1

The thrust of this tenth edition of Strategic Marketing Managements book is to develop business, brand, and marketing strategies that lead to enduring competitive advantage, a task that has become more daunting over the years. In most markets, competitors are reaching parity on basic functional benefits, so marshaling and protecting innovation is more important than ever and requires a strong organization and system to make happen.

Developing and implementing strategies is now very different than it was only a few decades ago when the business environments were more stable and simpler. Every market can now be described as dynamic. As a result, firms need to be able to adapt strategies in order to stay relevant. It is a challenging but exciting time, full of opportunities as well as threats.

The unique aspects of the book remain its inclusion of:

- A business strategy definition that includes product/market scope, value proposition, assets and competencies, and functional area strategies. Too often the business strategy concept is vague and ill-defined, leading to a diffused focus and weak communication.

- A structured strategic analysis, including a detailed customer, competitor, market, environmental, and internal analysis leading to understanding of market dynamics that is supported by a summary flow diagram, a set of agendas to help start the process, and a set of planning forms

- Concepts of strategic commitment, opportunism, and adaptability and how they can and should be blended together

- Growing the business by energizing the business, leveraging the business, creating new business, and going global. Each option has its own risks and rewards and all should be on the table.

- Bases of a value proposition and strong brands. A strategy without a compelling value proposition will not be market driven or successful. Brand assets that will support a business strategy need to be developed.

- Creating synergetic marketing with silo organizations defined by products or countries. All organizations have multiple products and markets, and creating cooperation and communication instead of competition and isolation is becoming an imperative.

Coping with a dynamic market requires customer-driven strategies and creativity. The book emphasizes a customer perspective and the fact that every strategy should have a value proposition that is meaningful to customers. It also details paths to break out of the momentum of the past to generate creative strategies and offerings.

THE TENTH EDITION

The tenth edition, which is again compact, retains the same chapter structure as the ninth edition. But there are significant additions and changes.

There is a new chapter on "Toward a Strong Brand Relationship." A business strategy depends on creating sustainable competitive advantage based in part of relevant assets and competences. A loyal customer base is the ultimate competitive advantage because it is as asset that shields the business from competitors. It makes it easier and more economical to retain existing customers and to create new ones. Three routes to the creation of such a loyal base are presented in the chapter:

- **Touchpoint management.** A brand experience is created by brand touchpoints that occur any time a person interacts with the brand. Five steps to improve touchpoints are identifying current and desired touchpoints, internally evaluating their importance, having customers evaluate them, prioritizing, and developing a touchpoint plan.

- **Customer's sweet spot.** In developing a marketing programs and a strong relationship, connect to the customer's "sweet spot," a topic or activity that is related to what is important and involving to customers. A "sweet spot" program is more likely to stimulate a social network, create brand energy and interest, enhance brand liability and credibility, and form a relationship. To proceed, identify a "sweet spot" and then create or locate a program that the brand can be imbedded.

- **Go beyond functional benefits.** Broaden the brand concept to include emotional benefits (When I buy this brand, I feel _____), self-expressive benefits (When I buy or use this brand, I am _____), or social benefits (When I buy or sue this brand, the type of people I relate to are _____).

In addition to updating throughout, there is new or substantially revised material based on recent research and writings by influential thinkers. New topics include:

- Pitfalls in strategy development
- Digitally enabled customer research
- Big data
- Going green
- Social programs as a value proposition
- Getting brand credit for social programs
- Creating "must haves" that define new categories or subcategories
- Category exemplars
- Sourcing innovation in emerging markets
- What makes a good CMO change agent.

There are also new case studies to illustrate such as the revitalization of Lincoln, the Haas School's brand identity, P&G's "Thank You Mom" campaign, Pampers' Village, Red Bull events, Coca-Cola World Wildlife partnership, California Casualty's energizer programs, Whole Foods Markets, Panasonic's experience in China, and more.

AN OVERVIEW

This book begins with an introduction that defines a business strategy, followed by an overview of the book and a discussion of the CMO and strategy. Part I of the book, Chapters 2 to 6, covers strategic analysis, with individual chapters on customer, competitor, market, environmental, and internal analysis. Part II of the book, Chapters 7 to 16, covers the development and implementation of strategy. Chapter 7 discusses the concept of a sustainable competitive advantage (SCA) and introduces three strategy styles—strategic commitment, strategic opportunism, and strategic adaptability. Chapter 8 provides an overview of the scope of strategic choices by describing several value propositions. Chapter 9 shows how brand equity can be created and leveraged. Chapter 10 discusses how to develop a deep relationship with customers. The next four chapters discuss growth options: Chapter 11 covers energizing the business, Chapter 12 leveraging the business, Chapter 13 creating new businesses, and Chapter 14 global strategies. Chapter 15 discusses setting priorities and the disinvestment option. Finally, Chapter 16 introduces organizational dimensions and their role in supporting strategy and moving silo organization toward cooperation and communication.

THE AUDIENCE

This book is suitable for any course in a school of management or business that focuses on the management of strategies. In particular, it is aimed at:

- The marketing strategy course, which could be titled strategic market management, strategic market planning, strategic marketing, or marketing strategy
- The policy or entrepreneur course, which could be titled strategic management, strategic planning, business policy, entrepreneurship, or policy administration

The book is also designed to be used by managers who need to develop strategies in dynamic markets—those who have recently moved into general management positions or who run small businesses and want to improve their strategy development and planning processes. Another intended audience is general managers, top executives, and planning specialists who would like an overview of recent issues and methods in strategic market management.

A WORD TO INSTRUCTORS

The tenth edition is accompanied by a revision of the extensive instructor's resource guide authored by David Aaker and Jim Prost, which is located on the book's companion Web site at www.wiley.com/college/aaker. The resource guide has a PowerPoint presentation organized by chapter, a set of lecture suggestions for each chapter, a test bank, several course outlines, case notes, and three extra cases: Xerox, Samsung, and Intel.

ACKNOWLEDGMENTS

This book could not have been created without help from my friends, students, reviewers, and colleagues at the Haas School of Business and at Prophet. Their help and support are appreciated. Special thanks to the insightful reviewers—Gilbert Frisbie, Indiana University, and Jeffrey Stoltman, Wayne State University—who helped me make some major changes in this edition.

I am pleased to be associated with the publisher, John Wiley, a class organization, and its superb editors—Rich Esposito (who helped give birth to the first edition), John Woods, Tim Kent, Ellen Ford, Jeff Marshall, Judith Joseph, Jayme Heffler, and Franny Kelly (who guided this as well as the last edition). It is a pleasure to be supported by competent, supportive professionals who are fun to be around. Eugenia Lee guided the manuscript through production with competence and good humor, and Brian Baker expertly coordinated the editorial and production process.

I owe a debt to some Nestlé people who helped with the pet food example used in the planning forms. Leah Porter, John Carmichael, and Mark Brodeur helped to develop the case study and updated it through several editions.

My thanks to my friend and colleague Jim Prost, a strategy teacher extraordinaire who made numerous suggestions about prior editions of the book and has helped me create a world-class teacher's resource manual.

This book is dedicated to the women in my life—my wife, Kay, and my three girls, Jennifer, Jan, and Jolyn, who all provide stimulation and support.

David A. Aaker
February 2013

CONTENTS

CHAPTER ONE

Strategic Market Management—An Introduction and Overview

Plans are nothing, planning is everything.
—*Dwight D. Eisenhower*

Even if you are on the right track, you'll get run over if you just sit there.
—*Will Rodgers*

If you don't know where you're going, you might end up somewhere else.
—*Casey Stengel*

All markets today are dynamic. Change is in the air everywhere, and change affects strategy. A winning strategy today may not prevail tomorrow. It might not even be relevant tomorrow.

There was a time, not too many decades ago, when the world held still long enough for strategies to be put into place and refined with patience and discipline. The annual strategic plan guided the firm. That simply is no longer the case. New products, product modifications, subcategories, technologies, applications, market niches, segments, media, channels, and on and on are emerging faster than ever in nearly all industries—from snacks to fast food to automobiles to financial services to software. Multiple forces feed these changes, including Internet technologies, the rise of China and India, trends in healthy living, energy crises, political instability, and more. The result is markets that are not only dynamic but risky, complex, and cluttered.

Such convoluted markets make strategy creation and implementation far more challenging. Strategy has to win not only in today's marketplace but also in tomorrow's, when the customer, the competitor set, and the market context may all be different. In environments shaped by this new reality, some firms are driving change. Others are adapting to it. Still others are fading in the face of change. How do you develop successful strategies in dynamic markets? How do you stay ahead of competition? How do you stay relevant?

The task is challenging. Strategists need new and refined perspectives, tools, and concepts. In particular, they need to develop competencies around five management tasks—strategic analysis, innovation, getting control of multiple business units, developing sustainable competitive advantages (SCAs), and developing growth platforms.

Strategic analysis. The need for information about customers, competitors, and trends affecting the market is now higher than ever. Further, the information needs to be continuous, not tied to a planning cycle, because a timely detection of threats, opportunities, strategic problems, or emerging weaknesses can be crucial to getting the response right. There is an enhanced premium on the ability to predict trends, project their impact, and distinguish them from mere fads. That means resources need to be invested and competencies created in terms of getting information, filtering it, and converting it into actionable analysis.

Innovation. The ability to innovate is one key to successfully winning in dynamic markets as numerous empirical studies have shown. Innovation, however, turns out to have a host of dimensions. There is the organizational challenge of creating a context that supports innovation. There is the brand portfolio challenge of making sure that the innovation is owned and not a short-lived market blip. There is the strategic challenge of developing the right mix of innovations that ranges from incremental to transformational. There is the execution challenge; it is necessary to turn innovations into offerings in the marketplace. There are too many examples of firms that owned an innovation and let others bring it to market.

Multiple businesses. It is the rare firm now that does not operate multiple business units defined by channels and countries in addition to product categories and subcategories. Decentralization is a century-old organizational form that provides for accountability, a deep understanding of the product or service, being close to the customer, and fast response, all of which are good things. However, in its extreme form, autonomous business units can lead to the misallocation of resources, redundancies, a failure to capture cross-business potential synergies, and confused brands. A challenge, explored in Chapter 16, is to adapt the decentralization model so that it no longer inhibits strategy adaptation in dynamic markets.

Creating sustainable competitive advantages (SCAs). Creating strategic advantages that are truly sustainable in the context of dynamic markets and dispersed business units is challenging. Competitors all too quickly copy product and service improvements that are valued by customers. What leads to SCAs in dynamic markets? One possible cornerstone is the development of assets such as brands, distribution channels, or a customer base or competencies such as social technology skills or sponsorship expertise. Another is leveraging organizational synergy created by multiple business units, which is much more difficult to copy than a new product or service.

Developing growth platforms. Growth is imperative for the vitality and health of any organization. In a dynamic environment, stretching the organization in creative ways becomes an essential element of seizing opportunities and adapting to changing circumstances. Growth can come from revitalizing core businesses to make them growth platforms as well as by creating new business platforms.

This book is concerned with helping managers identify, select, implement, and adapt market-driven business strategies that will enjoy a sustainable advantage in dynamic markets, as well as create synergy and set priorities among business units. The intent is to provide concepts, methods, and procedures that will lead to competencies in these five crucial management tasks—and, ultimately, to high-quality strategic decision making and profitable growth.

The book emphasizes the customer because in a dynamic market, a customer orientation is likely to be successful. The current, emerging, and latent motivations and unmet needs of customers need to influence strategies. Because of this, every strategy needs to have a value proposition that is meaningful and relevant to customers.

This first chapter starts with a very basic but central concept, that of a business strategy. The goal is to lend structure and clarity to a term that is widely employed but seldom defined. It continues with an overview of the balance of the book, introducing and positioning many of the subjects, concepts, and tools to be covered. Finally, the role of marketing in business strategy will be discussed. There is a significant trend for marketing to have a seat at the strategy table and to see the chief marketing officer (CMO) as empowered to create growth initiatives.

WHAT IS A BUSINESS STRATEGY?

Before discussing the process of developing sound business strategies, it is fair to address two questions. What is a business? What is a business strategy? Having groups of managers provide answers to these basic questions shows that there is little consensus as to what these basic terms mean. Clarifying these concepts is a necessary start toward a winning, adaptable strategy.

A Business

A business is generally an organizational unit that has (or should have) a defined strategy and a manager with sales and profit responsibility. The organizational unit can be defined by a variety of dimensions, including product line, country, channels, or segments. An organization will thus have many business units that relate to each other horizontally and vertically.

There is an organizational and strategic trade-off in deciding how many businesses should be operated. On one hand, it can be compelling to have many units because then each business will be close to its market and potentially capable of developing an optimal strategy. Thus, a strategy for each country or each region or each major segment may have some benefits. Too many business units become inefficient, however, and result in programs that lack scale economies and fail to leverage the strategic skills of the best managers. As a result, there is pressure to aggregate businesses into larger entities.

Business units can be aggregated to create a critical mass, to recognize similarities in markets and strategies, and to gain synergies. Businesses that are too small to justify a strategy will need to be aggregated so that the management structure can be supportable. (Of course, two business units can share some elements of operations, such as a sales force or a facility, to gain economies without merging.) Businesses that have similar market contexts and business strategies will be candidates for aggregation to leverage shared knowledge. Another aggregation motivation is to encourage synergies among business units when the combination is more likely to realize savings in cost or investment or create a superior value proposition.

There was a time when firms developed business strategies for decentralized business units defined by product, countries, or segments. These business strategies were then packaged or aggregated to create a firm strategy. That time has passed. There also now needs to be a firm strategy that identifies macro trends and strategy responses to these trends as a firm, allocates resources among business units, and recognizes synergy potentials. So there needs to be a strategy for the Ford company and perhaps the SUV group as well as the Ford Explorer, a major SUV brand.

A BUSINESS STRATEGY

Four dimensions define a business strategy: the product-market investment strategy, the customer value proposition, the assets and competencies, and the functional strategies and programs. The first specifies where to compete, and the remaining three indicate how to compete to win, as suggested by Figure 1.1.

The Product-Market Investment Strategy: Where to Compete

The scope of the business, and the dynamics within that scope, represent a very basic strategy dimension. Which sectors should receive investments in resources and management attention? Which should have resources withdrawn or withheld? Even for a small organization, the allocation decision is key to strategy.

The scope of a business is defined by the products it offers and chooses not to offer, by the markets it seeks to serve and not serve, by the competitors it chooses to compete with and to avoid, and by its level of vertical integration. Sometimes the most important business scope decision is what products or segments to avoid because such a decision, if followed by discipline, can conserve resources needed to compete successfully elsewhere. Peter Drucker, the management guru, challenged executives to specify—"What is our business and what should it be? What is not our business, and what should it not be?" Such a judgment can sometimes involve painful choices to divest or liquidate a business or avoid an apparently attractive opportunity. Chapter 15 discusses disinvestment judgments and why they are hard to make and easy to avoid.

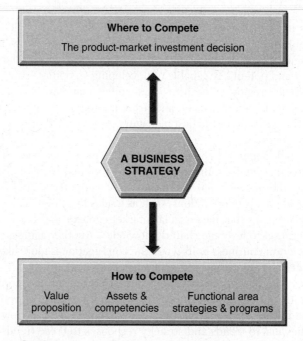

Figure 1.1 A Business Strategy

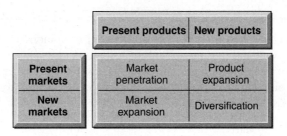

Figure 1.2 Product-Market Growth Directions

Many organizations have demonstrated the advantages of having a well-defined business scope. Williams-Sonoma offers products for the home and kitchen. IBM turned around its firm under the direction of Lou Gerstner in part by dialing up its service component and more recently by expanding its software footprint. P&G focuses on a broad spectrum of nonfood consumer goods with an emphasis on current or potential billion dollar brands such as Tide/Arial, Always/Whisper, Crest, Iams, Pampers, Charmin, Bounty, Pantene, Downy/Lenor, and Gillette. Wal-Mart and Amazon have a wide scope that generates both scale economies and a one-stop shopping value proposition.

More important than the scope is the scope dynamics. What product markets will be entered or exited in the coming years? As Figure 1.2 suggests, growth can be generated by bringing existing products to new markets (market expansion), bringing new products to existing markets (product expansion), or entering new product markets (diversification).

Expanding or changing the product-market mix can help the organization achieve growth and vitality and can be a lever to cope with the changing marketplace by seizing opportunities as they emerge. During the first five years of the Jeff Immelt era, GE changed its focus and character by investing in healthcare, energy, water treatment, home mortgages, and entertainment (by buying Universal) while exiting markets for insurance, industrial diamonds, business outsourcing based in India, and a motor division. In addition, the percentage of revenue sources outside the United States grew from 40 percent to nearly 50 percent.

There are risks as the scope expansion ventures further from the core business—the firm's offering may not be distinctive, problems in operations may arise, or the firm's brands may be inadequate to support the expansion. Despite similarities in manufacturing and distribution, Bausch & Lomb's attempt to move from eye care to mouthwash was a product and brand failure. An effort by a manufacturing equipment company to go into robots failed when it could not create or acquire the needed technology. Attention and resources may also be diverted from the core business, causing it to weaken.

The investment pattern will determine the future direction of the firm. Although there are obvious variations and refinements, it is useful to conceptualize the investment alternatives for each product-market as follows:

- Invest to grow (or enter the product market)
- Invest only to maintain the existing position
- Milk the business by minimizing investment
- Recover as many of the assets as possible by liquidating or divesting the business

The Customer Value Proposition

Ultimately, the offering needs to appeal to new and existing customers. There needs to be a value proposition that is relevant and meaningful to the customer and is reflected in the positioning of the product or service. To support a successful strategy, it should be sustainable over time and be differentiated from competitors. The customer value proposition can involve elements such as providing to customers:

- A good value (Wal-Mart)
- Excellence on an important product or service attribute such as getting clothes clean (Tide)
- The best overall quality (Lexus)
- Product line breadth (Amazon)
- Innovative offerings (3M)
- A shared passion for an activity or a product (Harley-Davidson)
- Global connections and prestige (CitiGroup)

Home Depot and Lowe's are home improvement retailers with very different value propositions. Home Depot has very austere, functional stores that are designed to appeal to contractors and homeowners on the basis of function and price. Lowe's strategy since 1994 has been to have a softer side, a look that would be comfortable to women. Thus, their stores are well lit, the signs colorful and clear, the floors spotless, and the people friendly and helpful. Years later, the Lowe's strategy has traction, and Home Depot, with a service issue caused by a cost reduction program, is attempting to adjust its own value proposition.

Assets and Competencies

The strategic assets or competencies that underlie the strategy often provide a sustainable competitive advantage (SCA). A *strategic competency* is what a business unit does exceptionally well—such as a customer relationship program, social technology, manufacturing, or promotion—that has strategic importance to that business. It is usually based on knowledge or a process. A strategic asset is a resource, such as a brand name or installed customer base, that is strong relative to that of competitors. Strategy formulation must consider the cost and feasibility of generating or maintaining assets or competencies that will provide the basis for a sustainable competitive advantage.

Assets and competencies can involve a wide spectrum, from Web sites to R&D expertise to a symbol such as the Michelin Man. For P&G, it is consumer understanding, brand building, innovation, go-to-market capability, and global scale.[1] Although a strong asset or competency is often difficult to build, it can result in an advantage that is significant and enduring.

The synergies obtained from operating a business that spans product markets can be an important asset and SCA source. Synergies, which are significant because they are based on organizational characteristics that are not easily duplicated, can come in many forms. Two businesses can reduce costs by sharing a distribution system, sales force, or logistics system, as when Gillette acquired Duracell (and later was itself acquired by P&G). Synergy can also be based on sharing the same asset, as with the HP brand shared by the dozens of business units or a competence such as Toyota's ability to manage manufacturing plants across brands and countries. Another source of synergy is the sharing of functional area strategies across business units. The Ford organization may be able to sponsor the World Cup, for instance, while Ford SUVs in the United Kingdom could not. Still another synergy source is the sharing of R&D. P&G aggregates brands such as Head & Shoulders, Aussie, Infusion, and Pantene into a hair care category not just to provide shelf space guidance to retailers and to create promotions more easily but also to manage the use of product innovations. Finally, a combination of products can provide a value proposition. Some software firms have aggregated products in order to provide a systems solution to customers; Microsoft Office is one example.

The ability of assets and competencies to support a strategy will in part depend on their power relative to competitors. To what extent are the assets and competencies strong and in place? To what extent are they ownable because of a symbol trademark or long-standing investment in a capability? To what extent are they based on organizational synergy that others cannot duplicate?

Assets and competencies can also provide points of parity. For dimensions such as perceived quality, distribution strength, or manufacturing cost, the goal may be not to create an advantage but to avoid a disadvantage. When an asset or competency is close enough to that of a competitor to neutralize the latter's strength, then a point of parity has been achieved. Such parity can be a key to success; if the perceived quality of a Wal-Mart offering is regarded as adequate, its price perception will then win the day.

Functional Strategies and Programs

A target value proposition, or a set of assets and competencies, should mandate some strategy imperatives in the form of a supportive set of functional strategies or programs. These strategies and programs, in turn, will be implemented with a host of tactical programs with a short-term perspective.

Functional strategies or programs that could drive the business strategy might include a:

- Customer relationship program
- Brand-building strategy
- Social technology strategy
- Communication strategy
- Information technology strategy
- Distribution strategy
- Global strategy
- Quality program
- Sourcing strategy
- Logistical strategy
- Manufacturing strategy

The need for functional strategies and programs can be determined by asking a few questions. What must happen for the firm to be able to deliver on the value proposition?

PITFALLS IN STRATEGY DEVELOPMENT

Richard Rumelt, noted strategy thinker, has identified some common pitfalls in developing a business strategy.[2] First, a central problem or threat is ignored. The problem could be a quality issue or a receding marketplace. A competitor's innovation or a customer trend could represent a threat. A strategy developed as if either did not exist will be doomed. Second, the strategy is a long to-do list with no sense of what is important. There needs to be a sense of priorities. Third, a set of goals is assumed to be a strategy. It is not. There can and should be goals, especially long-term goals that go beyond financial measures, but a strategy needs to address the four key dimensions in order to find a path to success. Finally, a strategy is a fluffy description of some desired state of affairs. We will become the industry leaders while increasing margins and addressing sustainability challenges. Rather, the strategies and accompanying action plans need to be specific.

Are the assets and competencies needed in place? Do they need to be created, strengthened, or supported? How?

Criteria to Select Business Strategies

The principal criteria useful for selecting alternatives can be grouped around five general questions:

- ***Is the ROI attractive?*** Creating a value proposition that is appealing to customers may not be worthwhile if the investment or operating cost is excessive. Starbucks opened in Japan in 1996 in the Ginza district and grew to over 400 units, many of which were in the highest rent areas. The result was a trendy brand but one that was vulnerable to competitors, who matched or exceeded Starbucks' product offerings and were not handicapped with such high overhead because they developed less costly sites.

- ***Is there a sustainable competitive advantage?*** Unless the business unit has or can develop a real competitive advantage that is sustainable over time in the face of competitor reaction, an attractive long-term return will be unlikely. To achieve a sustainable competitive advantage, a strategy should exploit organizational assets and competencies and neutralize weaknesses.

- ***Will the strategy have success in the future?*** A strategy needs to be able to survive the dynamics of the market, with its emerging threats and opportunities. Either the strategy components should be expected to have a long life or the strategy should be capable of adapting to changing conditions. In that context, future scenarios (described in Chapter 5) might be used to test the robustness of the strategy with respect to future uncertainties.

- ***Is the strategy feasible?*** The strategy should be within both the financial and human resources of the organization. It also should be internally consistent with other organizational characteristics, such as the firm's structure, systems, people, and culture. These organizational considerations are covered in Chapter 16.

EXPANDING THE BUSINESS SCOPE

In his classic article "Marketing Myopia," Theodore Levitt explained how firms that define their business myopically in product terms can stagnate even though the basic customer need they serve is enjoying healthy growth.[3] Because of a myopic product focus, others gain the benefits of growth. In contrast, firms that regard themselves as being in the transportation rather than the railroad business, the energy instead of the petroleum business, or the communication rather than the telephone business are more likely to exploit opportunities.

The concept is simple. Define the business in terms of the basic customer need rather than the product. Visa has defined itself as being in the business of enabling customers to exchange value (any asset, including cash on deposit, the cash value of life insurance, or the equity in a home) for virtually anything anywhere in the world. As the business is redefined, both the set of competitors and the range of opportunities are often radically expanded. After redefining its business, Visa estimated that it had reached only 5 percent of its potential given the new definition.

Defining a business in terms of generic need can be extremely useful for fostering creativity, generating strategic options, and avoiding an internally oriented product focus.

- ***Does the strategy fit with the other strategies of the firm?*** Are the sources and uses of cash flow in balance? Is organizational flexibility reduced by an investment in financial or human resources? Is potential synergy captured by the strategy?

STRATEGIC MARKET MANAGEMENT

Strategic market management is a system designed to help management create, change, or retain a business strategy and to create strategic visions. A *strategic vision* is a projection of a future strategy or sets of strategies. The realization of an optimal strategy may involve a delay because the firm is not ready or the emerging conditions are not yet in place. A vision will provide direction and purpose for interim strategies and activities and can inspire those in the organization by providing a purpose that is worthwhile and ennobling.

Strategic market management involves decisions with a significant, long-term impact on the organization. The resulting business strategies can be costly in terms of time and resources to reverse or change. In fact, emerging strategic decisions can mean the difference between success, mediocrity, failure, or even survival.

Developing the right business strategies is a basic goal, but it is not the end of the story. With a business strategy in hand, the task is to:

- Continuously challenge the strategy in order to make sure that it remains relevant to the changing marketplace and responsive to emerging opportunities
- Ensure that the organization develops and retains the necessary skills and competencies to make the strategy succeed
- Implement the strategy with energy and focus; the best strategy badly implemented will be a failure (or worse, jeopardize the firm)

Figure 1.3 provides a structure for strategic market management and for this book. A brief overview of its principal elements and an introduction to the key concepts will be presented in this chapter.

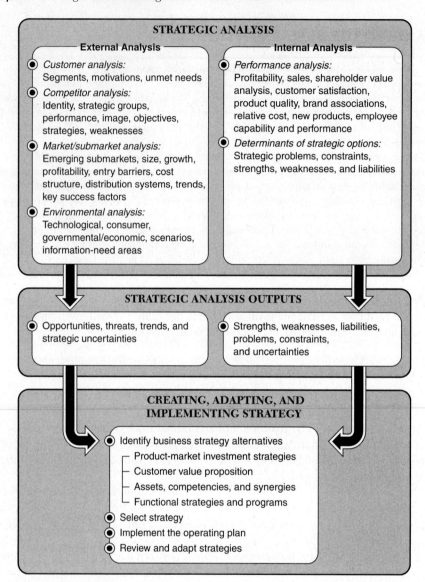

STRATEGIC ANALYSIS

External Analysis

- *Customer analysis:* Segments, motivations, unmet needs
- *Competitor analysis:* Identity, strategic groups, performance, image, objectives, strategies, weaknesses
- *Market/submarket analysis:* Emerging submarkets, size, growth, profitability, entry barriers, cost structure, distribution systems, trends, key success factors
- *Environmental analysis:* Technological, consumer, governmental/economic, scenarios, information-need areas

Internal Analysis

- *Performance analysis:* Profitability, sales, shareholder value analysis, customer satisfaction, product quality, brand associations, relative cost, new products, employee capability and performance
- *Determinants of strategic options:* Strategic problems, constraints, strengths, weaknesses, and liabilities

STRATEGIC ANALYSIS OUTPUTS

- Opportunities, threats, trends, and strategic uncertainties
- Strengths, weaknesses, liabilities, problems, constraints, and uncertainties

CREATING, ADAPTING, AND IMPLEMENTING STRATEGY

- Identify business strategy alternatives
  - Product-market investment strategies
  - Customer value proposition
  - Assets, competencies, and synergies
  - Functional strategies and programs
- Select strategy
- Implement the operating plan
- Review and adapt strategies

Figure 1.3 Overview of Strategic Management

External Analysis

External analysis, summarized in Figure 1.3, involves an examination of the relevant elements external to an organization—customers, competitors, markets and submarkets, and the environment or context outside of the market. Customer analysis, the first step of external analysis and a focus of Chapter 2, involves identifying the organization's customer segments and each segment's motivations and unmet needs. Competitor analysis, covered in Chapter 3, attempts to identify competitors (both current and potential) and describe their performance, image, strategy, and strengths and weaknesses. Market analysis, the subject of Chapter 4, aims to determine the attractiveness of the market and submarkets and to understand the dynamics of the market so that threats and opportunities can be detected and strategies adapted. Environmental analysis, the subject of Chapter 5, is the process of identifying and understanding emerging opportunities and threats created by forces in the context of the business.

The external analysis should be purposeful, focusing on key outputs: the identification of present and potential opportunities, threats, trends, strategic uncertainties, and strategic choices. There is a danger in being excessively descriptive. Because there is literally no limit to the scope of a descriptive study, the result can be a considerable expenditure of resources with little impact on strategy.

The frame of reference for an external analysis is typically a defined strategic business unit (SBU), but it is useful to conduct the analysis at several levels. External analyses of submarkets sometimes provide critical insights; for example, an external analysis of the mature beer industry might contain analyses of the import and nonalcoholic beer submarkets, which are growing and have important differences. It is also possible to conduct external analyses for groups of SBUs, such as divisions, that have characteristics in common. For instance, a food products company might consider analyses of the healthy-living segment and food trends that could span operating units within the firm.

Internal Analysis

Internal analysis, presented in Chapter 6 and summarized in Figure 1.3, aims to provide a detailed understanding of strategically important aspects of the organization. Performance analysis looks not only at sales and return on assets but also measures of customer satisfaction and loyalty, quality, brand image, costs, and new product activity. The identification and assessment of organizational strengths and weaknesses will guide strategic priorities, including both the development of new strategies and the adaptation of existing ones.

GALLO: A CASE STUDY

Gallo, despite producing roughly one of every four bottles of wine sold in the United States (primarily in the form of cheap wines sold under the Gallo name), thought it had to adapt to a strong market trend to premium varietals.

One vehicle was the launching of the premium Gallo of Sonoma brand, which enjoyed several significant potential SCAs. The grapes available to Gallo from Sonoma County in northern California (whose climate, some say, is superior to the famous Napa region), coupled with the company's willingness and ability to make great wine, have resulted in a product that has won some major international wine competitions. In addition, the brand gained synergies from Gallo's substantial distribution clout and operational scale efficiencies.

The decision to put the Gallo name on the new line undoubtedly created a huge liability, but it also had some compensating advantages. First, it permitted the business to leverage the credibility and personality of a third-generation family winemaker, Gina Gallo. Second, it boosted the pride of the organization and its partners in an aspect of the business (winemaking) that is at the core of its values. Finally, the seeming incongruity of Gallo making a fine wine could appeal to the wine tastemakers of the world by giving them a chance to prove that they are above labels.

The success of Gallo of Sonoma emboldened Gallo to radically change the business and brand strategy. Gallo of Sonoma became the Gallo Family Vineyards Sonoma, one of four Gallo Family brands. The Gallo value brands were retired, and other brands in the portfolio took on the value role.

Creating, Adapting, and Implementing Strategy

After describing strategic analysis, the book turns to the creation, adaptation, and implementation of strategy. How do you decide on the business scope? What are the alternative value propositions, and how do they guide strategy development? What assets and competencies will provide points of advantage, and which will aim for points of parity? What functional strategies and programs will lead to strategic success? What growth options will receive investment? Is the core business to be the source of growth, or is there a need to move beyond the core? What is to be the global strategy? How should the business units be prioritized? Should there be disinvestment in the business portfolio? How can the organization be adapted so that it supports rather than constrains strategy?

Chapter 7 discusses the concept of an SCA and the slippery concept of synergy before introducing three strategic philosophies—strategic commitment, strategic opportunism, and strategic adaptability. These strategy styles provide a good overview of ways to manage strategy in the face of dynamic markets. Chapter 8 provides an overview of the scope of strategic choices by describing over a dozen possible value propositions, each of which provides an umbrella over a business strategy. Chapter 9 shows how brand equity, a key asset and adaptability lever, can be created and used. Chapter 10 discusses how to develop a deep relationship with customers. The next four chapters discuss growth options: Chapter 11 covers energizing the business, Chapter 12 leveraging the business, Chapter 13 creating new businesses, and Chapter 14 global strategies. Chapter 15 discusses the disinvestment option, an important and often overlooked dimension of the investment decision. Finally, Chapter 16 introduces organizational dimensions and their role in strategy choice and implementation and discusses the problems engendered by product-autonomous and country-autonomous silo organizational units and how to replace competition and isolation with cooperation and communication.

Strategic Market Management—The Objectives

Strategic market management is intended to:

- *Precipitate the consideration of strategic choices.* What external events are creating opportunities and threats to which a timely and appropriate reaction should be generated? What strategic issues face the firm? What strategic options should be considered? The alternative to strategic market management is usually to drift strategically, becoming absorbed in day-to-day problems. Nothing is more tragic than an organization that fails because a strategic decision was not addressed until it was too late.

- *Help a business cope with change.* If a particular environment is extremely stable and the sales patterns are satisfactory, there may be little need for meaningful strategic change—either in direction or intensity. In that case, strategic market management is much less crucial. However, most organizations now exist in rapidly changing and increasingly unpredictable environments and therefore need approaches for coping strategically.

- *Force a long-range view.* The pressures to manage with a short-term focus are strong, but they frequently lead to strategic errors.

- *Make visible the resource allocation decision.* Allowing allocation of resources to be dictated by the political strengths or inertia (i.e., the same strategy as last year) is too easy. One result of this approach is that the small but promising business with "no problems" or the unborn business may suffer from a lack of resources, whereas larger business areas may absorb an excessive amount.

- ***Aid strategic analysis and decision making.*** Concepts, models, and methodologies are available to help a business collect and analyze information and address difficult strategic decisions.
- ***Provide a strategic management and control system.*** The focus on assets and competencies and the development of objectives and programs associated with strategic thrusts provide the basis for managing a business strategically.
- ***Provide both horizontal and vertical communication and coordination systems.*** Strategic market management provides a way to communicate problems and proposed strategies within an organization to product and country business units; in particular, its vocabulary adds precision and its processes help coordinate and encourage synergy.

The Planning Cycle

Too often an annual planning exercise is perceived as strategy development when the output is not strategy but an operating and resource budget that specifies financial targets, hiring plans, and investment authorizations. Research at McKinsey involving a survey of over 700 executives suggests ways to make the strategy development process more effective.[4] In particular, a strategy process should:

- **Start with the issues.** CEOs say that planning should focus on anticipating big challenges and spotting important trends. Strategy choice will be well served by identifying the key associated strategic issues. One CEO asks the business leaders in his firm to imagine how a set of specific trends will affect their business. Another creates a list of three to six priorities for each business to form a basis for discussion.
- **Bring together the right people.** In particular, it is not enough to have staff people involved but also the people who will implement the strategy, the decision makers. Also, in order to foster synergies and strategies that span product or country organizational silos, it is worthwhile to have relevant teams of businesses represented.
- **Adapt planning cycles to the businesses.** It is unrealistic to say that all businesses need to have planning exercises each year. Some may need it every other year or even every third year. Also, trends, events, or issues should trigger a strategy review even if it is not in the annual cycle.
- **Implement a strategy performance system.** Too many businesses fail to follow up on strategy development. As a result, it becomes a rather empty exercise. Major strategic initiatives should have measurable progress goals as well as end objectives. What will be the barrier to success? What needs to happen for the strategy to be on track?

MARKETING AND ITS ROLE IN STRATEGY

Marketing has seen its strategic role growing over the years. The question for each organization is whether the CMO (chief marketing officer) and his or her team have a seat at the strategy table or are relegated to being tactical implementers of tasks such as managing the advertising program. The view that marketing is tactical is changing; it is now more and more frequently being accepted as being part of the strategic management of the organization. Given the definition of a business strategy and the structure of strategic market management, the roles that marketing can and should play become clearer.

One marketing role is to be the primary driver of the strategic analysis. The marketing group is in the best position to understand the customers, competitors, market and submarkets, and environmental forces and trends. By managing marketing research and market data, it controls much of the information needed in the external analysis. Marketing should also take the lead in the internal analysis with respect to selected assets (such as the brand portfolio and the distribution channel) and competencies (such as new product introduction and the management of sponsorships).

A second role is to drive growth strategy for the firm. Growth options are either based on or dependent on customer and market insights, and marketing therefore should be a key driver. In fact, a study by Booz Allen and Hamilton of some 2,000 executives found that a small but growing number of firms (9 percent) describe the CMO as a growth champion involved in all strategic levers relating to growth.[5]

A third role is to deal with the dysfunctions of product and geographic silos. Although all functional groups need to deal with this problem, marketing is often on the front lines. The corporate brand and major master brands usually span silos, and a failure to exercise some central control and guidance will result in inefficiencies and inconsistencies that can be damaging to one or more business strategies. Business-spanning marketing programs such as sponsorships or distribution channels need to be actively managed if opportunities are to be realized and waste and inefficiency are to be avoided.

A fourth role of marketing is to participate in the development of business strategies. This role is best understood by detailing the relationship between marketing and business strategies.

Marketing vs. Business Strategies

A marketing strategy is a subset of a business strategy and involves the same four components, although the scope is restricted to marketing. It includes the allocation of the marketing budget across product markets, the customer value proposition by segment, marketing assets and competencies, and the strategies of the functional areas of marketing. The marketing budget allocation decision should follow the lead of the strategic priorities, but it should also consider the effectiveness of marketing programs. If there are two business units with equal strategic importance and one has marketing programs that are much more effective than the other, the allocation of the marketing budget should be affected. This implies that there is a process to project the effectiveness of marketing programs that is common across silos, a challenge for most firms.

There are contexts in which the marketing strategy adapts to the business strategy and other contexts in which it influences or even drives the business strategy.

The product-market investment decision will be influenced by judgments that marketing is best able to provide about the health and competitor vitality of product markets. Further, customer research–based segmentation strategies that both identify and prioritize customer segments will be relevant to the business investment decision.

The value proposition will in most cases be driven by the marketing strategy because it will be informed by the customer insights of the marketing team and its partners that are close to the customers. The marketing team should be charged with developing the value proposition and adapting it to the various product markets and the changing market contexts as opposed to being an organizational unit that simply implements the value proposition dictated by the business strategy. Marketing ought to be the voice of the customer in the strategy discussion, making sure that the value proposition is based on substance and is meaningful to the customer.

Because the marketing assets and competencies are always an important subset of those underlying a business strategy, marketing will have a role in their identification, creation, and prioritization. The marketing strategy will involve marketing assets such as brand (Unilever) or distribution (Frito-Lay) and competencies such as sponsorship expertise (Nike) or new product introduction capability (P&G). In contrast, a business strategy will include assets such as plants (HP), technology (Oracle), and outsourcing partners (GAP) and competencies such as R&D capability (TI), manufacturing expertise (Toyota), and logistics (Wal-Mart).

Finally, the ability of the marketing team to be effective in developing and implementing functional strategies will often be crucial to the success of a business strategy. Marketing strategies will employ the functional strategies of marketing such as branding, advertising, social technology, media, call centers, training of customer contact people, and so on. A business strategy, of course, will involve a wider array of functional strategies getting into manufacturing, plant locations, executive hiring outside marketing, firm wide compensation plans, and so on.

Thus, marketing is a partner, usually a key partner, in the development and implementation of a business strategy. The conceptualization of a business and marketing strategy as having four dimensions helps illuminate the nature of that relationship. The firms that are able to achieve success over time are those that realize that marketing should have a strong voice in business strategy.

KEY LEARNINGS

- Strategy needs to be developed and executed in the context of a dynamic market. To cope, it is important to develop competencies in strategic analysis, innovation, managing multiple business, and developing SCAs and growth platforms.

- A business strategy includes the determination of the product-market investment strategy, the customer value proposition, assets and competencies, and the functional area strategy. A marketing strategy involves the allocation of the marketing budget over product markets, the customer value proposition by segment, the marketing assets and competencies, and the strategies of the functional areas of marketing.

- Strategic market management, a system designed to help management create, change, or retain a business strategy and to create strategic visions, includes a strategic analysis of the business to identify existing or emerging opportunities, threats, trends, strategic uncertainties, information need areas, scenarios, and strategic alternatives. It should precipitate strategic choices, help a business cope with change, force a long-term view, make visible resource allocations, aid strategy analysis and decisions, provide management and control systems, and enhance communication and coordination.

- The CMO role has grown over the years and is now often charged with being a partner in developing strategies and a vehicle to deal with the dysfunctions of the product-market silos.

FOR DISCUSSION

1. What is a business strategy? Do you agree with the definition proposed? Illustrate your answer with examples. Consider one of the following firms. Read the description of a business strategy in the text. Go to the firm's Web site and use it to gain an understanding of the business strategy. Look at elements such as the products and services offered, the history of the firm, and its values. What is the business strategy? What are the firm's product markets? What are its value propositions? How are the value propositions delivered? What assets and competencies exist? What strategic options? Consider the scope question raised by Levitt. What would be a narrow and broad scope specification?

   a. Dell

   b. P&G (Tide, Pampers)

   c. Citicorp (Citibank)

   d. A firm of your choice

2. In question 1, identify the marketing as opposed to the business strategy.

3. Consider the Gallo strategic decision. Describe how you would go about evaluating that decision.

4. Apply the marketing-myopia concept to print media, magazines, and newspapers. What is the implication?

5. Which criteria to pick a strategy would you consider most important? Why? How would the context affect your answer?

6. Which quote at the front of the chapter do you find the most insightful? Why? Under what circumstances would its implications not hold?

NOTES

1. A. G. Lafley, "What Only the CEO Can Do," *Harvard Business Review*, May 2009, p. 58.

2. Richard Rumelt, "The Perils of Bad Strategy," *McKinsey Quarterly*, 2011, Number 1, pp. 30–39.

3. Theodore Levitt, "Marketing Myopia," *Harvard Business Review*, July–August 1960, pp. 45–56.

4. Renee Dye and Olivier Sibony, "How to Improve Strategic Planning," *McKinsey Quarterly*, Number 3, 2007, pp. 41–49.

5. Constantine von Hoffman, "Armed with Intelligence," *BrandWeek*, May 29, 2006, pp. 17–20.

STRATEGIC ANALYSIS

CHAPTER TWO

External and Customer Analysis

The purpose of an enterprise is to create and keep a customer.
—*Theodore Levitt*

Consumers are statistics. Customers are people.
—*Stanley Marcus*

Before you build a better mousetrap, it helps to know if there are any mice out there.
—*Mortimer B. Zuckerman*

Developing or adapting strategy in a dynamic market logically starts with external analysis, an analysis of the factors external to a business that can affect strategy. The first four chapters of Part One present concepts and methods useful in conducting an external analysis. The final chapter of Part One turns to internal analysis: the analysis of the firm's performance, strengths, weaknesses, problems, liabilities, and constraints.

EXTERNAL ANALYSIS

A successful external analysis needs to be directed and purposeful. There is always the danger that it will become an endless process resulting in an excessively descriptive report. In any business there is no end to the material that appears potentially relevant. Without discipline and direction, volumes of useless descriptive material can easily be generated.

Affecting Strategic Decisions

The external analysis process should not be an end in itself. Rather, it should be motivated throughout by a desire to affect strategy. As Figure 2.1 shows, an external analysis can impact strategy directly by suggesting strategic decision alternatives or influencing a choice among them. More specifically, it should address questions such as:

- Should existing business areas be liquidated, milked, maintained, or targeted for investment?
- Should new business areas be entered?

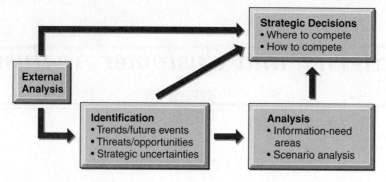

Figure 2.1   The Role of External Analysis

- What are the value propositions? What should they be?
- What assets and competencies should be created, enhanced, or maintained?
- What strategies and programs should be implemented in functional areas? What should be the positioning strategy, segmentation strategy, distribution strategy, brand-building strategy, manufacturing strategy, and so on?

Additional Analysis Objectives

Figure 2.1 also suggests that an external analysis can contribute to strategy indirectly by identifying:

- Significant trends and future events
- Threats and opportunities
- Strategic uncertainties that could affect strategy outcomes

A significant trend or event, such as concern about saturated fat or the emergence of a new competitor, can dramatically affect the evaluation of strategy options. A new technology, which can represent both a threat to an established firm and an opportunity to a prospective competitor, can signal new business arenas.

Strategic Uncertainties

Strategic uncertainty is a particularly useful concept in conducting an external analysis. If you could know the answer to one question prior to making a strategic commitment, what would that question be? If a property casualty insurance company were to consider whether to add earthquake insurance to its line, important strategy uncertainties might include the following:

- What will be the potential losses of a major earthquake?
- What will be the impact on the customer base of failing to offer coverage?
- Could coverage be provided in partnerships?

Strategic uncertainties focus on specific unknown elements that will affect the outcome of strategic decisions. "Should earthquake coverage be added?" is a strategic decision, whereas

Strategic Uncertainties	Strategic Decisions
• Will a major firm enter?	• Investment in a product market
• Will a tofu-based dessert product be accepted?	• Investment in a tofu-based product
• Will a technology be replaced?	• Investment in a technology
• Will the dollar strengthen against an offshore currency?	• Commitment to offshore manufacturing
• Will computer-based operations be feasible with current technology?	• Investment in a new system
• How sensitive is the market to price?	• A strategy of maintaining price parity

Strategic Uncertainties	Second-Level Strategic Uncertainties
• What will be the future demand of an ultrasound test?	• Performance improvements? • Competitive technological developments? • Financial capacity of healthcare industry?

Figure 2.2 Strategic Uncertainties

"What are the potential losses from a major earthquake?" is a strategic uncertainty. Most strategic decisions will be driven by a set of these uncertainties.

Below are some examples of strategic uncertainties and the strategic decisions to which they might relate. A single strategic uncertainty can often lead to additional sources of strategic uncertainty. One common strategic uncertainty, as portrayed in Figure 2.2, is what the future demand for a product (such as ultrasound diagnostic equipment) will be. Asking, "On what does that depend?" will usually generate additional strategic uncertainties. One uncertainty might address technological improvements, whereas another might consider the technological development and cost/benefit levels achieved by competitive technologies. Still another might look into the financial capacity of the healthcare industry to continue capital improvements. Each of these strategic uncertainties can, in turn, generate still another level of strategic uncertainties.

Analysis

There are three ways of handling uncertainty, as suggested by Figure 2.1. First, a strategic decision can be precipitated because the logic for a decision is compelling and/or because a delay would be costly or risky. Second, it may be worthwhile to attempt to reduce the uncertainty by information acquisition and analysis of an information-need area. The effort could range from a high-priority task force to a low-key monitoring effort. The level of resources expended will depend on the potential impact on strategy and its immediacy. Third, the uncertainty could be modeled by a scenario analysis.

A scenario is an alternative view of the future environment that is usually prompted by an alternative possible answer to a strategic uncertainty or by a prospective future event or trend. Is the current popularity of vitamin-enhanced waters a fad, or does it indicate a solid growth area? Such a question could be the basis for a positive and a negative scenario. Each could be associated with very different environmental profiles and strategy recommendations. In Chapter 5, information-need areas and scenario analysis are covered in more detail.

A host of concepts and methods are introduced in this and the following three chapters. It would, of course, be unusual to use all of them in any given context, and the strategist should resist any compulsion to do so. Rather, those that are most relevant to the situation at hand should be selected. Furthermore, some areas of analysis will be more fruitful than others and will merit more effort.

External Analysis as a Creative Exercise

In part, external analysis is an exercise in creative thinking. In fact, there is often too little effort devoted to developing new strategic options and too much effort directed to solving operational problems of the day. The essence of creative thinking is considering different perspectives, and that is exactly what an external analysis does. The strategist is challenged to look at strategy from the perspectives of customer, competitor, market, and environment as well as from an internal perspective. Within each there are several subdimensions; in Figure 1.3, more than two dozen are identified. The hope is that by examining strategy from different viewpoints, options will be generated that would otherwise be missed.

The Level of Analysis—Defining the Market

An external analysis of what? To conduct an external analysis, the market or submarket boundaries need to be specified. The scope of external analysis can involve an industry broadly defined (sporting goods), narrowly defined (high performance skis), or using a scope definition that falls in between such as:

- Ski clothing and equipment
- Skis and snowboards
- Downhill skis

The level of analysis will depend on the organizational unit and strategic decisions involved. A sporting goods company, such as Wilson, will be making resource decisions across sports and thus needs to be concerned with the whole industry. A ski equipment manufacturer may only be concerned with elements of sporting goods relating to skis, boots, and clothing. The maker of high-performance skis might be interested in only a subsegment of the ski industry. One approach to defining the market is to specify the business scope. The scope can be identified in terms of the product market and in terms of the competitors. Relevant, of course, are the future product market and competitors as well as the present ones.

There is always a trade-off to be made. A narrow scope specification will inhibit a business from identifying trends and opportunities that could lead to some attractive options and directions. Thus, a maker of downhill skis may want to include snowboards and cross-country skis because they represent business options or because they will impact the ski equipment business. On the other hand, depth of analysis might be sacrificed when the scope is excessively broad. A more focused analysis may generate more insight.

The analysis usually needs to be conducted at several levels. The downhill ski and snowboard industry might be the major focus of the analysis. However, an analysis of sporting goods might suggest and shed light on some substitute product pressures and market trends. Also, an analysis may be needed at the segment level (e.g., high-performance skis) because entry, investment, and strategy decisions are often made at that level. Furthermore, the key success factors could differ for different product markets within a market or industry. One approach is a layered analysis, with the primary level receiving the most depth of analysis. Another approach could be multiple analyses, perhaps consecutively conducted. The first analysis might stimulate an opportunity that would justify a second analysis on a submarket.

When Should an External Analysis Be Conducted?

There is often a tendency to relegate the external analysis to an annual exercise. Each year, of course, it may not require the same depth as the initial effort. It may be more productive to focus on a part of the analysis in the years immediately following a major effort.

The annual planning cycle can provide a healthy stimulus to review and change strategies. However, a substantial risk exists in maintaining external analysis as an annual event. The need for strategic review and change is often continuous. Information sensing and analysis therefore also need to be continuous. The framework and concepts of external analysis can still play a key role in providing structure even when the analysis is continuous and addresses only a portion of the whole.

External analysis deliberately commences with customer and competitor analyses because they can help define the relevant industry or industries. An industry can be defined in terms of the needs of a specific group of customers—those buying fresh cookies on the West Coast, for instance. Such an industry definition then forms the basis for the identification of competitors and the balance of external analysis. An industry such as the cookie industry can also be defined in terms of all its competitors. Because customers have such a direct relationship to a firm's operation, they are usually a rich source of relevant operational opportunities, threats, and uncertainties.

THE SCOPE OF CUSTOMER ANALYSIS

In most strategic market-planning contexts, the first logical step is to analyze the customers. Customer analysis can be usefully partitioned into an understanding of how the market segments, an analysis of customer motivations, and an exploration of unmet needs. Figure 2.3 presents a basic set of questions for each area of inquiry.

SEGMENTATION
- Who are the biggest customers? The most profitable? The most attractive potential customers? Do the customers fall into any logical groups based on needs, motivations, or characteristics?
- How could the market be segmented into groups that would require a unique business strategy?

CUSTOMER MOTIVATIONS
- What elements of the product/service do customers value most?
- What are the customers' objectives? What are they really buying?
- How do segments differ in their motivation priorities?
- What changes are occurring in customer motivation? In customer priorities?

UNMET NEEDS
- Why are some customers dissatisfied? Why are some changing brands or suppliers?
- What are the severity and incidence of consumer problems?
- What are unmet needs that customers can identify? Are there some of which consumers are unaware?
- Do these unmet needs represent leverage points for competitors or a new business model?

Figure 2.3 Customer Analysis

SEGMENTATION

Segmentation is often the key to developing a sustainable competitive advantage. In a strategic context, *segmentation* means the identification of customer groups that respond differently from other groups to competitive offerings. A segmentation strategy couples the identified segments with a program to deliver an offering to those segments. Thus, the development of a successful segmentation strategy requires the conceptualization, development, and evaluation of a targeted competitive offering.

A segmentation strategy should be judged on three dimensions. First, can a competitive offering be developed and implemented that will be appealing to the target segment? Second, can the appeal of the offering and the subsequent relationship with the target segment be maintained over time despite competitive responses? Third, is the resulting business from the target segment worthwhile, given the investment required to develop and market an offering tailored to it? The concept behind a successful segmentation strategy is that within a reduced market space, it is possible to create a dominant position that competitors will be unwilling or unable to attack successfully.

How Should Segments Be Defined?

The task of identifying segments is difficult, in part, because in any given context there are literally hundreds of ways to divide up the market. Typically, the analysis will consider five, ten, or more segmentation variables. To avoid missing a useful way of defining segments, it is important to consider a wide range of variables. These variables need to be evaluated on the basis of their ability to identify segments for which different strategies are (or should be) pursued.

The most useful segment-defining variables for an offering are rarely obvious. Among the variables frequently used are those shown in Figure 2.4.

CUSTOMER CHARACTERISTICS

- Geographic
  - Small Southern communities as markets for discount stores
- Type of organization
  - Computer needs of restaurants versus manufacturing firms versus banks versus retailers
- Size of firm
  - Large hospital versus medium versus small
- Lifestyle
  - Jaguar buyers tend to be more adventurous, less conservative than buyers of Mercedes-Benz and BMW
- Sex
  - Mothers of young children
- Age
  - Cereals for children versus adults
- Occupation
  - The paper copier needs of lawyers versus bankers versus dentists

PRODUCT-RELATED APPROACHES

- User type
  - Appliance buyer—home builder, remodeler, homeowner
- Usage
  - Concert—season ticket holders, occasional patrons, nonusers
- Benefits sought
  - Dessert eaters—those who are calorie-conscious versus those who are more concerned with convenience
- Price sensitivity
  - Economy-sensitive Honda Civic buyer versus the luxury Mercedes-Benz buyer
- Competitor
  - Users of competing products
- Application
  - Professional users of chain saws versus homeowners
- Brand loyalty
  - Those committed to Heinz ketchup versus price buyers

Figure 2.4 Examples of Approaches to Defining Segments

The first set of variables describes segments in terms of general characteristics unrelated to the product involved. Thus, a bakery might be concerned with geographically defined segments related to communities or even neighborhoods. A consulting company may specialize in the hospitality industry. A fast food firm in the United States may target Hispanics because this segment is projected to grow at a significant rate on its way to tripling its size by 2050.

Demographics are particularly powerful for defining segments, in part because a person's life stage affects his or her activities, interests, and brand loyalties. Another reason is that demographic trends are predictable. Such trends are discussed in Chapter 5. Gold Violin, recognizing this trend, has established itself as a source of products designed for the active elderly. Specialized items such as a talking watch, a bed-vibrating alarm clock, a doorknob turner, and a lighted hands-free magnifier (all with tasteful, attractive designs) are just some of the Gold Violin products that appeal to this long-ignored demographic segment.

Another demographic play is represented by the Toyota Scion xB, which is a small car with a funky design (tall, angular, and boxy), and the Scion iB, the world's smallest four seat car, both aimed at Generation Y, the so-called echo boomers. The average age of a Toyota buyer is 48, the company's inexpensive entries are considered boring, and Scion is an effort to become relevant and interesting to a key target segment. To create a buzz around Scion xB when it was introduced, Toyota targeted the 15 percent of the echo-boomer target market seen as "leaders and influencers"—those who encourage their peers to gravitate to a new style, whether it be in music, sports, or cars.[1]

The second category of segment variables includes those that are related to the product. One of the most frequently employed is usage. A bakery may follow a very different strategy in serving restaurants that rely heavily on bakery products than in serving those that use fewer such products. A manufacturer of lawn equipment may design a special line for a large customer such as Wal-Mart but sells through distributors using another brand name for other outlets. Four other useful segment variables are benefits, price sensitivity, loyalty, and applications.

Benefits

If there is a most useful segmentation variable, it would be benefits sought from a product, because the selection of benefits can determine a total business strategy. In gourmet frozen dinners and entrées, for example, the market can be divided into buyers who are calorie conscious, those who focus on nutrition and health, those interested in taste, and price-conscious buyers. Each segment implies a very different strategy.

The athletic shoe industry segments into serious athletes (small in number but influential), weekend warriors, and casual wearers using athletic shoes for street wear. Recognizing that the casual wearer segment is 80 percent of the market and does not really need performance, several shoe firms have employed a style-focused strategy as an alternative to the performance strategy adopted by such firms as Nike.

Price Sensitivity

The benefit dimension representing the trade-off between low price and high quality is both useful and pervasive; hence, it is appropriate to consider it separately. In many product classes, there is a well-defined breakdown between those customers concerned first about price and others who are willing to pay extra for higher quality and features. General merchandise stores,

THE MALE SHOPPER[2]

The male shopper has been long ignored. A segmentation scheme provides insight into how males differ and suggests strategies for appealing to very different segments.

The Metrosexual. An affluent urban sophisticate, age 20 to 40, who loves to buy and looks for trendy, prestigious, and high-quality products. Into men's grooming, expensive haircuts. Think Polo Ralph Lauren, Beiersdorf, and Banana Republic.

The Retrosexual. Traditional male behavior, into football and NASCAR, rejects feminism, nostalgic for the way things were, prefers below-casual clothing, not into moisturizers for men. Think Levi's, Nike, Old Spice, Burger King, and Target.

The Modern Man. Between "metro" and "retro," this shopper shares their interests but does not go overboard. A sophisticated consumer in his twenties or thirties, he is comfortable with women but does not shop with them. Think Gap, Macy's, and fast casual restaurants.

The Dad. Good income. Involved in the family shopping. Efficient shopper. More functional clothing. Think Nordstrom's, McDonald's, and Amazon.

The Maturiteen. More savvy, responsible, and pragmatic than earlier generations of teens. A technology master adept at online research and buying. Sony, Adidas, Old Navy, Circuit City, and Internet sites of all types do well.

for example, form a well-defined hierarchy from discounters to prestige department stores. Automobiles span the spectrum from the Honda Civic to the Buick LaCrosse to the Lexus 460. Airline service is partitioned into first class, business class, and economy class. In each case, the segment dictates the strategy.

Loyalty

Brand loyalty, an important consideration in allocating resources, can be structured using a loyalty matrix as shown in Figure 2.5. Each cell represents a very different strategic priority and can justify a very different program. Generally, it is too easy to take the loyal customer for granted. However, a perspective of total profits over the life of a customer makes the value of an increase in

	Low Loyalty	Moderate Loyalty	Loyal
Customer	Medium	High	Highest
Noncustomer	Low to Medium	High	Zero

Figure 2.5 The Brand Loyalty Matrix: Priorities

loyalty more vivid. Thus, the highest priority is to retain the existing loyal customer base and, if possible, increase their commitment intensity and perhaps encourage them to talk to others.

The key is often to reward the loyal customer by living up to expectations consistently, providing an ongoing relationship, and offering extras that surprise and delight.

The loyalty matrix suggests that the moderate loyals, including those of competitors, should also have high priority because they represent one route to increase the size of the loyal segment. Using the matrix involves estimating the size of each of the six cells, identifying the customers in each group, and designing programs that will influence their brand choice and loyalty level. The brand loyal noncustomer is a low priority because the cost to attract is usually prohibitive unless a competitor misstep provides an opportunity. The nonloyal group will have a reduced long-term value because they will be easily enticed by a price deal.

Applications

Some products and services, particularly industrial products, can best be segmented by use or application. A laptop computer may be needed by some for use while traveling, whereas others may use it at the office. One segment may use a computer primarily for Internet access, while others may use it for editing documents or for data analysis. Some might use a four-wheel drive for light industrial hauling, and others may buy primarily for recreation.

Christiansen et al. argue that an application focus is more likely to lead to successful new products and marketing programs then other segmentation schemes.[3] They illustrate by telling the story of a milkshake seller that found that many consumers bought the product in the morning in order to help them kill time while driving to work and provide energy to tide them over until lunch. Being efficient to buy and capable of being consumed with only one hand were therefore critical. Such an insight leads to ideas like making the shake thicker (so it takes longer to consume), making the purchase even more efficient with buyer cards, and adding fruit to make it more interesting in the context of a boring commute. The basic concept is that ideas for products and marketing programs are more likely to come from a deep understanding of how the product is used than by understanding the customer. The success of Arm & Hammer in extending its business can be credited to a focus on applications involving deodorizing (carpets, kitty litter, clothes, underarms, and refrigerators).

Multiple Segments vs. a Focus Strategy

Two distinct segmentation strategies are possible. The first focuses on a single segment, which can be much smaller than the market as a whole. Wal-Mart, now the largest U.S. retailer, started by concentrating on cities with populations under 25,000 in eleven south central states—a segment totally neglected by its competition, the large discount chains. This rural geographic focus strategy was directly responsible for several significant SCAs, including an efficient and responsive warehouse supply system; a low-cost, motivated workforce; relatively inexpensive retail space; and a lean and mean, hands-on management style. Union Bank, California's fifth largest bank, makes no effort to serve individuals and thus provides a service operation tailored to business accounts that is more committed and comprehensive than those of its competitors.

An alternative to a focusing strategy is to involve multiple segments. General Motors provides the classic example. In the 1920s, the firm positioned the Chevrolet for price-conscious buyers; the Cadillac for the high end; and the Oldsmobile, Pontiac, and Buick for well-defined segments in between. A granulated potato company has developed different strategies for reaching fast-food chains, hospitals and nursing homes, and schools and colleges.

In many industries, aggressive firms are moving toward multiple-segment strategies. Campbell Soup, for example, makes its nacho cheese soup spicier for customers in Texas and California and offers a Creole soup for southern markets and a red-bean soup for Hispanic markets. In New York, Campbell uses promotions linking Swanson frozen dinners with the New York Giants football team, and in the Sierra Nevada Mountains, skiers are treated to hot soup samples. Developing multiple strategies is costly and often must be justified by an enhanced aggregate impact.

There can be important synergies between segment offerings. For example, in the alpine ski industry, the image developed by high-performance skis is important to sales at the recreational-ski end of the business. Thus, a manufacturer that is weak at the high end will have difficulty at the low end. Conversely, a successful high-end firm will want to exploit that success by having entries in the other segments. A key success factor in the general aviation industry is a broad product line, ranging from fixed-gear, single-engine piston aircraft to turboprop planes, because customers tend to trade up and will switch to a different firm if the product line has major gaps.

CUSTOMER MOTIVATIONS

After identifying customer segments, the next step is to consider their motivations: What lies behind their purchase decisions? And how does that differ by segment? It is helpful to list the segments and the motivation priorities of each, as shown in Figure 2.6 for air travelers.

Internet retailers have learned that there are distinct shopper segments, and each has a very different set of driving motivations.[4]

- *Newbie shoppers*—need a simple interface, as well as a lot of hand-holding and reassurance.
- *Reluctant shoppers*—need information, reassurance, and access to live customer support.
- *Frugal shoppers*—need to be convinced that the price is good and they don't have to search elsewhere.
- *Strategic shoppers*—need access to the opinions of peers or experts and choices in configuring the products they buy.

Segment	Motivation
Business	Reliable service, convenient schedules, easy-to-use airports, frequent-flyer programs, and comfortable service
Vacationers	Price, feasible schedules

Figure 2.6 Customer Motivation Grid: Air Travelers

- ***Enthusiastic shoppers***—need community tools to share their experiences, as well as engaging tools to view the merchandise and personalized recommendations.
- ***Convenience shoppers***—(the largest group) want efficient navigation, a lot of information from customers and experts, and superior customer service.

Some motivations will help to define strategy. A truck, for example, might be designed and positioned with respect to power. Before making such a strategic commitment, it is crucial to know where power fits in the motivation set. Other motivations may not define a strategy or differentiate a business but may instead represent a dimension for which parity performance must be obtained or the battle will be lost. If the prime motivation for buyers of gourmet frozen-food dinners is taste, a viable firm must be able to deliver at least acceptable taste.

Determining Motivations

As Figure 2.7 suggests, consumer motivation analysis starts with the task of identifying motivations for a given segment. Although a group of managers can identify motivations, a more valid list is usually obtained by getting customers to discuss the product or service in a systematic way. Why is it being used? What is the objective? What is associated with a good or bad use experience? For a motivation such as car safety, respondents might be asked why safety is important. Such probes might result in the identification of more basic motives, such as the desire to feel calm and secure rather than anxious.

Customers can be accessed with group or individual interviews. Griffin and Hauser of the MIT Quality Function Deployment (QFD) program compared the two approaches in a study of food-carrying devices.[5] They found that individual interviews were more cost-effective and that the group processes did not generate enough extra information to warrant the added expense. They also explored the number of interviews needed to gain a complete list of motivations and concluded that twenty to thirty will cover 90 to 95 percent of the motivations.

The number of motivations can be in the hundreds, so a second task is to cluster them into groups and subgroups. Affinity charts developed by a managerial team are commonly used. Each team member is given a set of motives on cards. One member puts a motive on the table or pins it to a wall, and the others add similar cards to the pile until there is a consensus that the piles represent reasonable groupings. An alternative is to use customers or groups of customers to sort the motives into piles. The customers are then asked to select one card from each pile that best represents their motives. Although managers gain buy-in and learning by going through the process themselves, Griffin and Hauser report that in the twenty applications at one firm, the managers considered customer-based approaches better representations than their own.

Figure 2.7 Customer Motivation Analysis

BUYER HOT BUTTONS

Motivations can be categorized as important or unimportant, yet the dynamics of the market may be better captured by identifying current buyer hot buttons. Hot buttons are motivations whose salience and impact on markets are significant and growing. What are buyers talking about? What are stimulating changes in buying decisions and use patterns?

In consumer retail food products, for example, hot buttons include:

- **Freshness and naturalness.** Grocery stores have responded with salad bars, packaged precut vegetables, and efforts to upgrade the quality and selection of their fresh produce.
- **Healthy eating.** Low fat, particularly saturated and trans fat, is a prime driver, but concern about sodium, sugar, and processed foods is also growing and affecting product offerings in most food categories.
- **Ethnic eating.** A growing interest in ethnic flavors and cooking such as Asian, Mediterranean, and Caribbean cuisines has led to an explosion of new offerings. Brands usually start in ethnic neighborhoods, move into natural-food and gourmet stores, and finally reach the mainstream markets.
- **Gourmet eating.** The success of Williams-Sonoma and similar retailers reflects the growth of gourmet cooking and has led to the introduction of a broader array of interesting cooking aids and devices.
- **Meal solutions.** The desire for meal solutions has led to groups of products being bundled together as a meal and to a host of carryout prepared foods offered by both grocery stores and restaurants.
- **Low-carb foods.** The influence of low-carb diets has created a demand for reduced-carb food variants in both grocery stores and restaurants.
- **Convenience.** Shoppers have taken convenience to a new level with frozen dinners and cake mixes and even canned soup considered to demand too much preparation. Open and eat is the key. Snacks and yogurt deliver.

A third task of customer motivation analysis is to determine the relative importance of the motivations. Again, the management team can address this issue. Alternatively, customers can be asked to assess the importance of the motivations directly or perhaps through trade-off questions. If an engineer had to sacrifice response time or accuracy in an oscilloscope, which would it be? Or how would an airline passenger trade off convenient departure time with price? The trade-off question asks customers to make difficult judgments about attributes. Another approach is to see which judgments are associated with actual purchase decisions. Such an approach revealed that mothers often selected snack food based on what "the child likes" and what was "juicy" instead of qualities they had said were important (nourishing, easy to eat).

A fourth task is to identify the motivations that will play a role in defining the value proposition of the business. The selection of motivations central to strategy will depend not only on customer motivations but on other factors as well, such as competitors' strategies that emerge in the competitor analysis. Another factor is how feasible and practical the resulting strategy is for the business. Internal analysis will be involved in making that determination, as will an analysis of the strategy's implementation.

Changing Customer Priorities

It is particularly critical to gain insight into changes in customers' priorities. In the high-tech area, customer priorities often evolve from needing help in selecting and installing the right equipment to wanting performance to looking for low cost. In the coffee business, customer tastes and habits have evolved from buying coffee at grocery stores to drinking coffee at gourmet cafés to buying their own whole-bean gourmet coffees. Assuming that customer priorities are not changing can be risky. It is essential to ask whether a significant and growing segment has developed priorities that are different from the basic business model.

The Customer as Active Partner

Customers are increasingly becoming active partners in their relationship with the firm and brand rather than passive targets of product development and advertising. The trend is illustrated by patients taking control of medical issues, the control of media shifting as audiences move to DVRs such as TiVo, and the power-enhancing access to information and fellow customers provided by the Internet.

To harness this change, managers should create and support customer communities. One motivation is to hear customer experiences and opinions about a brand in a context that will engender unbiased, motivated thoughts. This involves interacting with the customer on the Internet requires skills in listening, engaging, and leading. Each has challenges. Often there is information overload. There is a mention of McDonald's on the Internet every 5 seconds or so. Software to summarize content can play a role if integrated into an information system. Engaging can be difficult because it depends on where the firm has permission to enter the space, and there can be risks of a misstatement or inflaming an issue if it is engaged. However, clearly identified firm spokespeople can be effective. Leading usually requires getting in front of the Internet discussion with products or programs.

UNMET NEEDS

An unmet need is a customer need that is not being met by the existing product offerings. OfficeMax, for example, found that people, especially women professionals, wanted a cubicle workplace with color, patterns, and textures. The result was four product lines that promised to enliven and personalize cubicle environments delivered under the tagline "Life Is Beautiful, Work Can Be Too." An unmet need provided not only a route to a successful offering but also a way to enhance a brand relationship.

Unmet needs are strategically important because they represent opportunities for firms to increase their market share, break into a market, or create and own new markets. They can also represent threats to established firms in that they can be a lever that enables competitors to disrupt an established position. Ariat, for example, broke into the market for equestrian footwear by providing high-performance athletic footwear to riders who were not well served by traditional riding boots. Driven by the belief that riders are athletes, Ariat developed a brand and product line that was responsive to an unmet need.

Sometimes customers may not be aware of their unmet needs because they are so accustomed to the implicit limitations of existing equipment. Who could have conceived of a need for an electric lightbulb or a tractor before technology made them possible? Unmet needs that are not obvious may

USER-DEVELOPED PRODUCTS

For an internal application, IBM designed and built the first printed circuit card insertion machine of a particular type to be used in commercial production.[6] After building and testing the design in house, IBM sent engineering drawings of its design to a local machine builder along with an order for eight units. The machine builder completed this and subsequent orders and applied to IBM for permission to build essentially the same machine for sale on the open market. IBM agreed, and as a result, the machine builder became a major force in the component insertion equipment business.

In the early 1970s, store owners and sales personnel in southern California began to notice that youngsters were fixing up their bicycles to look like motorcycles, complete with imitation tailpipes and chopper-type handlebars. Sporting crash helmets and Honda motorcycle T-shirts, the youngsters raced fancy 20-inchers on dirt tracks. Obviously onto a good thing, the manufacturers came out with a whole new line of motorcross models. California users refined this concept into the mountain bike. Manufacturers were guided by the California customers to develop new refinements, including the 21-speed gear shift that doesn't require removing one's hands from the bars. Mountain bike firms are still watching their West Coast customers.

be more difficult to identify, but they can also represent a greater opportunity for an aggressive business because there will be little pressure on established firms to be responsive. The key is to stretch the technology or apply new technologies in order to expose unmet needs.

Using Customers to Identify Unmet Needs

Customers are a prime source of unmet needs. The trick is to access them, to get customers to detect and communicate unmet needs. What product-use experience problems have emerged? What is frustrating? How does it compare with other product experiences? Are there problems with the total-use system in which the product is embedded? How can the product be improved? This kind of research helped Dow come up with Spiffits, a line of premoistened, disposable cleaning towels that addressed the need for a towel already moistened with a cleaning compound.

A structured approach, termed *problem research*, develops a list of potential problems with the product or service. The problems are then prioritized by asking a group of 100 to 200 respondents to rate each problem as to whether (1) the problem is important, (2) the problem occurs frequently, and (3) a solution exists. A problem score is obtained by combining these ratings. A dog-food problem research study found that buyers thought dog food smelled bad, cost too much, and was not available in different sizes for different dogs. Subsequently, products responsive to these criticisms emerged. Another study led an airline to modify its cabins to provide more leg room.

Eric von Hippel, a researcher at MIT who studies customers as sources of service innovations, suggests that lead users provide a particularly fertile ground for discovering unmet needs and new product concepts.[7] Lead users are users who:

- Face needs that will be general in the marketplace but face them months or years before the bulk of the marketplace. A person who is very into health foods and nutrition would be a lead user with respect to health foods if we assume that there is a trend toward health foods.

- Are positioned to benefit significantly by obtaining a solution to those needs. Lead users of office automation would be firms that today would benefit significantly from technological advancement.

An effective and efficient way to access customers is to use the Internet to engage them in a dialogue. Dell, for example, has a Web site called Ideastorm where customers can post ideas and observe and "vote" on the ideas of others. They also see the reaction of Dell, which can include responses such as "under review" or "partially implemented." Among the suggestions was to have backlit keyboards, to support free software such as Linux, and to design quieter computers. Starbucks with its MyStarbucksidea site is among many firms that are attempting to do something similar. A risk with customer-driven idea sites is that there can be a surge around an idea that is impractical or unwise, and the company would then be defensive. But it has the potential of leveraging many perspectives to generate ideas that can result in real energy and innovation.

A less direct way is to create communities of customers and let them converse with each other. The conversation will illuminate problems and unmet needs. P&G, for example, has the engagement platform BeingGirl, where preteen and teen girls can discuss coming of age issues with each other. It is an effective forum to spread awareness and knowledge about P&G feminine hygiene products and programs. Intuit's site, developed to allow tax professionals to answer each other's questions, provides insights into the kinds of questions being posed, which in turn informs Intuit's TurboTax refinement efforts.

Qualitative Research

Qualitative research is a powerful tool in understanding customers and potential customers, their unmet needs, and their motivation at a very basic level. It can involve focus-group sessions, in-depth interviews, customer case studies, or ethnographic research. The concept is to search for the real concerns and motivations that do not emerge from structured lists and that customers may not be consciously aware of. For instance, buyers of sports utility vehicles might really be expressing their youth or a youthful attitude rather than being a set of functional benefits. Getting inside the customer can provide strategic insights that do not emerge any other way.

Although a representative cross-section of customers is usually sought, special attention to some is often merited. Very loyal customers are often best able to articulate the bonds that the firm is capable of establishing. Lost customers (those who have defected) are often particularly good at graphically communicating problems with the product or service. New customers or customers who have recently increased their usage may suggest new applications. Organizational buyers using multiple vendors may have a good perspective of the firm relative to the competition.

The Internet has changed and enhanced qualitative research.[8] No longer is it time and location limited. You don't have to gather people into a conference room or send out interviewers to conduct one-on-one dialogues. Respondents do not have to rely on the memory of an experience weeks or months ago. A research study can now access experiences as they happen where they happen. Respondents do not have to be from one location but can be global. Further respondents, even if globally located, can be engaged with each other. Spontaneous interactions and moments of self-discovery can be stimulated. And it is more cost-effective and much faster than focus groups, in-depth interviews, or ethnographics.

Firms such as Revolution can address research tasks like the following.

- **Assume that you are interested in wine experiences.** Respondents can keep a journal and show by video or picture the context of their wine experience and their observations about it. A moderator can ask probing questions.

- **Assume that you want to understand the food inventory of consumers.** Instead of asking about a respondent's refrigerator contents, ask him or her to take you on a photo tour of the fridge.

- **Assume you want to get into deep emotions surrounding a brand.** Ask respondents to deprive themselves of it for a day and record the resulting emotions over the course of the day. Or ask the respondent to create or find images that reflect the feelings associated with a brand and post them. Encourage a discussion around the most interesting.

- **Assume you want some insight into a brand.** Post six pictures and ask which jumps out at you when you are in a certain brand context.

- **Assume you need to develop a new product to revitalize a frozen dinner brand.** First, you start seven days of respondents using an online diary recording their experiences and activities related to frozen dinners complete with videos and descriptions. A moderator interjects questions. Second, you expose another respondent set to ten concepts presented with a video showing the package and use experience. An online discussion with moderator interaction is part of the process. Finally, three finished concepts are put to an in-home test during which respondents film their test experience.

Ethnographic Research

A powerful qualitative research approach is ethnographic or anthropological research, which involves directly observing customers in as many contexts as possible. By accurately observing not only what is done involving the target or service but also *why* it is being done, companies can achieve a deeper level of understanding of the customer's needs and motivations and generate actionable insights. It is often done by actually having researchers spend real time with customers in their homes or offices. P&G has their executives regularly engage in such research. However, it can also be aided by a video camera or by the Internet-based research in which customers monitor themselves in a structured way.

For example, the financial data company Thomson Corporation regularly studies from 25 to 50 customers, examining their behavior from three minutes prior to using their data as well as three minutes afterward.[9] One such study, which found that analysts were inputting the data into a spreadsheet, led to a new service. Although this research approach has been around for nearly a century, it has taken on new life in the last few years not only in packaged goods firms such as P&G but also in business-to-business firms such as Intel and GE.

Ethnographic research is particularly good at identifying breakthrough innovations. Customers usually cannot verbalize such innovations because they are used to the current offerings. Henry Ford famously observed that had he asked customers what they wanted, they would have said faster horses. By watching people buy and use in the context of their lives or their businesses, however, experienced and talented anthropologists (or executives, in the case of P&G) can generate insights that go beyond what customers could talk about.

Ethnographic research works.[10] After one study observed the difficulty people had in cleaning the bathroom, P&G developed Magic Reach, a device with a long handle and swivel head. Visits to contactors and home renovators resulted in the development of the OXO hammer (with a fiberglass core to cut vibration and a rubber bumper on top to avoid leaving marks when removing nails) as part of a line of professional-grade tools. Sirius followed 45 people for a week, studying music listened to, magazines read, and TV shows watched, and then developed a portable satellite-radio player that can load up to 50 hours of music for later playback. Black & Decker's observation that electric drill users ran out of power led to the detachable battery pack. Intel's research in developing countries led it to develop a cheap PC that could run on truck batteries in 100-degree temperatures. GE found through ethnographic research that buyers of plastic fiber for fire-retardant jackets were more concerned with performance than price. That led to a completely different business model in GE's efforts to enter the field.

Ethnographic research can also be used to improve existing products or services. Marriott had a multifunctional team of seven people (including a designer and an architect) spend six weeks visiting twelve cities, hanging out with guests at hotel lobbies, cafés, and bars.[11] They learned that hotels were not doing well at service for small groups of business travelers. As a result, lobbies and adjacent areas were redesigned to be more suitable for transacting business, with brighter lights and "social zones" with a mix of small tables, larger tables, and semiprivate spaces.

The Ideal Experience

The conceptualization of an ideal experience can also help to identify unmet needs. A major publisher of directories polled its customers, asking each to describe its ideal experience with the firm. The publisher found that its very large customers (the top 4 percent who were generating 45 percent of its business) wanted a single contact point to resolve problems, customized products, consultation on using the service, and help in tracking results. In contrast, smaller customers wanted a simple ordering process and to be left alone. These responses provided insights into improving service while cutting costs.[12]

KEY LEARNINGS

- External analysis should influence strategy by identifying opportunities, threats, trends, and strategic uncertainties. The ultimate goal is to improve strategic choices—decisions as to where and how to compete.

- Segmentation (identifying customer groups that can support different competitive strategies) can be based on a variety of customer characteristics, such as benefits sought, customer loyalty, and applications.

- Customer motivation analysis can provide insights into what assets and competencies are needed to compete, as well as indicate possible SCAs.

- Unmet needs that represent opportunities (or threats) can be identified by asking customers, by accessing lead users, by ethnographic research, and by interacting with customers.

FOR DISCUSSION

1. Why do a strategic analysis? What are the objectives? What, in your view, are the three keys to making a strategic analysis helpful and important? Is there a downside to conducting a full-blown strategic analysis?

2. Consider the buyer "hot buttons" described on page 30. What are the implications for Betty Crocker? What new business areas might be considered given each hot button? Answer the same questions for a grocery store chain such as Safeway.

3. Consider the segments in the male shopper insert on page 26. Describe each further. What car would they drive? What kind of vacation would they take? What shirt brand would they buy?

4. What is a customer buying at Nordstrom? At Banana Republic? At Zara?

5. Pick a company or brand or business on which to focus, such as cereals. What are the major segments? What are the customer motivations by segments? What are the unmet needs?

NOTES

1. Andrew Tilim, "Will the Kids Buy It?" *Business 2.0*, May 2003, pp. 95–99.

2. This insert was inspired by Nanette Byrnes, "Secrets of the Male Shopper," *BusinessWeek*, September 4, 2006, pp. 45–53.

3. Clayton M. Christiansen, Scott Cook, and Taddy Hall, "Marketing Malpractice: The Cause and the Cure," *Harvard Business Review*, December 2005, pp. 74–83.

4. Melinda Cuthbert, "All Buyers Not Alike," *Business 2.0*, December 26, 2000.

5. Abbie Griffin and John R. Hauser, "The Voice of the Customer," *Marketing Science*, Winter 1993, pp. 1–27.

6. Eric von Hippel, "Lead Users: A Source of Novel Product Concepts," *Management Science*, July 1986, p. 802.

7. Ibid.

8. For more on web-based qualitative research, see revolutionglobal.com.

9. Richard J. Harrington and Anthony K. Tjan, "Transforming Strategy One Customer at a Time," *Harvard Business Review*, March, 2008, p. 67.

10. Spencer E. Ante, "The Science of Desire," *Business Week*, June 5, 2006, pp. 99–106.

11. Ibid., p. 104.

12. George S. Day, "Creating a Superior Customer-Relating Capability," *Sloan Management Review*, Spring 2003, pp. 82–83.

CHAPTER THREE

Competitor Analysis

Induce your competitors not to invest in those products, markets and services where you expect to invest the most . . . that is the fundamental rule of strategy.
—*Bruce Henderson, founder of BCG*

There is nothing more exhilarating than to be shot at without result.
—*Winston Churchill*

The best and fastest way to learn a sport is to watch and imitate a champion.
—*Jean-Claude Killy, skier*

*T*here are numerous well-documented reasons why the Japanese automobile firms were able to penetrate the U.S. market successfully, especially during the 1970s. One important reason, however, is that they were much better than U.S. firms at doing competitor analysis.[1]

David Halberstam, in his account of the automobile industry, graphically described the Japanese efforts at competitor analysis in the 1960s. "They came in groups. . . . They measured, they photographed, they sketched, and they tape-recorded everything they could. Their questions were precise. They were surprised how open the Americans were."[2] The Japanese similarly studied European manufacturers, especially their design approaches. In contrast, according to Halberstam, the Americans were late in even recognizing the competitive threat from Japan and never did well at analyzing Japanese firms or understanding the new strategic imperatives created by the revised competitive environment even though the Japanese car firms were very open about their methods.

Competitor analysis is the second phase of external analysis. Again, the goal should be insights that will influence the development of successful business strategies. The analysis should focus on the identification of threats, opportunities, or strategic uncertainties created by emerging or potential competitor moves, weaknesses, or strengths.

Competitor analysis starts with identifying current and potential competitors. There are two very different ways of identifying current competitors. The first examines the perspective of the customer who must make choices among competitors. This approach groups competitors according to the degree to which they compete for a buyer's choice. The second approach attempts to place competitors in strategic groups on the basis of their competitive strategy.

WHO ARE THE COMPETITORS?

- Against whom do we usually compete? Who are our most intense competitors? Less intense but still serious competitors? Makers of substitute products?
- Can these competitors be grouped into strategic groups on the basis of their assets, competencies, and/or strategies?
- Who are the potential competitive entrants? What are their barriers to entry? Is there anything that can be done to discourage them?

EVALUATING THE COMPETITORS

- What are their objectives and strategies? Their level of commitment? Their exit barriers?
- What is their cost structure? Do they have a cost advantage or disadvantage?
- What is their image and positioning strategy?
- Which are the most successful/unsuccessful competitors over time? Why?
- What are the strengths and weaknesses of each competitor or strategic group?
- What leverage points (or strategic weaknesses or customer problems or unmet needs) could competitors exploit to enter the market or become more serious competitors?
- How strong or weak is each competitor with respect to their assets and competencies? Generate a competitor strength grid.

Figure 3.1   Questions to Structure Competitor Analysis

After competitors are identified, the focus shifts to attempting to understand them and their strategies. Of particular interest is an analysis of the strengths and weaknesses of each competitor or strategic group of competitors. Figure 3.1 summarizes a set of questions that can provide a structure for competitor analysis.

IDENTIFYING COMPETITORS—CUSTOMER-BASED APPROACHES

One approach to identifying competitor sets is to look at competitors from the perspective of customers—what choices are customers making? A Cisco buyer could be asked what brand would have been purchased had Cisco not made the required item. A buyer for a nursing home meal service could be asked what would be substituted for granulated potato buds if they increased in price. A sample of sports car buyers could be asked what other cars they considered and perhaps what other showrooms they actually visited.

Brand-Use Associations

Another approach that provides insights is the association of brands with specific-use contexts or applications. Perhaps twenty or thirty product users could be asked to identify a list of use situations or applications. For each use context they would then name all the brands that are appropriate. Then for each brand, they would identify appropriate use contexts so that the list of use contexts would be more complete. Another group of respondents would then be asked to make judgments about how appropriate each brand is for each use context. Then brands would be clustered based on the similarity of their appropriate use contexts. Thus, if Doritos was perceived as a snack, its set of competitors would be different than if it was perceived as a party enhancer.

The same approach will work with an industrial product that might be used in several distinct applications.

Both the customer-choice and brand-use approaches suggest a conceptual basis for identifying competitors that can be employed by managers even when marketing research is not available. The concept of alternatives from which customers choose and the concept of appropriateness to a use context can be powerful tools in helping to understand the competitive environment.

Indirect Competitors

In most instances, primary competitors are quite visible and easily identified. Coke competes with Pepsi, other cola brands, and private labels such as President's Choice. CitiBank competes with Chase, Bank of America, and other major banks. NBC competes with ABC, CBS, and Fox. Boeing competes with Airbus. The competitor analysis for this group should be done with depth and insight.

In many markets, however, customer priorities are changing, and indirect competitors offering customers product alternatives are strategically relevant. Understanding these indirect competitors can be strategically and tactically important, as the following examples demonstrate.

- Coke focused on Pepsi and ignored for many years the emerging submarkets in water, energy drinks, and fruit-based drinks. The result was a missed opportunity and the eventual need to pursue an expensive and difficult catch-up strategy.

- While the major television networks struggle against each other, independent networks have emerged. Strong cable networks, such as ESPN, Fox, HBO, and CNN, have flourished; pay-per-view, Netflix, computer games, mobile applications, and the Internet are competing for the leisure time of viewers.

- While banks focused on competing banks, their markets were eroded by mutual funds, insurers, and brokers.

- While Folgers, Maxwell House, and others competed for supermarket business using coupon promotions, other firms, such as Starbucks, succeeded in selling a very different kind of coffee in different ways. And Starbucks has more recently been threatened by gourmet coffee makers sold for home use and by alternatives offered by chains like Dunkin' Donuts and McDonald's.

- Steel minimills were ignored by the major steel firms until they gradually became a major player.

The energy bar category, established in the mid-1980s by PowerBar, includes direct competitors such as Clif, Balance, and dozens of small, local niche firms. There are also a host of indirect competitors, many with very similar products: candy bars (Snickers was called "the energy bar" for many years), breakfast bars, meal replacement bars, diet bars, granola bars, and the cereal bar category. Understanding the positioning and new product strategies of these indirect competitors will be strategically important to businesses in the energy bar category.

Both direct and indirect competitors can be further categorized in terms of how relevant they are, as determined by similar positioning. Thus, candy bars will be more relevant to Balance than to PowerBar because of where the former has positioned itself (Balance Gold is even marketed as being "like a candy bar"). For the same reason, Clif will be a closer competitor to PowerBar than to Balance.

The competitive analysis in nearly all cases will benefit from extending the perspective beyond the obvious direct competitors. By explicitly considering indirect competitors, the strategic horizon is expanded, and the analysis more realistically mirrors what the customer sees. In the real world, the customer is never restricted to a firm's direct competitors but instead is always poised to consider other options.

A key issue with respect to strategic analysis in general, and competitor analysis in particular, is the level at which the analysis is conducted. Is it at the level of a business unit, the firm, or some other aggregation of businesses? Because an analysis will be needed at all levels at which strategies are developed, multiple analyses might ultimately be necessary. For example, when Clif developed Luna, an energy bar designed for women, PowerBar countered with Pria. The manager of the Luna business may need a competitive analysis of energy bars for women, in which case the other energy bars might be considered indirect competitors.

IDENTIFYING COMPETITORS—STRATEGIC GROUPS

The concept of a strategic group provides a very different approach toward understanding the competitive structure of an industry. A strategic group is a group of firms that:

- Over time pursue similar competitive strategies (for example, the use of the same distribution channel, the same type of communication strategies, or the same price/ quality position)
- Have similar characteristics (e.g., size, aggressiveness)
- Have similar assets and competencies (such as brand associations, logistics capability, global presence, or research and development)

For example, there have historically been three strategic groups in the pet food industry, which is the subject of an illustrative industry analysis in the appendix to this book. One strategic group consists of very large diversified, branded consumer and food product companies. All distribute through mass merchandisers and supermarkets, have strong established brands, use advertising and promotions effectively, and enjoy economies of scale. The major players include Nestlé Ralston Petcare, Del Monte, and Mars.

A second strategic group of highly focused ultra-premium producers, such as Hill's Petfood (Science Diet and Prescription Diet) and the Iams Company, sells product through veterinary offices and specialty pet stores. They have historically used referral networks to reach pet owners concerned with health. When P&G acquired Iams and introduced it into mass merchandisers and supermarkets, the distinction between the two strategic groups blurred, and new competitive dynamics were introduced. Iams became a threat to established brands in this space, and the Hill's brands found their competitive context very different.

The third strategic group, private-label producers, is led by a unit of Del Monte (formerly Doanne) that supplies Wal-Mart and other major retailers.

In fact, many industries are populated by several strategic groups: premium-dominated volume entries such as United in airlines or Budweiser in beer, low-cost entries such as JetBlue in airlines and Milwaukee's Best in beer, and niche groups such as timeshare planes and low alcohol and craft beers.

Each strategic group has mobility barriers that inhibit or prevent businesses from moving from one strategic group to another. An ultra-premium group in pet food producers has the brand reputation, product, and manufacturing knowledge needed for the health segment, access to influential veterinarians and retailers, and a local customer base. Private-label manufacturers have low-cost production, low overhead, and close relationships with customers. It is possible to bypass or overcome the barriers, of course. A private-label manufacturer could create a branded entry, especially if markets are selected to minimize conflicts with existing customers. The barriers are real, however, and a firm competing across strategic groups is usually at a disadvantage.

A member of a strategic group can have exit as well as entry barriers. For example, assets such as plant investment or a specialized labor force can represent a meaningful exit barrier, as can the need to protect a brand's reputation.

The mobility barrier concept is crucial because one way to develop a sustainable competitive advantage is to pursue a strategy that is protected from competition by assets and competencies that represent barriers to competitors. Consider the PC and server market. Dell and others marketed computers direct to consumers by telephone and the Internet. They developed a host of assets and competencies to support their direct channels, including an impressive product support system. Competitors such as HP—which has used indirect channels involving retailers and systems firms—have developed a very different set of assets and competencies. HP and Dell have both struggled to cross the channel barriers. Competition has largely been between the groups rather than brands. As the direct channel lost appeal while products matured and service problems emerged, HP gained in the marketplace.

Using the Strategic Group Concept

The conceptualization of strategic groups can make the process of competitor analysis more manageable. Numerous industries contain many more competitors than can be analyzed individually. Often it is simply not feasible to consider thirty competitors, to say nothing of hundreds. Reducing this set to a small number of strategic groups makes the analysis compact, feasible, and more usable. For example, in the wine industry, competitor analysis by a firm like Robert Mondavi might examine three strategic groups: jug wines, premium wines ($7 to $20), and super-premium wines (over $20). Little strategic content and insight will be lost in most cases because firms in a strategic group will be affected by and react to industry developments in similar ways. Thus, in projecting future strategies of competitors, the concept of strategic groups can be helpful.

Strategic groupings can refine the strategic investment decision. Instead of determining in which industries to invest, the decision can focus on what strategic group warrants investment. Thus, it will be necessary to determine the current profitability and future potential profitability of each strategic group. One strategic objective is to invest in attractive strategic groups in which assets and competencies can be employed to create strategic advantage.

The emergence of a new strategic group or subgroup is of particular importance. It can create a dynamic that will affect strategies of all competitors for a long time period. Major disruptions to an industry often start small with inferior products, so analysis needs to proceed with an eye toward projecting future offerings rather than assuming they will not evolve. Chapter 13 elaborates.

POTENTIAL COMPETITORS

In addition to current competitors, it is important to consider potential market entrants, such as firms that might engage in:

1. **Market expansion.** Perhaps the most obvious source of potential competitors is firms operating in other geographic regions or in other countries. A cookie company may want to keep a close eye on a competing firm in an adjacent state, for example.

2. **Product expansion.** The leading ski firm, Rossignol, has expanded into ski clothing, thus exploiting a common market, and has moved to tennis equipment, which takes advantage of technological and distribution overlap.

3. **Backward integration.** Customers are another potential source of competition. General Motors bought dozens of manufacturers of components during its formative years. Major can users, such as Campbell Soup, have integrated backward, making their own containers.

4. **Forward integration.** Suppliers attracted by margins are also potential competitors. Apple Computer, for example, opened a chain of retail stores. Suppliers, believing they have the critical ingredients to succeed in a market, may be attracted by the margins, the control, and the visibility that come with integrating forward.

5. **The export of assets or competencies.** A current small competitor with critical strategic weaknesses can turn into a major entrant if it is purchased by a firm that can reduce or eliminate those weaknesses. Predicting such moves can be difficult, but sometimes an analysis of competitor strengths and weaknesses will suggest some possible synergistic mergers. A competitor in an above-average growth industry that does not have the financial or managerial resources for the long haul might be a particularly attractive candidate for merger.

6. **Retaliatory or defensive strategies.** Firms that are threatened by a potential or actual move into their market might retaliate. Thus, Microsoft has made several moves (including into the Internet space) in part to protect its dominant software position.

COMPETITOR ANALYSIS—UNDERSTANDING COMPETITORS

Understanding competitors and their activities can provide several benefits. First, an understanding of the current strategy, strengths, and weaknesses of a competitor can suggest opportunities and threats that will merit a response. Second, insights into future competitor strategies may allow the prediction of emerging threats and opportunities. Third, a decision about strategic alternatives might easily hinge on the ability to forecast the likely reaction of key competitors. Finally, competitor analysis may result in the identification of some strategic uncertainties that will be worth monitoring closely over time. A strategic uncertainty might be, for example, "Will Competitor A decide to move into the western U.S. market?"

As Figure 3.2 indicates, competitor actions are influenced by eight elements. The first of these reflects financial performance, as measured by size, growth, and profitability.

Size, Growth, and Profitability

The level and growth of sales and market share provide indicators of the vitality of a business strategy. The maintenance of a strong market position or the achievement of rapid growth usually

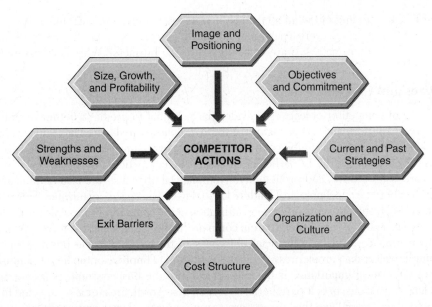

Figure 3.2 Understanding the Competitors

reflects a strong competitor (or strategic group) and a successful strategy. In contrast, a deteriorating market position can signal financial or organizational strains that might affect the interest and ability of the business to pursue certain strategies. To provide a crude sales estimate for businesses that are buried in a large company, take the number of employees and multiply it by the average sales per employee in the industry. For many businesses, this method is very feasible and remarkably accurate.

After size and growth comes profitability. A profitable business will generally have access to capital for investment unless it has been designated by the parent to be milked. A business that has lost money over an extended time period or has experienced a recent sharp decrease in profitability may find it difficult to gain access to capital either externally or internally.

Image and Positioning Strategy

A cornerstone of a business strategy can be an association, such as being the strongest truck, the most durable car, the smallest consumer electronics equipment, or the most effective cleaner. More often, it is useful to move beyond class-related product attributes to intangibles that span product class, such as quality, innovation, sensitivity to the environment, or brand personality.

In order to develop positioning alternatives, it is helpful to determine the image associations, including the brand personality of the major competitors. Weaknesses of competitors on relevant attributes or personality traits can represent an opportunity to differentiate and develop an advantage. Strengths of competitors on important dimensions may represent challenges to exceed them or to outflank them. In any case, it is important to know the competitive profiles.

Competitor image and positioning information can be deduced in part by studying a firm's products, advertising, Web site, and actions, but often customer research is helpful to ensure that an accurate current portrayal is obtained. The conventional approach is to start with qualitative customer research to find out what a business and its brands mean to customers. What are the associations? If the business were a person, what kind of person would it be? What visual imagery, books, animals, trees, or activities are associated with the business? What is its essence?

Objectives and Commitment

A knowledge of competitor objectives provides the potential to predict whether or not a competitor's present performance is satisfactory or strategic changes are likely. The financial objectives of the business unit can indicate the competitor's willingness to invest in that business even if the payout is relatively long term. In particular, what are the competitor's objectives with respect to market share, sales growth, and profitability? Nonfinancial objectives are also helpful. Does the competitor want to be a technological leader? Or to develop a service organization? Or to expand distribution? Such objectives provide a good indication of the competitor's possible future strategy.

The objectives of the competitor's parent company (if one exists) are also relevant. What are the current performance levels and financial objectives of the parent? If the business unit is not performing as well as the parent, pressure might be exerted to improve or the investment might be withdrawn. Of critical importance is the role attached to the business unit. Is it central to the parent's long-term plans, or is it peripheral? Is it seen as a growth area, or is it expected to supply cash to fund other areas? Does the business create synergy with other operations? Does the parent have an emotional attachment to the business unit for any reason? Deep pockets can sometimes be accompanied by short arms; just because resources exist does not mean they are available.

Current and Past Strategies

The competitor's current and past strategies should be reviewed. In particular, past strategies that have failed should be noted because such experiences can inhibit the competitor from trying similar strategies again. Also, a knowledge of a competitor pattern of new product or new market moves can help anticipate its future growth directions. Is the strategy based on product-line breadth, product quality, service, distribution type, or brand identification? If a low-cost strategy is employed, is it based on economies of scale, the experience curve, manufacturing facilities and equipment, or access to raw material? What is its cost structure? If a focus strategy is evident, describe the business scope.

Organization and Culture

Knowledge about the background and experience of the competitor's top management can provide insight into future actions. Are the managers drawn from marketing, engineering, or manufacturing? Are they largely from another industry or company? Clorox, for example, has a very heavy Procter & Gamble influence in its management, lingering from the years that Procter & Gamble operated Clorox before the courts ordered divestiture.

An organization's culture, supported by its structure, systems, and people, often has a pervasive influence on strategy. A cost-oriented, highly structured organization that relies on tight controls to achieve objectives and motivate employees may have difficulty innovating or shifting into an aggressive, marketing-oriented strategy. A loose, flat organization that emphasizes innovation and risk taking may similarly have difficulty pursuing a disciplined product-refinement and cost-reduction program. In general, as Chapter 16 will make clearer, organizational elements such as culture, structure, systems, and people limit the range of strategies that should be considered.

Cost Structure

Knowledge of a competitor's cost structure, especially when the competitor is relying on a low-cost strategy, can provide an indication of its likely future pricing strategy and its staying power. The following information can usually be obtained and can provide insights into cost structures:

- The number of employees and a rough breakdown of direct labor (variable labor cost) and overhead (which will be part of fixed cost)
- The relative costs of raw materials and purchased components
- The investment in inventory, plant, and equipment (also fixed cost)
- Sales levels and number of plants (on which the allocation of fixed costs is based)
- Outsourcing strategy

Exit Barriers

Exit barriers can be crucial to a firm's ability to withdraw from a business area and thus are indicators of commitment. They include:[3]

- Specialized assets—plant, equipment, or other assets that are costly to transform to another application and therefore have little salvage value
- Fixed costs, such as labor agreements, leases, and a need to maintain parts for existing equipment
- Relationships to other business units in the firm resulting from the firm's image or from shared facilities, distribution channels, or sales force
- Government and social barriers—for example, governments may regulate whether a railroad can exit from a passenger service responsibility, or firms may feel a sense of loyalty to workers, thereby inhibiting strategic moves
- Managerial pride or an emotional attachment to a business or its employees that affects economic decisions

NINTENDO—SUCCESS THAT STARTED WITH COMPETITOR ANALYSIS

The story of the Nintendo business strategy and brand is nothing short of astounding, and competitive analysis played an important part. BrandJapan, an annual survey of the strength of over 1,000 Japanese brands, saw a remarkable stability spanning nine years in the cast of characters occupying the top two dozen positions. Then came Nintendo. In the 2005 findings, Nintendo was ranked 135 in the survey. From that point it rose to 66 in 2006, to 5 in 2007, and finally to number one in 2008, a position it held with a value of over 93 while the next seven brands were bunched at 82 to 84, and a position it retained in 2009. During the 2004 to 2008 period, its stock price went up more than fivefold, and at one point its market cap was behind only Toyota in Japan. Why? What drove this performance?

(*continued*)

The products were clearly the drivers. Nintendo DS, released in December 2004, was a compact portable game console characterized by an innovatively intuitive touch-pen method. It was supported by games that got traction such as *Nintendogs, Animal Crossing,* and *Brain Age* aimed at a wide target market, including young females and even seniors. Then came Wii, a new form of game that incorporated user movement into gaming. With a wireless controller and the Wii remote that detects movement in three dimensions, the user can dance, golf, box, play a guitar, and on and on. Opponents can be sourced in other locations and even other countries. In fact, the DS and Wii with their supporting games created a new market categorized as "casual games," video games that require less skills and experience and are characterized by simple and intuitive rules. The new casual game category went from 1 percent of the market to over 20 percent by 2005.[4]

But what was behind the Nintendo innovation success? Why was it able to win facing Sony and Microsoft? One principle reason was the acceptance of a realistic and astute analysis of the two competitors: Sony (Playstation) and Microsoft (P3 players). Nintendo recognized that Sony and Microsoft had and will have equipment that had better technology—higher performance, higher resolution, and higher quality graphics that appeal to the heavy users—young males. They were focused on that objective and invested in chips, software, manufacturing, and hardware to keep delivering. As a result, Sony and Microsoft had a definitive edge with respect to male teen and early 20s users, the hard core heavy user group. Given this reality, Nintendo took a different course, a low-tech route, even though that meant that the heavy user segment might have to be ceded to the two competitors.

Nintendo decided to refocus away from the hard core young males who were into action games and high-quality graphics toward a broader audience, less concerned with better and better graphics. The key for this group would be a wide array of easy-to-use games that would move beyond the action genre and include some learning vehicles. One goal is to have the mother as a participant and an advocate rather than a cynic and opponent. Another is to involve the whole family so the games are not simply related to boys' retreats. The strategy went against the conventional one of focusing on heavy users and trying to better competitor's offerings.

Sony and Microsoft aggressively responded with innovations of their own, and the Nintendo lofty brand position did not hold. By 2011, the Nintendo brand had fallen but still was in the top 15 of 1,000 brands, while DS was in the top 25 and Wii in the top 50. But then Nintendo fought back with more innovations. A successor to the DS line, the Nintendo 3DS produced a three-dimensional effect with glasses and included games that can only be played on the device. A new WII, the WiiU, included a GamePad controller that can be the centerpiece of the home entertainment system as it allows the user to connect and control entertainment options such as games, television shows, and more. Both leveraged the Nintendo franchise games such as Mario and Zelda plus new brands as well. In addition, Nintendo8 provided access the games of the 1980s and provided a link to the brand's heritage. And there more was in the wings indicating that the Nintendo innovation that involves being user friendly is in action.

Assessing Strengths and Weaknesses

Knowledge of a competitor's strengths and weaknesses provides insight that is key to its ability to pursue various strategies. It also offers important input into the process of identifying and selecting strategic alternatives. One approach is to attempt to exploit a competitor's weakness in an area where the firm has an existing or developing strength. The desired pattern is to develop a strategy that will pit "our" strength against a competitor's weakness. Another approach is to bypass or neutralize a competitor's strength.

One firm that developed a strategy to neutralize a competitor's strength was a small software firm that lacked a retail distribution capability or the resources to engage in retail advertising.

It targeted value-added software systems firms, which sell total software and sometimes hardware systems to organizations such as investment firms or hospitals. These value-added systems firms could understand and exploit the power of the product, integrate it into their systems, and use it in quantity. The competitor's superior access to a distribution channel or resources to support an advertising effort was thus neutralized.

The assessment of a competitor's strengths and weaknesses starts with an identification of relevant assets and competencies for the industry and then evaluates the competitor on the basis of those assets and competencies. We now turn to these topics.

COMPETITOR STRENGTHS AND WEAKNESSES

What Are the Relevant Assets and Competencies?

Competitor strengths and weaknesses are based on the existence or absence of assets or competencies. Thus, an asset such as a well-known name or a prime location could represent a strength, as could a competency such as the ability to develop a strong promotional program. Conversely, the absence of an asset or competency can represent a weakness.

To analyze competitor strengths and weaknesses, it is thus necessary to identify the assets and competencies that are relevant to the industry. As Figure 3.3 suggests, four sets of questions can be helpful.

1. *What businesses have been successful over time? What assets or competencies have contributed to their success? What businesses have had chronically low performance? Why? What assets or competencies do they lack?*

    By definition, assets and competencies that provide SCAs should affect performance over time. Thus, businesses that differ with respect to performance over time should also differ with respect to their assets and competencies. Analysis of the causes of the performance usually suggests sets of relevant competencies and assets. Typically, the superior performers have developed and maintained key assets and competencies that have been the basis for their performance. Conversely, weakness in several assets and competencies relevant to the industry and its strategy should visibly contribute to the inferior performance of the weak competitors over time.

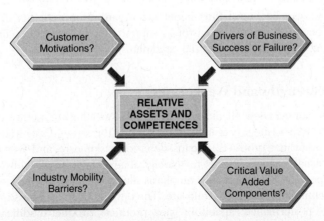

Figure 3.3 Identifying Relevant Assets and Competencies

For example, in the CT scanner industry, the best performer, General Electric, has superior product technology and R&D, scale economies, an established systems capability, a strong sales and service organization (owing, in part, to its X-ray product line), and an installed base.

2. ***What are the key customer motivations? What is needed to be preferred? What is needed to be considered?***

   Customer motivations usually drive buying decisions and thus can dictate what assets or competencies potentially create meaningful advantages. In the heavy-equipment industry, customers value service and parts backup. Caterpillar's promise of "24-hour parts service anywhere in the world" has been a key asset because it is important to customers. Apple has focused on the motivation of designers for user-friendly design platforms.

   There are motivations that lead to a brand being excluded from consideration. An offering characteristic may not determine winners, but a deficiency will eliminate it from being considered. Hyundai, for example, needs to be perceived as having adequate quality. A series of "best car" awards in 2009 did not necessarily vault the brand to a superior position, but for many, it did get rid of the "inadequate" perception.

3. ***What assets and competencies represent industry mobility (entry and exit) barriers?***

   Strategic groups are characterized by structural stability even when one group is much more profitable than the others. The reason is mobility barriers, which can be both entry barriers and exit barriers. Some groups have assets and competencies that will be difficult and sometimes impossible to duplicate by those seeking to enter. International deep water oil-well drilling firms, for example, have technology, equipment, and people that domestic, on-shore firms cannot duplicate. These assets also represent exit barriers because there is no other use to which they could be put.

4. ***What are the significant value added components in the value chain?***

   A firm that can excel on a critical value added component can have a sustainable advantage. The component can be critical because of its cost such as package handling for FedEx or the call center at Dell. Or it can be critical because of the customer benefit it generates or affects such as the ordering system at Amazon or the ingredients of a P&G detergent. In examining the value chain, it is helpful to start with suppliers and end with the customer use experience while charting all the components in between. The components can be found throughout the organization and that of its partners. For eBay, for example, operations, customer support, auction services, plus the operations of those selling goods are all potential candidates.

A Checklist of Strengths and Weaknesses

Figure 3.4 provides an overview checklist of the areas in which a competitor can have strengths and weaknesses. The first category is innovation. One of the strengths of Kao Corporation is its ability to develop innovative products in soaps, detergents, skin care, and even data storage disks. Its new products usually have a distinct technological advantage. In a highly technical industry, the percentage spent on R&D and the emphasis along the basic/applied continuum can be indicators of the cumulative ability to innovate. The outputs of the process in terms of product characteristics and performance capabilities, new products, product modifications, and patents provide more definitive measures of the company's ability to innovate.

INNOVATION
- Technical product or service superiority
- New product capability
- R&D
- Technologies
- Patents

MANUFACTURING/OPERATIONS
- Cost structure
- Effective and flexible operations
- Efficient operations
- Vertical integration
- Workforce attitude and motivation
- Capacity
- Outsourcing

FINANCE—ACCESS TO CAPITAL
- From operations
- From net short-term assets
- Ability to use debt and equity financing
- Parent's willingness to finance

MANAGEMENT
- Quality of top and middle management
- Knowledge of business
- Culture
- Strategic goals and plans
- Entrepreneurial thrust
- Planning/operation system
- Loyalty—turnover
- Quality of strategic decision making

MARKETING
- Product quality reputation
- Product characteristics/differentiation
- Brand name recognition
- Breadth of the product line—systems capability
- Customer orientation
- Segmentation/focus
- Distribution
- Retailer relationship
- Advertising/promotion skills
- Sales force
- Customer service/product support

CUSTOMER BASE
- Size and loyalty
- Market share
- Growth of segments served

Figure 3.4 Analysis of Strengths and Weaknesses

The second area of competitor strengths and weaknesses is manufacturing and operations. A major area of strength of Toyota, for example, based on its culture, work processes, and ability to reduce inventory and costs, has been manufacturing. Wal-Mart has developed operational capacity and efficiency, based in part by working closely with suppliers, that are significant advantages. In addition to potential cost advantages, superior processes and systems at both Toyota and Wal-Mart provide strategic and tactical flexibility.

The third area is finance, the ability to generate or acquire funds in the short as well as the long run. Companies with deep pockets (financial resources) have a decisive advantage because they can pursue strategies not available to smaller firms. This is especially true in times of stress. Firms with a strong balance sheet can seize opportunities. Operations provide one major source of funds. What is the nature of cash flow that is being generated and will be generated given the known uses for funds? Cash or other liquid assets and the deep pockets of a parent firm are important sources as well.

Management is the fourth area. Controlling and motivating a set of highly disparate business operations are strengths for GE, Disney, and other firms that have successfully diversified. The quality, depth, and loyalty (as measured by turnover) of top and middle management provide an important asset for others. Another aspect to analyze is the culture. The values and norms that permeate an organization can energize some strategies and inhibit others. In particular, some organizations, such as 3M, possess both an entrepreneurial culture that allows them to initiate new directions and the organizational skill to nurture them. The ability to set strategic goals and plans can represent significant competencies. To what extent does the business have a vision and the will and competence to pursue it?

The fifth area is marketing. Often the most important marketing strength, particularly in the high-tech field, involves the product line: its quality reputation, breadth, and the features that differentiate it from other products. Brand image and distribution have been key assets for businesses as diverse as Pizza Hut, Dell, and Bank of America. The ability to develop a true customer orientation can be an important strength. For P&G, two of its strengths are consumer understanding and brand building. Another strength can be based on the ability and willingness to advertise effectively. The success of Perdue chickens, MasterCard, and Budweiser were all due in part to an ability to generate superior advertising. Other elements of the marketing mix, such as the sales force and service operation, can also be sources of sustainable competitive advantage. One of Caterpillar's strengths is the quality of its dealer network. Still another possible strength, particularly in the high-tech field, is an ability to stay close to customers.

The final area of interest is the customer base. How substantial is the customer base, and how loyal is it? How are the competitor's offerings evaluated by its customers? What are the costs that customers will have to absorb if they switch to another supplier? Extremely loyal and happy customers are difficult to dislodge. What are the size and growth potentials of the segments served by a competitor?

THE COMPETITIVE STRENGTH GRID

With the relevant assets and competencies identified, the next step is to scale your own firm and the major competitors or strategic groups of competitors on those assets and competencies. The result is termed a competitive strength grid and serves to summarize the position of the competitors with respect to assets and competencies.

A sustainable competitive advantage is almost always based on having a position superior to that of the target competitors in one or more asset or competence area that is relevant both to the industry and to the strategy employed. Thus, information about each competitor's position with respect to relevant assets and competencies is central to strategy development and evaluation.

If a superior position does not exist with respect to assets and competencies important to the strategy, it probably will have to be created or the strategy may have to be modified or abandoned. Sometimes there simply is no point of difference with respect to the firms regarded as competitors. A competency that all competitors have will not be the basis for an SCA. For example, flight safety is important among airline passengers, but if airlines are perceived to be equal with respect to pilot quality and plane maintenance, it cannot be the basis for an SCA. Of course, if some airlines can convince passengers that they are superior with respect to antiterrorist security, then an SCA could indeed emerge.

The Luxury Car Market

A competitor strength grid is illustrated in Figure 3.5 for the luxury car market. The relevant assets and competencies are listed on the left, grouped as to whether they are considered keys to success or are of secondary importance. The principal competitors are shown as column headings across the top. Each cell could be coded as to whether the brand is strong, above average, average, below average, or weak in that asset or competence category. The figure uses an above average, average, and below average scale.

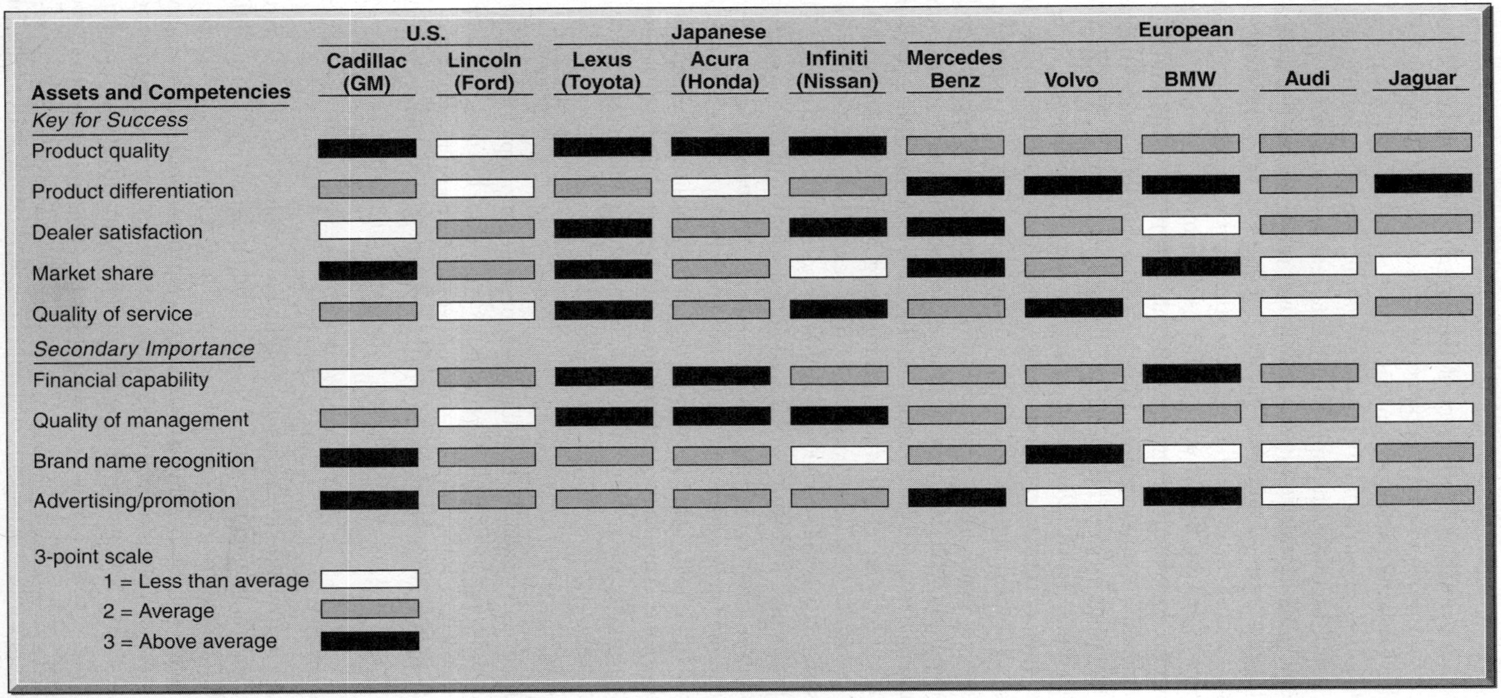

Assets and Competencies

Key for Success
- Product quality
- Product differentiation
- Dealer satisfaction
- Market share
- Quality of service

Secondary Importance
- Financial capability
- Quality of management
- Brand name recognition
- Advertising/promotion

	U.S.		Japanese			European				
	Cadillac (GM)	Lincoln (Ford)	Lexus (Toyota)	Acura (Honda)	Infiniti (Nissan)	Mercedes Benz	Volvo	BMW	Audi	Jaguar

3-point scale
1 = Less than average
2 = Average
3 = Above average

Figure 3.5 Illustrative Example of a Competitive Strength Grid for the U.S. Luxury Car Market

The resulting figure provides a summary of the hypothetical profile of the strengths and weaknesses of ten brands. Two can be compared, such as Ford and Lexus or BMW and Audi. BMW and Lexus have enviable positions.

In the grid, Lincoln is shown as not being well regarded. But that could change as Lincoln, blessed with an incredible heritage, attempted in 2013 a break-out reinvigoration. The effort rests in large part on the new MKZ midsize car that will deliver quality, looks right with an appealing fluid design described as "smooth and soft," has an interior that is competitive with the other brands, and includes a host of differentiating innovations such as push-button shifting and a panoramic glass roof. There is a hybrid version that gets 45 mpg.

The car is being introduced with an aggressive digital marketing program and a set of television ads that provides a link to the past heritage with glimpses of the some of the classic models and a full-page newspaper print ad that explains how Lincoln will become great again. People who test drive a Lincoln will receive a diner reward, a "Lincoln date night," and there will be a 24-hour concierge to help navigate model choice. The dealer experience got a significant upgrade. At the same time, the organization has been renamed as the Lincoln Motor Company (both a step up and a step back in time from the Lincoln Division), and the customer dealer experience is upgraded to Lexus levels.

A tough assignment but it has been done before. Cadillac came back from a similar point in 2003 with its CTS model. It was able to demonstrate the CTS could perform as well or better than any rival in terms of acceleration and drivability. It further got credibility and visibility by getting third-party quality recognition. It took years, but Cadillac came back. Hyundai is another brand that overcame a disastrous and well-earned reputation for poor quality and design. They changed course, created superior cars that won awards, and added some brilliant marketing. The result was impressive visibility, a revised image, and a remarkable increase in relevance.

So the image data has momentum but also is dynamic. It can change, especially if a major relaunch is anchored by an innovative new model that delivers value, gets recognition, and gets traction in the marketplace. It needs to get the delicate balance required to leverage the heritage into authenticity, personality, and self-expressive benefits rather than nostalgic charm

Analyzing Submarkets

It is often desirable to conduct an analysis for submarkets or strategic groups and perhaps for different products. A firm may not compete with all other firms in the industry but only with those engaged in similar strategies and markets. For example, a competitive strength grid may look very different for the safety submarket, with Volvo having more strength. Similarly, the handling submarket may also involve a competitive grid that will look different, with BMW having more strength.

The Analysis Process

The process of developing a competitive strength grid can be extremely informative and useful. One approach is to have several managers create their own grids independently. The differences can usually illuminate different assumptions and information bases. A reconciliation stage can disseminate relevant information and identify and structure strategic uncertainties. For example, different opinions about the quality reputation of a competitor may stimulate a strategic uncertainty that justifies marketing research. Another approach is to develop the grid in a group setting, perhaps supported by preliminary staff work. When possible, objective information based on laboratory tests or customer perception studies should be used. The need for such information becomes clear when disagreements arise about where competitors should be scaled on the various dimensions.

OBTAINING INFORMATION ON COMPETITORS

A competitor's Web site is usually a rich source of information and the first place to look. The strategic vision (along with a statement about values and culture) is often posted, and the portfolios of businesses are usually laid out. The way that the latter are organized can provide clues as to business priorities and strategies. When IBM emphasizes its e-servers, for example, that says something about their direction in the server business. The Web site also can provide information about such business assets as plants, global access, and brand symbols. Research on the competitor's site can be supplemented with search engines, access to articles, and financial reports about the business.

Detailed information on competitors is generally available from a variety of other sources as well. Competitors usually communicate extensively with their suppliers, customers, and distributors; security analysts and stockholders; and government legislators and regulators. Contact with any of these can provide information. Monitoring of trade magazines, trade shows, advertising, speeches, annual reports, and the like can be informative. Technical meetings and journals can provide information about technical developments and activities. Thousands of databases accessible by computer now make available detailed information on most companies.

Detailed information about a competitor's standing with its customers can be obtained through market research. For example, regular telephone surveys could provide information about the successes and vulnerabilities of competitors' strategies. Respondents could be asked questions such as the following: Which store is closest to your home? Which do you shop at most often? Are you satisfied? Which has the lowest prices? Best specials? Best customer service? Cleanest stores? Best-quality meat? Best-quality produce? And so on. Those chains that were well positioned on value, on service, or on product quality could be identified, and tracking would show whether they were gaining or losing position. The loyalty of their customer base (and thus their vulnerability) could be indicated in part by satisfaction scores and the willingness of customers to patronize stores even when they were not the most convenient or the least expensive.

KEY LEARNINGS

- Competitors can be identified by customer choice (the set from which customers select) or by clustering them into strategic groups (firms that pursue similar strategies and have similar assets, competencies, and other characteristics). In either case, competitors will vary in terms of how intensely they compete.

- Competitors should be analyzed along several dimensions, including their size, growth and profitability, image, objectives, business strategies, organizational culture, cost structure, exit barriers, and strengths and weaknesses.

- Potential strengths and weaknesses can be identified by considering the characteristics of successful and unsuccessful businesses, key customer motivation, mobility barriers, and value-added components.

- The competitive strength grid, which arrays competitors or strategic groups on each of the relevant assets and competencies, provides a compact summary of key strategic information.

FOR DISCUSSION

1. Consider the news industry. Identify the competitors to CNN and organize them in terms of their intensity of competition.

2. Evaluate Figure 3.5. What surprises are there in the figure? What are the implications for Cadillac? For Audi?

3. Pick a company or brand or business on which to focus. What business is it in? Who are its direct and indirect competitors? Which in each category are the most relevant competitors?

4. Consider the automobile industry. Identify competitors to Ford SUVs and organize them in terms of their intensity of competition. Also organize them into strategic groups. What are the key success factors for the strategic groups? Do you think that will change in the next five years?

5. Consider the Nintendo case on page 45. Why was Nintendo the firm to come up with the DS and the Wii products and not SONY or Microsoft? How did they do it? What assets and competences were required?

NOTES

1. David Halberstam, *The Reckoning*, New York: William Morrow, 1986, p. 310.
2. Ibid.
3. Michael E. Porter, *Competitive Strategy*, New York: The Free Press, 1980, pp. 20–21. The concept of exit barriers is discussed again in Chapter 15.
4. Study by Enterbrain mentioned in *Nikkei Business Daily*, July 23, 2007.

CHAPTER FOUR

Market/Submarket Analysis

As the economy, led by the automobile industry, rose to a new high level in the twenties, a complex of new elements came into existence to transform the market: installment selling, the used-car trade-in, the closed body, and the annual model. (I would add improved roads if I were to take into account the environment of the automobile.)
—*Alfred P. Sloan, Jr., General Motors*

Vision is the art of seeing things invisible.
—*Jonathan Swift*

To be prepared is half the victory.
—*Miguel Cervantes*

Market analysis builds on customer and competitor analyses to make some strategic judgments about a market (and submarket) and its dynamics. Should a firm invest, and what should the level of commitment be? Or should it disinvest? One of the primary objectives of a market analysis is to determine the attractiveness of a market (or submarket) to current and potential participants. Market attractiveness, the market's profit potential as measured by the long-term return on investment achieved by its participants, will provide important input into the product-market investment decision. The frame of reference is all participants.

A second and related objective of market analysis is to understand the dynamics of the market. It informs the investment decision but also sheds light on what it would take to be a winner in the space. The need is to identify emerging submarkets, key success factors, trends, threats, opportunities, and strategic uncertainties that can guide information gathering and analysis. A key success factor is an asset or competency that is needed to play the game. If a firm has a strategic weakness in a key success factor that isn't neutralized by a well-conceived strategy, its ability to compete will be limited. The market trends can include those identified in customer or competitor analysis, but the perspective here is broader, and others will usually emerge as well.

DIMENSIONS OF A MARKET/SUBMARKET ANALYSIS

The nature and content of an analysis of a market and its submarkets will depend on context but will often include the following dimensions:

- Emerging submarkets
- Actual and potential market and submarket size
- Market and submarket growth
- Market and submarket profitability
- Cost structure
- Distribution systems
- Trends and developments
- Key success factors

Figure 4.1 provides a set of questions structured around these dimensions that can serve to stimulate a discussion identifying opportunities, threats, and strategic uncertainties. Each dimension will be addressed in turn. The chapter concludes with a discussion of the risks of growth markets.

SUBMARKETS

Are submarkets emerging defined by lower price points, the emergence of niches, systems solutions, new applications, a customer trend, or new technology? How should the submarket be defined?

SIZE AND GROWTH

Important submarkets? What are the size and growth characteristics of a market and submarkets? What submarkets are declining or will soon decline? How fast? What are the driving forces behind sales trends?

PROFITABILITY

For each major submarket consider the following: Is this a business area in which the average firm will make money? How intense is the competition among existing firms? Evaluate the threats from potential entrants and substitute products. What is the bargaining power of suppliers and customers? How attractive/profitable are the market and its submarkets both now and in the future?

COST STRUCTURE

What are the major cost and value-added components for various types of competitors?

DISTRIBUTION SYSTEMS

What are the alternative channels of distribution? How are they changing?

MARKET TRENDS

What are the trends in the market?

KEY SUCCESS FACTORS

What are the key success factors, assets, and competencies needed to compete successfully? How will these change in the future? How can the assets and competencies of competitors be neutralized by strategies?

Figure 4.1 Questions to Help Structure a Market Analysis

EMERGING SUBMARKETS

The management of a firm in any dynamic market requires addressing the challenge and opportunity of relevance, as described in the box below. In essence, the challenge is to detect and understand emerging submarkets, identify those that are attractive to the firm given its assets and competencies, and then adjust offerings and brand portfolios in order to increase their relevance to the chosen submarkets. The opportunity is to influence these emerging submarkets so that competitors become less relevant.

In Chapter 13, characteristics of new business areas or submarkets will be detailed. Knowing these characteristics can help detect and analyze emerging submarkets. They include offerings that:

- Provide a lower price point—discount airlines
- Serve nonusers—Kodak Brownie camera
- Serve niche markets—performance snowboards
- Provide systems solutions—home theaters
- Serve unmet needs—Lexus car buying experience
- Respond to a customer trend—fortified energy drinks
- Leverage a new technology—Gillette Fusion Razors

RELEVANCE

All too frequently, despite retaining high levels of awareness, attitude, and even loyalty, a brand loses market share because it is not perceived to be relevant to emerging submarkets. If a group of customers want hybrid cars, it does not matter how good they think your firm's SUV is. They might love and recommend it, but if they are interested in a hybrid because of their changing needs and desires, then your brand is irrelevant to them. This may be true even if your firm also makes hybrids under the same brand. The hybrid submarket is different than SUVs and has a different set of relevant brands.

Relevance for a brand occurs when two conditions are met. First, there must be a perceived need or desire by customers for a submarket defined by some combination of an attribute set, an application, a user group, or other distinguishing characteristic. Second, the brand needs to be among the set considered to be relevant for that submarket by the prospective customers.

Winning among brands within a submarket, however, is not enough. There are two additional relevance challenges. One is to make sure that the submarket associated with the brand is relevant. The problem may not be that the customer picks the wrong brand but rather that the wrong submarket (and brand set) is picked. The second challenge is to make sure that the brand is considered by customers to be an option with respect to a submarket. This implies that a brand needs to be positioned against the submarket in addition to whatever other positioning strategies may be pursued. It must also be visible and be perceived to meet minimal performance levels.

Nearly every marketplace is undergoing change—often dramatic, rapid change—that creates relevance issues. Examples appear in nearly every industry, from computers, consulting, airlines, power generators, and financial services to snack food, beverages, pet food, and toys. Hardware, paint, and flooring stores struggle with the reality of Home Depot,. Xerox, and Kodak have found it difficult

(continued)

to address a relevance challenge as other firms are carving up the digital imaging world. Think about pay telephones, print newspapers, first class mail, and print discount supermarket coupons and the relevance issues posed to firms in those sectors. Relevance is an issue as well for brands attempting to open up new business arenas, such as Toyota's hybrid cars or Sony's Blu-ray player.

The key to managing such change is twofold. First, a business must detect and understand emerging submarkets, projecting how they are evolving. Second, it must maintain relevance in the face of these emerging submarkets. Businesses that perform these tasks successfully have the organizational skills to detect change, the organizational vitality to respond, and a well-conceived brand strategy. Chapter 9 elaborates, Chapter 11 explores the threat of a loss of brand energy to relevance.

The emergence of a new subcategory is also an opportunity for the firm that can dominate that submarket, control its perception, and make competitors less relevant or even irrelevant. IBM did this with e-business. Gillette did it with the Mach III and Fusion brands. Charles Schwab did it with Schwab OneSource. Creating and owning subcategories can only occur when the right firm, armed with the right idea and offering, is ready to act at the right time. But when it happens, it can be a strategic home run and the source of unusual profits over a long time period.[1]

Chapter 13 discusses how innovation can create new submarkets where competitors are less relevant.

ACTUAL AND POTENTIAL MARKET OR SUBMARKET SIZE

A basic starting point for the analysis of a market or submarket is the total sales level. If it is reasonable to believe that a successful strategy can be developed to gain a 15 percent share, it is important to know the total market size. Among the sources that can be helpful are published financial analyses of the relevant firms, customers, government data, and trade magazines and associations. The ultimate source is often a survey of product users in which the usage levels are projected to the population.

Potential Market—The User Gap

In addition to the size of the current, relevant market or submarket, it is often useful to consider the potential size. A new use, new user group, or more frequent usage could dramatically change the size and prospects for the market or submarket.

There is unrealized potential for the cereal market in Europe and among institutional customers in the United States—restaurants and schools/day-care facilities. All these segments have room for dramatic growth. In particular, Europeans buy only about 25 percent as much cereal as their U.S. counterparts. If technology allowed cereals to be used more conveniently away from home by providing shelf-stable milk products, usage could be further expanded. Of course, the key is not only to recognize the potential but also to have the vision and program in place to exploit it. A host of strategists have dismissed investment opportunities in industries because they lacked the insight to see the available potential and take advantage of it.

Small Can Be Beautiful

Some firms have investment criteria that prohibit them from investing in small markets. Chevron, Microsoft, Frito-Lay, and Procter & Gamble, for example, have historically looked to new products that would generate large sales levels within a few years. Yet in an era of micro-marketing, much of the action is in smaller niche segments. If a firm avoids them, it can lock itself out of much of the vitality and profitability of a business area. Furthermore, most substantial business areas were small at the outset, sometimes for many years, and as noted in Chapter 13, some become attractive niche submarkets. Avoiding the small market can thus mean that a firm must later overcome the first-mover advantage of others.

Further, there is evidence recounted in the book *The Long Tail* by Chris Anderson that many markets have changed so that the small niche business is economically viable and should not be automatically ignored.[2] The book, music, entertainment, and broadcasting areas illustrate the fact that the tail—the offerings that are not the large hit products—is extensive and collectively important. Cable networks serve smaller but worthwhile audiences. Companies limited by retailers to a small selection can provide access to a full line from their Web sites; KitchenAid, for example, offers its products in some 50 colors. With eBay, Amazon, Google, and others, the economics of marketing small niche items has changed. The fact that some 25,000 items are introduced in the grocery stores each year and car makers offer some 250 different models indicates that niche marketing is viable outside the Internet world as well.

There is a downside to having too many niche offerings. First, companies can create operating and marketing costs that can be debilitating when the offerings are too extensive. Second, customers can become overwhelmed by the confusion of too many choices and rebel—looking for the equivalent of Colgate's Total, a product that simplified decision making in a cluttered environment. Thus, many firms are trimming lines that have gotten too large. Nevertheless, the analysis of niche markets needs to reflect the new reality that customers have faster and more extensive access to information than before, and products are accessible in ways not feasible just a few years ago.

MARKET AND SUBMARKET GROWTH

After the size of the market and its important submarkets have been estimated, the focus turns to growth rate. What will be the size of the markets and submarkets in the future? If all else remains constant, growth means more sales and profits even without increasing market share. It can also mean less price pressure when demand increases faster than supply and firms are not engaged in experience curve pricing, anticipating future lower costs. Conversely, declining sales can mean reduced sales and often increased price pressure as firms struggle to hold their shares of a diminishing pie.

It may seem that the strategy of choice would thus be to identify and avoid or disinvest in declining situations and to identify and invest in growth contexts. Of course, the reality is not that simple. In particular, declining product markets can represent a real opportunity for a firm, in part because competitors may be exiting and disinvesting instead of entering and investing for growth. The firm may attempt to become a profitable survivor by encouraging others to exit and by becoming dominant in the most viable segments.

The other half of the conventional wisdom, that growth contexts are always attractive, can also fail to hold true. Growth situations can involve substantial risks. Because of the importance of correctly assessing growth contexts, a discussion of these risks is presented at the end of this chapter.

Identifying Driving Forces

In many contexts, the most important strategic uncertainty involves the prediction of market sales. A key strategic decision, often an investment decision, can hinge on not only being correct but also understanding the driving forces behind market dynamics.

Addressing most key strategic uncertainties starts with asking on what the answer depends. In the case of projecting sales of a major market, the need is to determine what forces will drive those sales. For example, the sales of a new consumer electronics device may be driven by machine costs, the evolution of an industry standard, or the emergence of alternative technologies. Each of these three drivers will provide the basis for key second-level uncertainties.

In the wine market, the relationship of wine to health and the future demand for premium reds might be driving forces. One second-level strategic uncertainty might then ask on what the demand for premium red will depend.

Forecasting Growth

Historical data can provide a useful perspective and help to separate hope from reality. Accurate forecasts for new packaged goods can be based on the timing of trial and repeat purchases. Durable goods forecasts can be based on projecting initial sales patterns. However, care needs to be exercised. Apparent trends in data such as those shown in Figure 4.2 can be caused by random fluctuations or by short-term economic conditions, and the urge to extrapolate should be resisted. Furthermore, the strategic interest is not on projections of history but rather on the prediction of turning points, times when the rate and perhaps direction of growth change.

Sometimes leading indicators of market sales may help in forecasting and predicting turning points. Examples of leading indicators include:

- **Demographic data.** The number of births is a leading indicator of the demand for education, and the number of people reaching age 65 is a leading indicator of the demand for retirement facilities.
- **Sales of related equipment.** Personal computer and printer sales provide a leading indicator of the demand for supplies and service needs.

Market sales forecasts, especially of new markets, can be based on the experience of analogous industries. The trick is to identify a prior market with similar characteristics. Sales of color televisions might be expected to have a pattern similar to sales of black-and-white televisions, for example. Sales of a new type of snack might look to the history of other previously introduced snack categories or other consumer products, such as some of the energy bars or

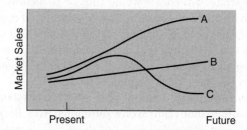

Figure 4.2   Sales Patterns

granola bars. The most value will be obtained if several analogous product classes and the differences in the product class experiences related to their characteristics can be examined.

Submarket Growth

Submarket growth is usually critical because it affects investment decisions and value propositions. That involves identifying and analyzing current and emerging submarkets. While the beer category is flat, imports are declining, and craft beers are showing significant growth. Among restaurants, fast casual chains such as Panera Bread, Chipotle Mexican Grill, and Panda Express are the fast growing.

Detecting Maturity and Decline

One particularly important set of turning points in market sales occurs when the growth phase of the product life cycle changes to a flat maturity phase and when the maturity phase changes into a decline phase. These transitions are important indicators of the health and nature of the market. Often they are accompanied by changes in key success factors. Historical sales and profit patterns of a market can help to identify the onset of maturity or decline, but the following often are more sensitive indicators:

- ***Price pressure caused by overcapacity and the lack of product differentiation.*** When growth slows or even reverses, capacity developed under a more optimistic scenario becomes excessive. Furthermore, the product evolution process often results in most competitors matching product improvements. Thus, it becomes more difficult to maintain meaningful differentiation.

- ***Buyer sophistication and knowledge.*** Buyers tend to become more familiar and knowledgeable as a product matures, and thus they become less willing to pay a premium price to obtain the security of an established name. Computer buyers over the years have gained confidence in their ability to select computers—as a result, the value of big names has receded.

- ***Substitute products or technologies.*** The sales of personal TV services like TiVo provide an indicator of the decline of VCRs.

- ***Saturation.*** When the number of potential first-time buyers declines, market sales should mature or decline.

- ***No growth sources.*** The market is fully penetrated and there are no visible sources of growth from new uses or users.

- ***Customer disinterest.*** The interest of customers in applications, new product announcements, and so on falls off.

MARKET AND SUBMARKET PROFITABILITY ANALYSIS

Economists have long studied why some industries or markets are profitable and others are not. Harvard economist and business strategy guru Michael Porter applied his theories and findings to the business strategy problem of evaluating the investment value of an industry, market, or submarket.[3] The problem is to estimate how profitable the average firm will be. It is hoped, of

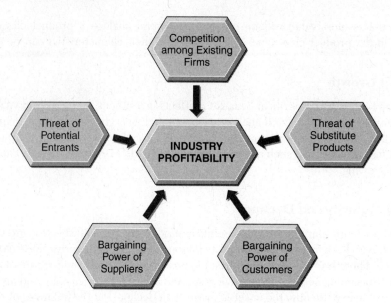

Figure 4.3   Porter's Five-Factor Model of Market Profitabiliy

Source: The concept of five factors is due to Michael E. Porter. See his book *Competitive Advantage*, New York: The Free Press, 1985, Chapter 1.

course, that a firm will develop a strategy that will bring above-average profits. If the average profit level is low, however, the task of succeeding financially will be much more difficult than if the average profitability were high.

Porter's approach can be applied to any industry, but it also can be applied to a market or submarket within an industry. The basic idea is that the attractiveness of an industry or market as measured by the long-term return on investment of the average firm depends largely on five factors that influence profitability, shown in Figure 4.3:

- The intensity of competition among existing competitors
- The existence of potential competitors who will enter if profits are high
- Substitute products that will attract customers if prices become high
- The bargaining power of customers
- The bargaining power of suppliers

Each factor plays a role in explaining why some industries are historically more profitable than others. An understanding of this structure can also suggest which key success factors are necessary to cope with the competitive forces.

Existing Competitors

The intensity of competition from existing competitors will depend on several factors, including:

- The number of competitors, their size, and their commitment
- Whether their product offerings and strategies are similar

- The existence of high fixed costs
- The size of exit barriers

The first question to ask is, how many competitors are already in the market or making plans to enter soon? The more competitors that exist, the more competition intensifies. Are they large firms with staying power and commitment or small and vulnerable ones? The second consideration is the amount of differentiation. Are the competitors similar, or are some (or all) insulated by points of uniqueness valued by customers? The third factor is the level of fixed costs. High fixed-cost industries such as telecommunications and airlines experience debilitating price pressures when overcapacity gets large. Finally, one should assess the presence of exit barriers such as specialized assets, long-term contract commitments to customers and distributors, and relationship to other parts of a firm.

One major factor in the shakeout of the Internet bubble firms was the excessive number of competitors. Because the barriers to entry were low and the offered products so similar, margins were insufficient (and often nonexistent), especially given the significant investment in infrastructure and brand building that was needed. Given the hysterical market growth and the low barriers to entry, the results should have been anticipated; at one time there were a host of pet-supply and drugstore e-commerce offerings competing for a still-embryonic market.

Potential Competitors

Chapter 3 discusses identifying potential competitors that might have an interest in entering an industry or market. Whether potential competitors, identified or not, actually do enter depends in large part on the size and nature of barriers to entry. Thus, an analysis of barriers to entry is important in projecting likely competitive intensity and profitability levels in the future.

Various barriers to entry include required capital investment (the infrastructure in cable television and telecommunication), economies of scale (the success of Internet portals like Yahoo! is largely based on scale economies), distribution channels (Frito-Lay and IBM have access to customers that is not easily duplicated), and product differentiation (Apple and Harley-Davidson have highly differentiated products that protect them from new entrants).

Substitute Products

Substitute products compete with less intensity than do the primary competitors. They are still relevant, however, as the discussion in Chapter 3 made clear. They can influence the profitability of the market and can be a major threat or problem. Thus, plastics, glass, and fiber-foil products exert pressure on the metal can market. Electronic alarm systems are substitutes for the security guard market. E-mail provides a threat to some portion of the express-delivery market of FedEx, UPS, and the U.S. Postal Service. Substitutes that show a steady improvement in relative price/performance and for which the customer's cost of switching is minimal are of particular interest.

Customer Power

When customers have relatively more power than sellers, they can force prices down or demand more services, thereby affecting profitability. A customer's power will be greater when its purchase size is a large proportion of the seller's business, when alternative suppliers are available, and when the customer can integrate backward and make all or part of the product. Thus, tire manufacturers face powerful customers in the automobile firms. Soft-drink firms sell to fast-food restaurant chains that have strong bargaining power. Wal-Mart has enormous power over its suppliers. It can dictate prices and product specifications; if companies resist, there is an Asian supplier that will comply. Wal-Mart is the leading seller of practically all appliances. Because something like 15 percent of all Procter & Gamble sales go through Wal-Mart (a proportion that approaches 30 percent for some categories), even P&G is subject to customer power.

Supplier Power

When the supplier industry is concentrated and sells to a variety of customers in diverse markets, it will have relative power that can be used to influence prices. Power will also be enhanced when the costs to customers of switching suppliers are high. Thus, the highly concentrated oil industry is often powerful enough to influence profits in customer industries that find it expensive to convert from oil. However, the potential for regeneration whereby industries can create their own energy supplies, perhaps by recycling waste, may have changed the balance of power in some contexts.

COST STRUCTURE

An understanding of the cost structure of a market can provide insights into present and future key success factors. The first step is to conduct an analysis of the value chain, presented in Figure 4.4, which shows the steps in the production and delivery of an offering that adds value. As suggested in Figure 4.4, the proportion of value added attributed to one value chain stage can become so important that a key success factor is associated with that stage. It may be possible to develop control over a resource or technology, as did the OPEC oil cartel. More likely, competitors will aim to be the lowest-cost competitor in a high value-added stage of the value chain. Advantages in lower value-added stages will simply have less leverage. Thus, in the metal can business, transportation costs are relatively high, and a competitor that can locate plants near customers will have a significant cost advantage.

It may not be possible to gain an advantage at high value-added stages. For example, a raw material, such as flour for bakery firms, may represent a high value added, but because the raw

Production Stage	Markets That Have Key Success Factors Associated with the Production Stage
• Raw material procurement	• Gold mining, winemaking
• Raw material processing	• Steel, paper
• Production fabricating	• Integrated circuits, tires
• Assembly	• Apparel, instrumentation
• Physical distribution	• Bottled water, metal cans
• Marketing	• Branded cosmetics, liquor
• Service backup	• Software, automobiles
• Technology development	• Razors, medical systems

Figure 4.4 Value-Added and Key Success Factors

material is widely available at commodity prices, it will not be a key success factor. Nevertheless, it is often useful to look first at the highest value-added stages, especially if changes are occurring. For example, the cement market was very regional when it was restricted to rail or truck transportation. With the development of specialized ships, however, waterborne transportation costs dropped dramatically. Key success factors changed from local ground transportation to production scale and access to the specialized ships.

DISTRIBUTION SYSTEMS

An analysis of distribution systems should include three types of questions:

- What are the alternative distribution channels?
- What are the trends? What channels are growing in importance? What new channels have emerged or are likely to emerge?
- Who has the power in the channel, and how is that likely to shift?

Sometimes the creation of a new channel of distribution can lead to a sustainable competitive advantage. A dramatic example is the success that L'eggs hosiery, with its egg-shaped package, achieved by its ability to market hosiery in supermarkets. Avon and other direct marketers have created a class of competitors that have become significant in several product categories such as cleaning products. Amazon has radically changed book selling and a host of other products as well.

An analysis of likely or emerging changes within distribution channels can be important in understanding a market and its key success factors. The increased sale of wine in supermarkets made it much more important for winemakers to focus on packaging and advertising. The consolidation of department stores meant that clothing brands had fewer retailers through which to sell their products

MARKET TRENDS

Often one of the most useful elements of external analysis comes from addressing the question, what are the market trends? The question has two important attributes: it focuses on change, and it tends to identify what is important. Strategically useful insights almost always result. A discussion of market trends can serve as a useful summary of customer, competitor, and market analyses. It is thus helpful to identify trends near the end of market analysis.

While the soft-drink market stagnated in the United States, sales of noncarbonated beverages grew sharply, and sales of herb- and vitamin-fortified beverages exploded. Not surprisingly, the major soft-drink companies sought to obtain a position in these trendy categories. Reports that dark chocolate was heart-healthy sent sales up 30 percent from 2003 to 2005. Chocolate makers scrambled to redo their lines and yet create products with authenticity.

Trends vs. Fads

It is crucial to distinguish between trends that will drive growth and reward those who develop differentiated strategies and fads that will only last long enough to attract investment (which is subsequently underemployed or lost forever). Schwinn, the classic name in bicycles, proclaimed mountain biking a fad in 1985, with disastrous results to its market position and, ultimately, its corporate health.[4] The mistaken belief that certain e-commerce markets, such as those for cosmetics and pet supplies, were solid trends caused strategists to undertake initial share-building strategies that eventually led to the ventures' demise.

One firm, the Zandl Group, suggests that three questions can help detect a real trend, as opposed to a fad.[5]

1. *What is driving it?* A trend will have a solid foundation with legs. Trends are more likely to be driven by demographics (rather than pop culture), values (rather than fashion), lifestyle (rather than a trendy crowd), or technology (rather than media).

2. *How accessible is it in the mainstream?* Will it be constrained to a niche market for the foreseeable future? Will it require a major change in ingrained habits? Is the required investment in time or resources a barrier (perhaps because the product is priced too high or is too hard to use)?

3. *Is it broadly based?* Does it find expression across categories or industries? Eastern influences, for example, are apparent in health care, food, fitness, and design—a sign of a trend.

Faith Popcorn observes that fads are about products, while trends are about what drives consumers to buy products. She also suggests that trends (which are big and broad, lasting an average of 10 years) cannot be created or changed, only observed.[6]

Still another perspective on fads comes from Peter Drucker, who opined that a change is something that people do, whereas a fad is something people talk about. The implication is that a trend demands substance and action supported by data rather than simply an idea that captures the imagination. Drucker also suggests that the leaders of today need to move beyond innovation to be change agents—the real payoff comes not from simply detecting and reacting to trends, even when they are real, but from creating and driving them.[7]

KEY SUCCESS FACTORS

An important output of market analysis is the identification of key success factors (KSFs) for strategic groups in the market. These are assets and competencies that provide the basis for competing successfully. There are two types. *Strategic necessities* do not necessarily provide an advantage, because others have them, but their absence will create a substantial weakness. The firm needs to achieve a point of parity with respect to strategic necessities. The second type, *strategic strengths*, are those at which a firm excels, the assets or competencies that are superior to those of competitors and provide a base of advantage. The set of assets and competencies developed in competitor analysis provides a base from which key success factors can be identified. The points to consider are which are the most critical assets and competencies now and, more important, which will be most critical in the future.

It is important not only to identify KSFs but also to project them into the future and, in particular, to identify emerging KSFs. Many firms have faltered when KSFs changed and the competencies and assets on which they were relying became less relevant. For example, for industrial firms, technology and innovation tend to be most important during the introduction and growth phases, whereas the roles of systems capability, marketing, and service backup become more dominant as the market matures. In consumer products, marketing and distribution skills are crucial during the introduction and growth phases, but operations and manufacturing become more crucial as the product settles into the maturity and decline phases.

RISKS IN HIGH-GROWTH MARKETS

The conventional wisdom that the strategist should seek out growth areas often overlooks a substantial set of associated risks. As shown in Figure 4.5, there are the risks that:

- The number and commitment of competitors may be greater than the market can support.
- A competitor may enter with a superior product or low-cost advantage.
- Key success factors might change and the organization may be unable to adapt.
- Technology might change.
- The market growth may fail to meet expectations.
- Price instability may result from overcapacity or from retailers' practice of pricing hot products low to attract customers.
- Resources might be inadequate to maintain a high growth rate.
- Adequate distribution may not be available.

Competitive Overcrowding

Perhaps the most serious risk is that too many competitors will be attracted by a growth situation and enter with unrealistic market share expectations. The reality may be that sales volume is insufficient to support all competitors. Overcrowding has been observed in virtually all hyped markets, from railroads to automobiles, airplanes, radio stations and equipment, television sets, and personal computers.

Overcrowding was never more vividly apparent (in retrospect, at least) than in the Internet bubble that occurred around 2000. At one point there were at least 150 online brokerages, 1,000

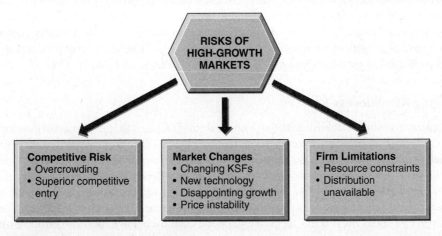

Figure 4.5 Risks of High-Growth Markets

travel-related sites, and 30 health and beauty sites that were competing for attention. Dot-com business-to-business (B2B) exchanges were created for the buying and selling of goods and services, information exchanges, logistics services, sourcing industry data and forecasts, and a host of other services. The number of B2B companies grew from under 250 to over 1,500 during the year 2000 and then fell to under 250 again in 2003. At the peak, there were estimated to be more than 140 such exchanges in the industrial supplies industry alone.[8]

The following conditions are found in markets in which a surplus of competitors is likely to be attracted and a subsequent shakeout is highly probable. These factors were all present in the B2B dot-com experience:

1. The market and its growth rate have high visibility. As a result, strategists in related firms are encouraged to consider the market seriously and may even fear the consequences of turning their backs on an obvious growth direction.

2. Very high forecast and actual growth in the early stages are seen as evidence confirming high market growth as a proven phenomenon.

3. Threats to the growth rate are not considered or are discounted, and little exists to dampen the enthusiasm surrounding the market. The enthusiasm may be contagious when venture capitalists and stock analysts become advocates.

4. Few initial barriers exist to prevent firms from entering the market. There may be barriers to eventual success (such as limited retail space); however, that may not be evident at the outset.

5. Some potential entrants have low visibility, and their intentions are unknown or uncertain. As a result, the quantity and commitment of the competitors are likely to be underestimated.

Superior Competitive Entry

The ultimate risk is that a position will be established in a healthy growth market and a competitor will enter late with a product that is demonstrably superior or that has an inherent cost advantage.

Thus, Honda was first to the U.S. market in 1999 with a hybrid car, but its offering struggled in part because it was a two-seater with a frumpy design and had some technological limitations. Toyota's Prius, introduced two years later, was a bigger car with better styling and technology and took over market leadership two years later. The success of late-entry, low-cost products from the Asia has occurred in countless industries, from automobiles to clothing to TVs.

Changing Key Success Factors

A firm may successfully establish a strong position during the early stages of market development, only to lose ground later when key success factors change. One forecast is that the surviving personal computer makers will be those able to achieve low-cost production through sourcing manufacture in low-cost countries, exploitation of the experience curve, and obtaining efficient, low-cost distribution—capabilities not necessarily critical during the early stages of market evolution. Many product markets have experienced a shift over time from a focus on product technology to a focus on process technology, operational excellence, and the customer experience. A firm that might be capable of achieving product technology-based advantages may not have the resources, competencies, and orientation/culture needed to develop the demands of the evolving market.

Changing Technology

Developing first-generation technology can involve a commitment to a product line and production facilities that may become obsolete and to a technology that may not survive. A safe strategy is to wait until it is clear which technology will dominate and then attempt to improve it with a compatible entry. When the principal competitors have committed themselves, the most promising avenues for the development of a sustainable competitive advantage become more visible. In contrast, the early entry has to navigate with a great deal of uncertainty.

Disappointing Market Growth

Many shakeouts and price wars occur when market growth falls below expectations. Sometimes the market was an illusion to begin with. Internet-based B2B exchanges did not provide value to firms that already had systems built with relationships that were, on balance, superior to the B2B exchanges. There was an absence of a compelling value proposition to overcome marketplace inertia. Sometimes an area becomes so topical and the need so apparent that potential growth seems assured. As a Lewis Carroll character observed, "What I tell you three times is true." However, this potential can have a ghostlike quality caused by factors inhibiting or preventing its realization. For example, the demand for computers exists in many under-developed countries, but a lack of funds and the absence of suitable technology inhibit buying.

The demand might be real but might simply take longer to materialize because the technology is not ready or because customers are slow to change. Demand for electronic banking, for example, took many years longer than expected to materialize.

Forecasting demand is difficult, especially when the market is new, dynamic, and gla-morized. This difficulty is graphically illustrated by an analysis of more than 90 forecasts of significant new products, markets, and technologies that appeared in *Business Week, Fortune*, and the *Wall Street Journal* from 1960 to 1979.[9] Forecast growth failed to materialize in about 55 percent of the cases cited. Among the reasons were overvaluation of technologies (e.g., three-dimensional color TV and tooth-decay vaccines), consumer demand (e.g., two-way cable TV, quadraphonic stereo, and dehydrated foods), a failure to consider the cost barrier (e.g., the SST and moving sidewalks), or political problems (e.g., marine mining). The forecasts for roll-your-own cigarettes, small cigars, Scotch whiskey, and CB radios suffered from shifts in consumer needs and preferences.

Price Instability

When the creation of excess capacity results in price pressures, industry profitability may be short-lived, especially in an industry such as airlines or steel, in which fixed costs are high and economies of scale are crucial. However, it is also possible that some will use a visible, popular product as a loss leader just to attract customer flow.

CDs, a hot growth area in the late 1980s, fueled the overexpansion of retailers that were very profitable when they sold CDs for about $15. However, when Best Buy, a home-electronics chain, decided to sell CDs for under $10 to attract customers to their off-mall locations. The result was a dramatic erosion in margins and volume and the ultimate bankruptcy of a substantial number of the major CD retailers. A hot growth area had spawned a disaster, not by a self-inflicted price cut but by price instability from a firm that chose to treat the retailing of CDs as nothing more than a permanent loss leader.

Resource Constraints

The substantial financing requirements associated with a rapidly growing business are a major constraint for small firms. Royal Crown's Diet-Rite cola lost its leadership position to Coca-Cola's Tab and Diet Pepsi in the mid-1960s when it could not match the advertising and distribution clout of its larger rivals. Furthermore, financing requirements frequently are increased by higher than expected product development and market entry costs and by price erosion caused by aggressive or desperate competitors.

The organizational pressures and problems created by growth can be even more difficult to predict and deal with than financial strains. Many firms have failed to survive the rapid-growth phase because they were unable to obtain and train people to handle the expanded business or to adjust their systems and structures.

Distribution Constraints

Most distribution channels can support only a small number of brands. For example, few retailers are willing to provide shelf space for more than four or five brands of a houseware appliance. As a consequence, some competitors, even those with attractive products and marketing programs, will not gain adequate distribution, and their marketing programs will become less effective.

A corollary of the scarcity and selectivity of distributors as market growth begins to slow is a marked increase in distributor power. Their willingness to use this power to extract price and promotion concessions from manufacturers or to drop suppliers is often heightened by their own problems in maintaining margins in the face of extreme competition for their customers. Many of the same factors that drew in an overabundance of manufacturers also contribute to over-crowding in subsequent stages of a distribution channel. The eventual shakeout at this level can have equally serious repercussions for suppliers.

KEY LEARNINGS

- The emergence of submarkets can signal a relevance problem or opportunity.
- Market analysis should assess the attractiveness of a market or submarket, as well as its structure and dynamics.
- A usage gap can cause the market size to be understated.
- Market growth can be forecast by looking at driving forces, leading indicators, and analogous industries.
- Market profitability will depend on five factors—existing competitors, supplier power, customer power, substitute products, and potential entrants.
- Cost structure can be analyzed by looking at the value added at each production stage.

- Distribution channels and trends will often affect who wins.
- Market trends will affect both the profitability of strategies and key success factors.
- Key success factors are the skills and competencies needed to compete in a market.
- Growth-market challenges involve the threat of competitors, market changes, and firm limitations.

FOR DISCUSSION

1. What are the emerging submarkets in the fast food industry? What are the alternative responses available to McDonald's, assuming that it wants to stay relevant to customers interested in healthier eating?

2. Identify markets in which actual sales and growth was less than expected. Why was that the case? What would you say was the most important reason that the bottom fell out of the dot-com boom? Why did all the B2B sites emerge, and why did they collapse so suddenly?

3. Why were some brands (like Google) able to fight off competitors in high-growth markets and others were not?

4. Pick a company or brand/business on which to focus. What are the emerging submarkets? What are the trends? What are the strategic implications of the submarkets and trends for the major players?

5. What considerations go into forecasting when dark chocolate will peak?

NOTES

1. For more details in the relevance concept, see David A. Aaker, "The Brand Relevance Challenge," *Strategy & Business,* Spring 2004, and David A. Aaker, *Brand Portfolio Strategy,* New York: The Free Press, 2004, Chapter 3.
2. Chris Anderson, *The Long Tail,* New York: Hyperion, 2006.
3. This section draws on Michael E. Porter, *Competitive Advantage,* New York: The Free Press, 1985, Chapter 1.
4. Scott Davis of Prophet Brand Strategy suggested the Schwinn case.
5. Irma Zandl, "How to Separate Trends from Fads," *Brandweek,* October 23, 2000, pp. 30–35.
6. Faith Popcorn and Lys Marigold, *Clicking,* New York: HarperCollins, 1997, pp. 11–12.
7. James Daly, "Sage Advice—Interview with Peter Drucker," *Business 2.0,* August 22, 2000, pp. 134–144.
8. George S. Day, Adam J. Fein, and Gregg Ruppersberger, "Shakeouts in Digital Markets: Lessons for GB2B Exchanges," *California Management Review,* Winter 2003, pp. 131–133.
9. Steven P. Schnaars, "Growth Market Forecasting Revisited: A Look Back at a Look Forward," *California Management Review* 28(4), Summer 1986.

CHAPTER FIVE

Environmental Analysis and Strategic Uncertainty

We are watching the dinosaurs die, but we don't know what will take their place.
—*Lester Thurow, MIT economist*

There is something in the wind.
—*William Shakespeare, The Comedy of Errors*

A poorly observed fact is more treacherous than a faulty train of reasoning.
—*Paul Valéry, French philosopher*

*T*homson Corporation, in 1997, was a Toronto media company that owned some 55 daily newspapers that were doing well.[1] CEO Richard Harrington, however, observed several trends in the environment that caused him to move the firm away from newspapers. He could see that the Internet was going to undercut classified advertising and that cable television and the Internet were going to steal readers. Despite the fact that the company was profitable, he made the rather dramatic decision to divest newspapers and to move the firm into delivering information and services online to the law, education, healthcare, and finance industries. As a result of that decision, Thomson thrived while other newspaper-based firms are struggling. The decision was based on projecting existing environmental trends and acting upon them.

In this chapter, the focus changes from the market to the environment surrounding the market. Being curious about the area outside the business is one route to generating creative ideas that could lead to products and strategies. It is also a way to anticipate threats and put a strategy in place, as Thomson did, to neutralize them. The goal is to identify and evaluate trends and events that will affect strategy either directly or indirectly.

The direct impact of an observed trend will be of interest, but it is important to look at indirect impact as well.[2] For example, increasing oil prices will affect the costs of a firm and its suppliers. However, pursuing the indirect implications can generate additional insights. What about the rising use of oil by China and India? Will they deal with their needs by some political alliances or actions? Will that affect prices and availability? Will conservation get traction and make a difference? Will new technologies affect the supply? What about wind and solar power?

TECHNOLOGY TRENDS

- To what extent are existing technologies maturing?
- What technological developments or trends are affecting or could affect the industry?

CONSUMER TRENDS

- What are the current or emerging trends in lifestyles, fashions, and other components of culture? Why? What are their implications?
- What demographic trends will affect the market size of the industry or its submarkets?
- What demographic trends represent opportunities or threats?

GOVERNMENT/ECONOMIC TRENDS

- What are the economic prospects and inflation risks for the countries in which the firm operates? How will they affect strategy?
- What changes in regulation are possible? What will their impact be?
- What are the political risks of operating in a governmental jurisdiction?

GENERAL EXTERNAL ANALYSIS QUESTIONS

- What are the significant trends and future events?
- What threats and opportunities do you see?
- What are the key areas of uncertainty as to trends or events that have the potential to impact strategy? Evaluate these strategic uncertainties in terms of their impact.

SCENARIOS

- What strategic uncertainties are worth being the basis of a scenario analysis?

Figure 5.1 Environmental Analysis

Where are the oil profits going to be invested? Such questions will result in a depth of understanding and raise options that take the strategic conversation to a whole new level.

Environmental analysis is by definition very broad and involves casting a wide net (see Figure 5.1). Any trend that will potentially have an impact on strategy is fair game. As a practical matter, the analysis requires some discipline to make sure that it does not become an out-of-control fishing expedition that occupies time and generates reports but provides little real insight and actionable information.

Although environmental analysis has no bounds with respect to subject matter, it is convenient to provide some structure in the form of three areas of inquiry that are often useful: technological trends, consumer trends, and government/economic forces. The analysis should not be restricted to these topics. Nevertheless, in the following sections, each of these three will be discussed and illustrated.

After describing environmental analysis, the last of the four dimensions of external analysis, the chapter will turn to the task of dealing with strategic uncertainty, a key output of external analysis. Impact analysis and scenario analysis are tools that help to evolve that uncertainty into strategy. Impact analysis—the assessment of the relative importance of strategic uncertainties—is addressed first. Scenario analysis—ways of creating and using future scenarios to help generate and evaluate strategies—follows.

TECHNOLOGY TRENDS

One dimension of environmental analysis is technological trends or technological events occurring outside the market or industry that have the potential to impact strategies. They can represent opportunities and threats to those in a position to capitalize. For example, technology advances have enabled customers and others to co-create offerings, have generated real options to cable-based television, and have changed the face of energy competition.

Big Data

There are trends, and there are megatrends, trends that are huge and influential and can be assumed to be unstoppable. The computer impact that started in the 1960s, the quality movement of the 1970s and 1980s, and the Internet movement of the 1990s and 2000s are examples. It appears that "big data" is such a trend.

Firms in general and marketing teams in particular are swamped by data and are struggling to turn that data into insights, products, and better decisions. One estimate is that 90% of all the data in the network in 2012 was created in the prior two years. It is truly an avalanche that has many sources, some new and some that have been around but not at the level of detail that they now are.

Among the sources are Internet search and shopping data; social media activity; blogging participation; cell phone use, including opt-in records of GPS locations; digital picture and videos; syndicated data; ad and promotion exposure data; survey data; purchase data; motion detectors; and much more. Further, the capability of accessing and melding data from multiple sources with sophisticated statistical tools has limited barriers to data analysis. Not easy but the potential is huge. Consider:

- A bank achieving more that 600% ROI by using predictive analytics to more intelligently target customer offers
- An apparel company using analytics to optimize product placement on its website based on social media inputs and product availability
- By examining buying patterns over time, a diary company refining its heavy user segment into a dozen operationally useful subsegments
- A beer firm measuring the ROI of new products by linking advertising campaigns and promotions to sales and profits
- Tracking pictures and videos provided a rich picture of brand dynamics in one marketplace
- The study of viral stories and videos informing positioning and creative efforts
- The examination of social media activity alerting a firm to threats from product deficiencies and opportunities from new applications
- A retailer linking customer traffic and social media behavior to in-store purchase patterns in order to optimize its pricing and product assortment
- A car firm using behavioral data to direct who gets what communication when

Firms trying to use "big data" to get an edge or just to keep up with competitors require a set of competences. First, it is critical to be able to ask the right questions, both strategic and tactical, because with big data, the questions is not obvious and the nature of the insights is often hidden. In part, finding the right questions requires creative thinking, marketing programs that have a wide scope, and clear objectives. Second, firms need to be competent in designing and interpreting ongoing flow of experiments as opposed to ad hoc single ones. Finally, they need to be good at data storage, data handling, analytics and the development of problem-driven statistical models because without such capabilities, they can't play the big data game.

Transformational, Substantial, and Incremental Innovations

Trends, both market and environmental, can stimulate innovation. It is useful to distinguish between incremental, substantial, and transformational innovation. These differ in terms of how new they are and how much wealth they represent for the business. An incremental innovation makes the offering more attractive or profitable but does not fundamentally change the value proposition or the functional strategy. In general, substantial innovations have ten times the impact of incremental innovations; the impact of transformational innovations is 10 times greater again. Substantial and transformational innovations need to be detected and tracked.

A transformation innovation will provide a fundamental change in the business model, likely involving a new value proposition and a new way to manufacture, distribute, and/or market the offering. It is likely to make the assets and competencies of established firms irrelevant. The advent of steam power, which ultimately spelled the end of sail-powered transport, was a transformational innovation. The automobile, Southwest Airlines, FedEx, the business model of Dell Computers, mini steel mills, and Cirque du Soleil represent innovations that have transformed markets. Transformational innovations, which sometimes take decades to emerge, are critical to analyze because they represent new competitive landscapes and often attract customers who were on the sidelines because the prior offering was too expensive or lacked some critical element.

Substantial innovations are in between in newness and impact. They often represent a new generation of products, such as the Boeing 747 or Windows Vista, that make the existing products obsolete for many. Cisco introduced a videoconference technology called telepresence that uses massive amounts of bandwidth to provide a high-fidelity experience and should expand the usage of videoconferencing. In these cases, the basic value proposition and business model were enhanced but not changed. Substantial innovations are much more common than transformational innovations and involve major changes in the competitive landscape.

Innovations that are transformational or even substantial are often championed by new entrants into the industry so it is important to monitor new, even small, firms and not let the large, established firms dominate the external analysis.[3] Incumbent firms—especially successful ones—are incented to focus on incremental innovation to protect and improve their profitable niche in the market. Their people, culture, and mix of assets and competencies are unlikely to support a transformational innovation. As a result, when transformational innovations make their appearance, the reaction of incumbent firms is denial, supported by a belief that improvements in the early offerings would not happen. So the horse-drawn buggy manufacturers never became automobile firms, telegraph companies missed out on the telephone, and 3M and others felt that the early and primitive Xerox copy technology would never replace heat-sensitive copier paper. Chapter 13 will discuss how the substantial and transformational innovation can define new subcategories and lead to enduring success.

Forecasting Technologies

It is often easy to compile a list of technologies in the wings; the hard part is sorting out the winners from the losers. The experience of the retail sector may provide some guidance. Among the big winners were the 1936 invention of the shopping cart (which allowed customers to buy more and do so more easily) and the UPC scanner (which improved checkout and provided a rich information source). Among the losers were Ted Turner's Checkout Channel (color monitors positioned by the checkout counters in grocery stores), the VideOcart (screens attached to shopping carts that could highlight specials and guide shoppers), and efforts to create home-deliver Internet supermarkets.

Ray Burke, a retail expert from Indiana University, drew upon a variety of research sources to develop a set of guidelines for separating winners from losers. Although his context is retailing, any organization exploring new technologies can benefit from considering each of the guidelines:[4]

- Use technology to create an immediate, tangible benefit for the consumer. The benefit, in short, needs to be perceived as such. The Checkout Channel was designed to help entertain, but consumers saw it as an intrusive annoyance.

- Make the technology easy to use. Consumers resist wasting time and becoming frustrated, and too often new technologies are perceived as doing exactly these things. Research shows that it takes customers an average of 20 to 30 minutes just to learn how to shop in most text-based Internet grocery-shopping systems.

- Execution matters: prototype, test, and refine. One in-store kiosk had no way to inform frustrated customers that it had run out of paper. A bank found customers more receptive to an interactive videoconferencing system when the screens were placed in inviting locations.

- Recognize that customer response to technology varies. One bank found that ATM customers rejected videoconferencing options because they actually did not want to interact with humans. Some retailers use loyalty cards to provide receipts and promotions tailored to individual customers.

Impact of New Technologies

Certainly, it can be important, even critical, to manage the transition to a new technology. The appearance of a new technology, however, even a successful one, does not necessarily mean that businesses based on the prior technology will suddenly become unhealthy.

A group of researchers at Purdue studied fifteen companies in five industries in which a dramatic new technology had emerged:[5]

- Diesel-electric locomotives vs. steam
- Transistors vs. vacuum tubes
- Ballpoint pens vs. fountain pens
- Nuclear power vs. boilers for fossil-fuel plants
- Electric razors vs. safety razors

Two interesting conclusions emerged that should give pause to anyone attempting to predict the impact of a dramatic new technology. First, the sales of the old technology continued for a substantial period, in part because the firms involved continued to improve it. Safety-razor sales have actually increased 800 percent since the advent of the electric razor. Thus, a new technology may not signal the end of the growth phase of an existing technology. In all cases, firms involved with the old technology had a substantial amount of time to react to the new technology.

Second, it is relatively difficult to predict the outcome of a new technology. The new technologies studied tended to be expensive and crude at first. The most spectacular erroneous forecast was attributed to Thomas Watson, the CEO of what is now IBM, who predicted in 1943 that the total world market for computers is maybe five. New technologies also sometimes start by invading submarkets and it can be hard to imagine their subsequent market potential. Transistors, for example, were first used in hearing aids and pocket radios. In addition, new technologies tended to create new markets instead of simply encroaching on existing ones. Throwaway ballpoint pens and many of the transistor applications opened up completely new market areas.

CONSUMER TRENDS

Consumer trends can present both threats and opportunities for a wide variety of firms. For example, a dress designer conducted a study that projected women's lifestyles. It predicted that a more varied lifestyle would prevail, that more time would be spent outside the home, and that those who worked would be more career oriented. These predictions had several implications

INFORMATION TECHNOLOGY

In nearly every industry it is useful to ask what potential impact new information technology based on new databases will have on strategies. How will it create SCAs and key success factors? Apparel manufacturers such as Levi-Strauss, drug wholesalers such as McKesson, and retailers such as the Limited all have developed systems of inventory control, ordering, and shipping that represent substantial SCAs. FedEx has stayed ahead of competitors by investing heavily in information technology. It was the first express delivery service to have the ability to track packages throughout its systems and the first to link its systems with customers' computers. Harrah's Casino has leveraged customer data to dramatically affect customer experience. For example, a losing customer may get a meal gift at just the right time.

In supermarket retailing, "smart cards," cards that customers present during checkout to pay for purchases, provide a record of all purchases that allow:

- Stores to build loyalty by rewarding cumulative purchase volume
- Promotions to target individual customers based on their brand preferences and household characteristics
- The use of cents-off coupons without the customer or store having to handle pieces of paper; the purchase of a promoted product can be discounted automatically
- The store to identify buyers of slow-moving items and predict the impact on the store's choice of dropping an item
- Decisions as to shelf-space allocation, special displays, and store layout to be refined based on detailed information about customer shopping

relevant to the dress designer's product line and pricing strategies. For example, a growing number and variety of activities would lead to a broader range of styles and larger wardrobes, with perhaps somewhat less spent on each garment. Furthermore, consumers' increased financial and social independence would probably reduce the number of follow-the-leader fashions and the perception that certain outfits were required for certain occasions.

Cultural Trends

Faith Popcorn has uncovered and studied cultural trends that, in her judgment, will shape the future. Her efforts provide a provocative view of the future environment of many organizations. Consider, for example, the following trends:[6]

- *Cocooning.* Consumers are retreating into safe, cozy "homelike" environments to shield themselves from the harsh realities of the outside world. This trend supports online and catalogue shopping, home security systems, gardening, and smart homes.

- *Fantasy adventure.* Consumers crave low-risk excitement and stimulation to escape from stress and boredom. Responsive firms offer theme restaurants, exotic cosmetics, adventure travel, fantasy clothes that suggest role-playing, fantasy-based entertainment, and fantasy cars.

- *Pleasure revenge.* Consumers are rebelling against rules to cut loose and savor forbidden fruits (for example, indulgent ice creams, cigars, martinis, tanning salons, and furs).

- *Small indulgences.* Busy, stressed-out people are rewarding themselves with affordable luxuries that will provide quick gratification: fresh-squeezed orange juice, chocolate-dipped Tuscan biscotti, crusty bread, and upscale fountain pens. For the financially well off, the range of possibilities might include Porsche flatware, a mahogany Cris-Craft canoe, or Range Rover night-vision binoculars.

- *Down-aging.* Consumers seek symbols of youth, renewal, and rejuvenation to counterbalance the intensity of their adult lives. The over-55 crowd going to school and participating in active sports (including iron man competitions and outdoor adventures) reflect this trend, but it really extends to a wide age group who favor products, apparel, activities, and entertainment that capture the nostalgia of youth.

- *Being alive.* Consumers focus on the quality of life and the importance of wellness, taking charge of their personal health rather than delegating it to the healthcare industry. Examples of this include the use of holistic medical approaches, vegetarian products and restaurants, organic products, water filters, and health clubs.

- *99 lives.* Consumers are forced to assume multiple roles to cope with their increasingly busy lives. Retailers serving multiple needs, ever-faster ways to get prepared food, a service that manages your second home and prepares it for visits, noise neutralizers, e-commerce, and yoga are all responsive to this trend.

There is a trend toward tribing, the affinity toward a social unit that is centered around an interest or activity and is not bound by conventional social links. Harley-Davidson events such as the annual rally in Sturgis, South Dakota, can attract hundreds of thousands of participants. The

Apple users group has been a strong part of Apple's survival in a PC world. The Internet has generated a host of communities and chat groups that play an influential role through information exchange and social networking. Tribing has significance for brand-building and communication programs, both positively and negatively.

Being Green

Another megatrend is the green movement of the 21st century. It will grow and impact and thus will deserve close scrutiny. In one study by MIT and Boston Consulting Group on which nearly 3,000 executives from 113 countries were interviewed, two thirds of the firms said that sustainability was critically important to being competitive. There are several drivers of "green."[7]

One driver is the concern with the threat of global warming and resource depletion. Many firms feel a responsibility to be part of the solution. The fact is that the private sector, especially in the U.S., is getting a lot done with respect to the environment and other social issues. Firms realize that they can make a difference.

Unilever has set a 10-year goal to half their environmental impact, and that includes their whole supply chain. Unilever's CEO Paul Polman observed that climate change cost Unilever well over 200 million Euros in just one year and that is enough motivation to do something about the problem. All the Unilever brands have a social as well as economic and product mission. He noted that "businesses that are responsible and actually make contributions to society a part of their business model will be successful."[8]

A second driver is its ability of green programs to provide functional benefits to firms largely in the form of cost savings from reduced energy consumption. Firms are often surprised at the extent to which green programs pay off. Wal-Mart, whose green story is told in the insert, discovered, to its surprise, that an ambitious environmental program was associated with meaningful, tangible cost savings plus positive sales response to green products.

A third driver, which will be explored more fully in Chapter 8, is a desire to be respected by customers and employees, both of which value a relationship with a firm that they admire. A 2009 study by the Grocery Manufacturers Association found that 59 percent of grocery store shoppers say that they actively consider a brand's sustainability characteristics, and about the same percentage intentionally bought more green products.[9] The interest in green products was across demographics. Ben & Jerry's has supported environmental causes in a colorful way that has enhanced the company's image. Frito-Lay's SunChips has created a point of differentiation with its visible use of solar power and compostable packaging.

More and more firms are getting involved. Firms with a legacy of concern for the environment and social responsibility have been the leaders in dialing up environmental programs. Other firms are following even though it might require a cultural change that is not easy.

One factor inhibiting progress is the complexity of the green movement. Consider Method, the household products company that is regarded as the pinnacle of "greenness." They trace the production process back to how a product's components, including any packaging, is created and transported. An ingredient, for example, might involve fertilizer and a tractor, both of which used serious amounts of energy. Another issue is the whether the end result, including the packaging, is recyclable and how that will be accomplished. It turns out that the analysis of a firm with the best intentions is not only complex but sometimes involves unknowns and ambiguity. Creating a sustainable business and measuring the effort is not easy even for the committed.[10]

WAL-MART TURNS GREEN

In 2005 Wal-Mart began to develop green programs, an amazing turnaround for a company that had prided itself on low costs and prices first and foremost.[11] The firm developed tangible energy reduction targets for its truck fleet and stores. Organic food and even clothes made from organic cotton became featured in Wal-Mart stores. Suppliers that had environmentally responsive products or packaging, from salmon fishermen in Alaska to Unilever (whose compact detergent used less space and package material), were not only favored but aided. Suppliers, some 60,000 of them around the world, were encouraged to become green. Fourteen sustainable-value networks around issues like logistics, packaging, and forest products were formed, consisting of Wal-Mart executives, suppliers, environmental groups, and regulators, with a goal to share information and ideas. Given Wal-Mart's footprint and influence around the world, these programs are likely to make a difference.

Also in 2005, a brand repositioning initiative was launched that resulted in a new brand position in 2008. Research found that customers really wanted value more than just low prices, value in the form of roomier stores, more high-quality products, and the lifestyle benefits of saving money. The result came together under a new slogan "Save money. Live better." It helped provide an umbrella theme for the new Wal-Mart and its sustainability program as well as its organic foods, higher quality products, and improved store look and feel.

The programs did affect the dialogue. Out of three thousand U.S. brands tracked by Y&R's Brand Asset Valuator (BAV) database, Walmart was number 12 on the social responsibility scale in 2008, an incredible achievement.[12] There was one 2010 article titled "Green Project Making it Harder to Hate Walmart," and another titled "Walmart's Environmental Game Changer." The hardcore Walmart critics were still there, but it was clear that their intensity and breadth were visibly lessened. The relevance challenge was not over for Wal-Mart, but it was greatly alleviated, and the trajectory was positive, a remarkable change given where the firm started only a few years before.

Why did Wal-Mart suddenly make such a U-turn? Three reasons. First, the CEO decided it was the right thing to do, based in part on the influence of an environmental professional who had vacationed with members of the outdoor-oriented Walton family. Second, a single-minded focus on costs and the resulting policies regarding employees, communities, and suppliers had generated press attention that was extremely negative and very visible and that affected the company's ability to grow and succeed. More communities were turning down Wal-Mart stores, and 8 percent of Americans were committed to shopping elsewhere. Wal-Mart executives felt that some positive press was needed. Finally, to the surprise of the executives, many of the green programs were helping the bottom line—a change in packaging resulted in significant savings, and the introduction of organic cotton fabrics was a customer hit.

Wal-Mart's experience raises some interesting issues. What is the responsibility for a for-profit organization to contribute to solving the problems of the nation and the world? Was Milton Friedman right when he said that the business of business is to make profits and that other objectives should be left to the government? What are the problems worth addressing? How should they be addressed? How does an individual business determine what programs will be effective or even helpful when the problems being addressed are so complex?

Demographics

Demographic trends can be a powerful underlying force in a market and can be predictable. Among the influential demographic variables are age, income, education, geographic location, and ethnicity.

The older demographic group is of particular interest because it is growing rapidly and is blessed with not only resources but also the time to use them. The over-65 population in the

United States will grow from 40 million or 13% of the population in 2010 to 55 million or 17% of the population in 2020. The over-85 group was at 5.5 -million in 2010 and was the fast growing demographic. Its members are much more likely to live independently than past generations. Women tend to outlive men, so their portion of the population increases sharply over age groups; within the 85-year-old group, there are only 41 men per 100 women. Research suggests that elderly women are dissatisfied at having to choose from products generally geared to younger segments.

Demographic trends are magnified when they are quantified by industry. The impact of aging is dramatically different across industries according to an Italian study.[13] The demand for health care, housing, and energy in Italy will increase 32 percent, 24 percent, and 21 percent, respectively, from 2005 to 2020. During that same time period the demand will fall for toys/sports by 41 percent, motorcycles by 36 percent, and education by 23 percent.

Ethnic populations are rising rapidly and support whole firms and industries, as well as affect the strategies of mainline companies. Hispanic populations, for example, are growing about five times faster than non-Hispanic populations and are gaining in income as well. Hispanics will soon be the largest minority group. The Asian American population, currently numbering over 6 million in the United States, is increasing rapidly.

GOVERNMENT/ECONOMIC TRENDS

Economic Recessions

Economic forecasts will affect strategy. A very different type of investment and strategy is needed when the economic climate is healthy than when it is under stress. Further, it is far better and sometimes imperative to put into place strategies before a strong or weak economy hits because when it is in progress, it can be too late. Thus, it becomes important to forecast the demand in general and the demand within the sectors that are most relevant to the business. Good forecasting means having links to authoritative voices, a broad-based information system, and a clear understanding of leading indicators.

Of particular importance is to forecast and adjust to recessions, particularly deep ones, because they can threaten survival and can provide rare opportunities for major changes in competitive position. That means that the balance sheet and cash position needs to be buttressed, which in turn means that firms need to cut budgets and programs, sometimes radically. Marketing is particularly vulnerable because its budget appears to be discretionary. Adjusting marketing to gain short-term financial benefits has its own risks. Some observations:

First, as the boxed insert details, a recession can be an opportunity to introduce products or marketing programs because the media environment will be less cluttered and competitors will be less motivated and able to respond.

Second, cutting marketing budgets and programs across the board, the easy route, is guaranteed to be suboptimal. Rather, a budget crunch is an opportunity to develop and nurture the effective and identify and defund the ineffective. There is almost always a significant portion of the budget that is going to products, countries, segments, media, or programs that have an unacceptable ROI. Funding is based on wishful thinking, historical momentum, or organizational power. The actual market impact of a budget reduction can be minimized by identifying and cutting support to budget areas in which marketing performance is mediocre or worse. The cost of ineffective marketing may exceed targeted budget cuts.

In measuring ROI, the difficult part is to ensure that measurement is not dominated by immediate sales promotion programs damaging to the brand franchise and inhibiting programs with a longer time horizon. One packaged goods firm developed an analytical model based on access to daily store sales. The model drove the firm to price promotions because they delivered immediate sales bumps. As a result, customers learned to wait for the next promotion, and after two years the business and brand were visibly deteriorating and the model was discarded. The fact is that some marketing efforts, both positive and negative, have been shown to have effects only with a two- and three-year delay. Surrogates for long-term health of the business such as the size and loyalty level of the loyal segment or brand health indicators such as image, differentiation, and energy of the brand can help.

Third, it is important to find ways to communicate value, often a necessity during tough economic times, without hurting the brand. Shouting price and deals is the wrong course because it announces that the brand is not worth the price. One way is to divert attention to value subbrands such as the BMW One Series or the Fairfield Inn by Marriott. Another is to bundle services to provide extra value at the same price, such as free shipping by Amazon or McDonald's Happy Meals. Still another is to demonstrate the value of quality—Bounty towels pay by doing more with less. Finally, the frame of reference can be changed—other products can become the comparison standard. For example: KFC's Family Value Meal vs. home cooking, or Crayola's 64 colors vs. expensive toys.

Fourth, the tendency is to think budgets (how much is spent) while the need is to change programs—finding new ones that are more effective. Marketing needs to elevate its game to move beyond competence to excellence. In many cases, how a budget is spent can be up to four times more important than how much is spent. When budgets become tight, the challenge of creating winning programs or reducing costs without sacrificing impact needs to be a priority. That means enhancing the creativity of the organization, sharing programs between organizational units, and considering different media, particularly digital media and social technology.

Hyundai in 2009 had most of these factors in hand.[14] Along with a heritage as a value brand, it had award-winning models, including the luxury Genesis; the first "car return" policy if you got laid off; a 10-year warranty; and a relatively strong financial position. Hyundai increased advertising 38 percent as its rivals on average decreased theirs 7 percent. Its sales sharply increased while their competitors' sales were declining, some close to 40 percent.

RECESSION OPPORTUNITIES TO GAIN MARKET POSITION

Opportunities to gain market position will occasionally emerge in times of economic stress. In that case, it might pay to be aggressive with some portion of the marketing budget.

In rare cases, it might be worthwhile to consider increasing the budget. In fact, numerous empirical studies of marketing budget changes during recessions have shown that, on average, there is a strong correlation between the marketing budget during a recession and the performance of the business both during and in the years after the recession. This evidence coupled with many case studies suggest that being aggressive rather than defensive can pay off—when there is a product, position, or program that can be leveraged to gain market position.

(continued)

What type of firms are likely to benefit from being aggressive? They include firms that:

- Can be positioned as a value brand. Wal-Mart in the recession of 1991 and 1992 aggressively told their value story and as a result took share away from Sears, a share gain that was never relinquished.
- Enjoy an offering that has points of relevant superiority. Merrill Lynch took share away from Bear Sterns by increasing marketing in a recession, telling a story that was based on real substance.
- Have a new product that is changing the industry or affecting the firm's competitive position— Starbucks launched a new interior in a recession.
- Have a particularly effective marketing program. Intel Inside, perhaps the most successful marketing program in the high-tech space, was launched in the 1991 recession.
- Have a balance sheet advantage over rivals—when competitors are unable to respond, the chances of improving market position with aggressive marketing increases. Consider, for example, Zurich Financial and Charles Schwab that today have financial strength superiority compared with some of their main competitors.

Government Regulations

The addition or removal of legislative or regulatory constraints can pose major strategic threats and opportunities. For example, the ban of some ingredients in food products or cosmetics has dramatically affected the strategies of numerous firms. The impact of governmental efforts to reduce piracy in industries such as software (more than one-fourth of all software used is copied), CDs, DVDs, and movie videos is of crucial import to those affected. Deregulation in banking, energy, and other industries is having implications for the firms involved. The automobile industry is affected by fuel-economy standards and by the luxury tax on automobiles. The relaxation of regulatory constraints in India and China can have enormous implications for global firms.

Global Events

In an increasingly global economy with interdependencies in markets and in the sourcing of products and services, possible political hot spots need to be understood and tracked. In a classic study of environmental trends and events that were forecast in *Fortune* magazine during the 1930s and 1940s, predictions were found to be remarkably good in many areas such as synthetic vitamins, genetic breakthroughs, the decline of railroads, and the advent of TVs, house-trailers, and superhighways. However, forecasting was extremely poor when international events were involved.[15] Thus, a mid-1930s article did not consider the possibility of U.S. involvement in a European war. A 1945 article incorrectly forecast a huge growth in trade with the Soviet Union, not anticipating the advent of the cold war. A Middle East scenario failed to forecast the emergence of Israel. International political developments, which can be critical to multinational firms, are still extremely difficult to forecast. A prudent strategy is one that is both diversified and flexible, so that a political surprise will not be devastating.

Cultivating Vigilance

There is a strong tendency to fail to understand important trends or predict future events.[16] Just consider how the warnings about the financial crises and the safety of Chinese products were ignored or minimized. One reason is that executives are focused on execution and have little attention span left for "might be." Another reason is there is a natural perceptual bias toward ignoring or distorting information that conflicts with the strategic model of the day and collecting supporting information. Still another is the support of "groupthink" within the organization—it is awkward to point out that basic assumptions may be wrong.

Research on organizational vigilance suggests some ways that leaders and organizations can improve. First, be curious, externally focused, and connected. What is happening in areas that will impact the business? Travel, observe, and interact with people of all types. Second, look to secondary as well as primary effects. Johnson & Johnson has a strategy process termed Frameworks that looks at regulations, insurance coverage, and competitive moves and considers their implications. Make sure that silo units are communicating so that in-house information is shared. Third, create discovery mechanisms. Texas Instruments holds a "Sea of Ideas" meeting each week to recognize emerging needs and innovation at the fringe of their business. One such meeting led to the development of a low power chip for mobile phones. Finally, force a long-term perspective; get away from the day-to-day executional issues and programs.

"YES, BUT . . ."

Some trends are real but have obvious implications that need to be qualified. For example:

Yes, the number of women in the workforce has been increasing, *but* . . .

- The increase is slow and long-term, with the total proportion rising from 42 percent in 1980 to 45 percent in 1990 and 47 percent in 2000 and 48 percent in 2010. Further, only a small percentage of these women fit the image of the young MBA.

Yes, Internet access and usage are growing rapidly, *but* . . .

- A significant proportion of the population still sees no need for the Internet, and some are outright hostile toward technology.

Yes, people can and will price shop on the Internet, *but* . . .

- Many are loyal to single sites and do not use price comparison services.

Yes, there is a strong trend to healthy eating and exercise, *but* . . .

- Indulgent foods like upscale chocolates, super-premium ice cream, and high-fat burgers are still a substantial and sometimes growing niche.

Yes, cell phones are a platform for multimedia marketing programs, *but* . . .

- In 2009 nearly half of U.S. mobile customers used their phones only to make calls.

DEALING WITH STRATEGIC UNCERTAINTY

Strategic uncertainty, uncertainty that has strategic implications, is a key construct in external analysis. A typical external analysis will emerge with dozens of strategic uncertainties. To be manageable, they need to be grouped into logical clusters or themes. It is then useful to assess the importance of each cluster in order to set priorities with respect to information gathering and analysis. Impact analysis, described in the next section, is designed to accomplish that assessment.

Sometimes the strategic uncertainty is represented by a future trend or event that has inherent unpredictability. Information gathering and additional analysis will not be able to reduce the uncertainty. In that case, scenario analysis can be employed. Scenario analysis basically accepts the uncertainty as given and uses it to drive a description of two or more future scenarios. Strategies are then developed for each. One outcome could be a decision to create organizational and strategic flexibility so that as the business context changes the strategy will adapt. Scenario analysis will be detailed in the final section of this chapter.

IMPACT ANALYSIS—ASSESSING THE IMPACT OF STRATEGIC UNCERTAINTIES

An important objective of external analysis is to rank the strategic uncertainties and decide how they are to be managed over time. Which uncertainties merit intensive investment in information gathering and in-depth analysis, and which merit only a low-key monitoring effort?

The problem is that dozens of strategic uncertainties and many second-level strategic uncertainties are often generated. These strategic uncertainties can lead to an endless process of information gathering and analysis that can absorb resources indefinitely. A publishing company may be concerned about cable TV, lifestyle patterns, educational trends, geographic population shifts, and printing technology. Any one of these issues involves a host of subfields and could easily spur limitless research. For example, cable TV might involve a variety of pay-TV concepts, suppliers, technologies, and viewer reactions. Unless distinct priorities are established, external analysis can become descriptive, ill-focused, and inefficient.

The extent to which a strategic uncertainty should be monitored and analyzed depends on its impact and immediacy.

1. The impact of a strategic uncertainty is related to:
   - The extent to which it involves trends or events that will impact existing or potential businesses
   - The importance of the involved businesses
   - The number of involved businesses
2. The immediacy of a strategic uncertainty is related to:
   - The probability that the involved trends or events will occur
   - The time frame of the trends or events
   - The reaction time likely to be available compared with the time required to develop and implement appropriate strategy

Impact of a Strategic Uncertainty

Each strategic uncertainty involves potential trends or events that could have an impact on present, proposed, and even potential businesses. For example, a strategic uncertainty for a beer firm could be based on the future prospects of the microbrewery market. If the beer firm has both a proposed microbrewery entry and an imported beer positioned in the same area, trends in the microbrewery beer market could have a high impact on the firm. The trend toward natural foods may present opportunities for a sparkling water product line for the same firm and be the basis of a strategic uncertainty.

The impact of a strategic uncertainty will depend on the importance of the impacted business to a firm. Some businesses are more important than others. The importance of established businesses may be indicated by their associated sales, profits, or costs. However, such measures might need to be supplemented for proposed or growth businesses for which present sales, profits, or costs may not reflect the true value to a firm. Finally, because an information-need area may affect several businesses, the number of involved businesses can also be relevant to a strategic uncertainty's impact.

Immediacy of Strategic Uncertainties

Events or trends associated with strategic uncertainties may have a high impact but such a low probability of occurrence that it is not worth actively expending resources to gather or analyze information. Similarly, if occurrence is far in the future relative to the strategic-decision horizon, then it may be of little concern. Thus, the harnessing of tide energy may be so unlikely or may occur so far in the future that it is of no concern to a utility.

Finally, there is the reaction time available to a firm compared with the reaction time likely to be needed. After a trend or event crystallizes, a firm needs to develop a reaction strategy. If the available reaction time is inadequate, it becomes important to anticipate emerging trends and events better so that future reaction strategies can be initiated sooner.

Managing Strategic Uncertainties

Figure 5.2 suggests a categorization of strategic uncertainties for a given business. If both the immediacy and impact are low, then a low level of monitoring may suffice. If the impact is thought

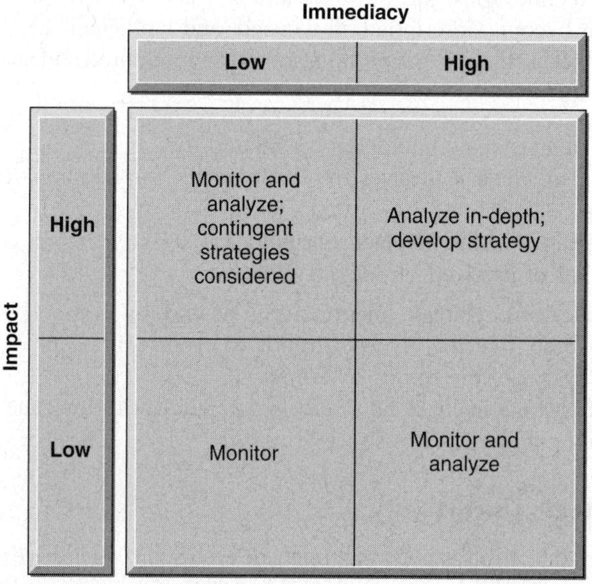

Figure 5.2   Strategic Uncertainty Categories

to be low but the immediacy is high, the area may merit monitoring and analysis. If the immediacy is low and the impact high, then the area may require monitoring and analysis in more depth, and contingent strategies may be considered but not necessarily developed and implemented. When both the immediacy and potential impact of the underlying trends and events are high, then an in-depth analysis will be appropriate, as will be the development of reaction plans or strategies. An active task force may provide initiative.

SCENARIO ANALYSIS

Scenario analysis can help deal with uncertainty. It provides an alternative to investing in information to reduce uncertainty that is often an expensive and futile process. By creating a small number of marketplace or market context scenarios and assessing their likelihood and impact, scenario analysis can be a powerful way to deal with complex environments.

There are two types of scenario analyses. In the first type, strategy-developing scenarios, the object is to provide insights into future competitive contexts and then use these insights to evaluate existing business strategies and stimulate the creation of new ones. Such analyses can help create contingency plans to guard against disasters—an airline adjusting to a terror incident, for example, or a pharmaceutical company reacting to a product safety problem. They can also suggest investment strategies that enable the organization to capitalize on future opportunities caused by customer trends or technological breakthroughs.

In the second type of analyses, decision-driven scenarios, a strategy is proposed and tested against several scenarios that are developed.[17] The goal is to challenge the strategies, thereby helping to make the go/no-go decision and suggesting ways to make the strategy more robust in withstanding competitive forces. If the decision is to enter a market with a technology strategy, alternate scenarios could be built around variables such as marketplace acceptance of the technology, competitor response, and the stimulation of customer applications.

In either case, a scenario analysis will involve three general steps: the creation of scenarios, relating those scenarios to existing or potential strategies, and assessing the probability of the scenarios (see Figure 5.3).

Identify Scenarios

Strategic uncertainties can drive scenario development. The impact analysis will identify the strategic uncertainty with the highest priority for a firm. A manufacturer of a medical imagery device may want to know whether a technological advance will allow its machine to be made at a substantially lower cost. A farm equipment manufacturer or ski area operator may believe that the weather—whether a drought will continue, for example—is the most important area of uncertainty. A server firm may want to know whether a single software standard will emerge or multiple standards will coexist. The chosen uncertainty could then stimulate two or more scenarios.

Figure 5.3 Scenario Analysis

A competitor scenario analysis can be driven by the uncertainty surrounding a competitor's strategy. For example, could the competitor aggressively extend its brand? Or might it divest a product line or make a major acquisition? Perhaps the competitor could change its value proposition or become more aggressive in its pricing.[18]

When a set of scenarios is based largely on a single strategic uncertainty, the scenarios themselves can usually be enriched by related events and circumstances. Thus, an inflation-stimulated recession scenario would be expected to generate a host of conditions for the appliance industry, such as price increases and retail failures. Similarly, a competitor scenario can be comprehensive, specifying such strategy dimensions as product-market investment, acquisition or joint ventures, pricing, positioning, product, and promotions.

It is sometimes useful to generate scenarios based on probable outcomes: optimistic, pessimistic, and most likely. The consideration of a pessimistic scenario is often useful in testing existing assumptions and plans. The aura of optimism that often surrounds a strategic plan may include implicit assumptions that competitors will not aggressively respond, the market will not fade or collapse, or technological problems will not surface. Scenario analysis provides a nonthreatening way to consider the possibility of clouds or even rain on the picnic.

Often, of course, several variables are relevant to the future period of interest. The combination can define a relatively large number of scenarios. For example, a large greeting-card firm might consider three variables important: the success of small boutique card companies, the life of a certain card type, and the nature of future distribution channels. The combination can result in many possible scenarios. Experience has shown that two or three scenarios are the ideal number with which to work; any more, and the process becomes unwieldy, and any value is largely lost. Thus, it is important to reduce the number of scenarios by identifying a small set that ideally includes those that are plausible/credible and those that represent departures from the present substantial enough to affect strategy development.

Relate Scenarios to Strategies

After scenarios have been identified, the next step is to relate them to strategy—both existing strategies and new options. If an existing strategy is in place, it can be tested with respect to each scenario. Which scenario will be the best one? How bad will the strategy be if the wrong scenario emerges? What will its prospects be with respect to customer acceptance, competitor reactions, and sales and profits? Could it be modified to enhance its prospects?

Even if the scenario analysis is not motivated by a desire to generate new strategy options, it is always useful to consider what strategies would be optimal for each scenario. A scenario by its nature will provide a perspective that is different from the status quo. Any strategy that is optimal for a given scenario should become a viable option. Even if it is not considered superior or even feasible, some elements of it might be captured.

Estimate Scenario Probabilities

To evaluate alternative strategies, it is useful to determine the scenario probabilities. The task is actually one of environmental forecasting, except that the total scenario may be a rich combination of several variables. Experts could be asked to assess probabilities directly. A deeper understanding will often emerge, however, if causal factors underlying each scenario can be determined. For example, the construction equipment industry might develop scenarios based on three alternative levels of construction activity. These levels would have several contributing causes. One would be the interest rate. Another could be the availability of funds to the homebuilding sector, which in turn would depend on the emerging structure of financial institutions and markets. A third might be the level of government spending on roads, energy, and other areas.

KEY LEARNINGS

- Environmental analysis of technology, consumer, and government/economic trends can detect opportunities or threats relevant to an organization.
- The green movement provides opportunities to connect to customers and employees.
- Impact analysis involves assessing systematically the impact and immediacy of the trends and events that underlie each strategy uncertainty.
- Scenario analysis, a vehicle to explore different assumptions about the future, involves the creation of two to three plausible scenarios, the development of strategies appropriate to each, the assessment of scenario probabilities, and the evaluation of the resulting strategies across the scenarios.

FOR DISCUSSION

1. What did the fax machine replace, if anything? What will replace (or has replaced) the fax machine? When will the fax machine disappear?

2. Develop a scenario based on the proposition that hydrogen-fueled cars will continue to improve and take 15 percent of the automotive market in a few years. Analyze it from the point of view of an energy company like Shell, or a car company like Mercedes.

3. Consider mobile computing using smart phones. Will this change the use of desktop computers? Laptop computers? How? Will it change the type of computers made?

4. Pick a company or brand/business on which to focus. What are the major trends that come out of an environmental analysis? What are the major areas of uncertainty? How would a major company in the industry handle those best?

5. Focusing on the airline industry, develop a list of strategic uncertainties and possible strategic actions.

6. Consider Cisco's "telepresence" in videoconferencing, which upgrades the quality of the experience. Will it change the incidence of usage? What is driving usage (or lack of usage) of videoconferencing?

7. Address the questions posed in the Wal-Mart insert.

8. Visible criticism has been leveled at the bottled water industry, including the claim that their product is not better than tap water in many locales (some brands are even said to have an unpleasant aftertaste) and that the plastic bottles are carbon costly to make and are not biodegradable. What programs would you consider to combat these arguments if you were Pepsi or the maker of Dasani?

NOTES

1. Ram Charan, "Sharpening Your Business Acumen," *Strategy & Business,* Spring 2006, pp. 49–57.
2. Ibid., p. 50.
3. Gerald J. Tellis, *Unrelenting Innovation: How to Build a Culture for Market Dominance,* San Francisco: Jossey-Bass, 2013.
4. Raymond Burke, "Confronting the Challenges That Face Bricks-and-Mortar Stores," *Harvard Business Review,* July–August 1999, pp. 160–167.
5. Arnold Cooper, Edward Demuzilo, Kenneth Hatten, Elijah Hicks, and Donald Tock, "Strategic Responses to Technological Threats," *Academy of Management Proceedings,* 1976, pp. 54–60.
6. Faith Popcorn and Lys Marigold, *Clicking,* New York: HarperCollins, 1997, pp. 11–12.
7. David Kiron, Nina Kruschwitz, Knut Haanaes, and Ingrid Von Streng Velken, "Sustainability Nears a Tipping Point," *MIT Sloan Management Review,* Winter 2012, pp. 69–74.
8. Captain Planet, *Harvard Business Review,* June 2012, pp. 112–118. Op cit. p. 114.
9. Sarah Mahoney, "Sustainability Counts: 54% of Grocery Shoppers Favor Greener Brands," *Marketing Daily,* April 29, 2009.
10. Adam Werbach, "When Sustainability Means More than Green," *McKinsey Quarterly,* 2009, Number 4, pp. 74–79.
11. Mac Gunther, "The Green Machine," *Fortune,* August 7, 2006, pp. 42–57.
12. Personal communication, John Gerzema, Y&Y's BAV, 2012.
13. Stefano Proverbio, Sven Smit, and S. Patrick Viguerie, "Dissecting Global Trends: An Example from Italy," *McKinsey Quarterly,* 2008, No. 2, pp. 14–16.
14. Janet Stilson, "Passing Lane," *Adweek Media,* April 6, 2009, pp. 7–10.
15. Richard N. Farmer, "Looking Back at Looking Forward," *Business Horizons,* February 1973, pp. 21–28.
16. George Day and Paul Schoemaker, "Are You a 'Vigilant Leader'?" *MIT Sloan Management Review,* Spring 2008, pp. 43–51
17. Hugh Courtney, "Decision-Driven Scenarios for Assessing Four Levels of Uncertainty," *Strategy & Leadership,* Vol. 31, No. 1, 2003, pp. 14–16.
18. Liam Fahey, "Competitor Scenarios," *Strategy & Leadership,* Vol. 31, No. 1, 2003, pp. 32–44.

CHAPTER SIX

Internal Analysis

We have met the enemy and he is us.
—*Pogo*

Self-conceit may lead to self-destruction.
—*Aesop, "The Frog and the Ox"*

The fish is last to know if it swims in water.
—*Chinese proverb*

Should the existing strategy be enhanced, expanded, altered, or replaced? Are existing assets and competencies adequate to win? An internal analysis of the business will help the strategist address these questions. This exploration is similar in scope to an analysis of a competitor or strategic group but much richer and deeper because of its importance to strategy and because much more information is available.

Just as strategy can be developed at the level of a business, a group of businesses, or the firm, internal analysis can also be conducted at each of these levels. Of course, analyses at different levels will differ from each other in emphasis and content, but their structure and thrust will be the same. The common goal is to identify organizational strengths, weaknesses, and constraints and, ultimately, to develop responsive strategies, either exploiting strengths or correcting or compensating for weaknesses.

Four aspects of internal analysis will be discussed in this chapter. The first, financial performance, provides an initial approximation as to how the business is doing. The second, an analysis of other performance dimensions such as customer satisfaction, product quality, brand association, relative cost, new products, and employee capability, can often provide a more robust link to future profitability. The third is an analysis of the strengths and weaknesses that are the basis of current and future strategies. The fourth is an identification and prioritization of the threats and opportunities facing the firm.

The final section explores the relationship between strategy and the analysis of the organization, its competitors, and the market. It suggests that successful strategy occurs when organization strengths are matched against market needs and competitor weaknesses.

FINANCIAL PERFORMANCE AND PROFITABILITY

Internal analysis often starts with an analysis of current financials, measures of sales, and profitability. Either can signal a change in the market viability of a product line and the ability to produce competitively. Furthermore, they provide an indicator of the success of past strategies and thus can often help in evaluating whether strategic changes are needed. In addition, sales and profitability at least appear to be specific and easily measured. As a result, it is not surprising that they are so widely used as performance evaluation tools.

Sales and Market Share

A sensitive measure of how customers regard a product or service can be sales or market share. After all, if the value proposition to a customer changes, sales and share should be affected, although there may be an occasional delay caused by market and customer inertia.

Sales levels can be strategically important. Increased sales can mean that the customer base has grown. An enlarged customer base, if we assume that new customers will develop loyalty, will mean future sales and profits. Increased share can provide the potential to gain SCAs in the form of economies of scale and experience curve effects. Conversely, decreased sales can mean decreases in customer bases and a loss of scale economies.

A problem with using sales as a measure is that it can be affected by short-term actions, such as promotions by a brand and its competitors. Thus, it is necessary to separate changes in sales that are caused by tactical actions from those that represent fundamental changes in the value delivered to the customer, and it is important to couple an analysis of sales or share with an analysis of customer satisfaction and loyalty, which will be discussed shortly.

Profitability

The ultimate measure of a firm's ability to prosper and survive is its profitability. Although both growth and profitability are desirable, establishing a priority between the two can help guide strategic decision making.

A host of measures and ratios reflect profitability, including margins, costs, and profits. Building on the assets employed leads to the return on assets (ROA) measure, which can be decomposed with a formula developed by General Motors and DuPont in the 1920s.

$$\text{ROA} = \frac{\text{profit}}{\text{sales}} \times \frac{\text{sales}}{\text{assets}}$$

Thus, return on assets can be considered as having two causal factors. The first is the profit margin, which depends on the selling price and cost structure. The second is the asset turnover, which depends on inventory control and asset utilization.

The determination of both the numerator and denominator of the ROA terms is not as straightforward as might be assumed. Substantial issues surround each, such as the distortions caused by depreciation and the fact that book assets do not reflect intangible assets, such as brand equity, or the market value of tangible assets.

Measuring Performance: Shareholder Value Analysis

The concept of shareholder value, an enormously influential concept during the past two decades, provides another perspective on financial performance. Each business should earn an ROA (based on a flow of profits emanating from an investment) that meets or exceeds the costs of capital, which is the weighted average of the cost of equity and cost of debt. Thus, if the cost of equity is 16 percent and the cost of debt is 8 percent, the cost of capital would be 12 percent if the amount of debt was equal to the amount of equity; if there were only one-fourth as much debt as equity, then the cost of capital would be 14 percent. If the return is greater than the cost of capital, shareholder value will increase, and if it is less, shareholder value will decrease.

Some of the routes to increasing shareholder value are as follows:

- Earn more profit by reducing costs or increasing revenue without using more capital.
- Invest in high-return products (this, of course, is what strategy is all about).
- Reduce the cost of capital by increasing the debt to equity ratio or by buying back stock to reduce the cost of equity.
- Use less capital. Under shareholder value analysis, the assets employed are no longer a free good. If improved just-in-time operations can reduce the inventory, it directly affects shareholder value.

The concept of shareholder value is theoretically valid.[1] If a profit stream can be estimated accurately from a strategic move, the analysis will be sound. The problem is that short-term profits (known to affect stock return and thus shareholder wealth) are easier to estimate and manipulate than long-term profits. Investors who assume that short-term profits predict longer-term profits pay undue attention to the former, as does the top management of a company with numerical targets to meet. The discipline to invest in a strategy that will sacrifice short-term financial performance for long-term prospects is not easy to come by, especially if some of the future prospects are in the form of options. For example, the investment in Saturn by General Motors should have been seen as an option to expand that nameplate if a gas shortage should occur and smaller cars became more popular. Unfortunately, Saturn was seen as a stand-alone business and did not receive the new car investment that would have made it a viable platform to compete with the Japanese firms. Similarly, when Black & Decker bought the small-appliance division of GE, it bought an option to take the business into related areas.

The impact of reducing investment is also not without risks. When, for example, Coca-Cola sold off its bottlers to reduce investment and improve shareholder value, its control of the quality of its product may have been reduced. In general, investment reduction often means outsourcing, with its balancing act between flexibility and loss of control over operations. A company that outsources its call center reduces its control over customer interaction.

One danger of shareholder value analysis is that it reduces the priority given to other stakeholders such as employees, suppliers, and customers, each of whom represents assets that can form the basis for long-term success. It can be argued that the shareholder has the least risk because he or she is very likely diversified and thus has only a small part of a portfolio at risk. In contrast, employees, suppliers, and sometimes customers have more to lose if the firm fails. Further, the shareholder does not in any practical way have any influence over the management of the firm. Thus, it might be reasonable to elevate the priority of other shareholders. P&G, for one, puts customers first, arguing in part that if customers are delighted with the products, shareholders will benefit in the long term. Other firms have explicitly put employees first, assuming that if they are productive, shareholders will eventually benefit. Making the share-holders the first priority can lead to programs such as cost reduction possibly involving degrading the customer experience. This results in short-term profits and therefore enhanced shareholder value but undercuts the firm's strength in the long-term.

In fact, shareholder value management has met with very mixed results. However, one study of the experience of 125 firms found similarities among those that had applied shareholder value concepts successfully.[2] These companies:

- Gave priority to shareholder value over other goals, particularly growth goals.
- Provided intensive training throughout the organization regarding shareholder value and made it a practical tool for business managers at all levels. The philosophy was not restricted to the executive suite.
- Were disciplined in identifying the drivers of shareholder value. For example, for a call center, drivers could be the length of time to answer calls and the quality of responses.
- Reduced overhead by adapting the current accounting system and integrating shareholder value analysis with strategic planning.

These firms found a variety of benefits. First, the concept led to value-creating divestments that otherwise would not have occurred. Second, firms were able to transfer corporate planning and decision making to decentralized business units because all units tended to use the same logic, metrics, and mindset. Third, the business investment horizon tended to be longer, with projects with multi-year time frames getting approved. Fourth, the new recognition that capital had a cost tended to generate better strategic decisions.

PERFORMANCE MEASUREMENT BEYOND PROFITABILITY

One of the difficulties in strategic market management is developing performance indicators that convincingly represent long-term prospects. The temptation is to focus on short-term profitability measures and to reduce investment in new products and brand images that have long-term payoffs.

The concept of net present value represents a long-term profit stream, but it is not always operational. It often provides neither a criterion for decision making nor a useful performance measure. It is somewhat analogous to preferring $6 million to $4 million. The real question involves determining which strategic alternative will generate $6 million and which will generate $4 million.

It is necessary to develop performance measures that will reflect long-term viability and health. The focus should be on the assets and competencies that underlie the current and future strategies and their SCAs. What are the key assets and competencies for a business during the planning horizon? What strategic dimensions are most crucial: to become more competitive with respect to product offerings, to develop new products, or to become more productive? These types of questions can help identify performance areas that a business should examine. Answers will vary depending on the situation, but, as suggested by Figure 6.1, they will often include customer satisfaction/brand loyalty, product/service quality, brand/firm associations, relative cost, new product activity, and manager/employee capability and performance.

Product and Service Quality

Internal analysis needs to start with the ability of the firm to deliver against the promise. The quality must meet or exceed expectations of the customer base and even do more if the customer

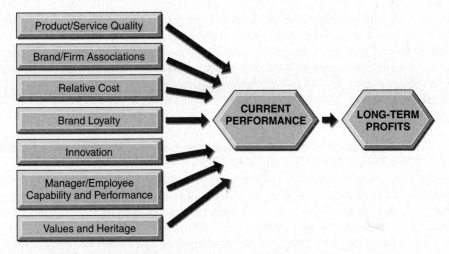

Figure 6.1 Performance Measures Reflecting Long-term Profitability

needs are different than expectations. Is the offering delivering value? How? Is it delivering superior quality?

It is important to compare the ability of a firm to deliver quality with current and future competitor offerings. One common failing of firms is to avoid tough comparisons with a realistic assessment of competitors' current and potential offerings. A newly appointed CEO of Frito-Lay once put all programs on hold for a year until the firm's manufacturing units around the world were able to make products that would win blind taste tests. He realized that product quality was a necessary condition for success.

In order to develop precision and diagnostics in the assessment of quality, the underlying dimensions should be identified and measured over time. For example, an automobile manufacturer can measure defects, ability to perform to specifications, durability, reparability, and features. A bank might be concerned with waiting time, accuracy of transactions, and the quality of the customer experience. A computer manufacturer can examine relative performance specifications and product reliability as reflected by repair data. A business that requires better marketing of a good product line is very different from one that has basic product deficiencies.

Brand/Firm Associations

An important asset of a brand or firm is its associations. What comes to mind with the brand or firm becomes visible? What is its perceived quality? Perceived quality, which is sometimes very different from actual quality, can be based on experience with past products or services and on quality cues, such as retailer types, pricing strategies, packaging, advertising, and typical customers. Is a brand or firm regarded as expert in a product or technology area (such as designing and making sailboats)? Innovative? Expensive? For the country club set? Is it associated with a country, a user type, or an application area (such as racing)? Such associations can be key strategic assets for a brand or firm.

Associations can be monitored by regularly asking customers to describe their use experiences and to tell what a brand or firm means to them. The identification of changes in important associations will likely emerge from such efforts. Structured surveys using a representative sample of customers can provide even more precise tracking information.

Chapter 9 provides a discussion of why associations are strategically important and describes the major types such as having a brand personality, organizational values and programs, being global, being contemporary, and being relevant to a customer need or application.

Brand Loyalty

Perhaps the most important asset of many firms is the loyalty of the customer base. Strategic investments will be influenced by an assessment of customer loyalty. Loyalty will affect profitability by supporting prices and by reducing cost of customer acquisition and retentions. Consequently, a firm should, in general, invest behind product-markets in which a strong loyal customer base exists. If a business lacks loyalty and a program cannot be economically be created to generate that missing asset, on average, that would not be a place to invest.

It is important to recognize that there are different forms and levels of loyalty. Especially in low-involvement categories, loyalty can be driven by satisfied customers that buy because of habit and because it is not worth spending time or resources reviewing whether that habit should be changed. In that case measures of distribution (making sure the purchase remains convenient), customer satisfaction (looking for warning signs that the brand is losing satisfaction), and repeat purchase (the ultimate measure) are needed. In higher involvement categories, loyalty often requires a scale that ranges from liking to having self-expressive benefits to being a brand that a person will talk about and recommend to others. In that case, measures of activity in brand communities and a willingness to recommend will be useful.

Two other comments. First, customers who have left the brand should be probed to identify the motivating problems and causes of dissatisfaction. The result is often insights that are sensitive and operational. Second, measures should be tracked over time and compared with those of competitors. Relative comparisons and changes are most important.

Chapter 9 has a discussion of brand loyalty and a component of brand equity that adds depth and texture to the concept and how it can be managed.

Relative Cost

A careful cost analysis of a product (or service) and its components, which can be critical when a strategy is dependent on achieving a cost advantage or cost parity, involves tearing down competitors' products and analyzing their systems in detail. The Japanese consultant Ohmae suggested that such an analysis, when coupled with performance analysis, can lead to one of the four situations shown in Figure 6.2.[3]

If a component such as a car's braking system or a bank's teller operation is both more expensive than and inferior to that of the competition, a strategic problem requiring change may exist. An analysis could show, however, that the component is such a small item in terms of both cost and customer impact that it should be ignored. If the component is competitively superior, however, a cost-reduction program may not be the only appropriate strategy. A value analysis, in which the component's value to the customer is quantified, may suggest that the point of superiority could support a price increase or promotion campaign. If, on the other hand, a component is less expensive than that of the competition, but inferior, a value analysis might suggest that it be de-emphasized. Thus, for a car with a cost advantage but handling disadvantage,

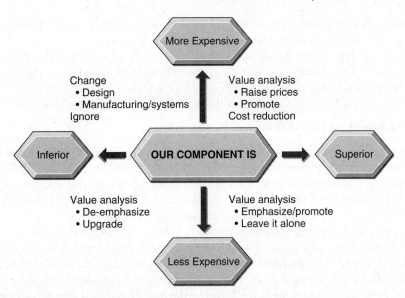

Figure 6.2 Relative Cost vs. Relative Performance—Strategic Implications

a company might de-emphasize its driving performance and position it as an economy car. An alternative is to upgrade this component. Conversely, if a component is both less expensive and superior, a value analysis may suggest that the component be emphasized, perhaps playing a key role in positioning and promotion strategies.

Sources of Cost Advantage

The many routes to cost advantage will be discussed in Chapter 8. They include economies of scale, the experience curve, product design innovations, and the use of a no-frills product offering. Each provides a different perspective to the concept of competing on the basis of a cost advantage.

Average Costing

In average costing, some elements of fixed or semivariable costs are not carefully allocated but instead are averaged over total production. Average costing can provide an opening for competitors to enter an otherwise secure market. Large customers can be much more profitable than small ones, and premium priced products can be more lucrative than value priced ones. A product line that is subsidizing other lines is vulnerable, representing an opportunity to competitors and thus a potential threat to a business.

Innovation

Does the R&D operation generate a stream of new product concepts? How does the flow of patents compare to that for competitors? Is the process from product concept to new product introduction well managed? Is there a track record of successful new products that has affected the product performance profile and market position?

Are the new products arriving in the marketplace in a timely fashion? Time to market is particularly important in many industries, from cars to software.

More broadly, does the organizational culture support innovation? Is it possible to generate substantial (if not transformational) innovations in addition to incremental innovations? Are there programs to precipitate innovation?

Manager/Employee Capability and Performance

Also key to a firm's long-term prospects are the people who must implement strategies. Are the human resources in place to support current and future strategies? Do those who are added to the organization match its needs in terms of types and quality or are there gaps that are not being filled? Is there enough diversity so that the organization can identify and respond to new threats and opportunities when they are not within the existing business arena?

An organization should be evaluated not only on how well it obtains human resources but also on how well it nurtures them. A healthy organization will consist of individuals who are motivated, challenged, fulfilled, and growing in their professions. Each of these dimensions can be observed and measured by employee surveys and group discussions. Certainly, the attitude of production workers was a key factor in the quality and cost advantage that Japanese automobile firms enjoyed throughout the past three decades. In service industries such as banking and fast foods, the ability to sustain positive employee performance and attitude is usually a key success factor.

Values and Heritage

The firms with strong performance over time usually have a well-defined set of values that are both known and accepted within the organization, values that are more than simply increasing financial return. Strong values that guide and even inspire are enhanced if they are supported by a well-known and relevant heritage. Values and a heritage not only create a strong and consistent brand but also support the business strategy. In fact, when business falters, one tact that often works is to return to the roots of the business—what made it strong in the first place. When McDonald's faltered, a turnaround was based in part on their historic core values of service, people, convenience, quality, and good prices.

Values provide a reason to believe in for employees and will influence the brand as a result. Among the values that are often influential are the organizational associations discussed in Chapter 9 such as innovation, social responsibility, concern for the customer, quality, service, and being globally and environmentally responsible.

Having a heritage based on a founder or on early success can be a guide and a value anchor. Consider L.L. Bean with a vision of their founder who designed a shoe for hunters that was waterproof. When the first batch had a problem, he took them all back. His focus on the customer and on the outdoors and the outdoorsmen continue to guide the firm. General Electric still has the innovation emphasis that was the hallmark of its founder Thomas Edison.

More generally, values are best communicated inside and outside a firm with stories. People remember and respond to stories. A firm should strive to have a story bank that collectively illustrates the values of the firm. The stories are not limited to the heritage of the firm but can reflect the actions of an employee or a program. The legend that Nordstrom's once took back a damaged tire even though they do not sell tires (although the store that did take back a tire formerly did sell ties, although under another owner) says so much about their customer service.

STRENGTHS AND WEAKNESSES

In developing or implementing strategy, it is important to identify the assets and competencies that represent areas of strength and weakness. A successful strategy needs to be based on assets and competencies because it is generally easier for competitors to duplicate what you do rather than who you are. Further, current assets and competencies, as illustrated in Chapter 12, can be leveraged to create new businesses.

Figure 3.4 is a partial list of the types of assets and competencies that an organization might develop. There are more than three dozen, organized under the categories of innovation, manufacturing, access to capital, management, marketing, and customer base. This checklist is a good place to start when identifying the most relevant assets and competencies. Another are the motivating questions introduced in Chapter 3 that identify assets and competencies important to customers, those developed by successful competitors, and those representing large or important parts of the value added chain.

Each asset or competence relevant to the business, such as a new product development capability, access to low-cost labor, an innovative culture, brand strength, or a loyal customer base, should be evaluated as to its strength and impact.

Is it dominant in that it provides a point of advantage that has endured and is likely to remain so in the future? The service delivery capability of Disney theme parks, for example, is so superior that other firms study its operation. Is the organization willing to invest to make the asset or competence dominant into the future? Certainly, Disney has shown this willingness over many decades. The investment commitment needs to be factored into the financial resource picture. It may mean that resources for new ventures will be limited.

Is it strong but vulnerable? Are others catching up? Should the firm attempt to invest to regain a dominant position so that it is a point of advantage? If so, what program at what cost is implied? Or should the firm retreat so that the asset or competence is simply a modest advantage over some competitors and a point of parity with respect to others?

Is the asset or competence adequate, a point of parity? Is it strong enough so that customers do not avoid the firm because of it? If so, is that a satisfactory long-term position? Can advantage be achieved on other dimensions? What investment is implied to maintain the current strength so that it does not become a point of disadvantage? Product quality is often in this situation. If Target, for example, can deliver quality adequate enough so that customers do not use a quality judgment as a reason to exclude Target from their consideration set, the battle will shift to other dimensions on which Target is likely to excel.

Is it a liability? Is it holding back the firm from gaining and retaining customers? Consider the Korean automobile firms whose quality and social acceptability deficit precluded people from buying their products. They needed to convert this liability to a point of parity.

THREATS AND OPPORTUNITIES

The other half of an internal analysis is the identification of threats and opportunities. In the external analysis, a host of potential threats and opportunities will have been identified. The internal challenge is to determine which are most relevant for the firm's business and to prioritize

BENCHMARKING

Comparing the performance of a business component with others is called *benchmarking*. The goals are to generate specific ideas for improvement and to define standards at which to aim. One target may be competitors: what cost and performance levels are they achieving, and how? Knowing your deficits with respect to the competition is the first step to developing programs to eliminate them. Best-practice companies are another target. Thus, many benchmark against Disney in terms of delivering consistent service in their theme parks or Amazon as the standard for Internet e-commerce operations and customer support. Looking outside one's own industry is often a way to break away from the status quo and thereby create a real advantage.

them. The dimensions used to manage strategic uncertainly in general, immediacy and impact, are appropriate when assessing threats and opportunities.

Those threats that are imminent and have high impact should drive a strategic imperative, a program that has the highest priority. If there is a visible quality problem (such as contaminated Perrier water or defective tires on Ford Explorers, for example), fixing that problem and thus addressing the associated threat needs to be a high priority. When the threat is of low impact or is not immediate, a more measured response is possible.

The most extreme threat is one that potentially makes the business model obsolete. Because of the decline in the use of printers, HP has seen its cash cow, printer supplies, decline with rather troubling strategic implications. AOL, with its "You've got mail" greeting and a route to the Internet for newbies and the intimidated, had a dominant business model with some 35 million subscribers. However, it failed to respond to the fact that its customers eventually obtained more sophistication and better equipment. AOL was in a position to be the social network Internet company but instead watched others like MySpace and Facebook assume that role and allowed its value proposition to erode. Dialing up the threat to the business model in a timely fashion and making the organization responsive might have led to a very different outcome for AOL.

Threats can come in the form of a strategic problem or a liability. Strategic problems, events, or trends adversely affecting strategy generally need to be addressed aggressively and corrected even if the fix is difficult and expensive. Strategic liabilities—the absence of an asset (such as good location) or competence (for example, new-product skills)—usually require a different response. A business often copes over time with a liability by adjusting strategies in a way that will neutralize that liability. A firm that lacks new product competencies might engage in a systematic product acquisition strategy.

An opportunity similarly can be evaluated as to whether its impact will be immediate and major. If so, the organization should be set up to move quickly and decisively. One study found that most organizations only get faced with a "golden opportunity" once or twice a decade. The mark of a firm that can adapt to new conditions and still come out a market leader is recognizing and reacting to such opportunities. Opportunities that have a low impact or are in the future may justify serious investment and perhaps an experimental entry into a new business area to gain information, but the resource commitment is likely to be more modest.

In general, lost opportunities are costly and are only too common. As Drucker wrote in several forms, managers need to spend more time on opportunities and less on solving problems.

FROM ANALYSIS TO STRATEGY

In making strategic decisions, inputs from a variety of assessments are relevant, as the last several chapters have already made clear. However, the core of any strategic decision should be based on three types of assessments. The first concerns organizational strengths and weaknesses. The second evaluates competitor strengths, weaknesses, and strategies because an organization's strength is of less value if it is neutralized by a competitor's strength or strategy. The third assesses the competitive context, the customers and their needs, the market, and the market environment in order to determine how attractive the selected market will be, given the business strategy.

The goal is to develop a strategy that exploits business strengths and competitor weaknesses and neutralizes business weaknesses and competitor strengths. The ideal is to compete in a healthy, growing industry with a strategy based on strengths that are unlikely to be acquired or neutralized by competitors. Figure 6.3 summarizes how these three assessments combine to influence strategy.

GE's decision to sell its small-appliance division illustrates these strategic principles. Small appliances were a part of GE's legacy and linked to its lamp and major-appliance product lines in the minds of retailers and customers. The small-appliance industry was not profitable, however, in part because of overcapacity and the power of the retailer. Also, cost pressures contributed to a reduction in product performance and reliability. Further, GE's strengths, such as its technological superiority and financial resources, were not leveraged in the small-appliance business, as any innovation could be copied. Thus, GE decided that a strategic fit did not exist, and it sold the small-appliance business to Black & Decker.

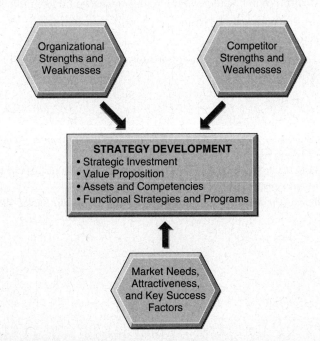

Figure 6.3 Structuring Strategic Decisions

KEY LEARNINGS

- Sales and profitability analysis provide an evaluation of past strategies and an indication of the current market viability of a product line.
- Shareholder value holds that the flow of profits emanating from an investment should exceed the cost of capital (which is the weighted average of the cost of equity and cost of debt). Routes to achieving shareholder value—such as downsizing, reducing assets employed, and outsourcing—can be risky when they undercut assets and competencies.
- Performance assessment should go beyond financials to include such dimensions as customer satisfaction/brand loyalty, product/service quality, brand/firm associations, relative cost, new product activity, and manager/employee capability and performance.
- Assets and competencies can represent a point of advantage, a point of parity, or a liability. Threats and opportunities that are both imminent and important should trigger strategic imperatives, programs with high priority.

FOR DISCUSSION

1. Explain shareholder value analysis. Why might it help firms? Why might it result in bad decisions?
2. Look at the quotations that begin Chapters 2 through 6. Which one do you find the most insightful? Why? Under what circumstances would its implications not hold?
3. What performance measure would you consider most important for McDonald's? For Chevrolet?
4. Conduct a strengths, weakness, opportunities, and threats (SWOT) analysis for Ford. For Frito-Lay.

NOTES

1. For an excellent review of the risks of shareholder value see Allan A. Kennedy, *The End of Shareholder Value,* Cambridge, MA: Perseus Publishing, 2000.
2. Philippe Haspeslagh, Tomo Noda, and Fares Boulos, "It's Not Just About the Numbers," *Harvard Business Review,* July–August 2001, pp. 65–73.
3. Kenichi Ohmae, *The Mind of the Strategist,* New York: Penguin Books, 1982, p. 26.

Understanding and Working with Industry Trends

TRENDS IN RETAILING

Consider the following trends in food and nonfood retailing.

Nonfood Retailing

1. ***Moving away from the middle.*** Retailers are offering a more upscale experience. Macy's locations are getting a face-lift and image advertising. Bath & Body Works is transforming into an affordable beauty boutique. High-end retailers such as Saks, Neiman's, Cole Hand, and Coach are clearly positioned to offer self-expressive benefits.

   At the same time, other retailers are moving down to compete with the discount stores. Discount stores such as TJ Maxx, Target, and outlet malls are becoming more important especially as consumers react to the recession.

2. ***Toward a better shopping lifestyle.*** Enclosed malls are in decline; they are being replaced by the "lifestyle center," which is a combination of stores such as Pottery Barn, Barnes & Noble, Gap, Victoria's Secret, and Williams-Sonoma, with open walkways and no department store. These are often in a revitalized urban setting.

3. ***Customers are looking and then buying where the price is lower.*** Retailers like Best Buy are simply showrooms for Amazon and others. Customers can scan the product code and instantly find and even buy the item over the Internet.

4. ***Faster fashion.*** The ability of retailers such as Zara, H&M, Forever 21, Target's Go International, and Uniclo to capture in-season trends by a fast-turnaround design and manufacturing cycle means that their stores are dynamic and interesting with new items flowing through.

Food Retailing

5. ***Private-label strength.*** Private-label goods continue to grow at a steady rate. The private-label brands such as Safeway's "S" and Wal-Mart's Super Value offer exceptional price savings and tend to thrive in categories that don't see a lot of innovation. The high-end private label brands such as Safeway Select often become competitive in terms of quality and even innovation while still offering lower prices

6. ***In-store media.*** Retailers are finding that conventional media are less effective and are going to in-store media including displays on shopping carts, couponing at the product site, and individualized couponing.

7. ***Organic offerings.*** Organic food, one of the success factors of Whole Foods, is going mainstream. Safeway's O Organics are sold outside Safeway, and Target's Archer Farms is adding energy to Target. But natural is being used more because organic sounds expensive.

8. Convenience redefined. Canned soup, frozen dinners, cereal, cake mixes, and instant potatoes are no longer convenient enough. People want items with little or no preparation, items like open-and-eat snacks and yogurt.

FOR DISCUSSION

1. What is driving each of these trends? Which are supported by underlying consumer trends? Identify them.

2. Which three trends will be around in five years? How would you forecast the probability that the trend will persist for that long?

3. What are the top two threats and opportunities represented by these trends for Macy's, Levi Straus, Safeway, and General Mills?

4. When might a retailer consider going against the trend?

5. Another potential trend is the return to a store's roots. Several retailers, such as Gap and Saks, lost core customers by attempting to appeal to younger buyers. As a result, they are now attempting to return to their roots and deliver the classic fashions that made them attractive to their now not-so-young customers. What possessed them to go trendy in the first place? Can they recapture the customers that they have alienated?

A New, Dynamic Industry

THE ENERGY BAR INDUSTRY

In 1986, PowerBar, a firm in Berkeley, California, single-handedly created the energy bar category. Positioned as an athletic energy food, it was distributed at bike shops and events that usually involved running or biking. The target segment was the athlete who needed an efficient, effective energy source.

Six years later, seeking to provide an alternative to the sticky, dry nature of the PowerBar, a competitor, also located in Berkeley, developed an energy bar with superior taste and texture and branded it the Clif bar. About the same time, another competitor introduced the Balance bar, which offered a blend of protein, fat, and carbohydrates based on the nutrition formula associated with the "Zone diet." Faced with these challengers, PowerBar responded with Harvest (a bar with a much more accessible taste and texture) and ProteinPlus (an entry into the high-protein subcategory closely related to that defined by Balance).

The makers of the Clif bar observed that many women were athletes and many more were involved in fitness. They further observed that this half of the population had unique needs in terms of vitamins and supplements and that the energy bar industry had yet to recognize or fill them—a classic case of unmet needs. As a result, they introduced Luna as the first nutritional (not energy) bar for women, using media and promotions targeting active females. The bar had a light, crunchy texture; came in flavors like "lemon zest" and chai tea; and contained nearly two dozen vitamins, minerals, and nutrients. The target market consisted of time-strapped women who wanted both taste and nutrition and would appreciate a bar tailored to their needs.

Both in reaction to Luna's success and to expand the segments for which the category was relevant, PowerBar studied why women did not buy its products, which the firm considered to be nutritious, convenient, tasty, and able to provide a quick pick-me-up in mid-morning or mid-afternoon. One answer was that the calorie hit from any member of the PowerBar family was simply too great. In response, the firm created the almost indulgent PowerBar-endorsed Pria. With only 110 calories, Pria was designed to respond to Luna while attracting new users into the category.

The Balance strategy was to introduce a series of products, all of which stuck to the original bar's 40/30/30 nutritional formula but had different taste and textures. These spinoffs included Balance Plus, Balance Outdoor (with no chocolate coating to melt), Balance Gold, Balance Satisfaction, and the Balance-endorsed Oasis, a bar designed for women. The big success was Balance Gold, which was positioned close to the candy bar category (indeed, its tagline was "like a candy bar") by containing ingredients such as nuts and caramel. Such a bar probably risked some of Balance's perceived authenticity as being an energy bar. However, because Balance entered the category from the diet perspective anyway and probably was never considered in the center of the energy bar world, the risk may have been acceptable.

In addition to the major brands, challengers from a variety of small and large firms advanced subcategories by positioning themselves around such factors as age (bars for seniors and kids) and health (products to fit dairy-free, diabetic, and heart-conscious diets), to say nothing of numerous textures, flavors, sizes, and coatings. Over a 10-year period, some 450 products were introduced. For example, the popularity of low-carbohydrate diets has prompted a host of entries, including Atkins Advantage, developed by the Atkins organization, which gained a substantial market share that peaked in 2003 and fell off sharply thereafter. Other participating brands include Zone-Perfect, Met-Rx, GeniSoy, EAS, CarboLite, Carb Solutions, and Gatorade energy bars.

Masterfoods' Snickers Marathon—a candy bar with a blend of vitamins, minerals, and protein—has blurred the division between candy and energy bars by seeking to gain share in the latter market. One concern of the energy bar industry is the skepticism among some quarters as to how qualitatively different its products are from candy bars in the first place.

The motivation for using an energy bar is primarily to provide a convenient energy boost. The original heritage of being a product to enhance the performance of top athletes engaged in demanding physical activities (like Lance Armstrong, a PowerBar endorser) created credibility and self-expressive benefits in the category's early years. Because household penetration was still under 20 percent, however, the major firms worked to generalize "performance" to be relevant to anyone who needs to perform well during the day. In fact, the industry dream is to get people to label the category "performance nutrition" and think of it as enhancing one's ability to complete any task.

New products in the category are going in several directions. A trend toward indulgent icings, coatings, and coverings has led some to morph toward candy bars. Others go the opposite way, using whole-grain ingredients for products somewhat like the original Clif bar and Quaker's Oatmeal Squares for women. The makers of the Clif bar also have introduced a Mojo line of salty snack bars to provide alternatives to sweet-tasting bars and the Clif Nectar bar, an entirely organic nut and fruit bar. PowerBar introduced Nut Naturals, a low glycemic index bar. There are bars positioned around ingredients such as protein or soy bars. A major Japanese brand of soy bars, SoyJoy is now in the market with a dry bar that will not be confused with a candy bar.

The energy bar category has gone mainstream, moving from the bike shops to the grocery stores and exploding from just over $100 million in revenue in 1996 to an estimated $2 billion or more a decade later, with expected future growth exceeding 10 percent per year. It is fueled both by the confluence of trends toward low-carb, portable, nutritious snacks and meal replacements (along with a general concern for health and weight control) and by the introduction of new products. Along the way, it became large enough to attract the attention of major packaged-goods firms. In 2000, Nestlé purchased PowerBar, which has remained the leading player, with the Clif bar (which has remained independent) emerging as its most formidable competitor. The Balance line of products was bought by Kraft, also in 2000.

Energy bars can be considered a part of a larger food bar category which is also growing rapidly. The market is divided fairly equally between granola bars (positioned as a snack food that is healthier than candy bars), breakfast/cereal/snack bars (used as a meal replacement), and energy bars. Energy bars have a far lower household penetration than the other food bar forms. The top marketers of food bars are Kellogg's (Nutri-Grain), Quaker Oats, General Mills, and Slim-Fast.

FOR DISCUSSION

1. Conduct a thorough analysis of this category's customers, competitors, market, and environment from the perspective of PowerBar. What are the key strategic questions? What additional information would you like to obtain? How would you obtain it? What are the threats and opportunities? In particular, address the following issues:

   a. How is the market segmented? What are the key customer motivations and unmet needs? What are the similarities and differences among the segments? How might a company link customer motivations to value propositions?

    b. Identify the competitors. Who are the most direct competitors? The indirect competitors? Substitute products? What are the strategic groups?

    c. What are the market trends? The growth submarkets? The key success factors?

    d. What are the environmental trends that will affect the industry? Generate two or three viable future scenarios.

2. How would you go about evaluating emerging submarkets? What criteria would you use to enter each? Consider PowerBar's reaction to the Clif organic bar.

3. Can brands such as Harvest, Luna, Balance Gold, Balance Satisfaction, and others be leveraged?

4. Will the energy bar category morph into food bars, with elements like diet, tasting like candy, and breakfast replacement dominating as the energy definition recedes? How can Nestlé's PowerBar keep that from happening and still maintain its mainstream/supermarket posture?

5. At what stage is the energy bar market relative to the product-life cycle? What strategies can be used to extend the life cycle? Do you see a consolidation on the horizon?

6. What are the prospects for the Japanese SoyJoy bar? It comes in multiple flavors but is rather dry. What strategy would you advise them to pursue?

Source: Adapted with the permission of the Free Press, a division of Simon & Schuster Adult Publishing Group, from David Aaker, *Brand Portfolio Strategy*, Chapter 4, "Brand Relevance," pp. 98–101.

Evaluating and Assessing the Implications of a Transformation Innovation

TRANSFORMATIONAL INNOVATIONS

Business 2.0 nominated several firms with the potential to be game changers with transformational innovations. The magazine noted that the telephone was dismissed in 1876 by Western Union Telegraph (which was offered the technology for $100,000) and by J. Pierpoint Morgan, who called it a novelty with no commercial application. Yet the telephone as we know now transformed the communication industry. Will these firms transform industries as well? Or will they be historical footnotes?

Zopa—Peer-to-Peer Lending

Banking is a highly profitable industry, based in large part on its capacity to lend money provided by savers and in part by its use of credit cards to generate loans at high interest rates. Zopa, which pioneered the new industry in U.K. in 2005, provides an alternative to banks by enabling people to lend to each other; both the borrower and lender potentially receive better rates than a bank would offer. People join Zopa either as borrowers or lenders. Zopa assesses the credit risk of borrowers using conventional information such as credit reports and verified income, as well as less conventional sources such as eBay ratings. Both borrowers and lenders are pooled so that an individual lender actually is part of a group that will lend money to a group of borrowers, thereby reducing default risks. Zopa processes the payments and receives a 1 percent fee shared by the borrower and lender. The Lending Club and Amone are U.S. startups in a similar mode.

EEStor—A New Automobile Power Source

EEStor, formed in 2001, is developing a new solid-state battery in the form of high-power-density ceramic ultra-capacitors called Electrical Storage Units (ESUs). Although the technology is kept confidential by Eestor, reports indicate that an ESU can store over 10 times the energy of lead acid batteries at one-tenth the weight, can be recharged in minutes, has virtually unlimited recharge cycles, and has no overheating risk or hazardous materials. In 2013, EEStor had yet to prove its technology but was hopeful that it would be able to do so without excessive delay. Assuming it can deliver, the implications are significant.

The automobile market is an important potential application. EEStor's ESUs can run not only small automobiles but also even large SUVs. It has been estimated that an EEStor-powered car could drive 500 miles on about $9 worth of electricity and that the engine would cost just over $5,000, where a conventional gasoline engine costs from $3,000 to $5,000. A Toronto maker of low-speed electric cars called Feel Good Cars has apparently obtained an exclusive worldwide right to purchase ESUs from EEStor.

NextMedium

NextMedium system, called Embed, facilitates the marketing of brand integration (a term that includes product placement but also brand presence without an actual product) in television shows, movies, and video games. NextMedium will help entertainment companies present their inventory of potential brand integration opportunities, with minimum bids set forth. It will then put that inventory in front of advertisers. When a brand integration opportunity is purchased, there is check-off approval by the creative entertainment professional. For advertisers, this will provide an easy way to view and select from the inventory of brand integration options. Through NextMedium, advertisers can view or listen to their placement in its context. In addition, NextMedium will monitor the placement and provide information on the size and composition of the audience exposed to the placement.

FOR DISCUSSION

For each potential transformational innovation, answer the following questions.

1. Who are the industries and firms for which this would be a threat? What is the nature of the threat? How would you go about evaluating it? How can you forecast the impact? What similar examples from history can provide insights? How do they differ? How can you avoid making a decision like the Western Union CEO in 1876? Could this be an opportunity as well for these same firms? What prevents them from participating in the new technology?

2. Will this technology expand the market, bringing in new customers, or will it simply replace the existing business?

3. What are the strategic options for the firms with the transformational technology? What are the pros and cons of each?

4. How would you go about branding and positioning the new product class being proposed? How should it be labeled?

Source: Erick Schunfeld and Jeanette Bovzo, "The Next Disruptors," *Business 2.0*, October 2006, pp. 80–96.

Interpreting Big Trends

ENVIRONMENTAL TRENDS THAT MATTER

The following are environmental trends that will have a substantial impact on many categories.

Democratization of education Thanks to new online platforms and free access to world-class content, people can experience education on any number of topics—anywhere, anytime. Stanford offered three courses in 2011, each of which had over 100,000 attendees. At the same time, MIT offered 46 courses that included complete video lectures. These efforts are termed Massive Open Online Courses (MOOCs). Because of the massive scale of learners, MOOCs require instructional design that facilitates large-scale feedback and interaction. One approach is to leverage learner connection by encouraging peer-to-peer review and crowd sources interaction and group collaboration. Another is to use automated feedback through objective, online assessments (for example, quizzes and exams).

FOR DISCUSSION

What is the business model for MOOCs? What should a business school do to adapt? What are the options? What are the threats and opportunities for a text publisher like Wiley? What changes will they have to make to be relevant?

Payment forms changing. Credit cards are increasingly vanishing to let alternative forms of payment—quicker, easier, and cheaper ones—become the new standards. With the strong growth of e-commerce, optimizing mobile payments both for consumers and online sellers is a key to being relevant.

FOR DISCUSSION

What is the future of credit cards? Will they decline? How many years will it take before their size is reduced by 25%? What are the new alternative forms? Which will win in retailing? In B2B transactions?

3Ps of digital health. Applications are enabling a new wave of innovation that is changing the face of the health care industry. The future trend for health care is **personalized, participatory, and preventive** with the help of mobile devices seamlessly integrating technology into our daily lives to drive healthy outcomes.

FOR DISCUSSION

What are the implications for Kaiser Permanente? How do you personalize? What are the good examples? What are getting others to participate and to engage in preventive actions? What really is the impact of these concepts? What percent of people really believe in them? Of those, how many actually follow them?

PART TWO

CREATING, ADAPTING, AND IMPLEMENTING STRATEGY

CHAPTER SEVEN

Creating Advantage: Synergy and Commitment vs. Opportunism vs. Adaptability

All men can see the tactics whereby I conquer, but what none can see is the strategy out of which great victory is evolved.
—*Sun-Tzu, Chinese military strategist*

Don't manage, lead.
—*Jack Welch, GE*

Where absolute superiority is not attainable, you must produce a relative one at the decisive point by making skillful use of what you have.
—*Karl von Clausewitz, On War, 1832*

*O*ur attention now shifts from strategic analysis to the development of a business strategy. What strategic alternatives should be considered? What assets and competencies, target segments, value propositions, and functional strategies? What investment and disinvestment decisions should be raised? These questions will be the focus of the balance of the book. One goal will be to provide a wide scope of available strategic alternatives in order to increase the likelihood that the best choices will be considered. Even a poor decision among superior alternatives is preferable to a good decision among inferior alternatives.

The ten chapters remaining in this book are portrayed in Figure 7.1. This chapter will discuss the concept and creation of a sustainable competitive advantage (SCA), the key to a successful strategy. It then turns to the challenge of creating and leveraging synergy as one basis for an SCA. Finally, three very different strategic philosophies—strategic commitment, strategic opportunism, and strategy adaptability—are presented that provide different routes to a strategic advantage.

Chapter 8 provides an overview of alternative value propositions. A value proposition is often an umbrella concept under which the supporting assets and competencies and functional strategies and programs can be grouped. In that sense, it represents a good overview of alternative

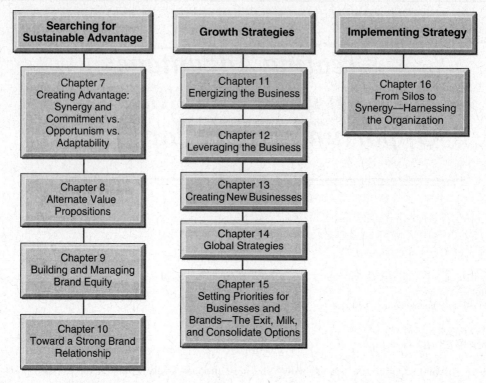

Figure 7.1   Creating and Implementing Strategy

strategies. Chapter 9 describes how to create and leverage a key asset, brand equity. Chapter 10 discusses how to develop a deep relationship with customers, the ultimate SCA. The next four chapters present growth strategies: energizing the business (Chapter 11), leveraging the business (Chapter 12), creating new business models (Chapter 13), and going global (Chapter 14). Chapter 15 discusses setting priorities among business units and making disinvestment decisions, a key determinate in providing growth resources. Finally, Chapter 16 introduces organizational issues focusing on creating cooperation and communication between organizational silos in order to gain synergy and efficiency.

THE SUSTAINABLE COMPETITIVE ADVANTAGE

As defined earlier in this book, a sustainable competitive advantage is an element (or combination of elements) of the business strategy that provides a meaningful advantage over both existing and future competitors (see Figure 7.2). Wal-Mart has a cost advantage because of its scale economies, market power and logistical efficiencies, value reputation, and site location assets. Southwest Airlines has a fun personality and a point-to-point model that provides for convenient, reliable, uncomplicated travel. Tesla, the premium battery-powered car, has a set of feature breakthroughs, an exceptional interior and exterior design, a powerful engine, a supportive buying experience, and the self-expressive benefit of driving an environmentally friendly car that looks and feels unique. This set of attributes combine to define a subcategory that will be defended by Tesla going forward.

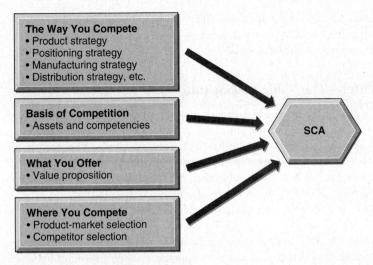

Figure 7.2   The Sustainable Competitive Advantage

An SCA needs to be both meaningful and sustainable. It should be substantial enough to make a difference; a marginal superiority in quality, especially when "good" quality is good enough for most customers, will not generate an SCA. Meanwhile, sustainability (in the absence of an effective patent) means that any advantage needs to be supported and enhanced over time. There needs to be a moving target for competitors. For example, Gillette maintained its technological superiority in razors over a long time period with innovation after innovation, making copying its competitive advantage difficult.

An SCA will in part depend on the functional strategies and programs, how you compete. Wal-Mart's discount store, Southwest's point-to-point system, and the Tesla car all have SCAs based in part on their functional strategies and programs. In these cases and others, however, an effective SCA will also involve other aspects of the business strategy—assets and competencies, the value proposition, and the selection of the product market.

The Basis of Competition: Assets and Competencies

The assets and competencies of an organization represent the most sustainable element of a business strategy because these are usually difficult to copy or counter. There is no point in pursuing a quality strategy, for example, without the design and manufacturing competencies needed to deliver quality products. Anyone can try to distribute cereal or detergent through supermarkets, but few have the competencies in logistics, shelf space management, and promotions or relationships with chain executives that make product distribution efficient and effective. Similarly, a department store's premium-service positioning strategy will not succeed unless the right people and culture are in place and are supported. Who you are, in other words, is as important as what you do.

As discussed in Chapter 3, several questions can help to identify relevant assets and competencies. What are the key motivations of the major market segments? What are the large value-added components? What are the mobility barriers? What elements of the value chain can generate an advantage? What assets and competencies are possessed by successful businesses and lacking in unsuccessful businesses?

What You Offer—The Value Proposition

An effective SCA should be visible to customers and provide or enhance a value position. The most widely employed value propositions such as quality, low price, social values, and customer relationships are described in the following three chapters. The key is to link a value proposition with the positioning of a business. A product's reliability may not be apparent to customers, but if it can be made visible through a brand strategy, it can support a reliability positioning strategy. Maytag is an example of a firm whose reliability positioning is supported by advertising that communicates the value proposition provided by its product design and performance.

A reputation for delivering a value proposition can be a more important asset than the substance that underlies that reputation. A business with such a reputation can falter for a time, and the market will either never become aware of the weakness or will forgive the firm. Conversely, competitors often have a much easier time in matching the quality or performance of a market offering than in convincing customers that they indeed have done so. Enduring impressions are why a visible value proposition that is meaningful to customers is strategically valuable.

A solid value proposition can fail if a key ingredient is missing. Procter & Gamble's Pringles potato chips had a host of assets, such as a consistent product, long shelf life, a crushproof container, and national distribution. The problem was that these attributes were valued only if the taste was perceived to be good. As a result, Pringles ability to penetrate the snack market was limited for decades until it made progress in terms of both actual and perceived taste. Kingsford Charcoal failed in the barbeque sauce market simply because there was no room for a third entrant in the premium segment.

Where You Compete: The Product Market Served

An important determinant for an SCA is the choice of the target product market. A well-defined strategy supported by assets and competencies can fail because it does not work in the marketplace. A product market needs to be selected for which the value proposition is relevant. As noted in Chapter 4, it does no good to offer the best SUV in the market if most of your target customers now want to buy a hybrid.

The scope of the business also involves the identity of competitors. Sometimes an asset or competency will form an SCA only given the right set of competitors. Thus, it is vital to assess whether a competitor or strategic group is weak, adequate, or strong with respect to assets and competencies. The goal is to engage in a strategy that will match up with competitors' weak points in relevant areas.

SCAs vs. Key Success Factors

What is the difference between key success factors (KSFs), introduced in Chapters 1 and 4, and SCAs? A KSF is an asset or competence needed to compete. An SCA involves an asset or competence that is the basis for a continuing advantage. It is a point of difference. For example, an automobile firm needs to have adequate distribution given its business model and objectives, so distribution is a KSF. Lexus has turned its dealer network into an SCA, however, because it is capable of delivering a superior customer experience. A KSF for value-priced economy cars is the ability to control costs in order to create profit margins. Hyundai's ability in this regard is markedly superior to its competitors, and thus it becomes an SCA.

To be a winner at poker requires skill, nerve, and money. In also requires a player to ante—to put up a certain amount of money just to see the cards and engage in betting. A KSF can be an ante in terms of the marketplace. Generating a superior quality car may have been an SCA for Lexus or Mercedes and a point of differentiation in the mid-1990s. As BMW and Cadillac improve their own quality, though, the quality dimension starts to be an attribute all luxury cars are assumed to have and thus becomes a KSF but not a basis for an SCA. Instead of winning the competitive hand, a KSF merely buys an organization a seat at the table.

The concept of a point of parity (POP), introduced in Chapter 1, is analogous to a KSF.[1] A POP is an association that is not necessarily unique to the brand but may be necessary to present a credible offering within a certain category. A bank may not be a credible option with ATMs and convenient hours. A POP might also be designed to negate a competitor's point of differentiation. A low-carb food brand, for example, seeks to create parity with regard to taste, thereby negating the taste point of differentiation (POD) of its competitors and leading customers to base their selection on its own POD (namely, low-carb ingredients).

What Business Managers Name as Their SCAs

Managers of 248 distinct businesses in the service and high-tech industries were asked to name the SCAs of their business.[2] The objectives were to identify frequently employed SCAs, to confirm that managers could articulate them, to determine whether different managers from the same businesses would identify the same SCAs, and to find how many SCAs would be identified for each business. The responses were coded into categories. The results, summarized in Figure 7.3, provide some suggestive insights into the SCA construct.

The wide variety of SCAs mentioned, each representing distinct competitive approaches, is shown in the figure. Of course, the list does differ by industry. For high-tech firms, for example, name recognition is less important than technical superiority, product innovation, and installed customer base. The next two chapters discuss several SCAs in more detail.

Most of the SCAs in Figure 7.3 reflect assets or competencies. Customer base, quality reputation, and good management and engineering staff, for example, are business assets, whereas customer service and technical superiority usually involve sets of competencies.

For a subset of 95 of the businesses involved, a second business manager was independently interviewed. The result suggests that managers can identify SCAs with a high degree of reliability. Of the 95 businesses, 76 of the manager pairs gave answers that were coded the same, and most of the others had only a single difference in the SCA list.

Another finding is instructive—the average number of SCAs per business was 4.58, suggesting that it is usually not sufficient to base a strategy on a single SCA. Sometimes a business is described in terms of a single competency or asset, implying that being a quality-oriented business or a service-focused business explains success. This study indicates, however, that it may be necessary to have several assets and competencies.

	High-Tech	Service	Other	Total
1. Reputation for quality	26	50	29	105
2. Customer service/product support	23	40	15	78
3. Name recognition/high profile	8	42	21	71
4. Retain good management and engineering staff	17	43	5	65
5. Low-cost production	17	15	21	53
6. Financial resources	11	26	14	51
7. Customer orientation/feedback/market research	13	26	9	48
8. Product-line breadth	11	23	13	47
9. Technical superiority	30	7	9	46
10. Installed base of satisfied customers	19	22	4	45
11. Segmentation/focus	7	22	16	45
12. Product characteristics/differentiation	12	15	10	37
13. Continuing product innovation	12	17	6	35
14. Market share	12	14	9	35
15. Size/location of distribution	10	11	13	34
16. Low price/high-value offering	6	20	6	32
17. Knowledge of business	2	25	4	31
18. Pioneer/early entrant in industry	11	11	6	28
19. Efficient, flexible production/operations adaptable to customers	4	17	4	25
20. Effective sales force	10	9	4	23
21. Overall marketing skills	7	9	7	23
22. Shared vision/culture	5	13	4	22
23. Strategic goals	6	7	9	22
24. Powerful, well-known parent	7	7	6	20
25. Location	0	10	10	20
26. Effective advertising/image	5	6	6	17
27. Enterprising/entrepreneurial	3	3	5	11
28. Good coordination	3	2	5	10
29. Engineering research and development	8	2	0	10
30. Short-term planning	2	1	5	8
31. Good distributor relations	2	4	1	7
32. Other	6	20	5	31
Total	315	539	281	1,135
Number of businesses	68	113	67	248
Average number of SCAs	4.63	4.77	4.19	4.58

Figure 7.3 Sustainable Competitive Advantages of 248 Businesses

THE ROLE OF SYNERGY

Synergy between business units can provide an SCA that is truly sustainable because it is based on the characteristics of a firm that are unique. A competitor might have to duplicate the organization in order to capture the assets or competencies involved.

A core element in the GE strategic vision has always been to achieve synergy across many businesses. The concept was that a GE business can call on the resources of the firm and of other GE businesses to create advantage. The turbine technology that GE pioneered as it established the infrastructure for electricity helped in the jet engine business. The SCAs of

General Electric in the CT scanner (an X-ray-based diagnostic system) business were in part based on its leadership in the X-ray business, in which it had a huge installed base and a large service network, and in part based on the fact that it operated other businesses involving technologies used in CT scanners. Technologies in one business can become innovations in another.

Sony exploits the synergy of its many product groups by showcasing them together in stores (such as one on Chicago's Michigan Avenue) and even on several Celebrity Cruise ships. The ships are outfitted with Sony entertainment products, including television sets, movie theaters, and sound equipment. The result is an integrated package that has the cumulative impact of reinforcing Sony's role of providing high quality and technologically advanced entertainment.

Synergy can be generated by leveraging assets and competences. Amazon leveraged its warehouse, ordering, and distribution system over hundreds of products and allows other firms to use their system, which generates more scale and margin dollars. Disney leverages its brand and its connection to kids and family over a wide variety of offerings, including Broadway shows and cruise ships.

Synergy means that the whole is more than the sum of its parts. In this context, it means that two or more businesses (or two or more product-market strategies) operating together will be superior to the same two businesses operating independently. In terms of products, positive synergy means that offering a set of products will generate a higher return over time than would be possible if each of the products was offered separately. Similarly, in terms of markets, operating a set of markets within a business will be superior to operating them autonomously.

As a result of synergy, the combined businesses will have one or more of the following:

1. Increased customer value and thus increased sales
2. Lower operating costs
3. Reduced investment

Generally, the synergy will be caused by leveraging some commonality in the two operations, such as:

- Customers and sometimes customer applications (potentially creating a systems solution)—IBM leverages its customer knowledge and relationships across products.
- A sales force or channel of distribution—P&G's channels support some 80 products.
- A brand name and its image—Samsung leverages its brand over products and countries.
- Facilities and methods used for manufacturing, offices, or warehousing—The Wal-Mart systems work in various countries.
- R&D efforts—The divisions of Texas Instruments draw on a central R&D operation.
- Staff and operating systems—All the divisions of Market Facts, the global market intelligence firm, access their statistical staff and operation systems.
- Marketing and marketing research—Coke market research technology helps all the Coke product lines.

Synergy is not difficult to understand conceptually, but it is slippery in practice, in part because it can be difficult to predict whether synergy will actually emerge. Often two businesses seem related, and sizable potential synergy seems to exist but is never realized. Sometimes the perceived synergy is merely a mirage or wishful thinking, perhaps created in the haste to put together a merger. At other times, the potential synergy is real, but implementation problems prevent its realization. Perhaps there is a cultural mismatch between two organizations, or the incentives are inadequate. In Chapter 12, the difficulties of realizing potential synergy will be revisited.

Alliances

Obtaining instant synergy is a goal of alliances. Pairing McDonald's with an oil company's convenience store, for example, provides traffic and added value for the oil company and valuable locations for McDonald's. Dentsu, the largest Japanese advertising agency, has more than a hundred alliances—many based on partial ownership—that allow it to offer a broader communication solution to clients.

Alliances are often the key to a successful Internet strategy. Yahoo! and Amazon have hundreds of major alliances and thousands of smaller ones that combine to help them reach their goals of driving Internet traffic and offering differentiated value to their visitors. Chapter 14, Global Strategies, covers the difficult process of putting together alliances and joint ventures and making them work.

Core Assets and Competencies

A firm's asset or competency that is capable of being the competitive basis of many of its businesses is termed a core asset or competency and can be a synergistic advantage. Consider a tree metaphor, in which the root system is the core asset or competency, the trunk and major limbs are core products, the smaller branches are business units, and the leaves and flowers are end products. You may not recognize the strength of a competitor if you simply look at its end products and fail to examine the strength of its root system. Core competence represents the consolidation of firm-wide technologies and skills into a coherent thrust. A core asset, such as a brand name or a distribution channel, merits investment and management that span business units.

Consider, for example, the core competencies of Apple in pioneering computer-based devices; 3 M in sticky-tape technology; Black & Decker in small motors; Honda in vehicle motors and power trains; Samsung in semiconductors (which underlies its product innovation in consumer electronics and cell phones); and Canon in precision mechanics, fine optics, and microelectronics. Each of these competencies underlies a large set of businesses and has the potential to create more. Each of these firms invests in competence in a variety of different ways and contexts. Each would insist on keeping its primary work related to the core competency in-house. Outsourcing would risk weakening the asset, and each firm would rightfully insist that there is no other firm that could match its state-of-the-art advances.

Highly effective business processes often represent a core competence that can be applied across businesses, leading to a sustainable advantage. One such process is the new product development and introduction process. Japanese automobile firms that have reduced the process from five years to three years while making it more responsive to the needs of the market have achieved a huge advantage. Another is the management of international operations, considered an SCA by IDV, the spirits subsidiary of Grand Metropolitan. Still another is the order and logistics process in retailing. By developing dramatic improvements in its order and logistics process through distribution center innovations, a dedicated trucking system, and computerized ordering, Wal-Mart developed huge cost and inventory handling advantages over its competition. Uniqlo, a Gap-like retailer in Japan, ties its retailers directly to suppliers in China, thereby creating the ability to respond to style trends in weeks instead of months.

Developing superior capabilities in key processes involves strategic investments in people and infrastructure, the use of cross-functional teams, and clear performance targets. True process improvement does not occur without control and ownership of the parts of the process. Thus, the virtual corporation, which draws pieces from many sources in response to the organizational task at hand, often struggles to deliver a capabilities-based synergy.

STRATEGIC COMMITMENT, OPPORTUNISM, AND ADAPTABILITY

There are three very different philosophies or approaches to the development of successful strategies and sustainable competitive advantages that can be labeled strategy commitment, strategy opportunism, and strategic adaptability. Descriptions of each, summarized in Figure 7.4, provide a good perspective on choices as to management style, processes, and philosophy of business. There is no one best way; given the right context, people, culture, and strategy, each can work. Further, in dynamic markets, most firms will need to employ all three. Firms need to learn to multitask.

Strategic Commitment

Strategic commitment involves a passionate, disciplined loyalty to a clearly defined business strategy that can result in an ever stronger and more profitable business over time. This "stick to your knitting" focus avoids being distracted by enticing opportunities or competitive threats that involve expending resources that do not advance the core strategy. Wal-Mart with its single-minded focus on costs and value has excelled with a strategic commitment philosophy. Starbucks has a focus on the coffee and the experience.

Google established its position with a single-minded focus on the search engine when its competitors such as Yahoo! and Microsoft were expanding their services in order to drive traffic and exploit their customer visits. Google based its strategy on several core beliefs. One is the unwavering drive to be the best search engine as exemplified by the concept that "it's best to do one thing really, really well" and "best is a starting point, not an end point."[3] Another is the value

Organizational Characteristics	Strategic Commitment	Strategic Opportunism	Strategic Adaptability
Perspective	Continuous improvement	Opportunistic	Adapt to changing marketplace
Orientation	Commitment	Fast response	Being relevant
Leadership	Charismatic	Tactical	Visionary
Structure	Centralized	Decentralized	Flat
Future perspective	Long term	Short term	Medium term
People	Eye-on-ball	Entrepreneurial	Diverse
Risk	Lose relevance	Also ran	Misread trends

Figure 7.4 Three Strategic Philosophies

of focus on the user to deliver a simple interface; fast loading; placement based on popularity, not bribes; and advertising content that appears to be relevant.

Strategic commitment is based on an assumption that the future will be enough like the past that today's effective business model will also be successful in the future. There is a long-term perspective; the focus is on the future in investment decisions and strategy development. The planning horizon may extend into the future two, five, or more than 10 years, depending on the business involved.

There should be an understanding and buy-in throughout the organization as to what the strategy is and why it is persuasive, achievable, and worthwhile. In particular, people should know and believe in the value proposition, the target market, the functional strategies, and the role of assets and competencies. The business rationale should be more than achieving financial objectives; there should be a purpose that is valued, if not inspirational.

Execution and improving the strategy are the keys to success. The emphasis is on continually improving (rather than changing) the existing implementations of the strategy, reducing the cost, improving efficiency, enhancing the value proposition, improving customer satisfaction, and strengthening the assets and competencies. Each year the operations and its output should be better than the last. Japanese firms such as Shiseido and Canon call this continuous improvement *kaizen* and have built successful companies around it. In pursuing continuous improvement, what is needed is incremental rather than transformational or even substantial innovation. The goal is improvement of the existing strategy rather than the creation of a new strategy. In that regard, the information needs are on technology developments and consumer attitudes within the framework of the existing competitive context.

Strategic commitment places demands on the organization and its people, culture, structure, and systems. In general, a centralized organization that can be disciplined in resource allocation and keep it "on strategy" will be helpful, as will the presence of a strong, charismatic leader who can sell the vision to relevant constituencies inside and outside the organization. The people should be specialized, each with skills that will advance the strategy and its underlying assets and competencies. The culture should revolve around the strategic vision that is supporting the strategy. It should go beyond financial goals to include those that will inspire those implementing the strategy.

Strategic Stubbornness

The risk of the strategic commitment route, as suggested by Figure 7.5, is that the vision may become obsolete or faulty and its pursuit may be a wasteful exercise in strategic stubbornness. Of the host of pitfalls that could prevent a vision from being realized, three stand out.

Implementation barriers. The picture of the future may be substantially accurate, but the firm may not be able to implement the strategy required. That was, in part, the problem with the efforts of GE and others to crack the computer market in the 1960s and with the attempt of Sony to promote its beta VCR format as the industry standard.

Faulty assumptions of the future. The vision might be misguided because it is based on faulty assumptions about the future. For example, the concept of a one-stop financial services firm was based, in part, on the erroneous assumption that customers would see value in a one-stop financial service. It turned out that consumers preferred to deal with specialists. GE's concept of factory automation was similarly faulty, as it discovered after some big losses. Customers wanted hardware and software components, not a factory system.

Strategic Approach	Strategic Risk
Strategic commitment	Strategic stubbornness
Strategic opportunism	Strategic drift
Strategic adaptability	Strategic blunders; misread trends

Figure 7.5 Vision vs. Opportunism

A paradigm shift. A third problem occurs when there is a paradigm shift, perhaps brought about by a transformational innovation. For example, computers changed from mainframes to minicomputers to workstations to servers. In the semiconductor industry, the vacuum-tube business first gave way to transistors and then, in sequence, to semiconductors, integrated circuits, and microprocessors. In both cases, each new paradigm brought with it a remarkable change in the cast of characters. It was extremely rare for a leader in one paradigm to be a leader in the next, often because of strategic stubbornness.

New operating models can also change the paradigm. Starbucks and others have changed the way coffee is purchased and consumed, leaving those selling canned coffee in supermarkets to fight in a declining, unprofitable segment. Dell changed the way both individuals and organizations buy their computers, leaving those selling through retail channels at a disadvantage. Nucor changed the steel industry by creating dispersed minimills that used scrap steel as raw material, leaving the big steel companies to compete on price and watch their sales decline and profits disappear. Firms employing the commitment strategy are likely to be too focused on improving last year's strategy to lead or even participate on a paradigm changing innovation. It is no coincidence that a new paradigm is almost always dominated by new entries or by entries that had been considered insignificant niche players by the leading companies.

Strategic Opportunism

Strategic opportunism is driven by a focus on the present. The premise is that the environment is so dynamic and uncertain that it is at least risky, and more likely futile, to predict the future and invest behind those predictions. The concept of building an SCA with a static strategy assumes a static marketplace just doesn't work in dynamic times. The more prudent and profitable route is to detect and capture opportunities when they present themselves, with a goal of achieving immediate profits. When short-term successes flow, the long term will take care of itself as at least some of these short-term winners will grow to major businesses, and the rest, in the aggregate, will not be a burden.

One key to success in strategic opportunism is an entrepreneurial culture and the willingness to respond quickly to opportunities as they emerge. The people should be entrepreneurial, sensitive to new opportunities and threats, and fast to react. The organization needs to be decentralized, with people empowered to experiment and invest behind emerging opportunities. The culture needs to support empowered managers, new ventures, and change. The strategy will be dynamic and change the norm. New products will be continuously explored or introduced and others de-emphasized or dropped. New markets will be entered, and disinvestment in existing ones will always be an option. The organization will be on the lookout for new synergies and assets and competencies to be developed.

Another key is to be close to the market. The management team needs to be talking to customers and others about changing customer tastes, attitudes, and needs. Information systems must monitor customers, competitors, and the trade to learn of trends, opportunities, problems, and threats as they appear. Information gathering and analysis should be both sensitive and continuous. Frequent, regular meetings to analyze the most recent developments and news may be helpful. The organization should be quick to understand and act on changing fundamentals.

Still other keys are the ability to experiment quickly and efficiently and the scale. Procter & Gamble has a "Connect + Develop" model that allows it to bring ideas to market quickly. It employs open-innovation networks (where design problems are thrown out to anyone with ideas) to resolve technical issues. It uses a walk-in, 3-D store to run quick, inexpensive experiments and then places test products with friendly audiences to get reaction. When a winner is found, it is scaled to the global marketplace. More than 80% of P&G's new products use the model.[4]

Strategic opportunism provides several advantages. One is that the risk of missing emerging business opportunities is reduced. Another is that the risk of strategic stubbornness is also reduced. Firms such as General Mills in cereals, Purina in pet foods, and Ziff Davis in media all seek emerging niche segments and develop brands tailored to specialty markets. Thus, Purina brands such as ALPO, Beneful, ProPlan, Mighty Dog, and Purina One and General Mills brands such as Berry Burst Cheerios and Cinnamon Toast Crunch are designed to appeal to a current taste or trend.

Strategic opportunism tends to generate a vitality and energy that can be healthy, especially when a business has decentralized R&D and marketing units that generate a stream of new products. Within 3 M, for example, new businesses are continually created and evaluated with respect to their prospects. Toshiba and Oracle are firms that believe in decentralized entrepreneurial management. These decentralized firms are often close to the market and technology and are willing to pursue opportunities.

Strategic opportunism results in economies of scope, with assets and competencies supported by multiple product lines. Nike, which applies its brand assets and competencies in product design and customer sensing to a wide variety of product markets, is a good example. A key part of the Nike strategy is to develop strong emotional ties and relationships with focused segments through its product design and brand name strengths. The organization is extremely sensitive to emerging segments (such as outdoor basketball) and the need for product refinements and product innovation. Nike has strategic flexibility, which characterizes successful strategically opportunistic firms.

Strategic Drift

The problem with the strategic opportunism model is that, as suggested by Figure 7.5, it can turn into strategic drift. Investment decisions are made incrementally in response to opportunities rather than directed by a vision. As a result, a firm can wake up one morning and find that it is in a set of businesses for which it lacks the needed assets and competencies and that provide few synergies.

At least three phenomena can turn strategic opportunism into strategic drift. First, a short-lived, transitory force may be mistaken for one with enough staying power to make a strategic move worthwhile. If the force is so short-lived that a strategy does not pay off or does not even have a chance to get into place, the result will be a strategy that is not suitable for the business or the environment.

Second, opportunities to create immediate profits may be rationalized as strategic when, in fact, they are not. For example, an instrumentation firm might receive many requests from some of its customers for special-purpose instruments that could conceivably be used by other customers but that have little strategic value for the company. Such opportunities might result in a sizable initial order but could divert R&D resources from more strategic activities.

Third, expected synergies across existing and new business areas may fail to materialize owing to implementation problems, perhaps because of culture clashes or because the synergies were only illusions in the first place. A drive to exploit core assets or competencies might not work. As a result, new business areas would be in place without the expected sustainable advantages.

Strategic drift not only creates businesses without needed assets and competencies, but it can also result in a failure to support a core business that does have a good vision. Without a vision and supporting commitment, it is tempting to divert investment into seemingly sure things that are immediate strategic opportunities. Thus, strategic opportunism can be an excuse to delay investment or divert resources from a core vision.

One example of strategic drift is a firm that designed, installed, and serviced custom equipment for steel firms. Over time, steel firms became more knowledgeable and began buying standardized equipment mainly on the basis of price. Gradually, the firm edged into this commodity business to retain its market share. The company finally realized it was pursuing a dual strategy for which it was ill suited. It had too much overhead to compete with the real commodity firms, and its ability to provide upscale service had eroded to the point that it was now inferior to some niche players. Had there been a strategic vision, the firm would not have fallen into such a trap.

Another example is a discounter that did well when operating a limited product line in a local market with a low-cost message. The customer value was clear, and the hands-on management style was effective. However, when the firm expanded its geographic and product scope (even going into groceries), the management systems were no longer adequate, and the value proposition become fuzzy as well. It had drifted into a business requiring assets and competencies it did not have.

Strategic Adaptability

Strategic adaptability, like strategic opportunism, is based on the assumption that the market is dynamic, the future will not necessarily mimic the past, and an existing business model, however successful, may not be optimal in tomorrow's marketplace. Unlike in strategic opportunism, however, there is also an assumption that it is possible to understand, predict, and manage responses to market dynamics that emerge and even create or influence them.

Strategic adaptability is about managing relevance, a topic introduced in Chapter 4. As the market dynamics evolve and the niches and submarkets emerge, one goal is to adapt the offering so that it maintains its relevance. The firm wants to avoid investing behind SUVs when the market is shifting to hybrids. Another is to seize opportunities to influence the creation of markets and submarkets. One study determined that such an opportunity occurs about once or twice a decade on average and that the window of opportunity is often short. A strategically adaptable firm does not want to miss such an opportunity. In that respect, it is more likely to go beyond incremental innovation to substantial and even transformational innovation if that is what it takes to create new markets.

A firm that aspires to be strategically adaptable needs to have competence in identifying and evaluating trends, a culture that supports aggressive response, and organizational flexibility so that business creation and modification can occur quickly.

Identifying and evaluating trends. The strategically adaptable firm needs to have a good external sensing mechanism to detect underlying customer trends and market dynamics involving drivers such as technology and distribution. In addition, the organization will need to be able to distinguish fads from trends and to evaluate the substance, dynamics, and implications of those trends. This is not an easy assignment. Being close to the customer, through direct contact and through research, will be important.

Adaptation-supporting culture. When trends are detected, the strategically adaptable firm needs to have a culture that supports aggressive response to opportunities represented by the trend analysis. That means that innovation, entrepreneurship, and experimentation should be valued and that it is okay to fail. Innovation is a mindset, but it also involves an R&D capability, in house or with alliance firms, to provide the potential to broaden the firm's offerings. The entrepreneurial style should be supported by organizational structures and reward systems that encourage managers to exploit opportunities with action-oriented strategies. There has to be some ability to tolerate a "ready, fire, aim" mentality and to allow pilot tests to thrive. Unlike strategic opportunism, the short-term product will be less important than the priority of getting the offering right and establishing a value position in the emerging market.

Strategic flexibility. Strategic adaptability usually requires flexibility so that the firm will be ready when a window of opportunity arises. Strategic flexibility—the ability to adjust or develop strategies to respond to external or internal changes—can be achieved in a variety of ways, including participating in multiple product markets and technologies, having resource slack, and creating a flexible brand portfolio.

Participation in multiple product markets or technologies means that the organization is already "on the ground" in different arenas and has purchased strategic options. Thus, if it appears that demand will shift to a new product market or that a newer technology will emerge, the organization can just expand its current product market rather than start from zero with all the risks and time required. An organization may also participate in business areas with weak returns in order to gain the strategic flexibility to deal with possible market changes.

Investing in underused assets provides strategic flexibility. An obvious example is maintaining liquidity (as with Toyota's $50 billion cash hoard or the $60 billion at Microsoft) so that investment can be funneled swiftly to opportunity or problem areas. Maintaining excess capacity in distribution, organizational staffing, or R&D can also enhance a firm's ability to react quickly.

A flexible brand portfolio may be needed so that brand assets will be in place to support a move in a new direction. Such flexibility can be based in a strong umbrella brand; GE not only has the GE brand but other brands, like NBC and Universal, that can be the basis of a growth platform. It can also be based on a system of endorsed brands, subbrands, and branded features such as Marriott's portfolio that includes Fairfield Inn, Courtyard, and others. The idea is to have a portfolio robust enough so that a new offering does not have to create a brand asset in order to compete.

Nucor has exhibited strategic adaptability over the years. In the 1970s, facing price pressures from fully integrated steel firms plus efficient Japanese brands, Nucor developed a strategy of producing joists (higher-value products used in construction) in rural minimills that employed nonunionized labor and used scrap steel as raw material. For a decade, this model made Nucor a strategic and financial success. By the mid-1980s, however, others had started to copy the strategy, scrap steel was no longer as plentiful, and aluminum had made serious inroads into traditional steel markets. In response to these changes, Nucor again reinvented the paradigm by focusing on flat-rolled, upmarket products using a scrap steel substitute and drawing on iron ore in Brazil and a processing plant in Trinidad.

Two other firms also illustrated strategic adaptability. Charles Schwab shifted from being a discount broker for individual investors to being an innovative supplier of no-load, no-transaction-fee mutual funds under the Schwab OneSource brand. It has now enlisted an army of fee-only financial advisers called Schwab Institutional to guide investors who are attracted to the Schwab investment options. Microsoft's focus progressed from operating systems to applications such as Office to Internet software. Both Schwab and Microsoft chose not to abandon the old vision but rather to augment it with a new direction.

Strategy Blunders—Misreading Trends

Investing behind trends and emerging submarkets is inherently risky because of the uncertainty and judgment involved and because the execution of the strategy is often difficult.

An error in interpreting a trend or emerging submarket can result in a substantial blunder that can damage or even cripple the firm. Not only will resources be wasted that could have been productively used elsewhere, but it can also have a deleterious impact on the brand assets and on the internal culture. A visible failure can inhibit future strategy choices. Consider, for example, Nabisco's Snackwells, which responded to a low-fat eating trend that turned out to be less of a long-term phenomenon than expected. The loss of equity for both the Snackwell and Nabisco brands was significant to the firm.

In addition to a trend being misinterpreted, there is an execution issue. The most astute and insightful analysis can lead to a strategy that simply cannot be implemented. Consider the merger of AOL with Time Warner. Time Warner hoped to provide content to the then-leading Internet portal and in the process become relevant in the Internet world. The failure of this concept was at least in part due to the inability to execute behind the strategy. The two organizations, with very different cultures and incentives, were unable to work together to execute the vision. Even had the vision been on target, the execution difficulties doomed the effort.

Blended Philosophies

There are firms that have a dominant strategic philosophy. It can be argued that Tesla and Starbucks are primarily strategic commitment firms, that General Mills is more in the strategic opportunistic group, and that P&G and GE are strategic adaptable. But it is not that simple. Most firms are and should be a blend.

Firms can engage in strategic commitment in one business arena, strategic opportunism in another, and strategic adaptability in still another. Starbucks ice cream is available in supermarkets, and Starbucks coffee can be had on United Airline flights, reflecting strategy opportunism. Further,

Starbucks has a soluble coffee, Via, in supermarkets and Starbucks kiosks at airports and in supermarkets, indicating some strategic adaptability. Google has adopted a strategic adaptability by acquiring a host of capabilities and firms along with some strategic opportunism based on knowing about traffic flows from its database. Among its many acquisitions were YouTube, Dodgeball (mobile social networking), and Double Click (an Internet advertising agency).

While General Mills has a strong opportunistic philosophy, it also has a strategic commitment with respect to the Cheerios brand and has pursued strategy adaptability with respect to health trends. And GE is strategic adaptable, but it too has commitment to business units such as jet engines and has been opportunistic in its acquisition strategy over the years.

The philosophies can also overlap within a business. Toyota, for example, has a very real strategic commitment with respect to some of its business strategy elements.[5] All Toyota businesses believe passionately that their ability to execute *kaizen* (continuous improvement), internal innovation enhanced by trial-and-error experimentation, and putting the customer first informed by first-hand customer contact are the basis for strategy. At the same time, Toyota has elements of strategic adaptability. In particular, it is in virtually all automotive and truck markets both with respect to models and countries. Thus, it is participating in a wide variety of niches and is unlikely to be caught on the wrong side of an emerging trend. Further, its conservative finance strategy with its cash hoard allows flexibility.

The real question is not which philosophy to have. The real challenges are to determine which philosophies make sense in which business units and to allow each the space to achieve success.

A blended organization represents a challenge. The need to be opportunistic and adaptable can undercut a commitment thrust, for example. But in dynamic markets, firms that can execute a successful blended philosophy will have a significant ongoing advantage.

KEY LEARNINGS

- To create an SCA, a strategy needs to be valued by the market and supported by assets and competencies that are not easily copied or neutralized by competitors. The most frequently employed SCAs are quality reputation, customer support, and brand name.
- Synergy is often sustainable because it is based on the unique characteristics of an organization.
- Strategic commitment, involving a stick-to-your-knitting focus on a clearly articulated strategy, is based on an assumption that the business model needs to be refined and improved, not changed.
- Strategic opportunism assumes that the environment is so dynamic and uncertain that it is futile to predict the future and invest behind those predictions. The more prudent and profitable route is to detect and capture opportunities when they present themselves, with a goal of achieving immediate profits.
- Strategic adaptability, based on the assumption that it is possible to understand, predict, and manage responses to market dynamics that emerge and even create or influence them, is about managing relevance.
- In dynamic markets, firms should strive to develop an organization that can blend commitment, opportunism, and adaptability.

FOR DISCUSSION

1. What is a sustainable competitive advantage? Identify SCAs for HP, P&G, Tide, and Wells Fargo.

2. Pick a product class and several major brands. What are each brand's points of parity and point of differentiation? Relate POPs to KSFs, and the POD to SCAs.

3. What is synergy? What are the sources of synergy? Give examples. Why is it so elusive?

4. What is strategic commitment? Can you name examples that fit besides those mentioned in the book? What examples of strategic stubbornness come to mind? Why are good strategists so blind to this problem? How does strategic commitment differ from strategic intent? Illustrate with examples.

5. What is the difference between strategic opportunism and strategic adaptability? Can you give examples of each? What is the difference between the risks of both? Can you give examples of firms that have experienced drift or misread trends?

6. Examine a major firm and determine its philosophy blend. Where does each of its philosophies become visible?

NOTES

1. Keller introduced points of parity in the branding context in Kevin Lane Keller, *Strategic Brand Management*, 2nd edition, Upper Saddle River, New Jersey: Prentice Hall, 2003, pp. 131–136.

2. David A. Aaker, "Managing Assets and Skills: The Key to a Sustainable Competitive Advantage," *California Management Review*, Winter 1989, pp. 91–106.

3. These quotes come from The Google Corporate Information site on Google.com. Accessed May 2009.

4. Martin Reeves and Mike Deimier, "Adaptability: The New Competitive Advantage," *Harvard Business Review*, July–August, 2011, p. 138.

5. A good source for the Toyota strategy is Emi Osono, Norihiko Shimizu, and Hirotaka Takeuchi, *Extreme Toyota: Radical Contradictions That Drive Success at the World's Best Manufacturer*, New York: John Wiley & Sons, 2008.

Alternative Value Propositions

Ever since Morton's put a little girl in a yellow slicker and declared, "When it rains, it pours," no advertising person worth his or her salt has had any excuse to think of a product as having parity with anything.
—*Malcolm MacDougal, Jordan Case McGrath & Taylor*

If you don't have a competitive advantage, don't compete.
—*Jack Welch, GE*

You can't depend on your eyes when your imagination is out of focus.
—*Mark Twain*

A business strategy, as defined in Chapter 1, involves four components—the product-market investment decision, the customer value proposition, the organization's assets and competencies, and functional strategies and programs. For a given industry and organizational context, a strategist will have uncountable ways to compete. Alternative markets, submarkets, product extensions, and new product arenas can always be considered. A bewildering variety of customer value propositions, each with its own nuances and spins, will represent strategy variants. Hundreds of conceivable assets and competencies can be developed, nurtured, exploited, and combined, and there are potentially thousands of viable functional strategies and programs.

Usually, however, business strategies cluster around a limited number of value propositions for a product market, supported by assets and competencies and functional strategies and programs. These value propositions include a superior attribute or benefit (BMW's drivability), appealing design (Apple's iPod), offering a complete systems solution (UPS Supply Chain Solutions), social responsibility (Avon Breast Cancer Crusade), a superior customer relationship (Nordstrom's), a specialist niche (Victoria's Secret), superior value (Wal-Mart), superior quality (Lexus), a familiar brand (Intel Inside), and a strong personality (Singapore Airlines). Each of these value propositions needs to be adapted to a given context, but all should potentially affect customer-firm relationships.

Looking at business strategies through the lens of value propositions provides a way to consider a broad set of strategies. As a summary indicator of complex strategies, value propositions provide a shorthand way to visualize a business strategy. Reflecting on a value proposition and its implied target markets, assets, competencies, and functional strategies is easier than dealing with a complete detailed business strategy. As a result, more strategies can be considered, and creating multiple alternatives is a way to make sure that superior ones are allowed to surface.

Considering strategies at the level of a value proposition also allows a firm to make preliminary evaluative judgments as to the problems that will have to be overcome, the investments required, the appeal in the marketplace, and the fit with the organization. Thus, some strategies can be rejected or put on hold before a lot of resources have been invested.

A business may select more than one value proposition—choosing to walk and chew gum at the same time, so to speak. It is not an either/or situation. In fact, most successful strategies will represent an integration of several value propositions. A solid understanding of each, however, can guide you not only in making the decision about which to include but also in specifying their respective roles and priorities in the overall strategy. Which should be dialed up? How should various propositions interact?

Although multiple value propositions can be supported and employed, there is a limit as to how many can be addressed—it is not credible or feasible to create or communicate too many value propositions simultaneously. More than two or three may risk making customers confused and skeptical.

BUSINESS STRATEGY CHALLENGES

Which value proposition or propositions—with their supporting target market, assets, competencies, and functional strategies—should form the basis for a business strategy? To answer this question, each value proposition should be challenged with respect to whether it contains a real and perceived value proposition and whether it is feasible, relevant, and sustainable. The goal of this analysis is to identify not only the potential impact of the strategic option but also its limitations and feasibility.

Is There a Real Customer Value Proposition?

A successful business strategy needs to add value for the customer, and this value needs to be real rather than merely assumed. The one-stop financial service vision, for example, had much less value to customers than was hoped when it was first tried in the early 1980s and again two decades later. Customers wanted excellence and competence from investment managers, and all-in-one convenience was relatively unimportant. Similarly, Bayer tried to apply its familiar brand name on nonaspirin products, only to find that the value of the Bayer name diminished greatly outside of the aspirin category.

Value is more likely to be real if it is driven from the customer's perspective rather than from that of the business operation. How does the point of differentiation affect the customer's experience of buying and using the product? Does it serve to reduce cost, add performance, or increase satisfaction? The concepts of unmet needs and customer problems, outlined in Chapter 2, are relevant. Does market research confirm that value is added from the customer's perspective?

Is There a Perceived Customer Value Proposition?

Further, the value proposition must be recognized and perceived as worthwhile by the customers. Delivering a value proposition is pointless unless customers know about it and believe it. For example, a customer may be unaware that Burger King has a convenient ordering process, that Cadillac is delivering quality equal to or better than Mercedes, or that Subaru has a superior braking system. This may occur because customers have not have been exposed to the information, because the information was not packaged in a memorable and believable way, or because the attribute or service was not considered to be relevant or of value.

The perceived value problem is particularly acute when the customer is not capable of judging the added value easily. Customers, for example, cannot evaluate airline safety or the skill of a dentist without investing significant time and effort. Instead the customer will look for signals, such as the appearance of the aircraft or the professionalism of the dentist's front office. The firm's task, then, is to manage the signals or cues that imply added value.

Is the Strategy Feasible?

If the value proposition is aspirational, is it feasible? It is one thing to create the perfect strategy with respect to customers, competitors, and the marketplace. It is another to execute that strategy effectively. The strategy may require assets and capabilities that are currently inadequate or do not exist, and programs to develop or upgrade them may turn out to be unrealistic. Alliance partners to fill the gap may be difficult to find or to work with. Further, an objective analysis of the customer trends, competitor strengths, or market dynamics may reveal that any strategic success will be short-lived.

Is the Value Proposition a Point of Difference That Is Sustainable?

Does the value proposition represent a point of superiority over the competition? Or is it simply a point of parity, with customers believing that the offerings are acceptable but not superior with respect to the value proposition? And if there is a point of difference, is it sustainable? Sustainability is often a tough challenge because most points of differentiation are easily copied. One route to a sustainable advantage is to own an important product dimension, perhaps with the aid of a branded differentiator (such as the Cadillac Northstar engine or the GM OnStar guidance systems), as described in Chapter 11. A second route would be creating a program of continuous investment and improvement that enables the strategy to remain a moving target, always ahead of competitors or poised to leapfrog them. Third, a business could create points of differentiation that are based on unique assets and competencies of the organization, which are inherently difficult to copy.

The most powerful value proposition is one that will redefine the product class, making those competitors that are perceived to be inferior on that dimension irrelevant. Crest enjoyed market leadership when it elevated decay prevention as a defining product characteristic for a large portion of the market.

Overinvestment in a value-added activity may pay off in the long run by discouraging competitors from duplicating a strategy. For example, competitors might be deterred from developing a service backup system that is more extensive than current customers expect. The same logic can apply to a broad product line. Some elements of that line might be unprofitable but still might be worth retaining if they plug holes that competitors could use to provide customer value.

ALTERNATIVE VALUE PROPOSITIONS

While there are an infinite number of business strategy variants in any context, certain value propositions with supporting strategy elements tend to be used most often. In this chapter, a snapshot of a handful of value propositions will be described, as shown in Figure 8.1. They are

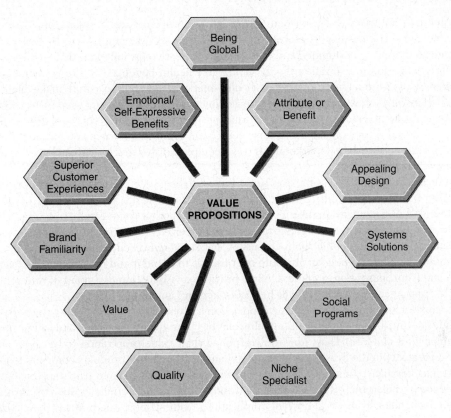

Figure 8.1 Strategic Options

among the most commonly used, and their description provides a glimpse of the scope of choices available to the business strategist.

Two of the value propositions—quality and value—will be discussed in some detail in this chapter. Each is frequently employed, has led to performance successes, and is associated with a body of knowledge and experience. Five others will also be considered in this chapter—product attributes or benefits, appealing design, systems solutions, corporate social programs, and being a niche specialist. Brand familiarity is covered in the next chapter; being global is the subject of Chapter 14. Delivering emotional/self-expressive benefits and superior customer experiences are examined in Chapter 10.

A Superior Attribute or Benefit

A functional benefit almost always needs to be part of the value proposition. Emotional, self-expressive, and social benefits with rare exceptions work only when there is a credible functional benefit that has parity with competition. When it is demonstrably better, a brand has the potential to dominate. Volvo has long owned safety by designing its cars and positioning its brand so that it has extremely strong credibility on that dimension. Pringles offers both a product form and package that allow convenient, compact storage of the product. Heinz has catsup that pours slowly because it is so thick and rich but easily because of innovative "Top Down" package designs. Emirates Airlines offers business-class passengers more comfortable living and sleeping space. In each case, the attribute is relevant to customers, and the brands are clearly positioned on that attribute.

Pfizer came to the realization that demonstrable health benefits could drive markets in the fragmented over-the-counter consumer health markets. So if they could make claims like "Benadryl is 54% more effective than the leading prescription allergy medics" or Listerine "reduced plaque significantly more than brushing or flossing alone," you would win globally. Toward that end, Pfizer enhanced their science-based innovation, their new product development, and their claims-based marketing. It was a comprehensive strategy driven by creating areal functional benefits.[1]

If such an option is to be viable over time, it needs to be protected against competitors. Having patent protection is one route. Dolby Laboratories has created a position based on an ever-expanding set of patents to support its sound offerings. Another route is to have a programmatic investment strategy in order to maintain the real and perceived edge. Thus, Volvo has an investment program and clear design philosophy to ensure that it can deliver on its safety promise.

Another route to owning an attribute over time is to brand it and then actively manage that brand and its promise. For example, OnStar provides a visible, branded point of differentiation for GM cars. Again, this concept will be elaborated in Chapter 11.

A superior and more relevant value proposition is often found by broadening the perspective beyond raw attributes and benefits.[2] Crayola has fine-quality crayons and other drawing instruments for children. They, however, reframed their value proposition to be about colorful fun and creativity in the lives of children and changed from an art products company to a visual expressions company. Lindsay Olives recognized that for some, olives can transform a social experience by being more fun, flavorful, and interesting than alternatives such as carrots and celery. Such changes have a host of implications with respect to products and customer relationships. They can include self-expressive and social benefits discussed in Chapter 10.

Appealing Design

An offering can appeal to a person's aesthetics, providing substantial self-expressive as well as functional benefits. Jaguar has long pursued this strategy and is somewhat unique among competitors that look all too similar, as if they all use the same wind tunnel. W Hotels have a unique look and feel (which extends to their rooms) that appeals to fashion-forward travelers. A string of Apple successes from the translucent Apple iMac to the iPad and iPhone showed that design could be an ongoing value proposition. (Steve Jobs has been quoted as saying, "Design is the soul of a manmade creation.") The Volkswagen Beetle came back with a new design that appealed while retaining the original Beetle look.

Pursuing a design option requires the firm to really have a passion for design and to support a home for a creative design team. Creating such a culture and infrastructure is a key to success for firms like Jaguar, W Hotels, and Apple, as well as other design-driven firms such as Disney and Ralph Lauren. Because achieving a home for design can be difficult, another route is to create an alliance with a design firm, which allows access to best-of-breed designers when needed. Outsourcing can succeed if the firm manages the alliance properly and establishes exclusive ownership of the output.

Making the design credible and visible is another challenge. The use of branded personality designers allowed Target to break through its utilitarian image. The well-known designer Isaac

Mizrahi in 2004 launched an affordable Target line of sweaters, blouses, pants, skirts, dresses, shoes, and purses that was well received. The renowned architect Michael Graves developed for Target a collection of cookware and other dining products.

Systems Solutions

A compelling value proposition can be based on moving from selling products to selling systems solutions, based on packaging products that work together to create a total system. Competitors selling ad hoc products, even though they might be superior, will be at a disadvantage. Sears offers a one-stop place to deliver home improvement projects. Sony, because it makes a complete line of home entertainment products, offers customers total system design and a single source for upgrades and service.

Especially in the business-to-business space, many firms are trying to move from being component suppliers to being systems solution players. One reason is that a systems-based organization will be more likely to control the customer relationship. Another is a need to capture greater margins in a context where components are becoming commodities. But the ultimate reason is that customers demand it. Simply bundling products, though, is rarely enough. To deliver value to the customer, a firm must offer not only product breadth but a systems orientation and expertise, but it must also be willing and able to deliver a high level of customer service. In Chapter 13, the potential of forming a new submarket of those desiring systems instead of components is discussed.

Social Programs

Social programs can provide a compelling value proposition, especially to the segment that is aware of issues and involved. Firms also initiate social programs to address real needs of society and, in the case of environmental programs as the discussion in Chapter 5 indicated, to reduce costs. However, influencing customers and employees while building the brand is often a significant motivation. A value proposition is created in several ways.

First, a social program, by engendering respect and trust, can make the firm more attractive to customers. People who feel that a firm is made of "good people" who are willing to expend resources on worthy activities that will help the larger world will be more inclined to have a positive judgment about the firm and brand and develop a strong relationship as well. This relationship, based in part on a perception of shared values, creates equity for the brand that can support loyal behavior and provide needed slack if something goes wrong.

Second, a strong and visible corporate social responsibility (CSR) program can deliver to customers self-expressive benefits, particularly for the core group of customers who have strong feelings about social issues. Certainly, many drivers of Toyota's Prius, the leading gas-electric hybrid car, achieve significant self-expressive benefits. In fact, the glamorous CEO of The Body Shop Japan famously drove a Prius as a statement about both herself and her firm. Women who participate or support the Avon Walk for Breast Cancer are expressing themselves and their values in an involving way.

Third, a social program can provide energy to a firm, particularly a firm that is, on balance, boring or in a boring category. Visible social programs can be interesting and new even with the offerings are not. Whether you make snack foods or insurance, a social program can involve and have energy. Lipton's Rainforest Alignment on sustainable tea and Dove's women's health awareness both provides energy to brands that the product itself could never do.

CEOs believe that CSR can pay off. In one survey, more than 90 percent thought that socially responsible management creates shareholder value.[3] In another study, 300 firms judged to have high commitment to CSR had a slightly higher stock return during a two-year period beginning in October 2000.[4] Providing a more direct measurement, a U.K. study compared the marketplace performance of three energy companies. Two of these, BP and Shell, were perceived as environmentally friendly, while the third, Esso, had visibly taken the position that renewable energy was not a viable solution and that the Kyoto international accords on the environment were flawed. Greenpeace subsequently attacked Esso with a high-profile "StopEsso" campaign. A subsequent Greenpeace poll found that the proportion of British gasoline buyers who said they regularly used Esso stations dropped by 7 percent during the year of the campaign.[5]

The social programs to work need to have real substance and continuity over time. An ad hoc promotion directed at some social good may be effective but will have little effect on long-term perceptions of the firm or the brand. And superficial efforts that are not perceived as effective will similarly be ineffective at creating a value proposition. Efforts cannot be seen as puffery without content or a short-term effort to gain attention and sales. However, even having an enduring program that has real substance is not enough. The programs also become visible and connected to the brand.

Sadly, few of the firms that actually deliver on their social program promise get credit for it in the marketplace. Their efforts, no matter how impactful and substantial, are usually not recognized outside the firm and often inside as well. Firms too often lack the ability to make their efforts visible in part because they have not generated compelling, credible stories. As a result, customers hear many firms making claims about their social responsibility values and programs and cope by ignoring all of them.

The lack of awareness of meaningful programs is astonishing. One survey found that 64 percent of Americans could not name a "green" firm, a percentage that was 51 percent even among those professing to be environmentally aware?[6] It is simply hard to communicate "greenness" in part because all firms are making that claim. There is a lot of clutter and some claims that do not seem impressive or even true. The result is a somewhat cynical and disinterested audience. The challenge is to create substantial branded programs that visibly make a difference. Not easy.

A few firms do break through the clutter and get credit from doing good. How they did it is instructive. The 11th annual brand equity study of some 1,000 brands in Japan has a CSR (corporate social responsibility) scale that was used to identify three such brands that suggest three routes to communicating an environmental values and programs.

One route is to have a product that tells a social concern story. The top brand by a big margin was Toyota. Toyota has an impressive array of environmental initiatives involving plants, suppliers, and show rooms, but these are nearly invisible. Their lofty social image comes from the Prius, a product that has held a dominate position in the hybrid subcategory that has come to represent its reduced omissions and gas consumption. It fact, it can be called the exemplar of the subcategory. Unlike other hybrids, it is also distinctive. While the Ford Focus might or might not be a hybrid, the Prius has no such ambiguity.

Another is Panasonic, a top brand along the CSR scale. Their route to making their environmental values visible is based on their spectrum of products and their ability to communicate their environmental product leadership. Panasonic has the eco-solutions umbrella brand that includes a host of products such as battery and solar cell energy sources, energy-efficient appliances, and energy management systems to optimize energy use in buildings. They have developed or participated in demonstration buildings and even cities such as the Dalian Best City in China to showcase their ideas and products. GE's ecomagination plays a similar role.

A third route is a visible and substantive involvement in a disaster or crises. Softbank made a huge contribution toward dealing with the aftermath of the tsunami. As a result, the firm vaulted them from 48th to third on the CSR scale list. Their ability to make such a move reflects the fact that few brands are established on the CSR scale.

Branding the social programs can help make it more visible. A brand can help communicate the program and its scope, objectives, and specific attributes. Knowing the brand makes it unnecessary to memorize all the details. The Avon Walk for Breast Cancer by itself can communicate a lot. A brand also gives the program credibility and substance and provides a label for any innovation news. Branding works, but only if it is worth branding.

There are challenges in pursuing a CSR strategy. Perhaps the most serious involves creating unreasonable expectations. If a firm is visible and active with regard to CSR, people will expect it to be flawless. Given the complexity of the issues, however, a firm can be making strides and still be criticized. BP can make significant investments in renewable energy relative to its competitors, for example, but some may correctly point out that the investment is still small relative to BP's size. Nike can make progress in addressing the labor practices of its offshore suppliers but can still draw fire because problems remain.

Niche Specialist

Being a niche specialist means that the firm concentrates on one part of the market or product line and can emerge in virtually any arena. Portman Hotels, which use a Rolls-Royce to transport guests, focus on the upscale segment. An industrial distributor may focus on large-volume users or even a single user. A clothing store might offer hot fashions for plus-sized teen girls. Armstrong Rubber has performed well over the years by focusing on replacement tires. Castrol Motor Oil focuses on male car owners who buy and change their own oil. Lets-go-fly-a-kite features kites. An online business with focus is Gold Violin, which provides products and services for the retired generation (whom it conceptualizes as modern-day heroes).

SHOULDICE HOSPITAL

Shouldice Hospital near Toronto only does hernia operations—some 7,500 per year. Since its founding in 1945, over 300,000 operations have been conducted, with a 99 percent success rate. Measured by how often repeat treatment is needed, Shouldice is 10 times more effective than are other hospitals. The surgical procedure used is branded as the Shouldice Technique.

The experience of the doctors and staff are appealing, but so are the Shouldice setting and its recovery program. Located on a country estate, the hospital has a calming ambience and facilities tailored to needs of recovering hernia patients. Patients walk to watch TV, to eat, and even to and from the operating room because walking is good therapy for hernias. There is thus no need to deliver food to rooms or to have wheelchair facilities. The length of a hospital visit at Shouldice is around half the norm elsewhere. No general anesthesia is administered because local anesthesia is safer and cheaper for hernia operations.

By concentrating on one narrow segment of the medical market. Shouldice has developed a hospital that is proficient, inexpensive, and capable of delivering an extraordinary level of patient satisfaction. Patients are so pleased that the Shouldice Hospital annual reunion attracts some 1,500 "alumni."

Because a niche specialist by its nature tends to avoid strategy dilution or distraction, it is more likely to pursue a strategic commitment strategy, leading to a sustainable advantage. When internal investments, programs, and culture have all been directed toward a single end and there is buy-in on the part of everyone in the organization, the result will be assets, competencies, and functional strategies that match market needs. There are no compromises or diluted investments. It is no accident that specialized retailers such as Williams-Sonoma and Victoria's Secret have been much more successful than department stores and others that are spread thin. One reason is the strategic and operational advantages of focusing.

A product focus can result in technical superiority because the people are developing and bringing to the market products that they are passionate about. When the products of a firm capture the imagination of its key people, they tend to be exciting, innovative, and of high quality.

A niche specialist strategy can translate into a value proposition for customers. First, a focused firm will have more credibility than a firm that makes a wide array of products, as demonstrated by Shouldice Hospital in hernia surgeries, Williams-Sonoma in cooking, Raymond Corporation in lift trucks, and the In-N-Out chain in making hamburgers. If you are really interested in the best, you will go to a firm that specializes in and has a passion for the business. Second, the bond between the loyal user and the brand will tend to be greater when the brand is focused and the people are seen to have passion for their product. The reunions of Shouldice Hospital patients and the passion of Harley-Davidson customers would not happen without a focus strategy.

This list of strategic options could be extended in any given context. For now, we will explore two options, quality and value, in more detail.

SUPERIOR QUALITY

A quality strategy means that the brand—whether it be hotels, cars, or computers—will be perceived as superior to other brands in its reference set. The point of superiority spans the brand offerings, delivering exceptional quality across products and individual attributes. Usually, such

LEXUS—A PASSION FOR EXCELLENCE

For more than a decade, Lexus has been among the leaders on a variety of objective quality indicators. Among the many reasons behind the Lexus achievement, several stand out. First, the Lexus concept was based on quality from its inception. Toyota launched Lexus in the early 1980s as a brand that would take automobile design, manufacturing, and retailing to a new level. Second, the brand delivered on the concept, as Lexus drew on assets and competencies developed by Toyota to make cars that were more reliable and had fewer defects. Third, a new dealer network offered the potential to break from industry norms and provide a pleasant buying experience. Fourth, the positioning of the Lexus brand (with the classic "relentless pursuit of perfection" tagline) delivered the quality message consistently over the years. Finally, Lexus excelled in the new standard of quality, clever features, and rideability.

The challenge facing Lexus now is that despite its success with a quality mission and message, it has failed to develop much personality in comparison with BMW, Mercedes, Jaguar, and Cadillac. When the latter brands gradually closed the quality gap over the years, the Lexus message became less compelling. In response, Lexus belatedly has tried to inject some emotional and self-expressive benefits, as demonstrated by its modified tagline, "The passionate pursuit of perfection." It has not been an easy task.

superiority will be associated with a price premium. As the Lexus insert illustrates, perceived quality can be the driver of a business strategy.

A quality value proposition, if based on substance, has a host of advantages. First, it provides an opportunity to be a leader in the category. Every category, including those with value offerings such as Target or Southwest Airlines, will have a market leader, and that leader will almost always have to have a superior quality image. Second, perceived quality can drive people's perceptions on a wide variety of attribute dimensions because of the powerful halo effect. Third, it provides the motivation, if not inspiration, for employees to do what they should do anyway, strive to deliver the best possible product or service. A quality culture affects what people strive for. And it affects how the organization reacts to missteps. Fourth, it can foster innovation because quality is always a moving target. If quality is not a priority as evidenced by the value proposition, innovation will likely not be ongoing.

A bottom line reason for a quality value proposition is that it simply pays off in terms of financial performance because it not only supports customer loyalty but also the price that can be charged. Aaker and Jacobson have demonstrated that perceived quality can drive stock return, a measure that truly reflects long-term performance.[7] They analyzed annual measures of perceived quality obtained from the Total Research EquiTrend database for 35 brands (including IBM, Hershey, Pepsi, and Sears) for which brand sales were a substantial part of firm sales. The impact of perceived quality on stock return, they found, was nearly as strong as the impact of ROI. Given that ROI is an established and accepted influence on stock return, the performance of perceived quality is noteworthy. It means that investors are able to detect and respond to programs that affect intangible assets such as perceived quality. Figure 8.2 shows the dramatic relationship between perceived quality and stock return.

Superiority will be defined by customers. In nearly all contexts, a single overall indicator of quality exists, is relevant to customers, and in fact drives other, more specific dimensions of performance. To understand what drives perceived quality and to actively manage it, however, the underlying dimensions in any given context need to be determined.

Figure 8.3 lists several dimensions of product quality that are often relevant. Of course, each of these dimensions has multiple components (for example, performance for a printer will involve attributes such as speed, resolution, and capacity). Further, the list itself will depend on the context. Still further, the drivers of quality will undergo changes over time. Thus, it is important to keep monitoring customer trends, preferences, sources of dissatisfaction, and unmet needs.

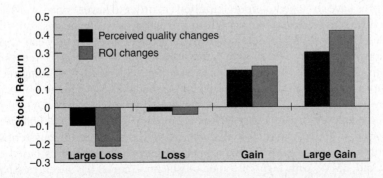

Figure 8.2 Perceived Quality and Stock Return

---

1. **Performance.** What are the specifications? How well is the task performed? Does the lawn mower cut grass well?
2. **Conformance to specifications.** Does the product or service perform reliably and provide customer satisfaction?
3. **Features.** Does the product offer the latest features? Are there any "Wow" attributes?
4. **Customer support.** Does the firm support the customer with caring, competent people and efficient systems?
5. **Process quality.** Is the process of buying and using the product or service pleasant, rather than frustrating and disappointing?
6. **Aesthetic design.** Does the design add pleasure to the experience of buying and using the product or service?

Figure 8.3   Product Quality Dimensions

Service Quality

In a service context—such as a bank, restaurant, or theme park—research has shown that quality is based in large part on the perceived competence, responsiveness, and empathy of the people with whom customers interact.[8] A successful organization therefore must deliver consistently on those dimensions. Delivering service quality, however, also means managing expectations. If expectations are too high, the service experience might be unsatisfactory even if it is at a high level. Generating clarity about the service promise, whenever possible, will thus be helpful.

Delivering service quality starts with the culture of the organization. With the right culture, innovation and motivation will happen. The top service firms in 2009 in a *Business Week* study conducted in conjunction with J.D. Power illustrate how culture affects performance and the variety of ways that firms can improve customer service.[9]

Amazon, the top service company, backs up the sales of outside merchants, which represent about 30 percent of its volume, and terminates any that fail to measure up to Amazon standards. Amazon also attempts to make the customer experience so good that they never need to contact an employee. When a contact does occur, Amazon makes sure it is positive. Toward that end, all employees spend two days every two years on the consumer response desk.

One key to service excellence is to reduce the frustration of accessing service. Many of the top service firms have stretched their organizations in order to have service available and easier to access. T. Rowe Price, for example has 300 former call service employees available to jump in when volume gets high. J.W. Marriott has cross-trained employees so they can step in at events that need extra service help. Still another is innovation. One innovation source is employees, if they are motivated. One way to motivate is to have formal rewards, including recognition for ideas that improve service. Lexus, for example, gives a $50,000 award to the dealer with the best new service ideas.

Motivated employees makes a huge difference in service. Enterprise Rental Car has pay and promotion based on the way that customers are treated as measured by mystery shoppers (or brand integrity assessors). American Express call centers have incentives based on customer satisfaction. And BMW, with high customer satisfaction scores, has incentives based on how dissatisfied customers are handled. It is possible, however, to create measures that are dysfunctional. For example, a company (not one of the top service firms) sought to improve the quality of its phone service by measuring the percentage of calls answered after the first ring. Unfortunately, the pressure to answer promptly caused agents to become abrupt and impatient with callers, and thus customer satisfaction suffered. The saying "Be careful what you wish for" is especially true in performance measurement.

How is a quality reputation obtained? The answer is context specific but involves creating the right culture, processes, and people and then managing the way the result is communicated. Total quality management, managing quality signals, and managing quality missteps are all relevant.

Total Quality Management

To pursue a quality strategic option successfully, a business must distinguish itself with respect to delivering quality to customers. To accomplish this goal, it needs a quality-focused management system that is comprehensive, integrative, and supported throughout the organization. Such a total quality management (TQM) system should incorporate a host of tools and precepts, including the following:

- The commitment of senior management to quality that creates a culture, if not passion, to deliver high quality
- Cross-functional teams empowered to make changes by initiating and implementing quality improvement projects
- A process (rather than results) orientation. The goal is not a one-time quality enhancement but to develop processes and cross-functional teams that will lead to quality improvements on an ongoing basis.
- A set of systems, such as suggestion systems, measurement systems, and recognition systems
- A focus on the underlying causes of customer complaints and areas of dissatisfaction. One approach used in TQM is to explore a problem in depth by repeatedly asking, "Why?" This process has been dubbed the five whys. Why is the customer unhappy? Why did the feature fail? Why was the design faulty? Etc.
- The tracking of key quality measures—going beyond customer satisfaction to measures of loyalty and the willingness to recommend. Updating quality measures so that the focus is not on dimensions that have become industry standards and points of parity.
- The involvement of suppliers in the system through supplier audits, ratings, and recognition, as well as joint team efforts

Signals of High Quality

Most quality dimensions, such as performance, durability, reliability, and serviceability, are difficult if not impossible for buyers to evaluate. As a result, consumers tend to look for attributes that they believe indicate quality. The fit-and-finish dimension of automobiles and appliances can be such a quality signal. Buyers assume that if a firm's products do not have good fit and finish, they probably will not have other, more important attributes. In pursuing a quality strategy, it is usually critical to focus on a visible dimension pivotal in affecting perceptions about more important dimensions that are very difficult to judge. Some examples:

- **Cable suppliers.** A professional attitude on the part of the installation team means quality.
- **Tomato juice.** Thickness means high quality.
- **Cleaners.** A lemon scent can signal cleaning power.
- **Supermarkets.** Produce freshness means overall quality.
- **Cars.** A solid door-closure sound implies good workmanship and a safe body.
- **Clothes.** Higher price means higher quality.
- **Airlines.** A stain on a seat can reflect on perceived maintenance standards.

Managing Quality Missteps

One somewhat ironic problem of achieving high actual and perceived quality is that expectations are raised and thus the potential of disappointing is higher. Because negative experiences are more salient than positive ones, a quality strategy needs to focus on avoiding them. The challenge is to seek points of annoyance and attempt to reduce their incidence and intensity. For example, in order to make even waiting in line at their respective locations bearable, Disney provides entertainment with its delightful characters, and Schwab provides stock news. More important than alleviating annoyances is to eliminate them. Disney has a system of reservations to eliminate the burden of long waits, and Schwab has a direct number to call agents so that the pain of menus does not occur at least during the second call.

A much more serious threat to a quality reputation is the visible and dramatic brand misstep. While obtaining trust is too often overvalued as a brand attribute because it is not differentiating or energizing, the loss of trust can be monumental. The Schlitz story shown in the insert illustrates how a decision to reduce costs led to a loss of perceived quality that was disastrous.

Disaster management requires not only the right quality culture but also a contingency plan to deal with it. The gold standard is how Johnson & Johnson handled the Tylenol poison incident—taking responsibility, removing the product from the shelves, and creating a visible packing solution. The action of US Airways after the miracle landing of a damaged plane on the Hudson River is a more recent role model. The airline dispatched a "Care Team" with over 100 members that have rehearsed for such incidents three times a year. They activated a special 800 number for passenger families and provided emergency cash, prepaid cell phones, and clothes. Passengers were escorted to alternative transportation or hotels. They followed up with a $5,000 advance to cover expenses and a ticket refund without requiring passengers to waive legal rights, an unprecedented action. The result was a sharp uptick on a reputation that had been somewhat marginal.

The impact of a disaster can depend on the positioning of the firm. In a fascinating experiment, academic researchers Jennifer Aaker of Stanford, Susan Fournier of Boston University, and Adam Brasel of Boston College created two online film processing firms with very different personalities; one was exciting and the other sincere—each experimental subject was randomly assigned to one of the sites.[10] In addition, after about 10 interactions, half of each of the two groups were informed with regret that their NetAlbum had been lost, and a week later they were informed that it had been found. Prior to the service disruption, the sincere site was

SCHLITZ: WHEN PERCEIVED QUALITY FALTERS

The story of Schlitz beer dramatically illustrates the strategic power of perceived quality and how fragile it is. From a strong number two position in 1974 (selling 17.8 million barrels of beer annually) supported by a series of well-regarded "go for the gusto" ad campaigns, Schlitz fell steadily until the mid-1980s, when it had all but disappeared (with sales of only 1.8 million barrels). The stock market value of the brand fell more than a billion dollars.

The collapse can be traced to a decision to reduce costs by converting to a fermentation process that took four days instead of 12, substituting corn syrup for barley malt, and using a different foam stabilizer. Word of these changes got into the marketplace. In early 1976, when bottles of flaky, cloudy-looking Schlitz beer appeared on the shelves, the condition was eventually traced to the new foam stabilizer. Worse still, in early summer of that same year, an attempted fix caused the beer to go flat after a few months on the shelf. In the fall of 1976, 10 million bottles and cans of Schlitz were "secretly" recalled and destroyed. Despite a return to its original process and aggressive advertising, Schlitz never recovered.

regarded more favorably than the exciting site. No surprise. However, after the service disruption, there was an unexpected finding. The exciting site was able to rebound from the disruption while the sincere site was not. One lesson is that building trust creates expectations and service problems had better be few and minimal.

VALUE

In nearly every market, from appliances to economy sedans to toothpaste to booksellers to brokerage services, there will be a segment that is motivated by price. Even in high-end markets such as luxury sports sedans, some brands (Acura, for example) will stake out a value position. During recessionary times, the "value segment" can become large. Whether it comprises 10 or 80 percent of the market, the value segment will usually be a significant one.

Ignoring the value segment can be risky because even healthy markets can evolve into situations where price grows in importance. A sharp recession can enhance the share of value offerings. In consumer electronics, appliances, and other product arenas, price pressures can be caused by overcapacity. Power retailers with their own brands as competitive tools are another potential contributing force. Thus, ignoring the value segment may not be an option. It may be necessary to participate, perhaps with a value brand or as a private label supplier, in order to maintain scale economies. In addition, competing in China, India, or other emerging market countries often requires a very low price point and a very different approach to product design and production.

As Figure 8.4 suggests, to compete successfully in the value arena, it is necessary to:

- Have a cost advantage (or at least avoid a cost disadvantage).
- Foster a cost culture in the organization.
- Create a perception of value without eroding the quality perception to the point that the brand is not considered.

Each of these imperatives is explored further below.

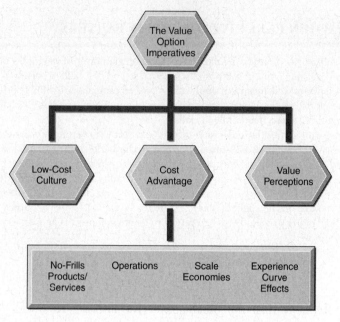

Figure 8.4   The Value Option

Creating a Cost Advantage (or Avoiding a Cost Disadvantage)

Although there is a tendency to think of low cost as a single approach, there are actually many dimensions to cost control and thus many routes to a cost reduction. The successful low-cost firms are those that can harness multiple approaches, including the use of no-frills products/services, operational efficiency, scale economies, and the experience curve.

SOUTHWEST AIRLINES

Southwest Airlines was founded in 1971, with three planes serving three Texas cities, as a low-fare airline whose goal was to make air travel efficient and pleasant. Its airfares were so aggressively low from the start that Southwest often competed as much with automobile travel as with other airlines. Even as it has grown, Southwest's point-to-point, no-frills approach has made it the consistent price leader in the markets it serves. The brand personality allows the staff to crack jokes and host games, injecting fun into what could be a boring time and further distinguishing Southwest from its competitors. The relationship of the staff to customers and its outstanding on-time record have helped Southwest win numerous customer satisfaction honors over the years.

The low-fare position often came under attack by aggressive and sometimes desperate competitors, who failed because Southwest had established a sustainable cost advantage supported by its no-frills operation. Southwest has no assigned seats, peanuts as meal service, and wages that are below the industry average. The company also shuns fancy hubs, reservation systems, and global schedules. Because of its service model, Southwest could turn around planes more quickly, which resulted in more trips and scale economies. The business model and brand personality were supported by a culture that valued cost containment and customer service.

No-Frills Product/Service

One direct approach to low cost is simply removing all frills and extras from a product or service and using materials and components that are functionally adequate. Membership warehouses, no-frills airlines, legal services clinics, and discount brokers all provide settings with limited amenities and personal service. Snap Fitness built a chain of 1,700 fitness centers in four years by offering access to a compact fitness gym for $35 a month with no long-term commitment. Not everyone needs a full service center.

A major risk, especially in the service sector, is that competitors will position themselves against a no-frills offering by adding just a few features. Motel 6 pioneered the concept of economy lodging in the early 1960s by giving the world a $6 hotel room with no phone or TV set. The industry has attracted a host of competitors since that time, many promising just a bit more in terms of creature comforts. The result of such strategies can be a feature war.

Firms competing in developing markets have to design products with the lowest possible cost. Panasonic, for example, developed a line of products including a $50 TV set and washing machines in the $100 to $200 range. They not only have to compete with other global firms but also with local firms that enjoy some labor cost advantages. They do tailor the products to local markets. For instance, a refrigerator sold in Vietnam where customers like ice cream has a large freezer and makes ice cubes in under two hours.[11]

Operations

Enduring cost advantages can also be created through efficiencies in operations based on government subsidies, process innovation, distribution efficiency access to target markets (USAA insurance is available only to military personnel), outsourcing competencies, and the management of overhead.

To obtain significant operational economies, it is useful to examine the value chain and look for inherently high-cost components that could be eliminated or reduced by changing the way that the business operates. The best example is the disintermediation of channel members. By selling direct, Dell and Amazon strip large components out of the value chain. For instance, in the conventional bookstore model, about 30 percent of sold books are returned, representing a huge deadweight on costs. In the Amazon model, that proportion is reduced to 3 percent—an enormous potential savings.[12]

Another place to find operations-based cost savings is in the interface with a supplier or customer. Uniqlo (a Japanese Gap-like retailer) links its store sales and inventory to its factories in China to create breathtaking efficiencies. Similarly, Procter & Gamble created an ongoing partnership with Wal-Mart, resulting in a continuous replenishment system for reordering, shipping, and restocking that minimizes shipping and warehouse costs, inventory, and out-of-stock conditions. Ten years after the partnership program began, stockkeeping units were down 25 percent, sales staffing was down 30 percent, inventory was down 15 percent, and the program was expanded to all major P&G customers.[13]

Scale Economies

The scale effect reflects the natural efficiencies associated with size. Fixed costs such as advertising, sales force overhead, R&D, staff work, and facility upkeep can be spread over more units. Furthermore, a larger operation can support specialized assets and activities (such as market research, legal staff, and manufacturing-engineering operations) dedicated to a firm's needs. Amazon has long based its business model on creating scale economies by driving sales higher.

When a business is too small to support needed assets or operations, the result can be a severe competitive disadvantage. The solution might be to prune or consolidate business units. Scale economy effects are particularly relevant in brand building, where each brand may seek a share of limited resources. Nestlé, Unilever, P&G, and other multibrand firms are deleting, consolidating, and prioritizing brands in their portfolios in order to make sure that the important brands are fully funded.

In retailing, scale can be obtained by combining business units. Yum! has introduced dual-branded stores from its stable of KFC, Pizza Hut, Taco Bell, Long John Silver's, and A&W. Such dual-brand outlets can compete with McDonald's and Burger King for expensive sites that require a large annual sales volume.

The Experience Curve

The experience curve, empirically verified in hundreds of studies, suggests that as a firm accumulates experience in building a product, its costs in real dollars will decline at a predictable rate. When the experience curve applies, the first market entry attaining a large market share will have a continuing cost advantage. The experience curve effect is based on the fact that over time people will learn to do tasks faster and more efficiently, that technological process improvements will occur, and that products will be redesigned to be simpler to build.

The classic experience curve is represented by the Ford Model T, introduced in 1908 as a reliable, easy-to-drive, and remarkably inexpensive car. The Model T, which sold over 15 million units, began its life priced at $850 (around $18,000 in modern dollars), but the price fell continuously until in 1922 it cost less than $300, a price that served to expand the market dramatically. Because of the production-friendly and unchanging design, vertical integration, and the building of the huge River Rouge plant, production cost declined according to an 85 percent experience curve (that is, costs fell roughly 15 percent every time cumulative production doubled). Figure 8.5 presents the pattern.

Several issues need to be understood in working with the experience curve concept. First, the experience curve is not automatic. It must be proactively managed with efficiency-improvement goals, quality circles, product design targets, and equipment upgrading. Further, a late entry can often gain the same advantage as the more experienced vendors simply by accessing the most

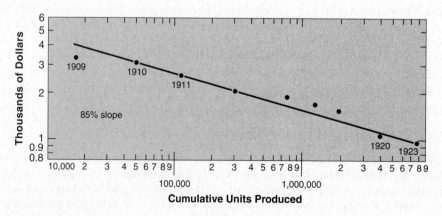

Figure 8.5　Price of Model T, 1909–1923 (Average List Price in 1958 Dollars)

recent design. Second, if the technology or market changes, the experience curve may become obsolete. The auto market in the early 1920s turned away from the Model T, and Ford had to close down for a year to retool to make what GM was offering, and the market wanted. Third, the experience curve model implies that cost improvements, whatever their source, should be translated into low prices and higher share so that the business can stay ahead on the experience curve. Lower prices can trigger price wars, however, leading to reduced margins, as has occurred in consumer electronics numerous times.

A Low-Cost Culture

A successful low-cost strategy is usually multifaceted and supported by a cost-oriented culture. Performance measurement, rewards, systems, structure, top management values, and culture are all fronts where cost reduction should be stressed. The single-minded focus needed is comparable to that required for total quality management. Such a commitment is evident at Target, Southwest, Wal-Mart, and other firms that have succeeded with a value strategy.

There are many examples of firms that decided to go into the low-cost world and failed because their cultures never could adapt. One large supermarket chain decided to create a discount beverage chain. When the chain failed to deliver on the promise and still be profitable, an analysis determined that the people and processes were not compatible with the cost structure needed to succeed in that market. A successful discount operation almost always requires a new organization with different culture, processes, and people.

Perceived Value

Managing prices and price perceptions is tricky because price is often a quality cue, and customers may perceive low price as a signal for inferior quality. If the quality is perceived to be unacceptably low, the offering will be deemed irrelevant to the customer's needs. This is particularly troublesome for offerings in categories where it is difficult to judge actual quality (perfume or motor oil, for example) and for premium brands in times of deep recessions where a value message is needed. So how to tell the value story without shouting price? Among the approaches that work:

- Communicate the substance behind the cost advantage—Dell's direct sales model, Southwest's point-to-point travel and no-frills service, Ford's mass production, the scale economies of Amazon and Wal-Mart, and the warehouse feel of Ikea, Home Depot, and Costco are all transparent to customers and thus reduce the risk of a perceived quality problem.

- Manage the relevance issue by positioning the offering with respect to the appropriate product category and set of competitors. Acura positions itself with BMW and Lexus, KFC's Family Value Meal is a bargain next to comparable home-cooked meals, Crayola's 64 colors are contrasted with expensive toys, and a DiGiorno Pizza is $6.69 vs. $16.13 for a delivered pizza.

- Highlight the affordability of products that may appear expensive. Gillette justifies the cost of its Fusion Power razor blades by suggesting that in a high-performance world, paying one dollar a week for the best is affordable. Campbell Soup talks about the original one dollar meal, and the price of milk is noted to be only 25 cents.

- Replace price reduction with bundled features or services that provide extra value at the same price such as free shipping by Amazon or McDonald's Happy Meals. Starbucks, the poster child for excess, responded with a breakfast sandwich or muffin plus a coffee for under $4.00.
- Demonstrate the value of quality—Bounty towels pay by doing more with fewer.
- Divert attention to value subbrands such as the BMW One Series or the Fairfield Inn by Marriott.
- Manage the visible price points. Grocery stores have long learned that customers tend to be knowledgeable about a few categories and brands. Similarly, the major book chains pay close attention to best-selling books because those are the ones most likely to receive a price comparison. Car manufacturers are concerned most with base prices and much less about accessories and options because prices for the latter will be harder to compare.

KEY LEARNINGS

- Business strategies usually cluster around a limited number of value propositions, such as a superior attribute, appealing design, systems solutions, social responsibility, a superior customer relationship, a niche specialist, superior quality, and superior value. The value proposition should be real, believed, feasible, relevant, and sustainable.
- Superior quality, which has been shown to drive stock return, has to be continuously addressed through processes and programs and transferred into quality perceptions.
- A value position needs to be communicated effectively and supported by a cost advantage, which can be based on a no-frills offering, operations, scale economies, and/or the experience curve.

FOR DISCUSSION

1. Consider three industries, such as hotels or appliances or automobiles. For several of the firms in the industry, identify what value propositions are represented in their strategies. Were there multiple propositions? Evaluate. Are they successful or likely to be successful?

2. Consider three of the following value propositions: systems solutions, corporate social responsibility, superior customer relationship, quality, and value. For each of these, think of two firms not mentioned in the book that have pursued them. Which of the two firms has done better with respect to the four business strategy challenges presented at the outset of the chapter? Discuss why and how that firm was able to do better.

3. Evaluate the quality strategy of Lexus with respect to the business strategy challenges. How might Lexus add more personality and emotion to its brand? Think of role models that have achieved a quality reputation and a strong personality.

4. Pick a product or service offering. How would you develop a set of customer survey questions that would measure its quality on an ongoing basis? How would you administer the survey?

5. Consider the NetAlbum experiment. What explanation would you propose?

NOTES

1. Paul Leinwand and Cesare Mainardi, "The Coherence Premium," *Harvard Business Review*, June 2010, p. 8792.

2. Fred Geyer, "Brand Challenge: Renovate Before It's Too Late," Prophet Web Site, March 2009.

3. Stan L. Friedman, "Corporate America's Social Conscience," *Fortune*, June 23, 2003, p. S6.

4. Ibid., p. S4.

5. "Esso—Should the Tiger Change Its Stripes?" *Reputation Impact*, October 2002, p. 16.

6. Wendy Melillo and Steve Miller, "Companies Find It's Not Easy Marketing Green," *Brand Week*, July 24, 2006, p. 8.

7. David A. Aaker and Robert Jacobson, "The Financial Information Content of Perceived Quality," *Journal of Marketing Research*, May 1994, pp. 191–201.

8. Valarie A. Zeithaml, *Service Quality*, Boston: Marketing Science Institute, 2004.

9. Jena McGregor, "When Service Means Survival," *Business Week*, March 2, 2009, pp. 26–40.

10. Jennifer Aaker, Susan Fournier, and S. Adam Brasel, "When Good Brands Do Bad," *Journal of Consumer Research*, June 31, 2008, pp. 1–18.

11. Daisuke Wakabayashi, "Panasonic Reaches Wide—and Low—With Appliances for Emerging Markets," *Wall Street Journal*, July 9, 2009, p. B1.

12. Timothy M. Laseter, Patrick W. Houston, Joshua L. Wright, and Juliana Y. Park, "Amazon Extracting Value from the Value Chain," *Strategy and Business*, First Quarter 2000, pp. 94–105.

13. Lawrence D. Milligan, "Keeping It Simple, The Evolution of Customer-Business Development at Procter & Gamble," remarks at the AMA Doctoral Symposium, Cincinnati, July 1997.

CHAPTER NINE

Building and Managing Brand Equity

You do not merely want to be considered just the best of the best. You want to be considered the only ones who do what you do.
—*Jerry Garcia, The Grateful Dead*

You cannot make a business case that you should be who you're not.
—*Jeff Bezos, Amazon*

The secret of success is constancy of purpose.
—*Benjamin Disraeli*

A business strategy is enabled by brand assets. A brand gives a firm permission to compete in product markets and services, and it represents the value proposition of the business strategy. Thus, it is strategically crucial to develop, refine, and leverage brand assets.

Anecdotes abound about the power of a brand to improve financial performance, but solid research also shows that, on average, building brands generates a payoff in terms of stock return. In fact, the brand effect on stock return is nearly as large as that of accounting ROI in such diverse settings as large-cap, Internet, and high-tech firms. Further, efforts to estimate the value of brand assets as compared with other intangible assets—such as people and IT technology—and tangible assets reveal that the brand assets represent from about 15 percent (Toyota and GE) to more than 75 percent (BMW and Nike) of the value of the firm. Even the lower number is significant strategically.

Brand equity is the set of assets and liabilities linked to the brand. The conceptualization of brand equity, which occurred in the late 1980s, was pivotal because it changed the way that marketing was perceived. Where brand image could be delegated to an advertising manager, brand equity—as a key asset of the firm—needed to be elevated to part of the business strategy, the purview of the CEO. Its management was strategic and visionary instead of tactical and reactive, long term in orientation rather than short term, and involved a different set of metrics. It truly changed the role of marketing and the chief marketing officer (CMO).

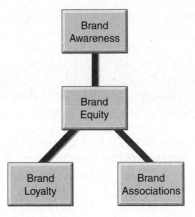

Figure 9.1   Brand Equity

There are three types of brand assets—brand awareness, brand loyalty, and brand associations (see Figure 9.1). Each creates formidable competitive advantages, and each needs to be actively managed.

BRAND AWARENESS

Brand awareness is often taken for granted, but it can be a key strategic asset. In some industries that have product parity, awareness—the third most mentioned SCA (see Figure 7.3)—provides a sustainable competitive difference. It serves to differentiate the brands along a recall/familiarity dimension.

Brand awareness can provide a host of competitive advantages. First, awareness provides the brand with a sense of familiarity, and people like the familiar. For low-involvement products, such as soap or chewing gum, familiarity can drive the buying decision. Taste tests of such products as colas and peanut butter show that a recognized name can affect evaluations even if the brand has never been purchased or used.

Second, name awareness can be a signal of presence, commitment, and substance, attributes that can be very important even to industrial buyers of big-ticket items and consumer buyers of durables. The logic is that if a name is recognized, there must be a reason. The "Intel Inside" program was remarkably successful at creating a perception of advanced technology and earned a significant price premium for Intel for well over a decade even though it did not communicate anything about the company or the product. Pure awareness power was at work.

Third, the salience of a brand will determine if it is recalled at a key time in the purchasing process. The initial step in selecting an advertising agency, a car to test drive, or a computer system is to decide on which brands to consider. The extreme case is name dominance, where the brand is the only one recalled when a product class is cued. Consider Kleenex tissue, Clorox bleach, Band-Aid adhesive bandages, Jell-O gelatin, Crayola crayons, Morton salt, Lionel trains, Philadelphia cream cheese, V-8 vegetable juice, Netflix, TiVo, and A-1 steak sauce. In each case, how many other brands can you name? How would you like to compete against the dominant brand?

Brand awareness is an asset that can be extremely durable and thus sustainable. It can be very difficult to dislodge a brand that has achieved a dominant awareness level. Customers' awareness of the Datsun brand, for example, was as strong as that of its successor, Nissan, four years after the firm changed its name.[1] An awareness study on blenders more than two decades after GE stopped making the product found that the GE brand was still the second-most preferred brand.[2] Another study of familiarity asked homemakers to name as many brands of any type as they could; they averaged 28 names each. The ages of the brands named were surprising: more than 85 percent were over 25 years old, and 36 percent were more than 75 years old.[3]

There is a great deal of difference between recognition (have you ever heard of Brand X) and unaided recall (what brands of SUVs can you name). Sometimes recognition for a mature brand is not even desirable when unaided recall is low. In fact, brands with high recognition and low recall are termed graveyard brands. Without recall, they are not in the game; their high recognition means they are considered yesterday's news, and thus it is difficult for them to gain visibility and energy.

Because consumers are bombarded every day by more and more marketing messages, the challenge of building awareness and presence—and doing so economically and efficiently—is formidable, especially considering the fragmentation and clutter that exist in mass media. One route to visibility is to extend the brand over product categories. For that reason, firms such as 3 M, Sony, Toshiba, and GE have an advantage because wide product scope provides brand exposure. Another route is to go beyond the normal media channels by using event promotions, publicity, sampling, Internet community, and other attention-grabbing approaches. For example, consider the impact of Samsung's Olympic sponsorship, the Niketown showcase stores, Swatch hanging a 165-yard-long watch from skyscrapers in Frankfurt and Tokyo, and the Pampers Village, the go-to site for resources and conversation about infant care All of these firms were able to increase their awareness levels much more effectively than if they had relied only on mass media advertising.

BRAND LOYALTY

An enduring asset for some businesses is the loyalty of the installed customer base (listed as item 10 in the list of SCAs in Figure 7.3). Competitors may duplicate or surpass a product or service, but they still face the task of making customers switch brands. Brand loyalty, or resistance to switching, can be based on simple habit (there is no motivation to change from the familiar gas station or supermarket), preference (people genuinely like the brand of cake mix or its symbol, perhaps based on use experience over a long time period), or switching costs. Switching costs would be a consideration for a software user, for example, when a substantial investment has already been made in training employees to learn a particular software system.

An existing base of loyal customers provides enormous sustainable competitive advantages. First, it reduces the marketing costs of doing business, since existing customers usually are relatively easy to hold—the familiar is comfortable and reassuring. Keeping existing customers happy and reducing their motivation to change are usually considerably less expensive than trying to reach new customers and persuading them to try another brand. Of course, the higher the loyalty, the easier it is to keep customers happy.

Second, the loyalty of existing customers represents a substantial entry barrier to competitors. Significant resources are required when entering a market in which existing customers must be enticed away from an established brand that they are loyal to or even merely satisfied with. The profit potential for the entrant is thus reduced. For the barrier to be effective, however, potential competitors must know about it; they cannot be allowed to entertain the delusion that customers are vulnerable. Therefore, signals of strong customer loyalty, such as customer interest groups, can be useful.

Third, a relatively large, satisfied customer base provides an image of a brand as an accepted, successful, enduring product that will include service backup and product improvements. A set of loyal customers also provides reassurance to others. Customers find comfort in the fact that others have selected the brand.

Finally, brand loyalty provides the time to respond to competitive moves—it gives a firm some breathing room. If a competitor develops a superior product, a loyal following will allow the firm the time needed to respond by matching or neutralizing the offering. With a high level of brand loyalty, a firm can allow itself the luxury of pursuing a less-risky follower strategy.

The management of brand loyalty is a key to achieving strategic success. Firms that manage brand loyalty well are likely to:

- Have a customer culture, whereby people throughout the organization are empowered and motivated to keep the customer happy.

- Manage customer touchpoints to ensure that the brand does not falter in key contexts.

- Have a relationship that goes beyond functional benefits to emotional, self-expressive, and social benefits.

- Make customers feel that they are part of the organization, perhaps through customer clubs.

- Have continuing communication with customers, using direct mail, the Internet, toll-free numbers, and a solid customer backup organization.

- Measure the loyalty of existing customers. Measurement should include not only sensitive indicators of satisfaction but also measures of the relationship between the customer and the brand. Is the brand respected? Liked? Trusted? The ultimate measure is, will the customer recommend the brand to others?

- Conduct exit interviews with those who leave the brand to locate points of vulnerability.

- Measure the lifetime value of a customer so expected future purchases are valued.

BRAND ASSOCIATIONS

The associations attached to a firm and its brands can be key enduring business assets, as they reflect the strategic position of the brand. A brand association is anything that is directly or indirectly linked in the consumer's memory to a brand (see Figure 9.2). Thus, McDonald's could be linked to Ronald McDonald, kids, the Golden Arches, Ronald McDonald House, Newman's Own Salad Dressing, having fun, fast service, family outings, or Big Macs. All these associations potentially serve to make McDonald's interesting, memorable, and appealing to its customers.

Product attributes and customer benefits are the associations that have obvious relevance because they provide a reason to buy and thus a basis for brand loyalty. Heinz is the slowest-pouring (thickest) ketchup, Bayer is faster acting, Texas Instruments has a faster chip, Jaguar is stylish, Volvo is durable and safe, and Wal-Mart delivers value. Companies love to make product claims, for good reason. They often engage in shouting matches, or specmanship, to convince customers that their offering is superior in some key dimension—Brand One is a high-fiber cereal, or a Boeing plane has more range.

Associations	Brands
Attributes/Benefits	Volvo, Crest
Design	Jaguar, Calvin Klein
Systems Solution	Siebel, IBM
Social Programs	Avon, McDonald's
Customer Relationships	Nordstrom's, Ritz Carlton
Niche Specialists	Ferrari, Gold Violin
Quality	Lexus, Hertz
Value	Wal-Mart, Hyundai
Product Category	TiVo, Toyota's Prius
Breadth of Product Line	Amazon, Marriott
Organizational Intangibles	3M, Accenture
Being Global	Visa, Ford
Being Contemporary	Google, Apple
Brand Personality	MetLife, Singapore Airlines

Figure 9.2　Brand Associations

There are several problems with a reliance on attribute and benefit associations. First, a position based on some attribute is vulnerable to an innovation that gives your competitor more speed, more fiber, or a greater range. In the words of Regis McKenna, the Silicon Valley marketing guru, "You can always get outspeced."

Second, when firms start a specification shouting match, they all eventually lose credibility. After a while, customers start to doubt whether any aspirin is more effective or faster acting than another. There have been so many conflicting claims that all of them are discounted.

Third, people do not always make decisions based upon a particular specification. They may feel that small differences in some attributes are not important, or they simply lack the motivation or ability to process information at such a detailed level.

Strong brands go beyond product attributes to develop associations on other dimensions that can be more credible and harder to copy. It is useful to understand some of these other dimensions and learn how they have been used by firms to create customer relationships and points of differentiation.

The value propositions described in the last chapter in addition to attributes or benefits—design, systems solutions, social programs, customer relationships, niche specialist, quality, and value—are all prominent candidates for actual or aspirational associations. Several additional ones, all with a proven ability to drive successful firms, will be described to provide a feel for the scope of potential associations.

Product Category

The choice of a product category or subcategory with which a business will associate itself can have enormous strategic and tactical implications. Schweppes positioned its tonic in Europe as an adult soft drink, and the popularity of new-age adult drinks carried it to a dominant position. In the United States, however, Schweppes (perhaps wanting to avoid the Coke/Pepsi juggernaut) positioned its entry as a mixer for alcoholic drinks, which relegated it to being a minor player when the market changed. Energy bars became a big business by creating a category distinct from candy. Wasa Crispbread, in contrast, expanded its market by positioning itself as an alternative to

Figure 9.3 Staying Relevant

bread rather than sharing a category with rice cakes and Ry-Krisp. Siebel created the customer relationship management (CRM) category and benefited from an association with it.

Maintaining Relevance

As suggested in Chapter 4, the relevance concept can help with the difficult task of managing an evolving category with emerging and receding subcategories. Relevance is, in essence, being perceived as associated with the product category in which the customer is interested. In the Brand Asset Valuator, the product of Young & Rubicam's mammoth study of global brands, relevance was one of four key dimensions identified (along with differentiation, esteem, and knowledge). Analysis of this data base revealed that relevance is necessary. If a business loses relevance, differentiation may not matter.

The ability of a firm to maintain relevance varies along a spectrum, as shown in Figure 9.3. At one extreme are trend neglectors—firms that miss or misinterpret trends, perhaps because they are too focused on a predetermined business model. Such firms are often characterized as having inadequate strategic analysis capability, organizational inflexibility, and/or a weak brand portfolio strategy; they eventually wake up in surprise to find their products are no longer relevant. At the other end of the spectrum are trend drivers, those firms that actually propel the trends that define the category (or subcategory). In the middle are trend followers, firms that track closely the trends and the evolution of categories and subcategories, making sure that their products stay current.

Virgin Atlantic Airlines, Toyota, and Schwab all have been trend drivers. Virgin created a new subcategory by introducing and owning new services such as massage services in first class. Toyota defined the hybrid category with its Prius. Schwab's OneSource defined a new subcategory of brokerage firm services.

Trend responders—those firms that can recognize and evaluate trends and then create and implement a response—can sustain success in dynamic markets. Some fashion brands such as Tommy Hilfiger have been nimble in staying abreast of fashion trends. Barbie has changed with the times, being an astronaut, a surgeon, a presidential candidate, and a high-fashion woman; incorporating ethnicity; and becoming relevant to the Internet with an involving Barbie site. L.L. Bean has evolved its position from hunting, fishing, and camping to a broader outdoors theme that is relevant to hikers, mountain bikers, cross-country skiers, and water-sports enthusiasts, the heart of its marketplace.

Being a successful trend responder, however, is not easy. As suggested in Chapter 4, it can be difficult to identify and evaluate trends and separate the trends from the fads. It is also difficult to respond to emerging subcategories, especially if they start small and if the existing business and brand are established. Consider the difficulty that McDonald's, Burger King, KFC, and the other fast food giants have had in responding to the healthy eating trend. They are simply not good at product development and delivery in that arena because it is not in their DNA—they lack the people and culture to be successful. Even worse, their brand becomes a liability as they attempt to change perceptions ingrained by decades of doing what they do. Nevertheless, McDonald's, after several unsuccessful efforts to create salads, broke through with not only salads that worked but also healthy desserts for concerned parents and even gourmet coffee to provide an alternative to Starbucks.

Breadth of Product Line

A broad product offering signals substance, acceptance, leadership, and often the convenience of one-stop shopping. For example, the strategic position that drove Amazon's operations and marketing was never about selling books, even at the beginning when it was simply a bookstore. (Amazon had the vision to avoid calling itself books.com.) Rather, the firm positioned itself as delivering a superior shopping/buying experience based on the "Earth's Biggest Selection"—an array of choices so wide that customers would have no reason to look anywhere else. This position allows Amazon to enter a variety of product markets, although it also puts pressure on the company to deliver in each venue.

Breadth also works well as a dimension for other firms, such as Chevrolet, Wal-Mart, and Black & Decker. Even under a strong brand, however, expanding the product offering involves risks. The firm may venture into business areas in which it lacks skills and competencies, the brand might be eroded, and resources needed elsewhere may be absorbed.

Organizational Intangibles

As already noted, attribute and benefit associations can often be easily copied. In contrast, it is difficult to copy an organization, which will be uniquely defined by its values, culture, people, strategy, and programs. Organizational attributes such as being global (Visa), innovative (3M), quality driven (Cadillac), customer driven (Nordstrom), involved in community or social issues (Avon), or concerned about the environment (Toyota) are usually more resistant to competitive claims than product-attribute associations.

A laboratory study of cameras demonstrated the power of an intangible attribute. Customers were shown two camera brands, one of which was positioned as being more technically sophisticated and the other as easier to use. Detailed specifications of each brand, which were also provided, clearly showed that the easier-to-use brand in fact had superior technology as well. When subjects were shown both brands together, the easy-to-use brand was rated superior on technology by 94 percent of the subjects. However, when this brand was shown two days after exposure to the supposedly (but not actually) more sophisticated brand, only 36 percent felt that it had the best technology. Using technology as an abstract attribute dominated the actual specifications.

Being Global

CitiGroup is a global financial institution. Visa is a global credit card. Toyota is a global car company. Being global provides functional benefits in that you can access the services of CitiGroup or Visa anywhere. It also provides the prestige and assurance that comes from knowing that the firm has the capability of competing successfully throughout the world. Knowing that Toyota is strong in the United States helps it in Europe, where customers might otherwise look at it as a modest player. More information on global associations and strategy is provided in Chapter 14.

Being Contemporary

Most established businesses face the problem of remaining or becoming contemporary. A business with a long heritage is given credit for being reliable, safe, a friend, and even innovative if that is part of its tradition. However, it also can be perceived as "your father's (or even grandfather's) brand." The challenge is to have energy, vitality, and relevance in today's marketplace—to be part of the contemporary scene. The answer usually entails breaking out of the functional-benefit trap. Approaches to add energy will be explored in Chapter 11.

Lane Bryant, a retailer to plus-sized women, developed a dowdy, apologetic image that was holding it back. To break out, it developed a new, contemporary strategic position. It spread the message with new, even sexy fashions; a Lane Bryant fashion show in New York; revitalized stores; and a new spokesperson, rapper/actress Queen Latifah, in ads, on its Web site, and in a voter-registration program. Ironically, Lane Bryant's sister company, Victoria's Secret, had to reposition itself previously from an edgy (Frederick's of Hollywood) brand to a more mainstream one, albeit at the edge of the mainstream market.

Brand Personality

As with human beings, a business with a personality tends to be more memorable and better liked than one that is bland, nothing more than the sum of its attributes. And like people, brands can have a variety of personalities, such as being professional and competent (CNN and McKinsey), upscale and sophisticated (Jaguar and Tiffany's), trustworthy and genuine (Hallmark and John Deere), exciting and daring (Porsche and Benneton), or active and tough (Levi's and Nike). Certainly, Virgin is a brand whose strategic position includes a statement personality.

Harley-Davidson has a strong personality reflecting a macho, America-loving, freedom-seeking person who is willing to break out of confining social norms. The experience of riding a Harley (or even the association that comes from wearing Harley-Davidson clothing) helps some people to express a part of their personality, which results in intense loyalty. More than 250,000 of these people belong to one of the 800 chapters of the Harley Owners Group (HOG). Twice a year, believers from all over the country gather for a bonding experience. Harley is much more than a motorcycle; it is an experience, an attitude, a lifestyle, a vehicle to express "who I am."

Joie de Vivre is a San Francisco firm whose boutique hotels are each inspired by a theme that reflects a personality. The "Rolling Stone" Phoenix hotel attracts rock-and-roll and other entertainment personalities with its irreverent sense of cool and funky, adventurous decor. The "New Yorker" Rex hotel is clever and sophisticated, with a literary sensibility. The "1920s luxury liner" Commodore Hotel, with its Titanic Café, looks and feels like a party straight out of *The Great Gatsby*. The "movie palace" Hotel Bijou has a miniature movie theater in the lobby, accompanied by dramatic Hollywood portraits.

VIRGIN ATLANTIC AIRLINES

In 1970, Richard Branson and a few friends founded Virgin as a small mail-order record company in London, England. By the mid-1980s, this modest beginning had led to a chain of record shops and the largest independent music label in the United Kingdom, with artists as diverse and important as Phil Collins, the Sex Pistols, Boy George, and the Rolling Stones. By the 1990s, there were more than a

(continued)

hundred Virgin "megastores," many making a significant brand statement with their signage, size, and interior design.

In February 1984, Branson decided to start Virgin Atlantic Airlines to make flying fun and enjoyable for all classes, not just first-class passengers. Defying the odds, Virgin became the number two airline in most of its markets by the end of the 1990s. Not only that, it enjoyed the same consumer awareness and reputation as much larger international carriers, including service-oriented airlines such as Singapore Airlines. Virgin Atlantic's success is due in part to its image of service quality, value for money, being the underdog, and having an edgy personality.

Extraordinary Service Quality

Virgin has delivered a high quality of service and, more important to perceptions, has often dazzled customers with original, "wow" experiences. Virgin pioneered sleeper seats in 1986 (British Airways followed nine years later with the cradle seat), limo services at each end of the flight (or motorcycle service for those flying light), in-flight massages, child safety seats, individual TVs for business class passengers, drive-through check-in at the airport, and new classes of service. First-class passengers are offered a new tailor-made suit to be ready at their destination, masseurs or beauty therapists, and a facility to shower or nap.

Value for Money

Virgin Atlantic's Upper Class is priced at the business-class level, but not much different from many other airlines' first-class service. Mid Class is offered at full-fare economy prices, and most Virgin Economy tickets are available at a discount. While this lower price point offers a clear consumer advantage, Virgin does not emphasize the price position in its promotion. Cheapness per se is not the message at Virgin.

The Underdog

Virgin's business model is straightforward. The company typically enters markets and industries with large, established players (such as British Airways, Coca-Cola, Levi-Strauss, British Rail, and Smirnoff) that can be portrayed as being somewhat complacent, bureaucratic, and unresponsive to customer needs. In contrast, Virgin presents itself as the underdog who cares, innovates, and delivers an attractive, viable alternative to customers. When British Airways attempted to prevent Virgin from gaining routes, Virgin painted British Airways as a bully standing in the way of an earnest youngster who offered better value and service.

The Virgin Personality

The Virgin brand has a strong, perhaps edgy personality, largely reflecting its flamboyant service innovations and the values and actions of Richard Branson. Virgin as a person would be perceived as someone who:

- Flaunts the rules
- Has a sense of humor that can be outrageous at times
- Is an underdog, willing to attack the establishment
- Is competent, always does a good job, and has high standards

Interestingly, this personality spans some extremes, from competent to a feisty, fun-loving, rule-breaker—an accomplishment envied by other businesses. The key is not only the personality of Branson himself but also the fact that Virgin has delivered on each facet of this personality.

Virgin is a remarkable example of how the right set of brand associations can allow a business to stretch far beyond what would be considered its acceptable scope of operations. Rather than restrict itself to records and entertainment, Virgin has used its associations to extend from record stores to airlines, colas (Virgin Cola), vodka (Virgin Vodka), a rail service (Virgin Rail), jeans (Virgin Jeans), and dozens of other categories. In each business, the Virgin associations work to provide differentiation and advantage.

In fact, the decision to extend Virgin, a business then associated with rock music and youth, to an airline could have become a legendary blunder if it had failed. However, because the airline was successful and was able to deliver value with quality, flair, and innovation, the master Virgin brand developed associations that were not restricted to a single type of product. The elements of the Virgin strategic position—extraordinary service quality, value for money, the underdog position, and a quirky personality—work over a large set of products and services. It has become a lifestyle brand with an attitude whose powerful relationship with customers is not solely based on functional benefits within a particular product category.

Virgin's success has been driven in part by pure visibility, largely based on publicity personally generated by Richard Branson. For the launching of Virgin Bride, a company that arranges weddings, he showed up in a wedding dress. At the 1996 opening of Virgin's first U.S. megastore in New York's Times Square, Branson (a balloonist holding several world records) was lowered on a huge silver ball from 100 feet above the store. These and other stunts have turned into windfalls of free publicity for Virgin, helping the brand in all contexts.

Branson has fully mastered his role. By employing British humor and the popular love of flouting the system, he has endeared himself to consumers. By never deviating from the core brand values, he has gained their loyalty and confidence. When BBC Radio asked 1,200 people who they thought would be most qualified to rewrite the Ten Commandments, Branson came in fourth, after Mother Teresa, the pope, and the archbishop of Canterbury. When a British daily newspaper took a poll on who would be most qualified to become the next mayor of London, Branson won in a landslide.

BRAND IDENTITY

Creating and managing a brand requires a brand strategy, the heart of which is the *brand identity*, which provides direction, purpose, and meaning for the brand. A brand identity is a set of brand associations that the firm aspires to create or maintain, an aspirational external brand image. These associations represent what the brand aspires to stand for and imply a promise to customers from the organization. It differs from brand image in that it could include elements that are not present in the current image (you now make trucks as well as cars) or even conflict with it (you aspire to have a quality reputation that is superior to the current perceptions).

The brand identity can best be explained in terms of three steps. These steps assume that a comprehensive strategic analysis has been done. Customer, competitor, and internal analyses are particularly critical to the development of a brand identity.

1. What the Brand Stands For

The first step is to create a set of from 6 to 12 distinct associations that are desired for the brand. The process starts by putting down all the associations that are desired given what is known about the customers, competitors, and the business strategy going forward. A list of more than two dozen is shown in Figure 9.4 for a business-to-business service company here termed Ajax. In

Value creation	In-depth understanding of customers
Flexible	Close to customers
Resourceful	Team oriented
Dynamic	Partner with customers
Broad capability	Collaborator
Committed to excellence	Open communication
Best-of-breed	Multicultural
World class	Risk-sharing partner
Gets job done	Diversified workforce
Experienced	Technology that works
Confident	Global
Competent	Bold (without arrogance)
Straightforward	World health

Figure 9.4   Partial List of Aspirational Associations for Ajax

actuality, the list is more often from 50 to 100. During this process there is no effort to zero in on categories of associations, although there is an effort to make sure that organizational intangibles and personality dimensions are at least considered.

These items are then grouped, and each group is given a label. Ajax was created with a set of a half-dozen acquisitions, each of which continued to operate somewhat autonomously. It was becoming clear, though, that customers preferred a single-solution firm with broad capabilities. The new Ajax strategy was to orient its service to broad customer solutions and to get its operating units to work together seamlessly. The strategy represented a significant change in culture and operations. With respect to the brand identity, the elements "partner with customers," "customized solutions," "collaborative," and "close to customers" were clustered and given the name Team Solutions, which became one of eight identity elements. The brand goal was to provide a face to customers that matched this new strategy.

2. The Core Identity

The second step is to prioritize the brand identity elements. The most important and potentially the most impactful are classified as *core identity* elements. The core identity will be the primary drivers of the brand-building programs. They will be the focus of the brand investments, as they are the most critical to the success for the businesses that they are supporting. The balance of the elements are termed the *extended identity*. They serve to help define the brand, make decisions as to what actions and programs are compatible with the brand, and drive minor programs that will have lesser impact and take modest resources.

In developing the core and extended identity, four criteria should guide the process. Identity elements are sought that:

- **Resonate with the target market.** Ultimately, the market dictates success, and thus the identity should resonate with customers. It is useful to think in terms of how customers relate to the brand over time rather than simply what drives purchase decisions. Also, consider emotional and self-expressive benefits in addition to functional ones.

- **Differentiate from competitors.** Differentiation is often the key to winning. There should be some points of differentiation throughout the brand identity so that there is always an answer to the question as to how the brand is different.
- **Provide parity where competitors have an advantage that is compelling to customers.** It is not always necessary to be different or better on all dimensions. There may be some dimensions where the goal is simply to be close enough so that this dimension is no longer a reason to not buy the brand. Hyundai need not, for example, be equal to Toyota in quality; it just needs to be close enough so that its quality image does not prevent purchase.
- **Reflect the strategy and culture of the business.** Ultimately, the brand needs to enable and support the strategy of the business. Particularly when the strategy represents a change from the status quo, and requires a change in brand image, the brand identity needs to reflect the new strategy. The brand identity should also support and reflect the culture and values of the firm because it is the organization that has to deliver on the aspirational brand promise.

The Haas Business School at UC Berkeley has created a brand identity the core of which is:

- Question the status quo (lead by championing bold ideas)
- Confidence without attitude (lead through trust and collaboration and not arrogance)
- Students always (lifelong pursuit of personal and intellectual growth)
- Beyond yourself (lead ethically and responsibly)

The "confidence with attitude" dimension, in particular, resonates with students and recruiters and differentiates.

3. The Brand Essence

The core identity compactly summarizes the brand vision. However, it is often useful to provide even more focus by creating a *brand essence*, a single thought that captures the heart of the brand. The purpose of an essence is to communicate the brand internally. Thus, while there are times when an external tagline, designed to communicate the message of the day externally, can and does represent the essence, that is often not the case. Figure 9.5 shows the final brand identity for Ajax, including the brand essence.

A good brand essence will capture much of the brand identity from a different perspective, will provide a tool to communicate the identity, and will inform and inspire those inside the organization. Consider "transforming futures," the brand essence of the London School of Business. It provides an umbrella over what the LBS is and what it does in a way that is uplifting and inspiring to students, alumni, and donors, as well as faculty and staff. The Haas School of Business has as its essence "We develop leaders who redefine how we do business." The Haas essence is a stretch goal encouraging faculty and students to think broadly about innovation.

A key essence choice is whether to focus on what the brand is or on what it does for customers. The former, such as Banana Republic's "casual luxury" or the Lexus essence reflected in the "passionate pursuit of perfection," would tend to involve functional benefits; the latter, such as American Express' "do more" or BMW's "ultimate driving machine," tend to look to emotional and self-expressive benefits.

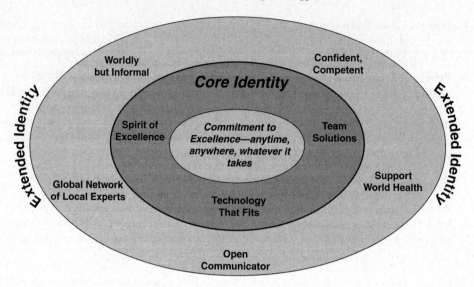

Figure 9.5 The Ajax Brand Identity

Proof Points and Strategic Initiatives

A brand identity should not simply reflect something that appeals to customers. Rather, the firm needs to be willing to invest behind it and create products and programs that will deliver on the promise. Toward that end, each identity element should have proof points and/or strategic initiatives associated with it.

Proof points are programs, initiatives, and assets already in place that provide substance to the strategy position and help communicate what it means. L.L. Bean has a position around outdoor enthusiasts. Proof points include the brand's heritage of outdoor activities, a flagship store geared to the outdoors, and the expertise and professionalism of the customer contact staff. Nordstrom has a customer service position supported by the following proof points:

- A current reputation for customer service
- A policy that attaches a service person to a customer rather than a product area
- A current return policy that is well known and has credibility
- A compensation program that makes the customer experience a priority
- The quality of the staff and the hiring program
- An empowerment policy permitting innovative responses to customer concerns

A gap between what the brand now delivers (even given the proof points) and the promise implied by the strategic position should lead to strategic imperatives. A *strategic imperative* is an investment in an asset or program that is essential if the promise to customers is to be delivered. What organizational assets and competencies are implied by the strategic position? What investments are needed in order to deliver the promise to customers?

If a regional bank aspires to deliver a relationship with customers, two strategic imperatives might be needed. First, a customer database might need to be created so that each customer contact person would have access to all of the customer's accounts. Second, a program might be needed to improve the interpersonal skills of customer contact people, including both training and measurement.

The Role of the Brand Identity

The need to articulate a brand identity and position introduces discipline and clarity into the strategy formulation process. The ultimate strategy is usually more precise and elaborated as a result. However, the brand identity and position have other, more explicit roles to play.

One role is to drive and guide strategic initiatives throughout the organization, from operations to product offering to R&D project selection. The overall strategic thrust captured by the identity and position should imply certain initiatives and programs. For example, given that we want to be an e-business firm, what tools and programs will customers expect from us? Initiatives and programs that do not advance the identity and position should be dialed down or killed.

A second role is to drive the communication program. A strategic identity and position that truly differentiates the product and resonates with customers will provide not only punch and effectiveness to external communication, but consistency over time because of its long-term perspective over organizational units that tend to march to their own drummers.

A third role is to support the expression of the organization's values and culture to employees and business partners. Such internal communication is as vital to success as reaching out to customers. Lynn Upshaw, a San Francisco communication consultant, suggests asking employees and business partners two questions:

- Do you know what the business stands for?
- Do you care?

Unless the answers to these questions are yes—that is, employees and business partners understand and believe in the business strategy—the strategy is unlikely to fulfill its potential. Too many businesses drift aimlessly without direction, appearing to stand for nothing in particular. Lacking an organizational sense of soul and a sound strategic position, they always seem to be shouting "on sale," attached to some deal, or engaging in promiscuous channel expansion.

Multiple Brand Identities

Arbitrarily insisting that a brand identity should apply to all products or market segments can be self-defeating. Rather, consideration should be given to adapting it to each context. One approach is to augment the brand identity to make it appropriate to a specific context. For example, Honda is associated with youth and racing in Japan while being more family oriented in the United States, but both positions share a focus on quality and motor expertise. Another is to define one of the brand identity elements differently in disparate contexts. Quality for GE Capital might be different than quality at GE Appliances, but high standards apply to both.

The Brand Position

The brand position represents the communication objectives—what parts of the identity are to be actively communicated to the target audience. The conceptualization of a brand position independent of a brand identity frees the latter to become a rich, textured picture of the aspirational brand. The brand identity does not have to be a compact view appropriate to guide communication.

The brand position will be inherently more dynamic than the brand identity. As the strategy and market context evolve and communication objectives are met, new ones become appropriate. A series of four or five positions over many years may be required to achieve the brand identity.

One fundamental choice often in front of strategists is whether to create a position that is credible or aspirational. In the case of Ajax, the firm's energy and over-the-top quality was legendary and created a value proposition with both functional and emotional components. An associated brand position would be credible, compelling, and relatively easy to implement. However, it would not move the needle as far as supporting the new strategy. A position around collaboration and team solutions, on the other hand, would be on-strategy but would also not be credible for a firm noted as being arrogant and silo-driven and would be expensive and maybe even infeasible. The choice depends on the answers to two questions. Does the firm have programs in place to deliver on the new promise? Is the market ready to accept the changed firm? If the answer to either question is no, it might be prudent to delay the aspirational position.

Another positioning choice is whether to emphasize points of differentiation or points of parity. The answer will depend on which direction will affect the target market. If the brand has a well-established image on a point of differentiation (such as value for Kmart, safety for Volvo), it may be more effective to attempt to create a point of parity on another dimension that is holding it back (quality for Kmart or styling for Volvo).

KEY LEARNINGS

- Brand equity, a key asset for any business, consists of brand awareness, brand loyalty, and brand associations.

- Awareness provides a sense of familiarity and credibility and makes it more likely that a customer will consider a brand.

- A core loyal customer base reduces the cost of marketing, provides a barrier to competitors, supports a positive image, and provides time to respond to competitor moves.

- Brand associations can and should go beyond attributes and benefits to include such associations as brand personality, organizational intangibles, and product category associations.

- The brand identity represents aspirational associations. The most important of these, the core identity, should be supported by proof points and/or strategic imperatives and should be the driver of strategic programs, including product development.

- While the identity represents long-term aspirational associations and is multidimensional, the position represents the short-term communication objectives and is more focused.

FOR DISCUSSION

1. Explain how each of the three brand equity dimensions provide value to the firm. Explain how they provide value to customers.

2. What is the difference between identity and position? Develop alternative positioning statements for Ajax. Include a tagline and the rationale for that tagline.

3. Create a brand identity for Virgin Atlantic Airlines. Are there potential dimensions, such as high quality and superior service, that are inconsistent with the brand's personality? If so, how is that handled? How has the identity been brought to life? What are the proof points? Why don't more brands emulate Virgin's brand-building programs?

4. Pick out three brands from a particular industry. How are they positioned? Which is the best in your view? Does that brand's positioning provide any emotional or self-expressive benefits? How would you evaluate each brand's positioning strategy? Hypothesize proof points and strategic imperatives for each brand.

5. Consider the Joie de Vivre hotel concept described on page 157. Think of themes stimulated by magazines or movies and discuss how you would design a hotel around each concept. For each theme, choose five words that reflect that theme.

NOTES

1. David A. Aaker, *Managing Brand Equity*, New York: Free Press, 1991, p. 57.
2. "Shoppers Like Wide Variety of Houseware Brands," *Discount Store News*, October 24, 1988, p. 40.
3. Leo Bogart and Charles Lehman, "What Makes a Brand Name Familiar?" *Journal of Marketing Research*, February 1973, pp. 17–22.

CHAPTER TEN

Toward a Strong Brand Relationship

They laughed when I sat down at the piano—but when I started to play. . . .
—*John Caples, copywriter, 1926*

A strong relationship develops not by driving brand involvement, but by supporting people in living their lives.
—*Susan Fournier, guru of the relationship metaphor*

Any CEO who cannot clearly articulate the intangible assets of his brand and understand its connection to customers is in trouble.
—*Charlotte Beers, J. Walter Thompson*

*I*ntegral to a business strategy is creating a cadre of loyal friends and customers to the brand based on a strong brand relationship. The larger the cadre and the stronger the relationship the better. It will provide a base business and, often as important, a potential source of brand advocacy, the most effective brand building that exists.

A loyal customer base is the ultimate competitive advantage because it is shielded from competitors. Loyal customers will have little motivation or interest in competitive offerings. As a result, competitors will find it expensive to try to gain converts among this group. If the customer base represents the most involved part of a categories market, a competitor may be in a highly disadvantageous position. In addition, because maintaining customers is much less expensive than attracting customers, the marketing effort to support the customer base will be relatively modest.

There are many routes to a customer relationship. Three of them are explored in this chapter. First, make the brand experience as positive as possible by employing a touchpoint analyses program. Second, instead of focusing on selling the brand or the firm, look to the customer sweet spot, something the customer is involved and even passionate about, and connect to it possibly as a partner. Third, look beyond functional benefits to provide a more intense and differentiating basis of a relationship.

UNDERSTANDING AND PRIORITIZING BRAND TOUCHPOINTS

The brand experience is at the essence of a relationship. It should be pleasant, exceed expectations, and even inspire people to talk about positive interactions. It should not be frustrating

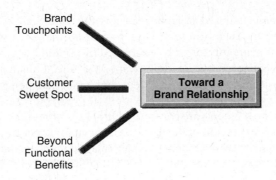

Figure 10.1 Toward a Brand Relationship

or disappointing and certainly should not motivate people to discuss negative incidents. The brand relationship can be compared to a personal relationship. If you have a friend or colleague or mentor relationship with another, you expect the interaction experiences to be consistent with the relationship as a minimum and hopefully be exceptional, thereby furthering and strengthening the relationship.

The brand experience is created by brand touchpoints. A brand touchpoint occurs any time a person in the marketplace interacts with the brand. Over time, all of those touchpoints combine to define the brand experience, which supports and hopefully enhances the brand relationship. It is therefore important to recognize that touchpoints need to be managed on an ongoing basis so that they deliver and support a strong on-brand relationship. This is especially true for a service business or one that has a service component to it.

A touchpoint perspective quickly makes it clear that the drivers of each touchpoint experience are the employees and firm partners who participate in the design and execute the experience. Thus, they need to understand and believe in the brand and in the value proposition. This is one reason why the brand vision should be communicated to employees and partners.

All touchpoints do not have the same impact, the same weakness in execution, or the same cost structure. So one task is to prioritize the touchpoints to determine which should receive resources to improve the experience. There should be a clear understanding as to which touchpoints should be improved, why they were selected, and how the improvement can be achieved.

Prioritizing the touchpoints and developing a plan to improve those that are considered most in need of change involves five steps.[1]

The first step is to identify all the touchpoints that exist and those that should exist but are not now in place. It is important to recognize that they can occur before, during, or after a purchase event. Before the purchase, a person can see an ad, hear a friend talk about an experience with the brand, visit the brand's Web site, see a package, or visit a trade show, and this is a partial list. A touchpoint can be connected to the purchase occasion with the quality of the salesperson experience, the existence of relevant items in inventory, how the price is communicated, and much more. After the purchase, there are the user experience, the service systems, and the social support, among a long list.

Touchpoints can be under the control of the firm such as the communication programs, the public relations efforts, the customer contact points such as service and accounting staffs, sponsorships, or customer-focused programs such as the Tide Stain Detective. Touchpoints can also be external to the firm, where at best there is an influence potential rather than a control context. Such touchpoints might be controlled by retailers, run by third parties such as *Consumer Reports*, or operated by a leading recipe Web site. Usually the list of touchpoints that exists or should exist can run to many dozens, but it can take persistence to avoid leaving some off.

Make sure that all the segments are covered. At Jiffy Lube, the shops were set up by men for men yet it turns out that 70 percent of the cars that came in for service were driven by women.[2] Women did not want to see dirty restrooms and men's magazines on the tables. Nor did they want to be asked to take a sleeping baby out of the car. Getting the segment right led the firm to make some easy changes.

The second step is to provide an internal evaluation of all of the touchpoints to determine which are managed well and which are deficient. What organizational unit owns each touchpoint, how is it managed, and what person is responsible? A key question is how well the touchpoint experience is being delivered with respect to internal expectations, external expectation, or the competition. If it is being delivered well, it will have a reduced chance of becoming a priority. Another is what will it take in terms of resources and program change to improve the performance? If the change is excessively costly, the benefit from implementing an improvement program will have to be higher to justify its value.

The third step looks to past, current, and future customers to determine which touchpoints have the greatest impact on their decision and experiences. What are their needs and expectations from the touchpoint experience? Which touchpoints affect them the most and how? How is the organization performing with respect to the brand touchpoints it deems most important relative to its expectations?

ASK THE RIGHT QUESTIONS

The CEO of Office Depot was puzzled about the fact that sales had been declining but the customer service scores from a third-party mystery shopper were extremely high.[3] To find out why, he proceeded to visit unannounced to some 70 stores in 15 states. He observed and talked to customers in the aisles. Customers leaving the store, especially if their shopping carts were empty or nearly so, were asked why they did not buy more. The mystery shopping scores were correct because they were based on cleanliness of the store, including the bathrooms, and whether the shelves were full. The stores got high marks on these dimensions.

More important, how was the customer experience? The answers were not good. The associates did not focus on the customers; in one case, they actually argued about whether an item was carried by the store. The stores were large and complex, so items were hard to find. The experience was not as efficient as was wanted; customers basically just wanted to get in and out. Customers wanted some items not offered such as shipping and computer repair.

As a result of these insights, stores were redesigned so they were easier to shop in, and some were downsized. Operations were made more efficient so that associates had more time to sell. The interaction pattern was changed. For example, questions such as, "What brings you in today?" and "How are you planning to use the product?" were added to help stimulate a dialogue. Finally, associates were encouraged to offer recommendations and to systematically cross-sell complementary items.

A few guidelines in conducting such an inquiry. Get the customers to use their own words to describe the touchpoints and their appraisal of the experiences; don't put words and ideas into their minds. Also ask them to describe the ideal touchpoint experience. Accepting the status quo as something they have to live with may prevent customers from identifying areas that should be improved.

The fourth step, to prioritize, is based on balancing three dimensions. A high-priority touchpoint program would have a high rating on the:

- Importance of the touchpoint experience in enhancing the brand, the value proposition, and customer loyalty
- Degree to which the experience is deficient
- Extent to which the cost and feasibility of improving the experience are reasonable

In making the evaluation, the business objective and organizational culture should provide reference points. Ultimately, priority touchpoint improvement should support the business and leverage the culture as well as enhance the brand experience.

The final step is to develop a touchpoint action plan. For the priority touchpoints, the goals of the touchpoint and who is responsible should be clearly identified. There will need to be accountability. Further, a development and execution plan to improve the touchpoint experience that includes performance metrics will be needed. The plans may have to involve multiple functional areas and coordinate with other touchpoint experiences.

The effort to improve the customer experience should strive to achieve simplicity and trustworthiness.

Customers want a touchpoint experience to be simple and easy to use, navigate, and understand. They do not want complexity, information overload, and frustration. The power of simplicity is shown by its effect on customer decisions. One study found that brands that scored in the top quarter in delivering simply, relevant information were 86 percent more likely to be purchased and 115 percent more likely to be recommended to others.[4]

Touchpoints around brand search are particularly prone to complexity and inconvenience. A buyer usually wants to compare brands, and communicating specifications and benefits of one brand is not that helpful. Several automobile brands, recognizing that reality, do offer the ability to compare their brand with a set of comparison brands of choice. Anything that can reduce the complicity of a decision will be welcome. DeBeers uses the four Cs (cut, color, clarity, and carat) to frame a complex decision. Herbal Essence provides a decision guide based on identifying hair type and color treatment needs that simplifies the decision. Also, information that is screened fro relevance will be valued. ShoeDazzle.com, for example, provides shoe suggestions based on personality information such as customers' favorite fashion icons and preference for heels.

Customers also want trustworthy, relevant information about brands and guidance as to how to compare them. Often customer input is seen as the most trustworthy because it is based on actual experience, and there is no commercial bias. Walt Disney World Moms Panel, for example, answers questions about the Disney vacations. J.C. Penney posts videos of teens talking about their purchases (termed "hauls") and provides insights into what and why purchases were made. TurboTax provides more than 100,000 of unfiltered reviews of its product and helps customers find the most relevant ones for their needs. Another source is experts. Saks Fifth Avenue, for example, has the fashion writer Dana Riggs give fashion advice to its customers. Betty Crocker has an "Ask Betty" section on its Web site that provides the specter of the heritage expert.

Improving the brand experience at every touchpoint is one way to build and solidify brand relationships. Any failure of a touchpoint to deliver an on-brand experience can put customer loyalty at risk and can provide an opening for competitors. Conversely, excelling at the touchpoint level will make customer loyalty an ongoing source of brand and business strength.

FOCUSING ON THE CUSTOMER'S SWEET SPOT

The instinct of executives developing a marketing program is to advance the offering, brand, and firm. This is especially true when the goal is to create a digital community around a brand. How can visibility be enhanced, associations reinforced, and user loyalty increased? This orientation is driven by financial performance goals and the assumption that customers are rational and want to know and act on information regarding a product or service.

When customers are highly involved in the brand and offering, an offering-driven program can work. For example, Dell has a series of programs for which customers are motivated to be engaged. These programs include Direct2Dell blog, where users can communicate directly to Dell; IdeaStorm whereby a user can post ideas for Dell to consider and evaluate the ideas of others; and the Dell Support Forums, where users to ask questions and get answers. The problem is that most brands and offerings are inconsequential within, tangential to, or detached from customers' lifestyles. As a result, offering-driven brand building and marketing rarely create a strong brand–customer relationship.

There is an alternative. Instead, look for a customer "sweet spot" and find a program that will allow the brand to connect with that sweet spot. A sweet spot, whether it is New York city adventures, healthy living, rock climbing, sustainability, ora college football team, or whatever else, should be related to what is important and involving to customers, what they are motivated to talk about. It should reflect how customers spend their "thinking and doing" time, their beliefs and values, their activities and passions, those possessions that express their personality, and their higher purpose. Ideally, it would be a part of, if not central to, their self-identity and lifestyle or reflect a higher-order purpose in their lives.

The goal should be to create or find an event, activity, interest area, or cause that connects to a true customer sweet spot. It needs to resonate, break out of the clutter, provide a hub around which a set of coordinated brand-building programs can be developed, and link to and enhance the brand. Consider Pampers and Coke, for example.

Pampers went beyond diapers by "owning" the Web site Pampers Village, which provides a "go to" place for all issues relating to babies and child care that gets more than 600,000 unique visitors each month. Its seven sections—pregnancy, new baby, baby development, baby toddler, preschool, me, and family—each has a menu of topics. For example, under baby development, there are 57 articles, 230 forums, and 23 play-and-learn activities. Its online community allows moms and soon-to-be moms to connect with each other to share their common experiences, issues, and thoughts about how to raise a healthy, happy child. The program demonstrates that Pampers understands mothers and works to establish a relationship between the brand and the mother that will potentially continue throughout a mother's Pampers-buying life.

Coca-Cola partnered with the World Wildlife Foundation, which is engaged in major initiatives to conserve water, reduce carbon emissions, and save polar bears. A visible Coke component is an effort to spotlight polar bears with research (customers can contribute and receive a virtual piece of arctic land from which they can monitor bears) and promotions such as the Polar Pick-me-up where person can send a Coke to a friend. The Coke Facebook page with

35 million likes coordinates the effort. The community provides Coke with likability, energy, and customer engagement. It resonates with a segment important to Coke that is likely to be different than the segment that responds to the humorous videos around Coke "happiness."

What Does the Sweet Spot–Driven Program Buy?

To connect with a customer sweet spot provides avenues to a relationship much richer than that of an offering-based relationship that, for most brands, is driven by a functional benefit and is relatively shallow and vulnerable. In particular, it can potentially do the following.

Stimulate a Social Network

A social community associated with a sweet-spot program often has the potential to have a high level of social activity, which is increasingly difficult in an era of social media fatigue. Focusing on what a person is passionate about, such as baby care as the Pampers Village has done or motorcycle trips as Harley-Davidson site does, will motivate customers to reach out for information or to share experiences and ideas. It can stimulate the major reasons to be socially active, to be involved in the contest (gain or spread information), self-involved (gain attention, show knowledge), and other involved (belonging to a community and helping others).

Create Brand Energy and Interest

One of the key challenges for most brands globally is to create energy and visibility. For Avon, for example, the product line is not an energy source, but the Avon Walk for Breast Cancer creates involvement; connects to an area the target audience has passion about; and attaches a higher purpose the to the Avon brand, which can lead to respect and liking. Millions of women have participated directly or indirectly over two decades, and the program has raised more than $600 million for cancer research. That is energy. If you make hot dogs, it is hard to manufacture energy. But if you focus on a shared interest with kids, namely their events and parties, and create the Oscar Mayer Wienermobile (or more accurately, eight of them) that joins the party and supports a jingle contest, you have real energy.

Enhance Brand Likability and Credibility

Finding a sweet spot and developing a connecting program with substance raises the brand way above the noise emanating from firms shouting" "My brand is better than your brand." The positive feelings associated with the shared-interest area can lead to positive feelings about the brand; people attribute all sorts of good characteristics to liked brands with whom they share interests. Hobart, a maker of high-end institutional kitchen equipment, became a thought leader and information source in regard to such issues as finding, training, and retaining good workers; keeping food safe; providing enticing dining experiences; eliminating costs; and reducing shrinkage. This program impacted perceptions of the brand and propelled Hobart into a leadership role that lasted well over a decade until the company was bought and integrated into a larger firm.

Form a Friend–, Colleague–, or Mentor–Brand Relationship

The existence of a sweet-spot program makes a friend, colleague, or mentor relationship metaphor likely to be applicable. California Casualty, an auto and home insurance firm that specializes in teachers, has a "School Lounge Makeover" program to provide $7,500 to upgrade teacher lounges for schools that make the most compelling case. Only a friend would take an interest in such a mundane but important issue area. California Casualty also acts as a colleague, sharing goals and programs by being a sponsor and partner in IMPACT, an organization that is designed to attack teenage distracted driving through in-school educational and involvement programs. Finally, the brand can be like a mentor. General Mills, which shares an interest in gluten-free living with its Web site GlutenFreely.com, for example, is in a position to offer advice and encouragement as well as support a community concerned with gluten issues.

HOW TO CREATE OR FIND A CUSTOMER SWEET SPOT

Creating a successful sweet spot–driven program involves identifying a customer sweet spot, creating or finding a connecting program, and linking the brand to the program. Each step has substantial uncertainties and challenges.

Identify a Customer Sweet Spot That Will Engage the Audience

The first challenge is to find a set of potential sweet spots by understanding the customers in depth. How do they spend their quality time? What activities do they enjoy? What possessions are important to them and reflect their personality and lifestyle? What do they talk about? What issues are absorbing their attention? In what areas do they hold strong opinions? What are their values and beliefs? Their higher purpose?

Create a Sweet Spot–Driven Program

With an understanding of the customer in hand, there are three on ramps to the identification of the right shared-interest program.

The offering is an integral part. The first on ramp is to determine if the brand can be integrated into a "sweet-spot" program and be a full partner that contributes assets and substance. Kaiser Permanente, for example, repositioned its brand away from a focus on health care (linked to bureaucracy and sickness) to a shared interest in healthy lifestyles (associated with control and wellness). The shared-interest program involves members controlling their own health by accessing a wide array of preventive health programs online and through classes that include areas such as weight control, stress management, insomnia, smoking issues, healthy eating, and many others, all supported by "My Health Manager," which can be used to record and monitor program participation. These programs have their own focus and objectives very different from selling compassionate staff and clean, effective hospitals.

A fit based on a natural association. A second on ramp is to build on a sweet spot that has a natural connection to the brand. There are a host of bases for a brand connection a such as a lifestyle (Zipcars and urban lifestyle living), an offering application (Harley-Davidson and touring on motorcycles), an activity (adidas Streetball Challenge, a local three-person basketball tournament surrounded by a weekend party with music, dance, etc.), a target customer (Pampers and baby care), a country (Hyundai makes and sponsors the Kimchi Bus, a 400-day effort to spread Korean cuisine), values (Dove on redefining beauty), or an interest (the Sephora BeautyTalk site for those interested in beauty tips and issues). The fit should work; it should not appear incongruous.

Disconnected: sponsorship only. A third on ramp is to find or create a sweet-spot program that has no connection with the brand or with a remote connection. The Avon Walk for Breast Cancer and the Red Bull Soapbox Racer video game have little relationship with the respective offerings. The brand, when distinct, should not distract or be a liability, of course. Relaxing the commonly held dictum that there must be some kind of brand fit or connection means that the search for a sweet-spot area that customers will be truly involved with will be unconstrained. Anything is eligible, and thus a winning idea is more likely.

With a disconnected sponsorship model, the problem of connecting the brand to the program can be a challenge. If the brand is included in the programs brand as it is for the Avon Walk or the Red Bull Soapbox Racer, the connection problem becomes modest. However, in other circumstances, the task requires persistent reminders in multiple ways, a task that can be expensive and difficult to be successful.

Find An Existing External Program to Which the Brand Could Connect

The classic "make or buy" decision should be on the table. An internal, owned sweet-spot program means that the substance, evolution, and investment can be controlled by the firm. However, establishing a new program can be costly, difficult, and even not feasible, especially if the sweet-spot program candidates have been already preempted in the marketplace or if the firm lacks the resources to create a competing program.

An option is to find an established branded sweet-spot program with proven visibility and effectiveness and link to it. Home Depot wanted a program to leverage its assets and expertise to help disadvantaged people build or rebuild homes. The solution was to connect to Habitat for Humanity, a branded program with an established record of success in building homes for those that need help. Home Depot connected by providing visible and tangible support with building supplies, volunteers from its knowledgeable staff, and signage in stores and on its Web site. For many customers of Home Depot, the link was well known. As an aside, it does not matter if Habitat for Humanity is linked to Home Depot, only the reverse, because the goal is to influence the Home Depot brand.

The Sweet Spot—A Big Idea

The sweet-spot program should have an immediate impact by stimulating customer involvement and purchases, thus affecting the short-term financials. Its more important impact, however, is likely to be enhancing the brand, building long-term customer relationships, and increased loyalty, all firm assets that will pay off even though they are sometimes not so easy to quantify or justify.

GET BEYOND FUNCTIONAL BENEFITS

When identifying the top print advertisements and best headline in the past century of advertising, the one written in 1926 by a young copywriter, only one year on the job, named John Caples is always in the conversation. The ad is known by its heading: "They laughed when I sat down at the piano—but when I started to play. . . ." His assignment was to entice people to buy piano lessons by correspondence from the U.S. School of Music.

Under a picture of a young man at a party sitting down to play the piano, the headline set the stage and indeed summarized the story, which was recounted in detail in the body of the ad. The hero was ridiculed by the guests when he sat down, but the ridicule turned to accolades and applause when he began to play, only a few months after starting the correspondence course. The ad was not only critically acclaimed but, more to the point, brought in a lot of customers.

There is a lot to learn today from this ad. There was almost nothing about the offering or the learning process that surrounded it. Rather, the ad told a story in graphic detail about what happened to someone who took the correspondence course. Most remarkable, the ad shows that functional benefits are not the sweet spot of persuasion and communication. Rather, what grabs people are emotional, self-expressive, and social benefits. There is the emotion felt not only by the piano player who excelled in a pressure context but also by those hearing the story that are bursting with pride that he did it. There is the self-expressive benefit, the ability of the person to express his talent, his perseverance, and his ability to face down doubters and those who ridiculed. And there is the social benefit when the man became not only accepted into a desirable reference group but also became an admired member.

All too common is what I call the "product-attribute fixation trap" in which the strategic and tactical management of the brand is excessively focused on product attributes and functional benefits. Product characteristics such as scope (Crest makes dental hygiene products), attributes (Volvo is safe), quality and value (Kraft delivers a quality product), and uses (Subaru is made for the snow) are assumed to dominate in the brand relationship. There is thus a failure to recognize that a brand includes these product characteristics but potentially much more. The results are less than optimal strategies and ineffective marketing programs.

The product-attribute fixation trap is based in part on the erroneous assumption that these attributes are the only relevant bases for customer decisions and competitive dynamics. This "rationale person" view of customers is comfortable but usually wrong. It gets reinforced when market research aimed at finding important drivers of brand preference has a significant bias toward attributes in part because they are easier to use by researchers and respondents alike. Attributes, however, often scale much higher in importance than they merit. Research on trucks, for example, suggests that rational attributes such as durability, safety features, options, and power are the most important. Yet more intangible attributes such as "cool styling," being "fun to drive," and "feeling powerful" are more likely to influence decisions of consumers who often cannot or will not admit that such frills are really important to them.

Even worse, strategies based on functional benefits are often strategically ineffective or limiting. First, customers may not believe that a brand has a functional advantage because of the conflicting claims of competitors and puffery or may not believe the benefit represents a compelling reason to buy the brand. In the hotel business, cleanliness is important, but all hotels are perceived to be clean. Second, if the functional benefit represents a point of differentiation, competitors may quickly copy it. A gas-millage advantage for a car brand may be a short-term differentiator because competitors will find ways to beat or bypass any performance specification. Third, the benefit may not represent a basis of a strong, long-term relationship because there is no emotional attachment. Finally, a strong functional association confines the brand, especially when it comes to responding to changing markets or in exploring brand extensions.

Thus, it makes sense to move beyond functional benefits and consider emotional, self-expressive, and social benefits as a basis for the value proposition.

BROADENING THE CONCEPT OF A BRAND

A brand, in addition to product attributes, can be defined by its user imagery (the Ralph Lauren man), symbols (LeBron James representing State Farm), country of origin (Audi is German made), organizational associations (such as innovation, a drive for quality, and concern for the environment), and brand personality (such as being perceived to be upscale, competent, trustworthy, formal, and intellectual).

A brand is also defined by some combination of emotional, self-expressive, and social benefits, three intertwined concepts that, along with functional benefits, are components of the value proposition. They provide a richer view of a brand and its relationship with customers.

Emotional Benefits

An emotional benefit relates to the ability of the brand to make the buyer or user of a brand feel something during the purchase process or use experience. "When I buy or use this brand, I feel. . . ." Thus, a customer can feel safe in a Volvo, excited in a BMW, energetic with Coke around, warm when receiving a Hallmark card, strong and rugged when wearing Levi's, relaxed when have Celestial Seasonings tea, or in control when using TurboTax. Evian is simply water, but through the slogan "Another day, another chance to feel healthy" and supporting advertising, Evian associates itself not only with working out (a common use occasion for the brand) but also with the satisfied feeling that comes from a workout.

Emotional benefits add richness and depth to the brand and the experience of owning and using the brand. Without the memories that Sun-Maid raisins evoke, the brand would border on commodity status. The familiar red package links many users to the happy days of helping mom in the kitchen (or the idealized childhood for some who wished that they had such experiences). The result can be a different use experience, one with feelings, and a stronger brand.

In a study of brand love, researchers from Michigan Rajeev Batra, Aaron Ahuvia, and Richard Bagozzi used some 90 in-depth interviews about object and brand love and followed them up with a quantitative study that provided structure the concept.[5] One finding was that respondents had no trouble identifying brands that they had a love relationship with. Another was that some of the key characteristics of that love relationship were emotional benefits such as feelings of happiness, excitement, calm, "like an old friend," having the right "fit," and having a strong desire to avoid being separated.

Self-Expressive Benefits

Russell Belk, a prominent consumer behavior researcher, once wrote, "That we are what we have is perhaps the most basic and powerful fact of consumer behavior."[6] Belk meant that brands and products can become symbols of a person's self-concept. A brand can thus provide a self-expressive benefit by providing a way for a person to express his or her self-image.

Brands and products, as symbols of a person's self-concept, can provide a self-expressive benefit by providing a vehicle by which a person can express his or her self. "When I buy or use this brand, I am___." A brand does not have to be Harley-Davidson to deliver self-expressive benefits. A person can be cool by buying clothes at Zara, successful by driving a Lexus, creative by using Apple, a nurturing mother by preparing Quaker Oats hot cereal, frugal and unpretentious by shopping at Kmart, adventurous and active by owning REI camping equipment, or competent by using Microsoft Office.

P&G's "THANK MOMS": A MODEL CAMPAIGN IN A GLOBAL WORLD

P&G's "Thank You Mom" Olympic marketing program was a brilliant effort to draw on a universal human value to create a program with energy, relevance, and emotional benefits that spanned brands and countries. Plus, it is ongoing with a life beyond one Olympics. Applied to the Vancouver Games of 2010 and the Special Olympics of 2011, it made it major push for the 2012 London Games. It is all about celebrating what moms do and to thank them for their efforts, their care, and their achievements.

The campaign came to life with the "Best Job," a short film that touches the heart and celebrates the role that moms play in raising Olympians and great kids. There were also videos of the moms of some of the 150 athletes sponsored by P&G brands. A mom would be shown watching her child excel by an exceptional performance or by winning an event. The campaign was promoted through a host of media channels. A companion in-store worldwide retailer program for five months before the London games involved four million retailers. It was tied to an effort to raise more than $25 million to support youth sports programs that would aid both the Olympics and moms everywhere. The promotions involved some 34 P&G brands, including Tide/Ariel, Pantene, Pampers, and Gillette. There was a "Thank You Mom" app that allowed people to thank their own moms with personalized content in the form of a video.

The marketing program was a winner for several reasons beside the fact that it scaled over dozens of brand silos and many countries and was estimated to have generated $500 million in sales. It provided the prestige and energy of being involved in the Olympics plus the "feel-good" aspect of supporting youth sports. Further, the connection with real moms provided a hearty dollop of authenticity and emotion. It is easy to empathize with moms who have fed babies, provided lunches, supported at swim meets, dealt with skinned knees, been there for recitals, and shared in the joy of winning gold at the Olympics. Everyone can relate to the best of a mom's role.

Why is some contemporary art sold at astronomical prices? Why would a stuffed dead shark be worth $40 million and hang in the New York Metropolitan Museum of Art? Why would a rectangular set of color spots created by an artist's staff sell for $600,000? It is not objective quality for sure. Experts could not agree as to whether a painting resembling a Jackson Pollock drip painting found at a flea market was authentic. Depending on their verdict, the painting would be worth a few thousand or $40 million. The same painting! How does an artist create a brand that can capture such a price premium? The answer is not simple, but without question, self-expressive benefits play a predominant role.

In the brand love study, another dimension that was identified was self-expressive benefits. There was a current self-identity where the brand says something about who you are, a desired self-identity when the brand helps you look or feel like you would aspire to, and a sense that a loved brand makes life meaningful.[7]

When a brand provides a self-expressive benefit, the connection between the brand and the customer is likely to be heightened. For example, consider the difference between using Oil of Olay, which has been shown to heighten one's self-concept of being gentle, sophisticated, mature, exotic, mysterious, and down to earth, and Jergens or Vaseline Intensive Care Lotion, either of which provides a comparable self-expression benefit.

Of course, each person has multiple roles; for example, a woman may be a wife, mother, writer, tennis player, music buff, and hiker. For each role, the person will have an associated self-concept and a need to express that self-concept. The purchase and use of brands is one way to fulfill this need for self-expression.

Benefits Offered	From Customer's Perspective
Emotional Benefits	When I buy or use this brand, I feel _____ .
Self-expressive Benefits	When I buy or use this brand, I am _____ .
Social Benefits	When I buy or use this brand, I relate to people like _____ .

Figure 10.2 Emotional, Self-Expressive, and Social Benefits

Social Benefits

The drive to have friends, colleagues, family, and groups with common interests is intense and satisfies a need of belonging and self-identity. Many brands have the capability of participating or even driving social benefits. "When I buy or use this brand, the type of people I relate to are_____." Social relationships not only are linked to fundamental human needs but provide a setting to influence as well. Word-of-mouth communication from friends or associates is often the most influential communication because it is perceived to be unbiased and based on knowledge or experience.

There are several types of social benefits. Some can involve actual or potential interactions with friends or others that share an interest or even a lifestyle and values. Bikers can post pictures of their last ride on the Harley Web site. BeautyTalk by Sephora, for example, provides a community for those interested in or even obsessed with skin care and cosmetics. They can directly talk about issues of concern with experts and peers who are every bit as involved as they are. Or Kraft Kitchens has a community around cooking dishes and meals that are tasty, healthy, and easy to prepare. The community shares information but, more important, feelings about a common interest

Some brands can provide social benefits by defining or linking to a reference group, a group in which an individual identifies and whose values he or she has adopted. Prius may reflect a person type that defines a reference group for some. Or a Starbucks loyalist may feel that he or she is part of a closed club of aficionados. This reference group social benefit, which occurs without any actual interaction even when the participant is anonymous as far as the group is concerned, can be very powered. The brand experience becomes the device to link the person with the group providing the belonging experience. Although there will be no actual word-of-mouth communication, the reference group is still influential in appraising brands because of their implied endorsement.

Another type of social benefit can come from an aspirational group. A person that plays golf using a Titlist Pro V1 is among a group that contains some really good golfers. The brand makes the link. These golfers are not assessable, but the brand provides a link that makes them a potential part of a person's identity and lifestyle. The group can also influence by being a type of person to emulate.

Social benefits also emerged from the brand love study.[8] Loved brands provide others with a sense of who you are or want to be. Also, loved brands are ones that a person will often talk to others about.

A social benefit is powerful because it provides a sense of identity and belonging as well as an influence platform. Most people need to have a social niche whether it is a family, a work team, a recreation groups, or whatever. If a brand can provide that, it can be a basis for a strong relationship.

Combining Benefits

These three benefits are often related, and a brand or its associated programs an activate two or all three benefits. BeautyTalk, for example, could provide a satisfying feeling from finding the right cosmetic and looking good, a self-expressive benefit of being knowledgeable, if not an expert, in an area of importance to you in addition to social benefits. That was the case in the ad "They laughed . . ." discussed at the outset.

When multiple benefits are present, it can be useful to prioritize them because it can matter which perspective dominates. It can impact the way that the benefits are enhanced and brought to light. For example, whereas emotional benefits tend to involve the act of using the product (wearing a cooking apron confirms oneself as a gourmet cook) self-expressive benefits would tend to focus on the consequence of using the product (feeling proud and satisfied because of the appearance of a well-appointed meal) and social benefits involving others affected by the use experience (the feelings of others participating in cooking or attending the meal). These differences suggest that it will be helpful to know which perspective is being used.

The Brand Ideal

One way to introduced higher-order benefits into your brand, according to Jim Stengel, the influential former CMO of P&G, is to develop a brand ideal, a shared goal of improving people's lives.[9] For P&G, it is to "touch lives and improve the lives of the world's consumers." Their Olympic sponsorship, the "proud sponsor of Moms," touched lives and resulted in a sales bump as well. P&G's Tide has its "Loads of Hope" program in which Tide people improve lives of disaster victims by literally doing their laundry. So instead of being a peanut butter brand, become a partner with Mom in a children's development.

Brand ideals come in five types:

- **Eliciting joy.** The Downey fabric softener (Lenor outside the U.S.) satisfies people's need to stimulate and renew the senses of touch smell and sight.
- **Enabling connection.** Think of the Zappos 24/7 call center that connects with customer on a personal level.
- **Inspiring exploration.** REI provides clothes and equipment for real exploration.
- **Evoking pride.** Jack Daniels has a deep heritage that makes users proud.
- **Impacting society.** Method delivers green products with passion and authenticity.

According to Stengel, leaders of brands, companies, or countries, should be able to conceptualize a vision that both inspires and provides practical direction for strategy. Operations proficiency is not enough. Vision is important.

Personal Relationship Models

Another "beyond functional benefit" route is to consider the human relationship metaphor. It has been shown that relationships observed in humans, such as arranged marriages, casual friends, marriages of convenience, committed partnership, best friends, compartmentalized friendships, kinships, rebound relationships, childhood friendships, courtships, flings, secret affairs, and enslavements, appear in brand settings as well. Customers can identify brands that fit these types of relationships and more.

Exploring whether a brand relationship can be modeled after a human analogue can provide insights. For example, if Microsoft is perceived to be a slave–master relationship, looking at the causes and ways to soften the relationship can be helpful. Or learning that some consumers believe that American Express looks down on them can lead to potential changes in substance and tone. Or knowing that a brand like Schwab is regarded as a mentor or a colleague suggests role models and a way of looking at relationship goals that can have a clarity that would not be possible if the brand vision did not include a relationship component.

KEY LEARNINGS

- Loyal customer groups based on strong brand relationship can be a significant competitive advantage in part because they are relatively easy to retain and expensive for competitors to attack.

- The customer experience is a key part of the relationship, and one way to enhance it is to prioritize brand touchpoints for improvement.

- Focus on the customer sweet spot—activities, beliefs and values, and a higher purpose. Find a way to connect to that sweet spot hopefully as a partner. Getting involved in a sweet spot is usually more effective that trying to sell a brand or firm.

- Get beyond the functional benefits to deliver emotional, self, or social benefits. The goal is to provide a deeper and more stable basis of a relationship.

FOR DISCUSSION

1. Consider the bank you have a relationship with. List all the brand touchpoints. Evaluate which are the most important to you and why.

2. What are your sweet spots? Pick an activity or interest. What brand-connected programs touch that activity of interest? If you were Ford, how would you design a program that would be relevant to your sweet spot?

3. Do you agree that marketing executions are subject to the attribute fixation trap? For what brands might that not be true? Why?

4. What brands deliver emotional benefits for you ? Self-expressive benefits? Social benefits? What is it about the brand that reinforces that ability to deliver benefits?

5. Think of some brands that have a relationship that you could describe as a fling, secret affair, or mentor relationships. Why?

6. What brands, if any, do you have a love relationship with? Why?

NOTES

1. This touchpoint process model is taken from Scott M. Davis and Michael Dunn, *Building the Brand Driven Business,* San Francisco: Jossey-Bass, 2002.

2. Allen P. Adamson, *The Edge: 50 Tips from Brand that Lead*, London: Palgrave MacMillan, 2013, p. 97.

3. Kevin Peters, "Office Depot's Resident on How 'Mystery Shopping' Helped Spark A Turn-around," *Harvard Business Review*, November 2011, pp. 47–50

4. Patrick Spenner and Karen Freeman, "Keep It Simple," *Harvard Business Review*, May, 2012, pp. 109–114.

5. Rajeev Batra, Aaron Ahuvia, and Richard P. Bagozzi, "Brand Love," *Journal of Marketing*, March, 2012, pp. 1–16.

6. Russell W. Belk, "Possessions and the Extended Self," *Journal of Consumer Research*, September 1988, p. 139.

7. Batra et.al., op cit, p. 8.

8. Batra et.al., op cit, p. 8.

9. Jim Stengel, "GROW: How Ideals Power Growth and Profit at the World's Greatest Companies," *Crown Business*, 2011.

CHAPTER ELEVEN

Energizing the Business

Only the paranoid survive.
—*Andrew Grove, Former CEO, Intel*

One never notices what has been done, one can only see what remains to be done.
—*Marie Curie*

Where there is no wind, row.
—*Portuguese proverb*

*B*usinesses need growth and not only for financial reasons. Certainly, shareholders, employees, and partners look to enhance sales and profits. However, growth also introduces vitality to an organization by providing challenges and rewards. An organization that cannot improve and grow may not even be viable. Further, improving performance by cutting costs and downsizing risks the morale of the employees and partners as well as cutting the muscle needed to create and support growth opportunities.

There are four ways to grow a business, as suggested by Figure 11.1. The first, covered in Chapter 12, is about leveraging the current business. That can mean taking the existing products into new markets, finding new products or services for the existing customer base, or leveraging assets such as brand equity or competencies such as managing the supermarket channel. The second, introduced in Chapter 13, involves creating a new business based on finding a white space in the market or by transformational innovation, a business for which a substantial competitive advantage will exist and persist. The third, presented in Chapter 14, entails going global, leveraging the business into new countries to create a broader market or creating new or improved assets and competencies that will lead to sustainable advantage in a global marketplace.

The fourth route to growth, the subject of this chapter, is to energize the existing business, an attractive growth avenue because an established firm has market and operating experience, assets, competencies, and a customer base on which to build. Developing new products or entering new markets is inherently risky and can stretch the firm in ways that may dilute the existing strategy and culture. An existing business can be energized by:

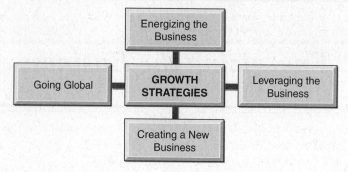

Figure 11.1   Growth Strategies

- Innovating to improve the offering
- Energizing the brand and marketing
- Increasing existing customer's usage

INNOVATING THE OFFERING

The ultimate business energizer is to improve the offering through innovation. An innovation, or better, a series of innovations, provides a sense that a firm is dynamic, creative, and always improving its offering. Innovation means new, interesting, and energetic.

A service company can improve the customer experience. The Memphis Redbirds minor league baseball team changed the spectator experience with cheerleaders, a mascot named Rocky, five party settings, and two kids' playgrounds—P.D. Parrot for under eight-year-olds and the Boardwalk with the Rocky Hopper ride for older kids. Add to that the Sonic Drive-In Kids Club, members of which get to run the bases, and more. The result is an experience that is involving and so unique that it engenders both loyalty and buzz.

Whole Foods Market is continuously innovating always on-brand. They took an industry leadership role with their seafood sustainability program. The chain stopped selling wild-caught fish species labeled "red," or threatened by overfishing, and introduced accepted labeling for sustainable seafood that is caught or farmed in ways that consider the long-term vitality of harvested species and the well-being of the oceans. The program not only had real substance but also engaged their customers in conversations around the sustainable seafood concept.

How can a firm innovate around the customer experience? One approach is to improve the important brand touchpoints as discussed in Chapter 10. Another is to exceed expectations with respect to the value proposition. What is expected, and what would surprise, delight, and even spur a "Wow!" reaction?

A product firm can enhance the product by adding a new dimension such as a feature or ingredient. P&G has introduced a steady stream of innovative diaper products from a Caterpillar Flex diaper and Feel 'n Learn training pants to Pampers Swaddlers, a diaper for newborns. Such activity provides vitality and credibility to the business. Product innovation, of course, does not just happen. It involves understanding unmet needs, organizational support, and the ability to evaluate proposed improvements in terms of customer relevance.

Line extensions can be a source of energy. New flavors, packaging, sizes, or services can add energy, interest, and the creation of new segments. Look for segments that are making do with the current offering and would prefer another option or more variety. Consider trends that are leaving your offering behind. Line extensions need to balance their value with the risk that the added cost might become a burden and that customers might rebel over the added confusion and complexity. Colgate made significant gains when it introduced Total, which simplified a purchase decision for consumers faced with a bewildering array of choices for toothpaste.

How can the organization create the sense and substance of continuous innovation rather than sporadic episodes of improvement in the product or service that are quickly copied and blend into the cluttered marketplace resulting in a transient advantage? A basic answer is to create an organizational culture that builds innovation into the business strategy and views it as a basis for winning over time. That is certainly true for the most innovative companies such as Google, Toyota, Microsoft, Nintendo, IBM, Wal-Mart, Amazon, and P&G. These firms also have become skilled in reaching outside their organization to other firms—even firms in other countries—to enhance their ability to innovate. P&G has a goal to source half of its innovation outside the company, a goal that potentially will double their R&D capability. In addition, the firms are good at branding their innovations.

Branding the Innovation

Innovations, no matter how exciting, novel, and relevant, will not energize the business unless they are communicated to the marketplace. Being innovative does not guarantee that a firm is so perceived. Somehow the innovations need to be attached to the brand and to have an extended impact. An innovation that influences for a few months is of limited value and usually represents a lost opportunity to create a long-term asset.

Branding the innovation can make a difference. It can enhance the impact of an innovation and extend its life in the minds of customers. When the innovation is not branded, the impact is usually short-lived if it occurs at all. Putting "new" or "improved" on a box of Tide detergent is unlikely to create a lasting point of differentiation.

Amazon developed a powerful feature, the ability to recommend books and other items based on customers' interests as reflected by their purchase history and the purchase history of those who bought similar offerings. But they never branded it. How tragic is that? As a result, the feature became basically a commodity that is an expected feature of many e-commerce sites. If Amazon had branded it and then actively managed that brand, improving the feature over time, it would have become a lasting point of differentiation that today would be invaluable. They missed a golden opportunity. They did not make that same mistake with One-Click, a branded service that plays a key role in defining Amazon in what has become a messy marketplace.

The problem with sliding innovations into the existing offering is twofold. First, the market is made up of those who are not motivated or perhaps not able to sort out claims and the rationale behind those claims. These people develop a coping strategy that ignores what are seen to be confused and contradictory competitive claims. As a result, the claims of "new and improved" simply fade in the muddled environment. Second, any dramatic visible improvement is likely to be quickly copied or appear to be copied by competitors so that any belief that a unique point of differentiation has been achieved will recede as the perception that competitors have matched the advance carry the day.

Branding changes all that. A new offering can have its own brand (Netflix), endorsed brand (Apple's iPod), or subbrand (Glad Press'n Seal). Further, an innovation that represents a feature (Cadillac's On-Star), ingredient (Dove's Weightless Moisturizer), or service (Best Buy's Geek

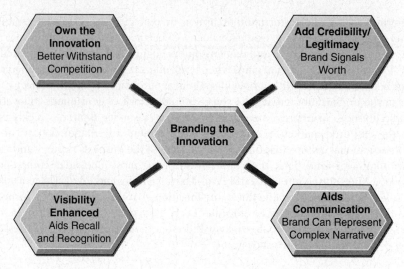

Figure 11.2 Why Brand Innovation?

Squad) could also be branded directly. A brand provides several powerful functions, most of which go back to the basic value of a brand in any context. A brand as summarized in Figure 11.2 allows ownership of the innovation, adds credibility and legitimacy, enhances visibility, and helps communicate sometimes detailed facts.[1]

First and foremost, a brand provides the potential to own an innovation because a brand is a unique indicator of the source of the offering. With the proper investment and active management of both the innovation and its brand, this ownership potential can be extended into the future indefinitely. A competitor may be able to replicate the offering or its new feature, ingredient, or service, but if it is branded, they will need to overcome the power of the brand. Another firm can copy the objective features of Apple's iPod or Westin's Heavenly Bed, but there will only be one authentic product, and that is the one carrying the brand name. In fact, it is sometimes possible to have such a strong brand that it gets credit for innovations by others. Dolby may be an example. An advance in audio technology may be attributed to Dolby no matter where it originates.

Second, a brand can add credibility and legitimacy to a claim. An unbranded claim—such as a "better fabric" or a "more reliable engine"—is likely to be interpreted as another example of puffery. The brand specifically says that the benefit was worth branding, that it is not only meaningful but also impactful. The observer will instinctively believe that there must be a reason why it was branded. Subaru has long emphasized four-wheel drive, and many car brands now offer this feature. Audi, however, has a branded version, Quattro, which gives them a credibility and relevance that the others lack. In essence, there are four-wheel drives, and then there is Quattro.

The ability of a brand to add credibility was rather dramatically shown in a remarkable study of branded attributes. Carpenter, Glazer, and Nakamoto, three prominent academic researchers, found that the inclusion of a branded attribute (such as "Alpine Class" fill for a down jacket, "Authentic Milanese" for pasta, and "Studio Designed" for compact disc players) dramatically affected customer preference toward premium-priced brands.[2] Respondents were able to justify the higher price because of the branded attributes. Remarkably, the effect occurred even when the respondents were given information implying that the attribute was not relevant to their choice.

Third, a brand name can help make the innovation visible because it provides a label for the "news." As a result, it is likely that it will be easier to achieve higher recall and recognition scores around the new offering or a branded feature, ingredient, or service. It is just much easier to remember a brand name such as the Louisville Redbird's baseball team Boardwalk for teens or its Rocky Hopper ride for kids than the details of a new feature or service. In fact, one of the characteristics of a good brand name is that it is easy to recall. Further, the job of linking the point of differentiation to the parent brand is also made much easier. The iPod will be more memorable than Apple's MP3 player.

Fourth, a brand makes communication more efficient and feasible. A new product or product feature, for example, even one regarded as a breakthrough by its designers, may engender a monumental lack of interest among the target audience. Even when the communication registers, it can be perceived as too complex to warrant processing and linking to an offering. The act of giving the product or feature a name can help by providing a vehicle to summarize a lot of information without learning the details. A name such as Oral B's Action Cup provides a way to crystallize detailed characteristics, making it easier to both understand and remember. Imagine if Chevron attempted to explain why "Chevron gasoline" was different without the use of the Techron brand. It would not be persuasive or even feasible.

There is the danger of overbranding, to put brands on innovations that do not warrant brand investments. So there is a yin and yang of branding innovation based on the Shakespeare-inspired conundrum—to brand or not to brand. The solution is to demand that any innovation that is branded have three characteristics. First, it should be a significant advance, not a marginal improvement. Second, it should be meaningful enough to customers to affect purchase and loyalty. Third, it should merit a long-term commitment to building and managing the brand.

The concept of a branded differentiator provides another more formal look at branded innovation.

Branded Differentiators

A *branded differentiator* **is an actively managed, branded feature, ingredient or technology, service, or program that creates a meaningful, impactful point of differentiation for a branded offering over an extended time period.**

For example, the Westin Hotel Chain created the "Heavenly Bed" in 1999, a custom-designed mattress set (by Simmons) with 900 coils, a cozy down blanket adapted for climate, a comforter with a crisp duvet, high-quality sheets, and five goosedown pillows. The Heavenly Bed became a branded differentiator in a crowded category in which differentiation is a challenge.

A branded differentiator does not occur simply by slapping a name on a feature. The definition suggests rather demanding criteria that need to be satisfied. In particular, a branded differentiator needs to be meaningful (that is, it matters to customers) and impactful (that is, not a trivial difference). The Heavenly Bed was meaningful in that it was truly a better bed and addressed the heart of a hotel's promise—to provide a good night's sleep. It was also impactful. During the first year of its life, those hotel sites that featured the Heavenly Bed had a 5 percent increase in customer satisfaction; a noticeable increase in perceptions of cleanliness, room decor, and maintenance; and increased occupancy.

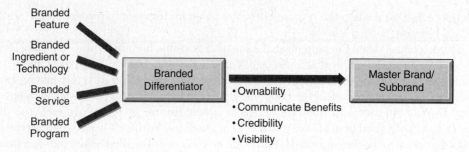

Figure 11.3 Branded Differentiators

A branded differentiator also needs to warrant active management over time and justify brand-building efforts. It should be a moving target. The Heavenly Bed has received that treatment with an active and growing set of brand-building programs. The reception to the bed was so strong that Westin started selling thousands per year. Imagine, selling a hotel bed. Think of the buzz. Further, in 2005 the bed became available in Nordstrom's At Home department. The concept has been extended to the Heavenly Bath, with dual shower heads plus soap and towels. The Heavenly Online Catalog is a place to connect and order all the branded products.

The Heavenly Bed was developed and owned by Westin. It is not always feasible to develop such products and brands, in part because the time and resources may not be available and in part because it is simply difficult. An alternative is to explore alliances in order to create branded differentiators with instant credibility. The Ford Explorer Eddie Bauer Edition, for example, was an offering that sold more than one million vehicles over two decades. It was successful from the outset because the Eddie Bauer brand was established with associations of style, comfort, and the outdoors. Ford never could have achieved that success with its own brand (the Ford Explorer LeatherRide, for example). It would be difficult to imbue such a brand with the self-expressive benefits offered by the Eddie Bauer brand even if the necessary brand-building resources and time had been available.

A branded differentiator, as suggested by Figure 11.3 and the definition, will be a feature, ingredient or technology, service, or program affecting the offering. A branded feature such as General Motor's OnStar often provides a graphic way to signal superior performance. The OnStar system provides automatic notification of air bag deployment to roadside assistance agencies, stolen vehicle location, emergency services, remote door unlocking, remote diagnostics, and concierge services.

A branded ingredient (or component or technology) such as Uniqlo's Heattech, the fabric that absorbs body moisture and turns it into heat so that clothing can keep people worm without layering, has been a key differentiator for the fast-growing retailer. A branded service such as the Tide Stain Detective, which provides stain removal information on the Tide Web site, provides product reinforcement and credibility to Tide. A branded program such as the Harley-Davidson Ride Planner can provide a way to deepen customer relationships.

ENERGIZING THE BRAND AND MARKETING

Relevance and differentiation have long been considered the basis of success for a brand. But recent studies involving the mammoth Y&R's Brand Asset Valuator (BAV) database—70 brand

CREATIVE THINKING METHODS

Not all growth strategies are obvious. In fact, the obvious ones may well be marginal in terms of likely success and impact, so it is useful to look for breakthrough ideas. Methods and concepts of creative thinking can help in this process. Among the guidelines suggested most often are:

- Pursue creative thinking in groups, as multiple perspectives and backgrounds can stimulate unexpected results.
- Begin with warm-up exercises that break down inhibitions. To make whimsy acceptable, for example, ask individuals to identify what animal expresses their personality and to imitate the sound made by that animal. To stretch minds, ask someone to start a story based on two random words (e.g., *blue* and *sail*); then ask the group to create a position for a brand based on that story.
- Focus on a particular task, such as how to build or exploit an asset (a brand name, for example) or a competence (such as the ability to design colorful plastic items).
- Develop options without judging them. Discipline in avoiding evaluation while generating alternatives is a key to creative thinking.
- Engage in lateral thinking to change the perspective of the problem. Make a list of associations with the brand or the use setting and take sets of two as a point of departure, the more incongruous the fit the better, or simply pick a random object or activity (such as *tiger* or *picnic*) to stimulate a new line of thought.
- Evaluate the options based on potential impact without regard to how feasible they are.
- Engage in a second stage of creative thinking aimed at improving the success chances of an attractive option—possibly one with high potential impact that seems too expensive or too difficult to implement.
- Evaluate the final choices not just rationally ("What do the facts say?") but emotionally ("What does your gut say?").
- Create an action plan to go forward.

metrics for each of 40,000 brands spread over 44 countries—find that another component is needed—energy.[3] An analysis of the total database from 1993 to 2007 showed that brand equities as measured by trustworthiness, esteem, perceived quality, and awareness have been falling sharply over the years. For example, in the past 12 years, trustworthiness dropped nearly 50 percent, esteem fell by 12 percent, brand quality perceptions fell by 24 percent, and, remarkably, even awareness fell by 24 percent. Only those brands with energy remained healthy and retained their ability to drive financial return.

Inadequate energy can also lead to relevance problems in two ways. First, as energy declines, so does visibility. The brand is no longer among those that come to mind when considering a purchase. It is lost in the noise of the environment and is therefore no longer considered, which means, by definition, it is not relevant.

Second, many brands that lack energy struggle with impressions that they are old fashioned, out of touch, and boring, an impression that can affect their relevance for some segments. That risk is especially high for the traditional brands of the world such as AT&T, John Deere, Dow, Brooks Brothers, Toshiba, and Wells Fargo Bank, which are usually portrayed as being reliable, honest, dependable, assessable, and often innovative as well. Remember Oldsmobile, which had an ill-fated effort to become "Not your father's Oldsmobile. The remedy for this all too common profile is to inject energy and vitality. The need for energy for mature respected brands is especially true for the key younger segment, the lifeblood of the future.

The best way to energize a business is by improving the offering through innovation. However, that route is not always open. In many cases, successful innovation even with well-conceived efforts and adequate budgets is elusive and infrequent. And innovations that really make a difference, that rise above those that simply maintain a market position, are even rarer. Further, some businesses compete in product categories that are either mature, boring, or both. If you make hot dogs or market insurance, it is hard to conceive of new offerings that are going to energize the brand.

The need is to look beyond the offering for ways to give the brand energy, to make it:

- **Interesting/exciting.** There is a reason to talk about the brand (Disney, AXE, Avon Walk for Breast Cancer, Pixar, FedEx Cup).
- **Involving/engaging.** People are engaged; the brand can be part of a valued activity or lifestyle (Lego, Disney. Starbucks, Google, Amazon).
- **Innovative/dynamic.** The brand is likely to be continually innovative or capable of creating "must-have" innovations that create new subcategories (Apple, Virgin, Dove, GE, 3M).
- **Passionate/purpose driven.** There is a higher purpose that propels passion (Whole Foods Market, Patagonia, Muji, Nike).

Some suggestions follow.

- **Create an involving promotion.** Coke Zero, for example, asked basketball fans to upload their most fanatical videos and photos supporting their favorite teams, and winners were shown in a special show before the championship game.
- **Create a promotion to attract new customers.** Denny's gave away more than two million Grand Slam Breakfasts in one day with the help of a Super Bowl commercial and online buzz. Free breakfasts broke through.
- **Go retail.** The Apple store is a good part of the success of its products and brand because it presents the Apple line in a way that is completely on-brand. Nike and Sony have statement stores that serve to present the brand and offering story in a compelling and integrative way.
- **Bring the brand to the customer.** TaylorMade golf equipment representatives travel to golf clubs to demonstrate and sell its equipment, giving customers a more vivid and on-brand way to experience them than they would get in a sporting goods store. Target created the 30-day Bullseye Bazaar in Chicago to introduce the Tracy Feith Clothing collection, the private-label food line from Archer Farms, and Target furniture.
- **Hold publicity events.** Consider the balloon adventures of Virgin's Richard Branson, the BMW short films created by top directors, or the incredible Red Bull sponsorship of a person jumping out of a balloon 24 miles above the New Mexico desert.
- **Support the higher order purpose.** Whole Foods Markets provides information and support to those interested in organic and natural foods.

The development of a customer community is one of the best ways to energize a brand. It can connect the brand to an activity that a customer sweet spot, as discussed in Chapter 10, that stimulates interest, involvement, and even passion. Consider America Express's Open Forum where small businesses can interact about issues. On the General Mills LiveGlutenFreely site, visitors can access a social network for those interested in gluten-free eating. Bikers on the Harley-Davidson Web site can post pictures of their most recent ride and plan new ones. Beinggirl, the Procter & Gamble feminine care sponsored site, is about the tribulations of 11- to 14-year-old girls.

The key to an effective site is not only to be motivated by the customer's sweet spot rather than the offering or firm but also to engender trust, to have real substance, to have dynamic content, to stimulate interaction, and to be on-brand. Not easy, but the payoff can be significant.

Another approach, very different than trying to make the brand or business interesting or involving, is to find something with energy and attach your brand to it and build a marketing program around the connection. Find a branded energizer.

Branded Energizers

A *branded energizer* **is a branded product, sponsorship, endorser, promotion, symbol, social program, CEO, or other entity that by association significantly enhances and energizes a target brand. The branded energizer and its association with the target brand are actively managed over an extended time period.**

As Figure 11.4 and the definition suggest, a branded energizer can be a wide variety of branded entities and should have several characteristics. First, a branded energizer should itself have energy and vitality as opposed to being lethargic. An effective branded energizer should do well when asked whether it would be described as being:

- Interesting vs. stale
- Youthful vs. mature
- Interesting vs. boring
- Dynamic vs. unchanging
- Contemporary vs. traditional

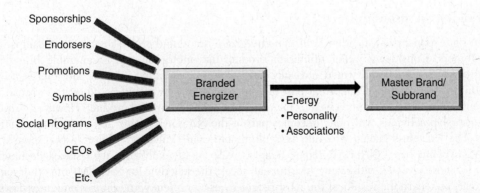

Figure 11.4 Branded Energizers

- Assertive vs. passive
- Involving vs. separated

Second, the branded energizer needs to be connected to the master brand even if, unlike a branded differentiator, it is not part of the master brand offering and does not promise any functional benefits. This connection task can be difficult and expensive. Even the Energizer bunny, one of the top icons among U.S. brands, is associated by some with Duracell rather than Energizer despite the exposure over a long time period.

One connection route is to use a subbrand such as Ronald McDonald House, where the master brand has a connection in the name. A second is to select a program or activity that is so "on-brand" that it makes the link easier to establish. A baby-oriented program would require little effort to connect to Gerber. A third is to simply forge the link by consistently building it over time with significant link-building resources, as MetLife has done with the Peanuts characters.

Third, a branded energizer should significantly enhance as well as energize the target brand and should not detract or damage the brand by being "off-brand" or making customers uncomfortable. Offbeat, underdog brands such as Virgin, Apple, and Mountain Dew, which are perceived as quirky to begin with, have more leeway. "Senior" brands, in contrast, can develop branded energizers that are edgier than the parent brand but with a lot of options foreclosed.

Fourth, the problems of finding and managing internal branded energizers leads firms to look outside the organization. The challenge is to find an external energizer brand that is linked into the lifestyle of customers, that will have the needed associations to energize and enhance, that is not tied to competitors, that can be linked to the target brand, and that represents a manageable alliance. The task takes discipline and creativity.

Fifth, branded energizers (like branded differentiators) represent a long-term commitment; the brands involved should be expected to have a long life and merit brand-building investments. If the energizers are internally developed, the cost of brand building will have to be amortized over a long enough period to make it worthwhile. If they are externally sourced, the cost and effort of linking them to the parent brand will take time as well. And they need to be actively managed over time so that they can continue to be successful in their roles. The concepts of branded energizers and differentiators do *not* provide a rationale to add brands indiscriminately.

There are many types of branded energizers. Some of the most useful include sponsorships, symbols, endorsers, promotions, programs, and even CEOs.

Branded Sponsorships

The right sponsorship, handled well, can energize a brand and create strong relationships with customers. Consider a rather utilitarian product like motor oil and a venerable brand like Valvoline. Such a brand would normally have trouble generating interest and energy, to say nothing of becoming an important part of a person's life. Few would be motivated to read ads about motor oil, which is perceived by many to be an undifferentiated product. However, through sponsorship activities, Valvoline becomes part of the NASCAR scene, and everything changes.

The Valvoline racing program is multidimensional. Valvoline is not just a sponsor of NASCAR but has a NASCAR racing team as well. At the Valvoline Web site, a destination site for those involved with racing, a visitor can access the schedule for NASCAR and other racing circuits and learn the results of the most recent races, complete with pictures and interviews. A "Behind Closed Garage Doors" section provides inside information and analyses. The visitor can adopt the Valvoline NASCAR racing team and learn about their current activities and recent finishes. In addition, it is possible to send Valvoline racing greeting cards, buy Valvoline racing gear, download a Valvoline racing screensaver, and sign up for a weekly newsletter (*TrackTalk*) that provides updates on the racing circuits. Valvoline thus becomes closely associated with the racing experience, much more than simply being a logo on a car.

The core segment for Valvoline is buyers who change their own oil, are very involved in cars, and live for NASCAR races. The Valvoline racing program has the potential to influence this group in several ways. At a most basic level, it provides credibility and associations of being a leader in motor oil technology. Top teams would not use Valvoline if it was not superior—there is too much riding on the engine's performance. But there are more subtle possibilities. A customer, by choosing Valvoline, can receive self-expressive benefits, as it is a way to tangentially associate oneself with the top drivers and teams. And research shows that it has tangible benefits. One study found that 47 percent of the U.S. public had an interest in watching NASCAR racing. In another, 60 percent of NASCAR fans said they trusted sponsors' products (compared with 30 percent of NFL fans), and more than 40 percent switch brands when a company becomes a sponsor.[4]

A sponsorship can provide the ultimate in relevance, the movement of a brand upward into the acceptable if not leadership position. A software firm trying unsuccessfully to make a dent in the European market became a perceived leader in a few months when it sponsored one of the top three bicycle racing teams. Part of Samsung's breakthrough from being just another Korean price brand to becoming a real player in the U.S. market was its sponsorship of the Olympics, which began with the Winter games in 1988. It says so much about the brand, so much more than product advertising could ever say. Tracking data confirm that well-conceived and well-managed sponsorships can make a difference. The Visa lead in perceived credit card superiority went from 15 percentage points prior to the Olympics to 30 points during to 20 points one month after— huge movements in what are normally very stable attitudes.[5]

A significant problem with sponsorship—indeed, with any external branded energizer—is linking it to the brand. DDB Needham's Sponsor-Watch, which measures such linkage, has shown that sponsorship confusion is common.[6] Of the 102 official Olympic sponsors tracked since 1984, only about half have built a link (defined as having sponsor awareness of at least 15 percent and at least 10 percent higher than that of a competitor that was not a sponsor—hardly demanding criteria). Those successful at creating links, such as Visa and Samsung, surround the sponsorship with a host of brand-driven activities, including promotions, publicity events, Web site content, newsletters, and advertising, over an extended time period.

Although most sponsorships are external to the firm, there are cases of internally controlled sponsorships. The Adidas Streetball Challenge is a branded weekend event centered around local three-person basketball tournaments and featuring free-throw competitions, a street dance, graffiti events, and extreme sports demonstrations, all accompanied by live music from bands from the hip-hop and rap scenes. The Challenge was right in the sweet spot of target customers, a party. And it was connected to Adidas by its brand and supporting signage and Adidas-supplied caps and jackets. It revitalized Adidas at a critical time in its history. Owning a sponsorship means that the cost going forward is both controllable and predictable and the event can evolve over time.

Endorsers

A brand may lack energy, but there are plenty of personalities who are contemporary, on-brand, energetic, and interesting. Think of what LeBron James brings to not only Nike but also

Coca-Cola, State Farm, and McDonald's. And Roger Federer to Gillette, Mercedes, Rolex, Credit Swiss, and Wilson.

Selecting and engaging an endorser is a critical first stop in creating a strategic brand energizer. There are a host of considerations. An endorser target should have:

- An appealing image
  - Visible among the target audience (low visibility will limit the impact)
  - Attractive, liked (simple liking can and does get transferred to the endorsed brand)
  - Sincere (will there be a feeling that the endorser is doing it for money and lacks a sincere belief in the product?)
  - Fresh, not overexposed (an endorser's impact can be diluted by overexposure as an endorser)
- On-brand associations
  - Matching the brand identity goals
  - A natural match to the brand (does the link make sense?)
  - Confidence that the positive associations can be leveraged and that the negative ones can be managed
- Potential for a long-term relationship (how long will the endorser have the desired associations and how likely will it be that a compatible relationship will endure?)
- Potential to create programs surrounding the endorser
- Cost effectiveness and availability, which need to take into account the cost of the programs surrounding the endorser

Branded Promotional Activities

Kraft's Oscar Mayer Wienermobiles provide energy to a very boring category. There are eight vehicles shaped like a huge Oscar Mayer Weiner touring the United States, with license plates with appropriate wording like "HOT DOG." They turn up at events and parties and support the annual contest to find a child to sing the signature Oscar Mayer jingle. The Wienermobile, which has been shown to bump the product sales, also lives on the Web, where visitors can be taken on a tour of Oscartown featuring the Oscar Museum, the OscarMart, and Town Hall. The brand Weinermobile, by its linkage to the product category, also links it to Oscar Mayer.

Memorable Branded Symbols

Brands that are blessed with strong relevant symbols such as the Pillsbury Doughboy, the Maytag repairman, P&G's Mr. Clean, the Redbird's Rocky, or the Michelin Man can actively manage and use the symbols to become energizer brands. Such symbols can give a personality to even the blandest of brands. They can also suggest attributes. The Doughboy is upbeat, with a sense of humor, and means freshness and superb quality. The Maytag repairman is relaxed and confident and symbolizes the reliability of Maytag. The Michelin Man is strong and positive and means safety. Mr. Clean is strong and reliable. Rocky is fun, friendly, and energetic.

Symbols can be leased as well as developed. MetLife adopted the Peanuts characters in 1985. Their goal was to provide a warm, light, nonthreatening approach to insurance—a tough sell in the context of an industry perceived by many to be boring, greedy, and bureaucratic. The familiar, funny characters provide a vehicle toward those objectives while also providing interest and energy. Snoopy's appearance on the Web site, on a blimp (which costs $2.5 million each per year), in ads, and even on the logo also serves to inhibit what psychologists call counterarguing. The natural tendency to be cynical toward an insurance company's ad or claim is reduced for MetLife in the presence of the likable Snoopy, in part because it would make no sense to argue with a cartoon character.

Another tact is to introduce or enhance a lively, humorous personality. Most competitors are serious about their offerings, and a business that takes itself lightly will often stand out. This is especially true in the insurance industry. Aflac made great strides on the awareness front by developing the Aflac duck, and MetLife has benefited from associations with the Peanuts characters.

It is important to understand the role of the symbol. Is it to create a personality? To suggest or reinforce associations? To be a vehicle to interject humor and likability into an otherwise bland and uninteresting message? To create interest and visibility, like the duck has done for Aflac? With the role in mind, it is possible to proactively look for or develop the right one.

Branded Social Programs

Branded social programs can pay off by providing the basis of a customer relationship based on trust and respect. However, they can also provide energy by generating interesting ideas and programs and even passion, tangible results, and opportunities for customer involvement. Consider the energy created by the Avon Breast Cancer Crusade with its signature Avon Walk for Breast Cancer, a program with substance (they have raised over $550 million for the fight against breast cancer) and incredible involvement not only with participants of the walks but the family members and sponsors as well. That interest and energy could never have been created by new Avon products, however different they might be. And it is branded as Avon, which means that its track record is linked to Avon.

Creating branded social programs can effectively be costless in that existing philanthropy dollars that are being spent without focus or impact can be diverted into branded social programs. However, they are also extremely hard to generate; there are firms that would like to create an Avon Walk program but simply can't come up with one. Kellie McElhaney, the Director of the Center for Responsible Business at the Haas School at UC Berkeley, has suggested several principles to guide development of a branded social program:[7]

Know thyself. The goal is to create branded programs that are authentic and effective. Ideally, they should support the business strategy, draw on firm assets and competencies, and enhance the image of the brand. That means that the firm should address very basic questions as to who they are, their strengths and weaknesses, and what they want to stand for.

Get a good fit. Being authentic, being connected to the program, and being effective will all be easier if there is a fit. Avon's program hits on a key concern of their target market and reflects a relationship with their customers that goes beyond product. The same can be said with Crest's Healthy Smiles (low-cost dental care for poor children), Home Depot's relationship with Habitat for Humanity, and Dove's Real Women. In contrast, the Ford association with the "Susan G. Komen for the Cure" breast cancer foundation (with its donations attached to buying a pink-trimmed Mustang) lacks a logical fit.

Brand it. If the program has a strong visible brand, it will be much more likely that people will learn and remember. Whirlpool is linked to the Habitat for Humanity program of building homes for less fortunate, a strong brand. Another challenge is to link the program brand to the brand to which it is lending energy. In the case of Home Depot, that is done with in-store communication and promotion and by having its employees involved in working on Habitat projects. An owned brand such as Ronald McDonald House or Avon Breast Cancer Crusade has the advantage of having the corporate brand as part of the program brand.

Create emotional connection. An emotional connection in general communicates much stronger than does a set of facts and logic. The message is punchier and simpler. Further, an emotional connection will tend to enhance the relationship between the brand to which it is attached and the customer. So Pedigree Adoption Drive with its pictures of adorable dogs triggers an emotional response. Ronald McDonald House presents a program that helps children with serious medical conditions and their families.

Communicate the program. There are a host of companies that are spending real money on programs that are unknown to their customers and, often, even to their employees. To achieve its objectives of advancing a social cause, energizing the employees, and enhancing the reputation of a corporate brand, the program needs to be communicated. That involves accessing the right set of communication vehicles including the Web site, social technology, PR, and active employees. Beware of making it too complex, too detailed, too quantitative. Simple with understandable symbols, taglines, and stories is what is needed. Metaphors can help—too much CO_2, for example, might be likened to a bathtub, now half full, that will eventually overflow.

Involve the customers. Involvement is the ultimate way to gain supporters and advocates. Method, a maker of environmentally safe cleaning products, has a brand ambassador program in which customers who sign on will get products and T-shirts and information about why their friends should use the product. Avon's Walk for Breast Cancer involves hundreds of thousands each year either as participants or supporters of walkers.

Branded CEOs

Some firms have branded CEOs who can serve to capture and magnify the energy in the brand or even create energy that can be transferred to the brand. Lee Iacocca helped save Chrysler by exuding confidence and competence when customers and investors had assumed the firm would collapse. Richard Branson's outlandish stunts (some involving hot-air balloons) have been a large part of the energy and personality of the Virgin brand. Herb Kelleher personified the Southwest Airlines brand with his visible and colorful expression of its culture. Steve Jobs and Bill Gates have driven much of the energy of Apple and Microsoft with their visible thought leadership.

The right CEO with the right message can often create news with credibility and has the advantage of being able to access media. To be an energizer, however, the CEO should have energy with respect to ideas, have a distinctive personality, and be around for a long enough time period to become a recognized representative of the brand.

INCREASING THE USAGE OF EXISTING CUSTOMERS

Attempts to increase market share will very likely affect competitors directly and therefore precipitate competitor responses. An alternative, attempting to increase usage among current customers, is usually less threatening to competitors.

When developing programs to increase usage, it is useful to begin by asking some fundamental questions about the user and the consumption system in which the product is

Strategy	Examples
Motivate heavy users to use more	Perks with more season tickets
Make the use easier	Microwaveable containers
Provide incentives	Frequent flyer miles
Remove or reduce reasons not to buy	Gentle shampoo for frequent use
Provide reminder communication	E-mail birthday reminder
Position for regular use	Floss after meals
Find new uses	Snowmobiles for delivery

Figure 11.5   Increasing Usage in Existing Product Markets

embedded. Why isn't the product or service used more? What are the barriers to increased use? Who are the light users, and can they be influenced to use more? What about the heavy users?

Greater usage can be precipitated in two ways, by increasing either the frequency of use or the quantity used. In either case, there are several approaches that can be effective (see Figure 11.5). All are based on becoming obsessed with what stimulates use and the use experience itself.

Motivate Heavy Users to Use More

Heavy users are usually the most fruitful target. It is often easier to get a holder of two football season tickets to buy four or six than it is to get an occasional attendee of games to buy two. It is helpful to look at the extra-heavy user subsegment—special treatment might solidify and expand usage by a substantial amount. Examples include Schwab's Gold Signature Services, the special dinner parties and courier service offered by Chase Manhattan to its biggest accounts, or the first-class treatment provided to high rollers by Las Vegas casinos.

Make the Use Easier

Asking why customers do not use a product or service more often can lead to approaches that make the product easier to use. For example, a Dixie cup or paper-towel dispenser encourages use by reducing the usage effort. Packages that can be placed directly in a microwave make usage more convenient. A reservation service can help those who must select a hotel or similar service. The classic but long-dormant Crock-Pot slow cookers were in 80 percent of homes but used by only 20 percent. A hot product in the early 1970s, it fell victim to out-of-home eating but is making a sharp comeback in part due to a desire to have home-cooked meals with minimal preparation. A catalyst is the Banquet line of frozen entrees called Banquet Crock-Pot Classics, which have made the process of cooking with the Crock-Pot much easier.

Provide Incentives

Incentives can be provided to increase consumption frequency. Promotions such as double mileage trips offered by airlines with frequent-flyer plans can increase usage. A fast-food restaurant might offer a large drink at a discounted price if it is purchased with a meal. A challenge is to structure the incentive so that usage is increased without creating a vehicle for debilitating price competition. Price incentives, such as two for the price of one, can be effective, but they also may stimulate price retaliation.

Remove or Reduce the Reasons Not to Buy

A business often reaches a ceiling because there are potential buyers who have a reason not to buy or to buy more. Thus, bags of snacks with 100 calories provide a way for users to partake without losing control of their eating habits. Hyundai addressed the problem of job insecurity with the breathtaking offer to buy back a car if the buyer lost his or her job. A gentle shampoo could be used daily.

Provide Reminder Communications

For some use contexts, awareness or recall of a brand is the driving force. People who know about a brand and its use may not think to use it on particular occasions without reminders.

Reminder communication may be necessary. An e-mail program to remind Wine.com customers about an upcoming birthday may ensure that they buy a present. Several brands, including Jell-O, have conducted advertising campaigns aimed at getting their product out of the cupboard and onto the table. It is not enough for people to have recipes if they never get around to using them. Routine maintenance functions such as dental checkups or car lubrication are easily forgotten, and reminders can make a difference.

Position for Regular or Frequent Use

Provide a reason for more frequent use. On Web sites, what works is to have information that is frequently updated. People go to My Yahoo to see the latest headlines or learn how their stocks are doing, as often as every few minutes when important things are happening. Other incentives might include a new cartoon each day at a teen Web site or a best-practices bulletin board at a brand consulting site.

The image of a product can change from that of occasional to frequent usage through a repositioning campaign. For example, the advertising campaigns for Clinique's "twice-a-day" moisturizer and "three glasses of milk per day" both represent efforts to change the perception of the products involved. The use of programs such as the Book-of-the-Month Club, CD clubs, DVD clubs, and flower-of-the-month or fruit-of-the-month delivery can turn infrequent purchasers into regular ones.

Find New Uses

The detection and exploitation of a new functional use for a brand can rejuvenate a business that has been considered a has-been for years. Jell-O, for example, began strictly as a dessert product but found major sources of new sales in applications such as Jell-O salads. Another classic story is that of Arm & Hammer baking soda, which saw annual sales grow 10-fold by persuading people to use its product as a refrigerator deodorizer. An initial 14-month advertising campaign boosted the use as a deodorizer from 1 to 57 percent. The brand subsequently was extended into other deodorizer products, dentifrices, and laundry detergent. A chemical process used in oil fields to separate waste from oil found a new application when it was applied to water plants to eliminate unwanted oil. Kraft encouraged people to use cream cheese, stuck in the bagels for breakfast slot, with crackers or celery as a snack.

New uses can best be identified by conducting market research to determine exactly how customers use a brand. From the set of uses that emerge, several can be selected to pursue. Customer application tracking allowed BENGAY to learn that much of its volume was going toward arthritis sufferers. A separate marketing strategy was developed, and the result was a wave of growth. Another tactic is to look at the applications of competing products. The widespread use of raisins prompted Ocean Spray to create dried cranberries, which can be found in cookies and in cereal such as Müeslix with a "made with real Ocean Spray cranberries" seal on the package. They are also being sold as a snack food called Ocean Spray Craisins.

Sometimes a large payoff will result for a firm that can provide applications not currently in general use. Thus, surveys of current applications may be inadequate. Firms such as General Mills have sponsored recipe contests, one objective of which has been to create new uses for a product by discovering a new "recipe classic." For a product that can be used in many ways, such as stick-on labels, it might be worthwhile to conduct formal brainstorming sessions or other creative exercises.

If some application area is uncovered that could create substantial sales, it needs to be evaluated. Consideration needs to be given to the possibility that a competitor will take over an application area, whether through product improvement, heavy advertising, or engaging in price warfare. Can the brand achieve a sustainable advantage in its new application to justify building the business? Ocean Spray is associated with cranberries, which might protect its entry into a cranberry snack, but the firm's name will be less helpful in a processed application such as cookies or cereals.

KEY LEARNINGS

- Energizing an existing business is a fruitful source of growth because it avoids the risks of venturing into new competitive arenas requiring new assets and competencies.

- Improving the offering through innovation is always the best route to growth and profitability. However, innovations can represent short-lived advantages unless branded. A brand provides ownability, credibility, visibility, and communicability. A branded differentiator is an actively managed, branded feature, ingredient or technology, service, or program that creates a meaningful, impactful point of differentiation for a branded offering over an extended time period.

- Sometimes innovation is not feasible, and then energizing the brand/marketing or creating a branded energizer is the best option. A branded energizer is a branded product, promotion, sponsorship, symbol, program, or other entity that by association significantly enhances and energizes a target brand—the branded energizer and its association with the target brand are actively managed over an extended time period.

- Growth less vulnerable to competitive response can also come from increasing product usage by motivating heavy users to use more, making the use easier by removing or reducing reasons not to buy, providing usage incentives, reminder communications, positioning for frequent use, and finding new use.

FOR DISCUSSION

1. Why are Apple, Google, Toyota, Microsoft, Nintendo, IBM, HP, Wal-Mart, Amazon, and P&G considered innovative? Did branding play a role? For which brands? What other brands would you nominate? Why? What role did branding play in your judgment for those brands?

2. Think of some highly differentiated brands. Do they have branded differentiators? If not, how did they achieve differentiation? Will it be lasting?

3. Think of some branded differentiators. How differentiated are they? Do the customers care? Are they impactful? Have they been managed well over time? Do they have legs? Evaluate Best Buy's Geek Squad.

4. Think of some brands that have high energy. What gives them that energy? Will that continue into the future?

5. Think of some brands that have branded energizers that made a difference. Evaluate them in terms of whether they are "on-brand," energetic, and linked to the master brand.

6. Using the creative thinking guidelines, think about how you would increase the usage of products or services if you were the manager of:
   a. Doritos
   b. Charles Schwab
   c. GAP

NOTES

1. Branded differentiators and branded energizers are introduced and discussed in more detail in Chapter 5 of David Aaker, *Brand Portfolio Strategy*, New York: The Free Press, 2005.

2. Gregory S. Carpenter, Rashi Glazer, and Kent Nakamoto, "Meaningful Brands from Meaningless Differentiation: The Dependence on Irrelevant Attributes," *Journal of Marketing Research*, August 1994, pp. 339–350.

3. John Gerzema and Ed Lebar, *The Brand Bubble*, San Francisco: Jossey-Bass, 2008, Chapters 1 and 2.

4. Kevin Lane Keller, *Strategic Brand Management*, 2nd ed. Saddle River, NJ: Prentice Hall, 2003, p. 317.

5. James Crimmins and Martin Horn, "Sponsorship: From Management Ego Trip to Marketing Success," *Journal of Advertising Research*, July–August 1996, pp. 11–21.

6. Ibid.

7. Kellie A. McElhaney, *Just Good Business*, San Francisco: Berrett-Koehler Publishers, 2008.

CHAPTER TWELVE

Leveraging the Business

Results are gained by exploiting opportunities, not by solving problems.
—Peter Drucker

The more opportunities I seize, the more opportunities multiply before me.
—Sun Tzu

The most dangerous moment comes with victory.
—Napoleon

*U*ltimately, growth avenues outside the existing business need to be explored. While it is risky to leave the comfort of the familiar and the tested, it also removes the ceiling on the firm's growth potential. There is virtually unlimited potential when you agree to extend the business.

The goal discussed in this chapter is to leverage the existing business into new product markets. The assets and competencies of the business, in particular, are potential sources of advantage in a new marketplace. The capabilities around marketing skills, distribution clout, developing and manufacturing products, R&D, and brand equities are among the potential bases for advantage for a new growth business. The idea is to build on the core business to create a synergy. The challenge, though, is to achieve real synergy with real impact on the customer value proposition, costs, or investments. Too often, apparent synergy is not realized.

The spectrum of available choices can be categorized generally as to how removed they are from the core business. Those that are close will represent less risk and have the greatest chance of leveraging business assets and competencies to achieve a real advantage. As more distance is allowed from the current business, opportunities become more plentiful, but the risk goes up as well. It can be difficult to gain the necessary knowledge and operational competence to run a business successfully that is far removed from one's core abilities. Of course, creating a new core business can have a huge upside, and taking the risk of moving far from the core business may pay off. But the risk should be visible and part of the analysis.

There are many ways to generate growth options that leverage the core business. Creative thinking processes, introduced in Chapter 11, can help. Good outcomes more often come from having good options on the table rather than making optimal decisions among mediocre ones.

The creative-thinking exercises can best be engaged around the following series of questions, which have proved to be a good source of options.

- Which assets and competencies can be leveraged?
- What brand extensions are possible?
- Can the scope of the offering be expanded?
- Do viable new markets exist?

After these questions have been discussed, some option evaluation issues will be addressed and, finally, the critical concept of synergy will be analyzed.

WHICH ASSETS AND COMPETENCIES CAN BE LEVERAGED?

A focus on assets and competencies starts by creating an inventory in order to identify the real strengths of the business. In doing so, the discussion in Chapter 3 around identifying and evaluating assets and competencies can be helpful. What are the key assets and competencies that are supporting the core business? What are their characteristics? How strong is each?

The second step is to find a business area where the assets and competencies can be applied to generate an advantage. A line of greeting cards sold through drugstores might have an artistic capability and a distribution asset that could be leveraged. What other items are in drugstores that might employ artistic talents? Are there items in the drugstore that the retailers have difficulty sourcing, for whatever reason? A retailer problem might suggest an opportunity.

One fruitful exercise is to examine each asset for excess capacity. Are some assets underutilized? A legal firm that considered this question took advantage of excess office space to offer tax services. A supermarket chain with obsolete sites went into the discount liquor business. A cookie plant began making muffins. If a growth initiative can use excess capacity, a substantial, sustainable cost advantage could result.

The final step is to address implementation problems. Assets and competencies may require adaptations when applied to a different business. Further, new capabilities may have to be found or developed. Existing core businesses are sometimes best leveraged by making an acquisition because developing the business internally may not be economic or even feasible. When acquisitions are involved, two organizations with different systems, people, and cultures will have to be merged. Many efforts at achieving synergy falter because of implementation difficulties.

As the partial list profiled in Chapter 3 suggests, there are a wide range of exportable assets and competencies. To give a flavor of the opportunities, consider the following: marketing skills, sales and distribution capacity, design and manufacturing skills, and R&D capabilities.

Marketing Skills

A firm will often either possess or lack strong marketing skills for a particular market. Thus, a frequent motive for expanding into new product markets is to export or import marketing skills. Black & Decker had developed and exploited an aggressive new-products program (e.g., cordless screwdrivers and HandyChopper), effective consumer marketing (for brands such as Space-Maker, DustBuster, and ThunderVolt cordless tools), and intensive customer service and dealer relations. The acquisition of Ernhart, with its branded door locks, decorative faucets, outdoor lighting, and racks, provided Black & Decker with an opportunity to apply its marketing skills and distribution clout to a firm that lacked a marketing culture.

Applying marketing skills is not always as easy as it appears. Philip Morris, a successful marketer of Miller Lite and other brands, failed with 7-Up, which it attempted to position as a caffeine-free soft drink in response to health interests of consumers. After a seven-year battle, Philip Morris gave up and sold the line. The problems that beset Philip Morris included the reaction of competitors who rushed caffeine-free drinks to the market, the power of existing distributors, and the limited appeal of lemon-lime drinks. Coca-Cola made a similar misjudgment when it created Wine Spectrum and failed in its efforts to overcome Gallo, in part because of Gallo's control over distribution.

Capacity in Sales or Distribution

A firm with a strong distribution capability may add products or services that could exploit that capability. Thus, Black & Decker's distribution strength helped provide a boost to the Ernhart lines. A joint venture between Nestlé and Coca-Cola in the canned tea business combined Coke's distribution strength with the product knowledge and name of Nestlé.

E-commerce firms such as Amazon or Wine.com often have operations that can add capacity just by adding a button to access another product group. The result can be additional sales and margins to offset the fixed costs of the operation.

Design and Manufacturing Skills

Design and manufacturing ability can be the basis for entry into a new business area. The ability to design and make small motors helped Honda succeed in the motorcycle business and led to its entry into lawn-care equipment, outboard motors, and a host of other products. The ability to make small products has been a key for Sony as it has moved from product to product in consumer electronics. Schwinn's experience with bicycles provided a basis to market the stylish Tailwind electric bike that features a 30-minute fast charge.

R&D Skills

Expertise in a certain technology can lead to a new business based on that technology. GE's early research has spawned very successful businesses. For example, its research on turbines for electricity generation provided the basis for its aircraft engine business, and its light bulb research provided the foundation for what became the medical instrumentation business. P&G has actively applied technology from one business area to another such as fragrance technology applied to detergents to create both incremental and game-changing innovation. In general, breakthroughs in a business area tend to come from technologies owned by other industries. Creativity, often in short supply, is needed to provide opportunities for basic technology and the R&D capability that supports it.

BRAND EXTENSIONS

One common exportable asset is a strong, established brand name—a name with visibility, associations, and loyalty among a customer group. The challenge is to take this brand asset and use it to enter new product markets. The name can make the task of establishing a new product more feasible and efficient because it makes developing awareness, trust, interest, and action all easier.

Lenox, a maker of fine china, exploited its traditional, high-quality image and its distribution system by expanding into the areas of jewelry and giftware. H&R Block added legal services to its chain of income tax services, hoping to gain synergy by exploiting (and enhancing) its brand. A ski boot manufacturer leveraged its brand into skis and then ski clothing.

Many firms have built large, diverse businesses around a strong brand, including Sony, IBM, Siemens, GE, Schwab, Virgin, Mitsubishi, and Disney. More than 300 businesses carry the Virgin name, and all gain from the public-relations flair of Richard Branson, its owner. Mitsubishi has its name on thousands of products, each of which contributes two benefits that are often under-appreciated, name exposure and cumulative new-product vitality.

Disney, founded in 1923 as a cartoon company with Mickey Mouse (made famous in the cartoon "Steamboat Willie") as its initial asset, might be the most successful firm ever at leveraging its brand. In the 1950s, the company built Disneyland and launched a long running TV show (*The Wonderful World of Disney*), dramatically changing the brand by making it much richer and deeper than before. Particularly after extending the theme parks to Florida, Paris, and Japan; establishing its own retail stores, resorts, and a cruise line; and supporting a host of Disney-endorsed offerings such as the California Adventure Park, Disney can deliver an experience that goes far beyond watching cartoons. As a result of this brand power, the Disney Channel has become a strong, differentiated TV network, an incredible achievement if you consider what others have put into that space.

It is instructive to see why Disney has done so well with an aggressive brand extension strategy. First, from the beginning, the company has known what it stands for—magical family entertainment, executed with consistent excellence. Everything Disney does reinforces that brand identity; when it went into adult films, it did so under the name Touchstone rather than Disney. Second, Disney has a relentless, uncompromising drive for operational excellence that started with Walt Disney's fanatical concern for detail in the earliest cartoons and theme parks. The parks are run so well that Disney holds schools for other firms seeking to learn how to maintain energy and consistency. The cruise line was delayed, despite ballooning costs, until everything was judged perfect. Third, the organization actively manages a host of subbrands that have their own identities, including Mickey Mouse, Donald Duck, a mountain (the Matterhorn), a song ("It's a Small World"), film characters such as Mary Poppins and the Lion King, and on and on. Fourth, Disney understands synergy across products. *The Lion King* is not only a film but also supports a Broadway musical and an exhaustive set of promotions at fast-food chains and elsewhere.

Brand extension options can be created by determining the current brand image and what products and services would fit these associations (see Figure 12.1). In what arenas would the

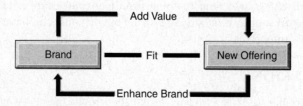

Figure 12.1   Brand Extension Logic

brand be considered relevant? McDonald's has associations with fun and kids, fast delivery of consistent food, Big Macs, and fries. The fun and kids might suggest a theme park, a line of toys, or a day-care center.

A brand, of course, can evolve over time in part by the brand extensions and then get permission to drive a broader assortment of offerings. So the addition of a healthy submenu to McDonald's may allow the firm to venture into areas that would have not made sense before. Virgin was a record company, and an airline under that brand name made no sense. But after the organization became not only successful but also known for an over-the-top attitude, customer service and innovation, and an ability to face up to large, established competitors, its new associations provided the basis to go into a host of business areas.

The evaluation of each extension alternative is based on three questions. Each must be answered in the affirmative for the extension to be viable.

1. *Does the brand fit the new product context?* If the customer is uncomfortable and senses a lack of fit, acceptance will not come easily. The brand may not be seen as having the needed credibility or expertise, or it may have the wrong associations for the context. In general, successful extensions will have one or more bases of fit such as a:

- Base product—Starbucks Frappuccino (a packaged drink), VIA (instant coffee), and Dreyer's Starbucks Coffee Ice Cream
- Companion product—Coppertone sunglasses, Duracell Durabeam flashlights
- Common user—Gerber baby clothing, The Mint Cookie (Girl Scout) Blizzard
- Distinctive attribute/benefit—Arm & Hammer Carpet Deodorizer, Sunkist Vitamin C
- Expertise—Mr. Clean Performance Car Washes, Zagat Physician Rating, David Beckham (Soccer) Academy
- Personality/self-expressive benefits—Pierre Cardin Wallets, Hooter's Airline

In general, a brand that has strong ties to a product class and attributes (for example, Boeing, Netflix, or Kleenex) will have a more difficult time stretching than a brand that is associated with intangibles such as a brand personality. Thus, brands like Disney, Virgin, and Gucci have permission to extend further. In a TippingSprung survey of brand extensions, consumers were not enthused about Burger King men's apparel, Kellogg hip-hop streetwear, Allstate Green insurance, and Playboy energy drink in part because of a fit problem.[1]

2. *Does the brand add value to the offering in the new product class?* A customer should be able to express why the brand would be preferred in its new context. Despite the fact that cruise ships are difficult to tell apart, nearly anyone could verbalize rather clearly how a Disney cruise ship would be different from others—it would have Disney characters aboard, contain more kids and families, and provide magical family entertainment. Coppertone sunglasses, the top rated extension in the TippingSprung survey, would be expected to benefit from the years of experience that Coppertone has with activities in the sun.[2] Mr. Clean Performance Car Washes, the second rated extension in the same survey, offers the credibility of the Mr. Clean brand to an area that can have high variability of service. Starbucks provides a premium quality association to its Frappuccino and VIA lines and a sense of authenticity to coffee-flavored ice cream.

If the brand name does not add value in the eyes of the customer, the extension will be vulnerable to competition. For example, Pillsbury Microwave Popcorn initially benefited from the Pillsbury name but was vulnerable to the entry of an established popcorn name. Thus, although Orville Redenbacher entered the microwave category late, it still won with a name that meant quality and authenticity in popcorn. Rice-a-Roni's Savory Classics did not fit the consumer's notion of the role of Rice-a-Roni in the kitchen. The Arm & Hammer name also spawned two failures—a spray underarm deodorant, for which the Arm & Hammer name may have had the wrong connotations, and a spray disinfectant.

A concept test can help determine what value is added by the brand. Prospective customers can be given only the brand name and then asked whether they would be attracted to the product and why. If they cannot articulate a specific reason why the offering would be attractive to them, it is unlikely that the brand name will add significant value.

3. *Will the extension enhance the brand name and image?* With the focus on the extension, its impact on the brand can be overlooked. An extension that fails or has inappropriate associations can damage the brand. The ideal is to have extensions that will provide visibility, energy, and associations that support the brand. Coach was a successful but a bit stodgy maker of leather bags until it hired a new designer and extended the brand to hats, shoes, sunglasses, coats, watches, and even straw beach hats, all with the signature "C" in leather. The extensions provided energy to the brand and helped attract younger customers, who are vital to the firm's long-term future. Sunkist's associations with oranges, health, and vitality are reinforced by the promotion of Sunkist juice bases and vitamin C tablets, while Sunkist fruit rolls may be a risk. Coppertone sunglasses, Mr. Clean Performance Car Washes, and Starbucks Frappuccino and VIA all provide meaningful visibility to the brand. These extensions need to deliver on the brand promise to avoid harming the brand. Coppertone sunglasses need to have sun protection and not just be a stylish design, and Mr. Clean and the Starbucks extensions need to deliver the experience that will be expected for the brand to be enhanced rather than compromised.

If an extension will damage the brand but represents a viable business opportunity, another brand option needs to be found. When Gap introduced a value chain and called it Gap Warehouse, the Gap brand was in danger of being confused and tarnished. Gap quickly reconsidered and protected its namesake brand by changing the name of the new chain to Old Navy. The use of subbrands and endorsed brands provides alternatives to creating a new brand with all its costs and risks.

Subbrands and Endorsed Brands

Subbrands and endorsed brands become options when two unfortunate realities exist. First, the existing brands are judged to have the wrong associations or to have a risk of being damaged by the extension. Second, the organization does not have the size or resources to build a new brand, perhaps because the task is too difficult in a cluttered context or because the business does not justify the needed investment.

In such a situation, the answer may lie in the use of subbrands or endorsed brands. The GE Profile subbrand allowed General Electric to stretch into a premium segment in order to participate in the energy and high margins afforded by that submarket. Similarly, the Pentium Zeon subbrand allowed Intel to offer a high-end server microprocessor. A subbrand lets the offering separate itself somewhat from the parent brand, and it offers the parent brand some degree of insulation.

An endorsed brand offers even more separation. The Schwinn brand name in bicycles has given its Johnny G. Spinner bike an edge with its endorsement. And Marriott needed to enter the huge and growing business hotel arena. Because it would have been extremely expensive to create a stand-alone brand in that area and the existing brands were all too messy to buy, the company created Courtyard by Marriott. The endorsement indicated that Marriott as an organization stood behind the Courtyard brand, so visitors could be confident that the chain would deliver a reliable experience. Leveraging a brand by using it to endorse other brands provides a trust umbrella.

EXPANDING THE SCOPE OF THE OFFERING

A firm may look to its in-depth knowledge of and access to a market segment as an under-leveraged asset. Dometic, a Swedish company that pioneered absorption refrigerators characterized by silent operation, built a business selling them to hotels for use as minibars and to the RV industry.[3] The RV industry success led Dometic to add other products directed at the RV industry, such as air conditioning; automated awnings; generators; and systems for cooking, sanitation, and water purification. The product scope was broadened from refrigeration to RV interior systems, enabling Dometic to create a direct-to-dealer distribution system that became an ongoing competitive advantage. The Dometic experience illustrates how success in a market can be leveraged.

Considering the broader use context is a powerful idea. Thus, instead of being in the orange juice business, be in the breakfast business. Instead of selling only basketballs, consider making baskets and courts. GE's Jack Welch was quoted as saying that dominant companies in slow-growing businesses should redefine their markets, looking at a broader scope that will have more opportunities.

Slywotsky and Wise make a similar suggestion in their book *How to Grow When Markets Don't.*[4] They recommend identifying and serving the customer needs that emanate from the use of existing products. Cardinal Health, for example, moved beyond distributing drugs to pharmacies to managing hospital drug dispensing and related record-keeping and creating medical-supply kits for surgeons. Clarke American Checks went from check printing for banks to managing their customer relations, including running call centers and helping banks come up with incentives to increase customer retention. John Deere, the equipment manufacturer, decided to offer a one-stop shop for landscaping.

An analysis of the total set of tasks surrounding the customer use experience is a good way to begin determining whether there is a viable growth option in expanding the view of the offering. The use experience can be modeled by walking through exactly what the customer needs to do in order to use the product or service. This task set for a Healthy Choice frozen meal could include buying, paying, transporting, storing, preparing for use, using, and disposal. Can any of these tasks be made easier or eliminated by adding a feature or service to the product strategy? P&G, for example, has worked with Wal-Mart to provide a seamless integration of the two firms to determine what product is needed where and arrange the shipping so that administrative expenses, store outages, and inventory costs are all reduced. The net result is that P&G has an expanded scope beyond its products and a strong link to customers.

The analysis of a consumption system may not result in an end-to-end solution. But even if two parts can be combined, replaced by an alternative, or made to work better, the result may have added value or a point of differentiation for the customer. Annie Chun created a meal kit whereby the sauce and noodles are combined into an easily microwaved dinner dish. In doing so, several steps for the cook were eliminated or combined, and the easy cook/serve features were appealing.

Another perspective on expanding the offering scope is simply to serve additional needs of the customer. What other products or services do existing customers buy that could be provided by the firm's operations? Fast-food chains have expanded their offerings to attract customers in a time slot for which they have capacity. McDonald's, for example, has gourmet coffee for afternoon snack needs. Jamba Juice and Starbucks both added oatmeal so that they would be appealing as breakfast locations. Dometic added products RV owners bought.

NEW MARKETS

A logical avenue of growth is to move existing products into new markets by duplicating the business operation, perhaps with minor adaptive changes. With market expansion, the same expertise and technology and sometimes even the same plant and operations facility can be used. Thus, there is potential for synergy and resulting reductions in investment and operating costs. Of course, market development is based on the premise that the business is operating successfully; there is no point in exporting failure or mediocrity.

Expanding Geographically

Geographic expansion may involve changing from a regional operation to a national operation, moving into another region, or expanding to another country. KFC, McDonald's, GE, IBM, and Visa have successfully exported their operations to other countries. Most of these companies and many others are counting on countries such as China, India, and Russia to fuel much of their growth for the coming decades. They realize that success will involve significant investment in logistics, distribution infrastructures, and organization building and adaptation. (Chapter 14 will elaborate.)

Moving from local to regional to national is another option. Samuel Adams and other microbreweries have generated growth by geographic expansion. The challenge is to build a brand in the face of established competitors. See's Candies faced this hurdle as they expanded into the East Coast. They were aided as their reputation had seeped into markets because of their story had appeared in movies and print and because people had moved from areas in which they were strong. See's also used "holiday gift centers," seasonal carts that appeared in shopping malls, to locate the most hospitable markets for the brand.

Expanding into New Market Segments

A firm can also grow by reaching into new market segments. If the target segments are well defined, there are always a host of other segments to consider that would provide growth directions. Consider, for example:

- **Distribution channel.** A firm can reach new segments by opening up a second or third channel of distribution. A retail sporting goods store could market to schools via a direct sales force. A direct marketer such as Avon could introduce its products into department stores, perhaps under another brand name.
- **Age.** Johnson & Johnson's baby shampoo was languishing until the company looked toward adults who wash their hair frequently.
- **Home vs. office.** A supplier of office equipment to businesses might look to the home office market.

- **Move upscale.** Olay, which was a tired mass market P&G brand, was injected with innovation (such as Regenerist, Definity, and Pro-X), eye-catching packaging, and new positioning and was able to demonstrate that the mass market would be willing to pay premium prices if the offering merited them. In the process, a $2.5 billion business was created.

A key to detecting new markets is to consider a wide variety of segmentation variables. Sometimes looking at markets in a different way will uncover a useful segment. It is especially helpful to identify segments that are not being served well, such as the women's computer market or the fashion needs of older people. In general, segments should be sought for which the brand can provide value. Entering a new market without providing any incremental customer value is very risky.

EVALUATING BUSINESS LEVERAGING OPTIONS

There will be no shortage of ways to leverage the existing business. Ultimately, these need to be evaluated to see whether one or more should be pursued either immediately or within a planning horizon. This section proposes several questions that represent important criteria to consider.

These criteria are all supported by a series of studies of initiatives that leverage existing businesses conducted by Chris Zook of Bain and Company (as reported in two books, *Profit from the Core* with James Allen and *Beyond the Core*).[5] In the first study, case studies were created of 25 companies that had achieved sustainable growth performance from 1992 to 2002 far in excess of their peers. In the second study, 12 pairs of firms were examined. Each pair was within the same industry and with a similar starting point but with very different financial trajectories over a 10-year period. The resulting database contained 150 attempts to leverage a business. The third study focused on 180 attempts to leverage a core business sourced from the United States and the United Kingdom. The focus of these studies was to attempt to determine what was associated with successful initiatives to leverage core businesses.

Is the Product Market Attractive?

Successful initiatives involve a foray into a market that has a robust profit pool going forward. Recall the five-factor Porter model introduced in Chapter 4. The most logical expansion will fail if there simply are no profits to be had because competitors control them or because the margins have been squeezed by overcapacity or the nature of the customer demand. The stampede of utility companies into telecommunications turned out to be a disaster because the profit pool was shrinking to the point that their ventures were uneconomic. In contrast, the controlled product expansion of EAS, the vitamin supplement firm, was always into areas in which the margins were healthy. Projecting a market forward, particularly a new one with potential new entrants, is difficult, but the risk of entering a hostile market can be significant. Recall the discussion of the risks of growth markets in Chapter 4.

Is the Core Business Successful?

There is no point in extending mediocrity. A weak business will seldom have either resources or assets and competencies to spin out to a growth initiative. The chances of success of leveraging a business has been estimated by the Zook studies to be around 25 percent.[6] And this falls to well under 8 percent when the core business is weak.[7] Budget Rent-A-Car, for example, attempted a host of strategies without success to improve on their also-ran status, including efforts to enter the travel arena and the truck rental business.

Can the Core Business Be Transferred to the New Product Market? How Much of a Stretch Is It?

The ability of the business to adapt to a new product market and the chances for success increase the closer the leveraged business is to the core business. Tesco, the United Kingdom grocery chain, refined its retail offering by improving the checkout experience, parking, and the fresh produce. They grew in part by expanding into in-store pharmacies, optical product stations, auto fuel, kitchen products, and coffee shops. Each of these leverage efforts enhanced their core business. Such synergy is healthy not only because the core business benefits but because the new business is more likely to draw on the strengths of the core as well. In contrast to this disciplined expansion, their competitor Sainsbury, whose performance lagged Tesco, strayed further from its core, investing in a grocery chain in Egypt and two do-it-yourself chains in the United Kingdom.

This effect has been quantified by the Zook studies in which the new business initiative was separated from the core in terms of whether the involved customers, competitors, channels of distribution, cost structure, and assets and competencies were the same or different. The sum of differences could range from zero to five (there could be a partial match on some dimensions). The success probability sinks from over 25 percent to under 10 percent if the sum of differences was two or more.[8]

The task of adapting a business into a new market is easy to underestimate as illustrated by the experience of FedEx when it attempted to duplicate its concept in Europe. Setting up a hub-and-spoke system in Europe was inhibited by regulatory roadblocks at every turn. Attempts to short-circuit regulations by acquiring firms with related abilities resulted in something of a hodgepodge—FedEx at one point owned a barge company, for example. The firm also lacked a first-mover advantage in Europe because DHL and others had employed the FedEx concept years earlier. A reliance on the English language and a decision to impose a pickup deadline of five o'clock in Spain (where people work until eight o'clock) caused additional implementation problems.

Will the New Business Be Successful, Become a Market Leader?

The first question, which is not trivial, is whether the new business can avoid failure because it simply lacks market acceptance for whatever reason. The acceptance of new products is low. Even for firms with high levels of competence in a market and with real synergy to buttress the new entry, failure rates are extremely high. And we know the primary reason. Dozens of studies in very different contexts and in different markets have concluded that the main reason for failure is that the new products lacked a point of difference, a reason to succeed. Too often they were "me-too" products, at least as perceived by customers. There was in essence no reason to succeed, so they didn't. There should be evidence that customers will value the product or service and that the offering can withstand the response of existing and potential competitors.

Even real advances may not be so perceived by customers. They may even read an advance as a reason not to buy. Clairol failed with Small Miracle hair conditioner, which could be used through several shampoos, in part because customers could not be convinced that the product would not build up on their hair if it was not washed off with each use. Even the use of an established brand cannot guarantee success. The concept of a colorless cola, Crystal Pepsi, did not achieve acceptance, and the appearance had a negative flavor connotation.

The goal, of course, should not be simply to survive but to become a market leader at least with an attractive submarket. Simply becoming the fourth or fifth or even third player creates the danger that it will be impossible to keep up with the ongoing investment needed. Without substantial market and financial success, needed resources from the firm may be hard to justify. There is always a competition for resources even in "wealthy" organizations.

Is the Leverage Strategy Repeatable?

There is great value in creating initiatives that are repeatable. Repeatability leads to learning curve effects, speed of execution, organizational simplicity, strategic clarity, and the ability to get the details right. In the Zook database, around two-thirds of the most successful, sustained growth companies had one or two repeatable formulas.[9] Nike, for example, has done much better over time than Reebok. While Reebok was buying a boat company, Nike was duplicating its success in basketball with moves into tennis, baseball, football, volleyball, hiking, soccer, and golf. In all these efforts, the strategy was very similar, starting with a prominent credible endorser from Michael Jordan to Tiger Woods and systematically moving from shoes to clothing to equipment.

THE MIRAGE OF SYNERGY

Synergy, as suggested in Chapter 7, is an important source of competitive advantage. However, synergy is often more mirage than real. Synergy is often assumed when in fact it does not exist, is unattainable, or is vastly overvalued.

Potential Synergy Does Not Exist

Strategists often manipulate semantics to delude themselves that a synergistic justification exists. But when a packaged-goods manufacturer bought Burger Chef, a chain of 700 fast-food restaurants, the fact that both entities were technically in the food business was of little consequence. Because the packaged-goods firm never could master the skills needed to run restaurants, there was considerable negative organizational synergy.

There are many examples of expected synergy based on a superficial analysis that did not materialize. A large school bus operator, bought into the ambulance business thinking that since both involved vehicles and drivers there would be synergy but because ambulances were more complex and heavily regulated, the synergy never happened. A supermarket chain struggled to expand into other countries because of the lack of common suppliers and the difficulty of creating an information system prevented synergies from emerging. EBay bought Skype thinking that it might be another way to connect buyers and sellers, but the connection did not work in e-commerce, and the Skype had to be divested.[10]

THE ELUSIVE SEARCH FOR SYNERGY

The concept of a total integrated communications firm that comprises advertising, direct marketing, marketing research, public relations, design, sales promotions, and Internet communications has been a dream of many organizations for two decades. The concept has been that synergy will be

(continued)

created by providing clients with more consistent, coordinated communication efforts and by cross-selling services. Thus, Young & Rubicam had the "whole egg," and Ogilvy & Mather talked about "Ogilvy orchestrations."

Despite the compelling logic and considerable efforts, though, such synergy has been elusive. Because each communication discipline involved different people, paradigms, cultures, success measures, and processes, the disparate groups had difficulty not only working together but even doing simple things such as sharing strategies and visuals. Their inclination was to view other disciplines as inferior competitors rather than partners. Further, they were often reluctant to refer clients to sister units that were suspected to deliver inferior results, which created client-relationship ownership issues.

The firms with at least some success stories to their credit—Young & Rubicam, Denstu, and McCann Ericson—have a set of communication modalities such as direct marketing, public relations, Internet communications, and advertising in one organization, with shared locations and client-relations leadership. These firms make sure there is a strong, credible team leader with a dedicated space and a team-oriented performance measure. Even with such assets, sustained success is extremely rare. When a virtual team is formed with separate companies under one umbrella even if they are within the same communication holding company, success is even rarer.

The lesson here is that synergy does not just happen despite logic and motivation. It can require real innovation in implementation—not just trying harder.

Potential Synergy Exists But Is Unattainable

Sometimes there is real potential synergy, but implementation difficulties—usually far greater than expected—inhibit or block this synergy from being realized. When two organizations (perhaps within the same firm) have different cultures, strategies, and processes, there are significant issues to overcome. The effort to combine United Airlines, Westin Hotels and Resorts, and Hertz into one organization was a classic case in which the operational problems coupled with presenting a confused brand face to customers doomed the idea. The efforts to create multi-service telecommunication companies and fully integrated entertainment companies in order to achieve synergies have struggled.

Even when progress occurs, the patience and resources may not last long enough to see success. And it can take a long time. The ultimate integration challenge occurs when a group of entities are integrated to provide a comprehensive customer solution. Lou Gerstner indicated that integrating the country, product, and service silos at IBM, in part in order to provide integrated customer solutions, was his most significant task and legacy.[11] He noted that it took five years to make this progress. The synergies expected from the merger of Daimler-Benz and Chrysler never materialized; they finally gave up and engaged in a costly separation.

Potential Synergy Is Overvalued

One risk of buying a business in another area, even a related one, is that the potential synergy may seem more enticing than it really is. Perhaps carried away by its success with Gatorade, Quaker Oats purchased the Snapple business in 1994 for $1.6 billion, only to sell it two years later for a mere $300 million. Quaker had difficulties in distribution and was inept at taking a quirky personality brand into the mainstream beverage market (its program was based on pedestrian advertising and a giant sampling giveaway). Moreover, the fact that Quaker paid several times more than Snapple was worth was a fatal handicap.

The acquisition of The Learning Company—a popular children's software publisher with titles such as *Reader Rabbit*, *Learn to Speak*, and *Oregon Trail*—seemed like a logical move by Mattel, the powerful toy company with Barbie among its properties. Yet less than a year and a half after paying $3.5 billion for it, Mattel basically gave The Learning Company away to get out from under mounting losses.

One study of 75 people from 40 companies that were experienced at acquisition led to several conclusions. First, few companies do a rigorous risk analysis, looking at both the least and the most favorable outcomes. When optimistic vibes abound, it is particularly wise to look at the downside: What can go wrong? Second, it is useful to set a maximum price that you will not exceed. Avoid getting so exuberant about the synergistic potential that you ultimately pay more than you will ever be able to recoup.[12]

KEY LEARNINGS

- Leveraging assets and competencies involves identifying them and creatively determining in what business areas they might be able to contribute.
- Brand extensions should both help and be enhanced by the new offering in addition to being perceived to have a fit with it.
- The business can be leveraged by introducing new products to the market or expanding the market for the existing products.
- Entering a new product market is risky, as the new offering might lack market acceptance or needed resources. Success likelihood goes up if the core business is healthy, if the new product market is attractive (competitors will be profitable), if the business model is repeatable, if market leadership is possible, and if the stretch from the core is small.
- Synergy can be a mirage. Too often, it does not exist, or it exists but is unattainable or overvalued.

FOR DISCUSSION

1. Pick an industry and a product or service. Engage in a creative-thinking process, as outlined on pages 187 in Chapter 11, to generate an improved offering. Do the same to create an entirely new offering that uses one or more of the assets and competencies of the firm.

2. Evaluate the following extension proposals.

   Bank of America going into home safes

   Crest going into a chain of dentist offices

   Caterpillar going into automobiles

   Snackwells going into exercise clubs

   Mr. Clean going into car washes

   Hooters going into charter airlines

3. Pick a branded offering such as Southwest Airlines. Come up with 20 products or services that are alternative extension options. Include some that would be a stretch. Then evaluate each using the three criteria provided in the chapter.

4. Consider the following mergers or acquisitions. What synergy was or would be logically possible? What would inhibit synergy? Consider operations, culture, and brand equities.

   a. Citicorp acquired Providian, a credit card firm serving low-income segments

   b. Pepsi (the owners of Frito-Lay) acquired Quaker Oats

   c. Toyota acquiring Jeep

5. Evaluate Starbucks' extension decisions: to put Starbucks on United Airlines, to open Starbucks in bookstores and supermarkets, to license Starbucks ice cream to Dreyer's, to offer oatmeal in Starbucks stores, to sell the soluble coffee VIA in supermarkets, and to sell Frappuccino as a packaged drink. What were the risks both as individual decisions and cumulatively?

6. Identify and evaluate a combination of businesses that have achieved synergy and another that has failed to do so.

NOTES

1. "TippingSprung Publishes Results for Fifth Annual Brand-Extension Survey," PRWEB, January 7, 2009.

2. Op. cit.

3. Chris Zook, "Finding Your Next Core Business," *Harvard Business Review*, April 2007, p. 70.

4. Adrian Slywotsky and Richard Wise, *How to Grow When Markets Don't*, New York: Warner Business Books, 2003.

5. Chris Zook with James Allen, *Profit from the Core*, Boston: Harvard Business School Press, 2001; Chris Zook, *Beyond the Core*, Boston: Harvard Business School Press, 2004.

6. Zook, *Beyond the Core*, p. 22.

7. Ibid, p. 112.

8. Ibid, pp. 87–88.

9. Ibid, p. 36.

10. "How eBay Developed a Culture of Experimentation," *Harvard Business Review*, March 2011, pp. 93–97.

11. Louis V. Gerstner, Jr., *Who Says Elephants Can't Dance*, New York: Harper Business, 2002, pp. 251–252.

12. Robert G. Eccles, Kirsten L. Lanes, and Thomas C. Wilson, "Are You Paying Too Much for That Acquisition?" *Harvard Business Review*, July–August 1999, pp. 136–143.

CHAPTER THIRTEEN

Creating New Businesses

The most effective way to cope with change is to help create it.
—*I. W. Lynett*

When I arise in the morning torn between a desire to improve the world and a desire to enjoy the world. This makes it hard to plan the day.
—*E. B. White*

The unexpected is the best source of inspiration.
—*Peter Drucker*

*E*nterprise Rent-A-Car, which passed Hertz in sales during the 1990s, had sales of $10.1 billion in 2008 compared with Hertz's $6.7 billion and was much more profitable. Enterprise, formed in 1957 in St. Louis, focused on the off-airport market, catering to leisure travelers and (more important) to insurance companies that needed to supply a car to customers whose car was being repaired, a market that Enterprise created and nurtured. With a signature "We'll pick you up" offer, its inexpensive off-airport sites were run by entrepreneur managers motivated in part by a bonus system tied to customer satisfaction. Not until the late 1980s when it was already nipping at the heels of Hertz did Enterprise begin national advertising and get on the radar screen of its competitors, who were all after the prime market of business travelers who wanted a car at the airport.

Cirque du Soleil started in 1984 with a few street performers. A traditional circus with animals, trapeze artists, clowns, three-ring entertainment, and tents was oriented to families with children. Competitors were always tweaking the acts and setting. Cirque du Soleil ("We reinvented the circus") was qualitatively different, appealing to a different customer group—adults and corporate clients, who would pay a significantly higher price. The performers were talented acrobats, the clowns were more sophisticated, and there was a motivating story line somewhat like a theater production. Further, much of the expense was eliminated: There was only one "ring," no animals, no star performers, and no aisle concessions. It was so different that it made the traditional circus irrelevant and changed what the customer was buying.

Yamaha revitalized a declining piano market by developing the Disklavier, which functioned and played like other pianos except that it also included an electronic control system, thus creating a modern version of the old player piano. The system allowed a performance to be recorded and stored in memory. It provided a professional piano experience (with an artist who did not charge or get tired) for the home, hotel lobby, restaurant, or wherever entertainment would be welcome.

During the past century, the automobile industry experienced a dozen or more innovations that have created new business arenas—the Model T, the enclosed car, the GM spectrum of cars from Chevrolet to Cadillac, installment buying, the automatic transmission, the original Ford Thunderbird, the VW bug, the inexpensive and reliable Japanese cars of the 1970s, minivans, SUVs, and hybrids. In each case the innovators achieved above-average profits that extended for years. In particular, the Chrysler minivan, introduced in 1983 with first year sales over 200,000, maintained leadership in the category for at least a decade and was a critical contributor to the very survival of the firm.

CREATE "MUST HAVES," RENDERING COMPETITORS IRRELEVANT

The brand home run is an innovative offering containing a "must have" that defines a new category or subcategory for which competitors are not relevant. A substantial group of customers will not consider any brand lacking the "must have."

As the book *Brand Relevance: Making Competitor' Irrelevant* details, such an innovation will not happen frequently, but when it does, brand strategists need to seize that opportunity, recognizing that something bigger than a point of differentiation is present, and manage it accordingly. The firm needs to not only develop a "must have" but also bring it to market and then build barriers to competitors so the luxury of having market for which their brand has a monopoly or near monopoly position will not be short lived. It is not easy, but the upside is enormous.[1]

To generate a "must have," there needs to be an offering innovation that is so substantial or transformational that some customers will not do without it. Transformational innovation, as described in Chapter 5, is a game changer such as SalesForce.com championing cloud computing or Cirque du Soleil reinventing the circus. Substantial, also described in Chapter 5 (unlike transformational), innovation will not change the basic characteristics of the offering but will significantly enhance it either through the addition of a new "must have" or an improvement of one of its characteristics that is so significant that customers will now reject any option without it. A new category or subcategory will then be formed. The branded ingredient Kevlar provided a substantial innovation, defining a subcategory in the body armor market. Sometimes the distinction between the two is blurred, but the innovation should clearly not be incremental, one that will improve or strengthen brand preference with a "like to have" in the context of the existing categories or subcategories.

The "must have" can take improve or enhance the offering such as:

- A feature such as the high-fiber content in Fiber One
- A benefit such as that provided by Nike Plus' running shoe with a built-in chip that allows user to track and share their training data
- An appealing design such as the Apple products have created
- A systems offering that combines such as Siebel's CMR integrates suite of customer contact programs
- A new technology such as cloud computing that Salesforce.com pioneered

- A product designed for a segment such as Luna, the energy bar for women
- A dramatically low price point such as JetBlue airlines

A "must have" can also involve basis for customer relationship that is not involved with a functional benefit of the offering but is important functionally and symbolically to the customer such as:

- A shared interest such as Pampers Village, a go-to site for baby care
- A personality that connects such as the energy of Red Bull, the competence of Charles Schwab, the irreverence of Virgin, the humor of Southwest, or the exotic service of Singapore Airlines
- A passion such as that shown by Whole Foods Market for healthy foods
- Organizational values such as being customer centered (Zappos.com), innovative (3M), global (Citibank), involved in community or social issues (Avon), or being concerned about the environment (Patagonia)

In any case, the "must have" is a characteristic or element of the brand relationship that is regarded as necessary for a brand to be considered and thus relevant.

The "Must Have" Pay-Off

Creating "must haves" through substantial or transformational innovation, making competitors irrelevant or less relevant, is not only desirable but, in fact, is with rare exceptions the only way to grow. With rare exceptions, the only way! By far the more common strategy is to engage in what I call brand preference competition, focusing on making a brand preferred among the choices considered by customers in a defined subcategory. The goal is to beat competition through the use of incremental innovation to make the brand ever more attractive or reliable or the offering less costly. "Faster, cheaper, better" is the mantra. Resources are expended on communicating more effectively with cleverer advertising, more impactful promotions, more visible sponsorships, and more involving social media programs. You win by making your brand preferred as opposed to making your brand the only relevant brand, the only brand considered.

The problem is that "my brand is better than your brand" marketing rarely changes the marketplace no matter how much marketing budget is available or how clever the incremental innovation. The stability of brand positions in nearly all markets is simply astonishing. There is just too much customer and market momentum. Brand preference competition is also just so not fun.

With few exceptions, the only time that a market structure experiences any meaningful change is when a new "must have" was introduced with a major innovation. For example, the market share trajectory within the Japanese beer industry changed only four times during five decades, three when a brand created or got traction for a new subcategories (Asahi Dry Beer in 1986, Kirin Ichiban in 1990, and Kirin's Happoshu brand in the late 1990s) and once in 1995 when two subcategories were both repositioned. All of the marketing in other years simply did not move the needle.

You can look at any category, and the result is the same. Only when new "must haves" are introduced, with rare exceptions, does a brand achieve real growth. In automobiles, for example, market dynamics are driven by innovations represented by brands such as Ford's Mustang and

Taurus, the VW bug, Mazda's Miata, Chrysler's minivans, Toyota's Prius and Lexus, BMW's Minicooper, and Enterprise Rent-A-Car. In computers, the market was altered by new sub-categories such as DEC's minicomputer, Silicon Graphic's workstations, Sun's network servers, Dell's build-to-order PCs, and Apple's interface. In services, there is Westin's Heavenly Bed, which defined the premium bed hotel. In packaged goods, there are Odwalla, So-Be, and Dreyer's Slow Churned Ice Cream. In retailing, there are Whole Foods Markets, Zara, Best Buy's Geek Squad, IKEA, Zappos.com, and Muji (the no-brand store).

Creating a marketplace with weak or nonexistent competition has a huge potential payoff. It is econ 101, the ticket to real growth in sales and profits. Consider the Chrysler minivan introduced in 1982 as the Plymouth Voyager and Dodge Caravan, which sold 200,000 during first year and 12.5 million since and enjoyed 16 years with no viable competitors. It literally carried Chrysler for nearly two decades.

In addition to numerous case studies, empirical evidence shows that creating new categories or subcategories pays off. Perhaps the most robust law in marketing is that new product success is correlated with how differentiated products are, and a highly differentiated offering is likely to define a new category or subcategory. A McKinsey study is one of many that supports this. It showed that new entrants into a market that likely involve a high percentage of new categories or subcategories had a return premium of 13 points the first year sliding to 1 percent in the tenth year.[2] A more telling study found that of 150 strategic moves, the 14 percent that were categorized as creating a new category or subcategory contributed 38 percent of the revenues and 61 percent of the profits of the group.[3]

Evaluating Potential "Must Haves"

The pay-off of a successful "must have" can be substantial real growth if not a game changer. A key aspect of the process is to evaluate innovations to determine if there is a "must have" or whether the innovation is in fact incremental. It turns out that the analysis is fraught with personal, professional, and organizational biases. Evacuation is based on two judgments.

Is the concept significant to the marketplace?
Does the new concept represent a substantial or transformation innovation or an incremental one? One error, which can be termed the "rosy picture bias," is to assume that a substantial innovation exists when in fact the market regards it as incremental. Innovation champions tend to inflate the prospects because they become psychologically committed and because, professionally, the concept's success might be pivotal in a career path and a failure a step back. There is also organizational momentum; an offering that has been funded and part of the plan is sometimes hard to terminate. So there needs to be a hard-headed, research-based judgment made on the market response to the innovation.

Another often more serious mistake is the "gloomy picture bias" leading to an erroneous judgment that an innovation will not succeed when, in fact, it represents an opportunity to own a major category or subcategory. The judgment could rely on market size estimates based on existing flawed products. The wrong application or market might be targeted and the potential thus missed. Joint Juice, a product designed to reduce joint pain by making glucosamine in liquid from, found life when it went after an older demographic instead of young to middle-aged athletes. There could be a flawed assumption that a niche market could not be scaled and the resulting market is too small. For that reason, Coca-Cola avoided the water market for decades, a decision that, in retrospect, was a strategic disaster. Estimates can be colored by the fact that people and organizations tend to be risk adverse because the cost of failure is only too evident.

Can the offering be created?

Is the concept even feasible, especially if a technological breakthrough is needed? And even if the offering is feasible, does the organization have, or can it create, the needed people, systems, culture, and assets that may be required? And does the organization have the will to commit to the idea even with barriers and difficulties in development or in the marketplace? There will be times when the risks seem great and the rewards uncertain, and alternative uses of the resources are appealing and have political support. Without commitment, the new innovation may well become underfunded and potentially doomed. Creating a new category or subcategory is difficult enough. A solid vision with commitment in key parts of the organization is often needed and not easy to obtain and retain.

Is the timing right? Being first into the market is not necessary or even always desirable. In fact, the pioneering brand is often premature because the market, the technology, or the firm was not ready. Apple was not the pioneer for the iPod (Sony beat Apple by two years), the iPhone (the technology was up and running in Europe years before), or the iPad (Bill Gates of Microsoft introduced the "Tablet PC" some 10 years earlier), but in each case, Apple had the timing right. The technology was in place or around the corner, the firm had the assets and experience, and the value proposition had been market tested albeit with inferior technology. For all the talents of Steve Jobs, his genius at timing is underappreciated.

The ability of an organization to develop "must have" opportunities depends on its being able to generate and nurture substantial and transformational innovation even when the large organizational units are favoring incremental innovation. Not easy. Further, the ability to capitalize on a successful creation of "must haves" and the new subcategory they define will depend on building barriers to competitors, the subject of a subsequent chapter.

THE INNOVATOR'S ADVANTAGE

A prime reason that new business innovators earn more than the average firm is the innovator's advantage. Innovation can create what is often termed a first-mover advantage based on several factors. First, competitors will often be inhibited from responding in a timely manner. They may believe that the new business will cannibalize their existing business. Thus, competitors to Chrysler held back in responding to the minivan because they wanted to protect their station wagon business. Chrysler was "blessed" with a weak position in station wagons and thus had less to lose. Further, they could be worried about the impact on their brand; Xerox did not want to be associated with the low-end desktop copiers that were being offered by Canon even though Xerox had access to one from its Japanese affiliate Fuji-Xerox. Because of these two concerns, firms are tempted to minimize the long-term impact of the innovation and make themselves believe that it is a passing fad.

Second, competitors often are simply not able to respond. They may be playing catch-up technologically, especially if the technology is evolving or if patents are involved. Sometimes there might be natural monopolies (an area might be able to support only one muliplex cinema, for example). More common are organizational constraints. Responding to an innovation might require changes in organizational culture, people, and systems, which can be all but impossible. Many retailers attempted to duplicate Nordstrom's customer service but were unsuccessful because, although they could copy what Nordstrom did, they could not duplicate what Nordstrom was as an organization—its reward system, culture, heritage, in-store organization, and more.

Third, the innovator can create customer loyalty based on the exposure and experience with its product or service. If the concept and experience are satisfactory, there may be no incentive for a customer to risk trying something that is different. The innovator can also earn the valuable "authentic" label. This was a factor facing competitors such as Kirin when they tried to duplicate Asahi Dry Beer's success in Japan. Customer-switching costs, perhaps involving long-term commitments, can create a distinct disadvantage for a follower. Or there could be network externalities. If a large community begins to use a service such as eBay, it may be difficult for a competitor to create a competing community.

To capture a first-mover advantage, it is important to hit the market first and invest to build position. While high initial prices may be an attractive way to capture margin and recover development costs, a low-price strategy may serve to build share and thus increase the barrier to followers. Followers will have the benefit of seeing the innovation but will often need to be significantly better to have a chance of dislodging the first mover among the user base. So it is helpful to make that user base as large as possible.

It turns out that true market pioneers often do not survive, perhaps because they entered before the technology was in place or because they got blown away by larger competitors.[4] Pioneers such as Dreft in laundry detergent, daguerreotypes in photography, Star in safety razors, and Harvard Graphics in presentation software did not or could not capitalize on their first-mover status. In contrast, Golder and Tellis found that early market leaders, firms that assume market leadership during the early product growth phase, had a minimal failure rate and an average market share almost three times that of market pioneers and a high rate of continuing market leadership.[5] They noted that successful early market leaders tended to share certain traits:

- *Envisioning the mass market.* While pioneers such as Ampex in video recorders and Chux in disposable diapers charged high prices, the early market leaders (such as Sony and Matsushita in video recorders or P&G in diapers) priced the product at a mass market level. Timex in watches, Kodak in film, Gillette in safety razors, Ford in automobiles, and L'eggs in women's hosiery all used a vision of a mass market to fuel their success.

- *Managerial persistence.* The technological advances of early market leaders often took years of investment. It took 10 years of research for P&G to create the successful Pampers entry and two decades for the Japanese firms to develop the video recorder.

- *Financial commitment.* The willingness and ability to invest are nontrivial when the payoff is in the future. For example, when Rheingold Brewery introduced Gablinger's light beer, it had a promising start, but financial downturns in other sectors caused it to withdraw resources from the brand. In contrast, Philip Morris invested substantially in Miller Lite for five years in order to achieve and retain a dominant position.

- *Relentless innovation.* It is clear that long-term leadership requires continuous innovation. Gillette learned its lesson in the early 1960s when the U.K. firm Wilkinson

1. Bluetooth	6. DreamWorks	11. Disney
2. Pixar	7. TiVo	12. Google
3. iPod	8i. iMac	13. Swifter
4. Imax	9. Discovery Channel	14. Wikipedia
5. Microsoft	10. Blackberry	15. Dyson

Figure 13.1   Perceived Innovativeness—2007

Sword introduced a stainless steel razor blade that lasted three times longer than Gillette's carbon steel blade. After experiencing a sharp share drop, Gillette returned to its innovative heritage and developed a new series of products, from the Trac II to the Altra, Sensor, Mach 3, and finally to the Fusion.

- **Asset leverage.** Early market leaders often also hold dominant positions in a related category, allowing them to exploit distribution clout and a powerful brand name to achieve shared economies. Diet Pepsi and Coke's Tab, for example, were able to use their distribution power and brand names to take over the diet cola market from the pioneer, Royal Crown Cola.

Being a first mover and owning an emerging market or submarket does more than provide a competitive edge in that market. It also leads to a perception of being innovative. Gaining perceptions of innovativeness is a priority for nearly all businesses because it provides energy and credibility for new products. But few brands break out and reach that goal. In Figure 13.1, examine the top 15 brands on an innovativeness scale according to the 2007 BAV (Brand Asset Valuator from Y&R) database covering over 3,000 brands.[6] Nearly all had created and/or owned a new submarket using transformational innovation.

MANAGING CATEGORY PERCEPTIONS

When a new product category or subcategory such as iPods, smart phones, Pringles, or hybrid cars, emerges, the innovators need to be aware that their challenge is not only to create an offering and a brand but also to manage the perception of the new category or subcategory. A new business will change what people are buying. Instead of buying a car, some customers will be looking for a hybrid. As new entrants come in, there will be different types of hybrids. So Toyota, the early hybrid leader, has an opportunity to manage the perceptions of the category while simultaneously linking itself to the category as the leading brand, one with authenticity and ability to deliver. For a business innovator, the focus is no longer just on what brand to buy (the preference question) but rather what product category or subcategory to buy (the relevance question).

The best way to define and manage perceptions of a new category or subcategory is to become its exempla, the brand that represents it in the minds of the customers. An exemplar will develop not manage perceptions but will provide credibility and authenticity for the brand. It will often be perceived to be an innovator and the brand that sets the quality standard. Others will usually be perceived to be imitators and inferior. Competitors will be in the awkward position of defining their relevance in a way that only reaffirms the authenticity of the exemplar.

To become an exemplar, a brand needs to advance the category or subcategory rather than the brand. It needs to focus on the category or subcategory characteristics, point out its

PETER DRUCKER'S DO'S AND DON'TS OF INNOVATION[7]

Do:
- Analyze the opportunities.
- Go out and look, ask, and listen.
- Keep it simple and keep it focused.
- Start small—try to do one specific thing.
- Aim at market leadership.

Don't:
- Try to be clever.
- Diversify, splinter, or do too many things at once.
- Try to innovate for the future.

advantages, and promote loyalty not to the brand but to the category or subcategory over other categories or subcategories. Second, the brand's organization needs to be a thought leader and innovator. Improvement and change will make the category or subcategory dynamic, the brand more interesting, and the role of the exemplar more valued. Disneyland is the exemplar of theme parks, and it is always innovating. Third, the brand should be willing to invest in capacity and marketing to be the early market leader in terms of sales and market share. It is hard to be an exemplar and to leverage that role without market share leadership and the large voice that goes with it.

In managing perceptions of a category, there are some guidelines. First, there may be a need to focus on attributes and functional benefits at the outset to make sure that the category and its value proposition are communicated. The emotional and self-expressive benefits can have secondary status at the outset. Second, labels such as minivan, camcorder, SUV, etc. help unless the first-mover brand such as TiVo or Xerox becomes the de facto subcategory label. Incidentally, these guidelines apply whenever the category is new to the market even if it is established elsewhere. For example, many categories of products (such as vans) are new to China long after they have been established in the Western world.

CREATING NEW BUSINESS ARENAS

The first step to the creation of a new business arena is to get ideas on the table and refine the best ones to obtain potential business concepts. Good ideas are more likely to happen if they are valued by the organization and if there is a process to stimulate them. GE has set a goal that each business should generate technology breakthrough ideas, concepts that could lead to a $50 million to $100 million idea in the foreseeable future. As a result, time and resources are given to idea generation.

In Chapter 12, the starting point was the assets and competencies of the firm and how they could be leveraged. Here, the starting point is the customer in relation to offerings. In what way are the offerings disappointing? What are the unmet needs? What activities are the existing product or service a part of, and what are the goals?

New business ideas can come from anywhere. However, the history of blue-ocean ventures contains patterns and can suggest possibilities. Among them are technological innovation, going from components to systems, unmet needs, niche submarkets, customer trends, and creating a dramatically lower price point.

Technological Innovation

A new technology—such as disposable razors, notebook computers, a new fabric, or hybrid cars—can drive the perception of a submarket. By creating a subcategory of dry beer, Asahi Super Dry Beer made Kirin, the leading lager beer brand, irrelevant for a significant and growing segment in Japan. A minor player with less than 10 percent of the market in 1986, Asahi grew to gain market share leadership in the late 1990s, in large part by taking share from Kirin. Kirin finally mounted a comeback by introducing Kirin Ichiban, a different beer formulation, and taking leadership of the low-malt subcategory, *happoshu*, a beer brewed with ingredients that warranted a sharply lower tax, and another no-malt beer with an even lower tax, termed the third beer. Amazingly, considering an average of three new product introductions per month and the marketing dollars spent in the Japanese beer market each year for 30 years, three of the four changes in marketing share momentum were due to these innovations: dry beer, Kirin Ichiban, and low-malt beer. The fourth change was due to Asahi's repositioning of the dry beer subcategory. The market share dynamic was explained entirely by the emergence or evolution of subcategories.

Technological innovation can take many forms. Packaging innovation led to Yoplait's Go-Gurt, the yogurt in a tube that kids slurp up, which created a new business with a different target market, value proposition, and competitors than conventional yogurt makers. Software innovation created eBay's online auction category where a host of imitators had difficulty matching both the operational performance and the critical mass of users established by eBay.

From Components to Systems

A classic way to change the market is to move from components to systems. The idea is to look at the system in which the product or service is embedded, to expand perceptions horizontally. Siebel, for example, changed what people bought by creating customer relationship management (CRM). CRM combined a host of software programs (such as call center management, loyalty programs, direct mail, customer acquisition, customer service, sales force automation, and much more) into a single umbrella package. It no longer was enough to provide the best direct mail program because firms were now buying something much broader and were simply not interested in stand-alone programs that would require idiosyncratic training and would not be linked to other complementary programs.

KLM Cargo's offering was providing space on its airplanes, a commodity that was becoming a low-margin business.[8] After studying the total system needs for customers who were shipping perishables, KLM determined that significant value could be added by providing not just cargo space but a transportation solution that would include end-to-end responsibility for the product. These customers, importers and retailers, were experiencing spoilage, and it was never clear who in the logistics chain was responsible. Under its Fresh Partners initiative, KLM provided an unbroken "cool chain" from the producer to the point of delivery, with three levels of service—fresh regular, fresh cool, and fresh supercool (where products are guaranteed to have a specific temperature from truck to warehouse to plane to warehouse to truck to the retailer). Firms importing orchids from Thailand and salmon from Norway were among those using the service. This initiative allowed KLM to move from a commodity business to one that could capture attractive margins based on the value delivered to customers.

Unmet Needs

Unmet needs provide insight that when translated into products or services will be highly likely to be relevant to the customer and can lead to new business. When Saturn and Lexus, for example, changed the way customers interacted with car dealers, they were addressing a significant unmet need. The result made some other brands less relevant for an important segment. Betty Crocker's Hamburger Helper addressed the need to have a shelf-stable meal preparation tool.

Cemex, a concrete company, realized that its customers had a lot of money riding on predictable delivery because concrete is highly perishable.[9] As a result, Cemex created capabilities of using digital systems that allowed drivers to adjust in real time to traffic patterns and changing customer timetables. It can now deliver product within minutes and process change orders on the fly. It addressed an unmet need, and the totally new business model that resulted has led to Cemex going from a regional player to the third largest concrete company in the world, serving 30 countries.

Customers are not always a good source for some kinds of unmet needs, especially those involving emotional and self-expressive benefits, and so insight from creative and knowledgeable people might be required. The attractiveness of an SUV, for example, did not really result from its functional benefits. Further, customers have a difficult time getting around the boundaries of the current offering and may not have been much help in going from a horse to a car to an airplane. So in analyzing the customer, it is important for the analysis to have both breadth and depth, and that is where ethnographic research excels.

Ethnographic (or anthropological) research, introduced in Chapter 2, is a good way to uncover and analyze unmet needs. Simply observing customers in their "native habitat" can provide a fresh and insightful look at the problems customers are facing.

Niche Markets

The market can be broken into niches with each niche having its own dominant brand. The energy bar market created by PowerBar ultimately fragmented into a variety of submarkets, including bars designed for women (Luna), high protein (Balance), low calories (Pria), and candy bar taste (Balance Gold).

A niche can be defined by an application. Bayer helped define a new subcategory—taking baby aspirin regularly to ward off heart attacks—with its Bayer 81 mg. It attempted to further define the subcategory by introducing Enteric Safety Coating to reassure those who might be concerned about the effects of regular aspirin use on the stomach.

A niche can be also defined by a unique position that appeals to a distinct submarket. In the United Kingdom, the Ford Galaxy minivan was positioned away from the functional soccer moms or family outing slot. It was instead introduced as being roomy and comfortable, like first-class air travel, and therefore suitable for busy executives. Starbucks similarly created a different retail coffee experience that made other competitors irrelevant.

Customer Trends

A customer trend can be a driver of a submarket. The expression "Find a parade and get in front of it" has some applicability. That was part of the strategy of Whole Foods with organic foods and Apple's iPod with music sharing.

It is even better if multiple trends can be accessed because the competitors will be more diffuse. The dual trends toward wellness and the use of herbs and natural supplements have supported a new category, healthy refreshment beverages (HRBs). This arena now contains a host of subcategories, such as enhanced teas, fruit drinks, soy-based drinks, and waters. The pioneer and submarket leader is SoBe, which started in 1996 (with SoBe Black Tea 3G, containing ginseng, ginkgo, and guarana) and now has an extensive line of teas, juices, and energy drinks. The large beverage companies ignored this trend for too long and have been playing a frustrating and expensive game of catch-up. Annie Chun developed a line of packaged Asian food that capitalized on a host of trends, including the rise of Asian foods, healthy eating, convenience, and quality meals.

Creating a Dramatically Lower Price Point

Many blue-ocean businesses occur when an offering appears that is simpler and cheaper than that of established firms. Clayton Christensen, a noted Harvard strategy researcher, has studied a wide variety of industries with a series of colleagues and developed two theories about disruptive innovations. His research is reported in three books: *The Innovator's Dilemma*, *The Innovator's Solution* (with Michael Raynor), and *Seeing What's Next* (with Scott Anthony and Erik Roth).[10]

The first theory is termed *low-end disruptive innovation*, where industries are altered by emerging products whose price appears dramatically low. In these industries, established firms target the best customers and attempt to sell them better products for more money. More features, services, and reliability are all aimed at capturing a higher level of loyalty and margin. The firms that are successful develop structures, staffs, incentives, and skills designed to generate and implement a continuous flow of "sustaining innovations" to improve the offering. They invest in building deeper relationships with their best customers, wealthy clients in the case of financial institutions. Packaged goods firms offer line extensions to provide variety and interest to loyal customers. Retailers and others invest in loyalty programs.

This drive to service the most profitable customers provides an opening in the form of the low-end customer. These customers, often ignored or considered a nuisance by the established firms, are typically "overserved" and would be happy with a simpler, cheaper product that delivers satisfactory performance. Capitalizing on this opportunity, firms (often new to the industry) engage in "low-end disruptive innovation." They introduce an entry that is easier to use and much less expensive. Typically, the entrant's product is so inferior that its appeal is to a limited number of applications and customers, which incumbent firms consider marginal anyway. But often these firms then improve their offering over time and become competitors in a broad section of the market. A study of stall points, where steady sales growth abruptly changes to prolonged decline, of some 500 firms over 50 years showed that the leading cause, occurring in 23 percent of the cases, was low-end disruption innovation.[11]

The steel minimills in the 1960s initially made low-quality steel, serving a market for rebar (reinforcing concrete) that did not require high quality and was a low-margin, unattractive business. Over the decades, they improved their technology and products, however, and began to challenge the incumbents on a broad front. There are many similar examples. The Japanese car companies entered the market in the late 1960s and provided an option for buyers who did not need the features and self-expressive benefits of the large American firms. The copier market in the 1970s was changed by Canon's low-end disruptive innovation strategy, which met the needs of small businesses that did not need the power of Xerox products.

The Christensen team also advances a second theory, that of *new-market disruptive innovations* aimed at noncustomers. In many markets, large groups of noncustomers either do not buy because the products or services are considered too expensive or complex or buy much less than they would like because the process is inconvenient. A more accessible offering that is priced right can open up the market. Apple's Macintosh attracted new users into the computer market, and online retail stockbrokers enabled day traders to thrive. The single-use camera provided a new market just as the Kodak Brownie did a century earlier. Vanguard's low-cost index funds attracted new buyers into the industry. The noncustomers have typically been ignored by the established firms who, again, tend to focus their efforts on the current "heavy users," the most profitable customers.

An attractively priced option can appeal to both the low-end and noncustomer segments simultaneously. Southwest Airlines targeted not only customers looking for a value airline but also people who could be lured from their automobiles, a segment that was ignored by the established airlines of the day. Dell Computer also succeeded both serving the low end and attracting new users.

Evaluation—Real, Win, Worth it

The evaluation of a major or transformational innovation is difficult because it will stray from the comfort zone and knowledge base of a business. A structured, disciplined evaluation approach is helpful not only to provide a termination decision but also to identify the roadblocks to success so that they can be addressed. The "real, win, worth it" structure suggested by Wharton's George Day involves the following sets of questions:[12]

- Is the market real? Is there a need or desire for the product? Can and will the customer buy it? Is the market size adequate? Segway's personal transporter was an ingenious technical innovation but did not solve transportation problems for any target market.

- Is the product real? Is there a clear concept that will satisfy the market? Can the product be made? Putting nuclear energy plants in the ocean presented construction barriers.

- Can the product be competitive? Does it have a competitive advantage, one that is sustainable? If a competitor can copy or neutralize the new product, it may have only a short window to establish a loyal customer base.

- Can our company be competitive? Do we have superior assets and competencies? Appropriate management? The success of the digital animation company Pixar depended on a unique blend of culture and people; it would not have worked in most film organizations.

- Will the product be profitable at an acceptable risk? Is the forecast ROI acceptable? Overoptimistic sales forecasts and unrealistic pricing expectations need to be considered.

- Does launching the product make strategy sense? Does it fit our overall strategy? Will top management support it? 3 M launched a privacy computer screen that opened up markets for anti-glare filters.

Keeping the Edge

The goal is to maintain dominance in the new submarket and the returns that go along with dominance. Not so easy when success breeds competitors. Those that have kept dominance have one or more characteristics. Some, like Apple, keep innovating so that they are a moving target. Others, like Snuggles and Asahi Dry, are the "authentic" choice. Still others like Cirque du Soleil have created significant entry barriers in terms of competencies and scale. And there are those like Southwest Airlines that surround their innovation with a personality. The list goes on, but there needs to be an edge to avoid a transformational innovation becoming only a short-term win.

FROM IDEAS TO MARKET

The payoff for creating a successful new business is huge. Historically, most financially successful firms are based on the creation of a new business. Yet few firms can have a history of creating multiple new businesses. It turns out that it is not easy for an organization to be successful with an established business and still provide an environment that will foster new business ideas and allow them to flourish. That is exactly what is required, though, when markets get dynamic. The challenge is to create an organization that can excel in existing businesses and still allow a new business, especially a transformational business, to survive if not thrive. In the terms of Chapter 8, strategic adaptability needs to play a more prominent role, either in addition to or perhaps in place of strategic commitment or strategic opportunism.

Most organizations lack a healthy mix of transformational and incremental innovation. One study concluded that the percentage of major innovation in development portfolios dropped from 20.2 to 11.5 from 1990 to 2004.[13] And from the mid-1990s to 2004, the percent of total sales due to major innovations fell from 32.6 percent to 28 percent. Why should there be such a bias toward incremental "little i" innovations? To answer that question, we turn to a discussion of the several reasons why organizations fail to support transformational innovations at an optimal level.

Fatal Biases Inhibiting New Business Creation

Understanding the several biases that inhibit firms from innovating new business areas is a first step to dealing with them. These biases can be expressed in terms of six related "curses"— short-term pressures, silo, success, incumbency, commitment, and size.

The short-term financial pressure curse. When the organization is doing well, there is pressure to create short-term growth and margins, in part driven by the desire for stock return and in part driven by managers with short job tenures. Short-term results can best be obtained by diverting R&D funds to sustaining innovation and focusing effort on improving the business model, enhancing the value proposition, and improving efficiency and productivity. Creating a new business platform is risky and expensive and likely to result in short-term financial pain. A new firm, perhaps funded by venture capitalists, will have a time horizon to start making profits.

The silo curse. The power of product silos within organizations often leads to a delegation of innovation and development from the corporation to the silo unit in part to gain accountability and funding ability. Silos by their nature have limited resources and are focused on a particular product line with its associated customer base, operations, assets, and competencies. The natural goal is to respond to opportunities to improve the offering or to leverage the existing business. A transformational innovation will require more resources, will often need to operate between existing silos, and can be a threat to the existing profit stream.

The curse of success. When times are good and the business is doing well, resources should be available to take risks and create new business areas. Curiously, however, complacency usually wins the day. Why change if the current business is generating growth and profits? Why not instead invest in a sure thing, to make the costs even lower and the profits even higher? It is much easier to change when there is a crisis than when things are going well, although in a crisis, both resources and time may be in short supply.

The incumbent curse. When a transformational innovation is aimed at the marginal customer or the noncustomer, there is a tendency to ignore the threat to the basic business. The natural strategy is to focus on the good, high-margin customers. If the new concepts steal marginal customers, so what? Those customers were more of a nuisance anyway. Further, it does not seem wise to invest in an offering that will kill the golden goose. Why invest in an offering that may cannibalize your business?

The commitment curse. Successful incumbent firms often have a tunnel focus on their strategic vision. In the terms of Chapter 7, they engage in strategic commitment. They invest vigorously in incremental innovation to reduce costs, improve the offering, and satisfy their loyal customers. The people hired, the culture created, the systems developed, and the organizational structure employed all are tailored to the task of making the existing business better. In that context, it is difficult for any new business concepts to get resources or serious traction within the firm.

The size curse. A new business by definition will start small. If a firm has been successful and grown to a meaningful size, it will look to business concepts that can make a difference to shareholders. McDonald's, for example, is inhibited from trying new restaurant concepts because even a successful concept aggressively expanded will have no impact on its financials; the core business is simply too huge. As a result, it became stuck in a model that was not supported by customer trends. Coke resisted marketing waters and other beverages in part because it was so unlikely for such business ventures to materially affect its shareholder value. A related problem is that a huge business like McDonald's or GE has built assets, processes, and organizations that are not adapted to run smaller businesses. One snack company once proclaimed that it was not capable of handling a business that was under $250 million. That inhibited it from participating in potential growth areas.

Making New Business Viable in Established Organizations

The basic problem is that a new business, particularly a transformational one, will require an organization that is very different from that of the core business. It will require people, systems, a culture, and a structure that must adapt quickly to an emerging market area, one that is almost by definition going to be very different from the core business.

One approach is to create a separate organization, either by acquiring the industry innovator and retaining its autonomy or by creating a stand-alone entity within the corporate framework. In either case, the separate organization will be free—indeed, encouraged—to create its own people, systems, culture, and structure. Of course, it can borrow elements of the core business, such as its accounting systems or perhaps marketing skills, but it needs to be committed to the strategic vision of the new organization while still being entrepreneurial and flexible. As the business matures, the link with the core business can become greater.

The other approach is to create a dual organization within the same firm. People who excel at "start-up" adaptability and change, as well as those who have proven to be good at incremental innovation, will need to be developed side by side. A more diverse set of people will likely be the result. Entrepreneurial cultural values will need to be tolerated within the organization. Experimentation and trial and error will need to be accepted if not encouraged. Different cost control systems and performance metrics will be needed. The new ventures will probably require a flatter organization.

Developing a dual organization is difficult and requires active management. However, it is possible and can result in providing new ventures with access to significant assets and competencies while also breathing energy into the core businesses.

In any case, an innovative new business cannot be starved for resources. The reason that most new businesses succeed as start-ups is because they have access to money from the stock market and from venture capitalists. Internally funded ventures are often at a disadvantage in obtaining needed resources. Too often, executives in large firms are said to have deep pockets but short arms.

To overcome resource shortfalls, top management has to make a commitment to grow through internal innovation and allocate resources toward that goal. Then a new venture will be able to compete for these resources with other new ventures and not from the existing business units. GE, with its program of encouraging and supporting breakthrough initiatives, does just that. Another key to resource availability is the disciplined process to disinvest in businesses that are not going to be the future of the firm, so that they do not exert their priority over future resources. Chapter 15 discusses the disinvestment decision process.

KEY LEARNINGS

- Over time, businesses that are new and different enough to have reduced or no competition will earn much more than average profits.

- The innovator has the potential to create a marketing position because competitors are reluctant to damage their own businesses, cannot match the technology, or believe it too costly to compete against a firm with an established customer base. Often it is not the innovator but the early market leader that captures these advantages.

- In creating a new business, managing the perceptions of the category is important.

- A new business can be based on technological innovation, moving from components to systems, by satisfying unmet needs, by creating niche marketing, by responding to customer trends, or by having a dramatically lower price point.

- There are organizational biases that inhibit the development of a new business. These can be described as the short-term financial pressure curse, the silo curse, the curse of success, the incumbent curse, the commitment curse, and the size curse.

FOR DISCUSSION

1. Why didn't Hertz or Avis start an off-airport business directed at insurance companies and vacationers? What advantages would they have had over Enterprise? Why didn't Steinway come up with the electronic organ? Why didn't Barnum and Bailey create Cirque du Soleil?

2. In order to revitalize the Reebok brand with women, the company that rode the aerobics craze two decades ago introduced Jukari Fit to Fly, an exercise program designed with Cirque du Soleil. A piece of equipment, the Fly Set, allows a person to fly through the air hanging on to a low trapeze. The goal is to invent a new fitness fad in exercise establishments with a program that is supported by a line of Reebok clothing.

   a. Is this a transformational or substantial innovation that defines a new category or subcategory?

   b. Evaluate its pros and cons for Reebok.

3. Think of some transformational new businesses such as Starbucks, TiVo, or Amazon.

   a. How was each different from what came before? What was similar? Scale them in terms of "newness" from truly transformational to substantial (some elements common to what came before but enough new to create a new subcategory).

   b. Was there an innovator advantage? How long did it last, and why?

   c. Did the business originate from an established business? If not, why not?

   d. Where did the idea for the business come from? If you don't know, try to speculate.

4. Consider some new businesses that have managed category perceptions well. Consider others that have not.

5. Pick a firm such a Bank of America, Patagonia, or L.L. Bean. Develop some potential innovations that would generate a "must have." How would you evaluate them?

NOTES

1. David Aaker, *Brand Relevance: Making Competitors Irrelevant*, San Francisco: Jossey-Bass, 2011.
2. Richard Foster and Sarah Kaplan, *Creative Destruction*, New York: Doubleday, 2001, p. 47.
3. W. Chan Kim and Renee Mauborgne, *Blue Ocean Strategy*, Boston: HBS Press, 2005, p. 7.
4. Peter N. Golder and Gerard J. Tellis, "Pioneer Advantage: Marketing Logic or Marketing Legend?" *Journal of Marketing Research*, May 1993, pp. 158–170.
5. Gerard J. Tellis and Peter N. Golder, "First to Market, First to Fail? Real Causes of Enduring Market Leadership," *Sloan Management Review*, Winter 1996, pp. 65–75.
6. Susan Nelson, "Who's Really Innovative," *Marketing Daily*, September 2, 2008.

7. James Daly interview with Peter Drucker, "Sage Advice," *Business 2.0*, August 22, 2000, p. 139.

8. The example is recounted in James C. Anderson and James A. Narus, "Selectively Pursuing More of Your Customer's Business," *MIT Sloan Management Review*, Spring 2003, pp. 43–49.

9. Rita Gunther McGrath and Ian C. MacMillan, "Market Busting," *Harvard Business Review*, March 2005, pp. 81–89.

10. Clayton M. Christensen, The Innovator's Dilemma: *When New Technologies Cause Great Firms to Fail*, Boston: Harvard Business School Press, 1997; Clayton M. Christensen and Michael E. Raynor, *The Innovator's Solution: Creating and Sustaining Successful Growth*, Boston: Harvard Business School Press, 2003; and Clayton M. Christensen, Scott D. Anthony, and Erik A. Roth, *Seeing What's Next: Using the Theories of Innovation to Predict Industry Change*, Boston: Harvard Business School Press, 2004.

11. Matthew S. Olsen, Derek van Berer, and Seth Verry, "When Growth Stalls," *Harvard Business Review*, March, 2008, pp. 51–61.

12. George S. Day, "Is It Real? Can We Win? Is It Worth Doing," *Harvard Business Review*, December, 2007, pp. 110–120.

13. Robert G. Cooper, "Your NPD Portfolio May Be Harmful to Your Business Health," *PDMA Visions*, April 2005.

CHAPTER FOURTEEN

Global Strategies

Most managers are nearsighted. Even though today's competitive landscape often stretches to a global horizon, they see best what they know best: the customers geographically closest to home.
—*Kenichi Ohmae*

A powerful force drives the world toward a converging commonality, and that force is technology. . . . The result is a new commercial reality—the emergence of global markets for standardized consumer products on a previously unimagined scale of magnitude.
—*Theodore Levitt*

My ventures are not in one bottom trusted, nor to one place.
—*William Shakespeare, The Merchant of Venice*

*T*he global reality. Few businesses can escape the reality that customers, competition, and markets have a global face. To compete successfully, firms need global strategies.

Global strategies need to create competitive advantage but also need to be opportunistic and flexible in the face of incredible complexity. Consider Groupe Danone, whose primary brands are Dannon Yogurt, Evian Waters, and Lu Biscuits, all among the world leaders in their categories. Danone bought a Brazilian cookie company and water companies in Indonesia and the United States, partnered with a local Turkish water company, and had a joint venture with Nestlé (a major competitor) that included biscuits in the Czech Republic. Before Danone gave the three product businesses global responsibility, there was an Asian-Pacific division that marketed all the products in Asia. An ongoing problem is that most innovation tends to originate in Europe and is not well suited for other markets. Another is that the Danone position around health works better in some countries than others. And this is only a glimpse of the strategic options and implementation issues facing one global firm.

A global strategy represents a worldwide perspective in which the interrelationships among country markets are drawn on to create synergies, economies of scale, strategic flexibility, and opportunities to leverage insights, programs, and production economies. A global strategy is different from a multidomestic or multinational strategy, in which separate strategies are developed for different countries, implemented autonomously, and managed as a portfolio of independent businesses.

A global strategy can result in strategic advantage or neutralization of a competitor's advantage. For example, products or marketing programs developed in one market might be used in another. Or a cost advantage may result from scale economies generated by the global market or from access to low-cost labor or materials. Operating in various countries can lead to enhanced flexibility as well as meaningful sustainable competitive advantages (SCAs). Investment and operations can be shifted to respond to trends and developments emerging throughout the world or to counter competitors that are similarly structured. Plants can be located to gain access to markets by bypassing trade barriers.

Even if a global strategy is not appropriate for a business, making the external analysis global may still be useful. A knowledge of competitors, markets, and trends from other countries may help a business identify important opportunities, threats, and strategic uncertainties. A global external analysis is more difficult, of course, because of the different cultures, political risks, and economic systems involved.

A global strategy requires addressing a set of issues that include the following:

1. What are the motivations (objectives) for a global strategy?
2. To what extent should products and service offerings be standardized across countries?
3. To what extent should the brand name and marketing activities (such as brand position, advertising, and pricing) be standardized across countries?
4. How can the global footprint be expanded successfully?
5. To what extent should strategic alliances be used to enter new countries?
6. How should the brand be managed globally?

Each of these issues will be explored in turn. The next section, in which the motivations for global strategies are presented, will be followed by discussions of standardization vs. customization, how to select which countries to enter, the use of alliances in developing global strategies, and global marketing management.

MOTIVATIONS UNDERLYING GLOBAL STRATEGIES

A global strategy can result from several motivations in addition to simply wanting to invest in attractive foreign markets. The diagram of these motivations shown in Figure 14.1 provides a summary of the scope and character of global strategies. Understanding what motivations have priority will inform how global strategies should be developed and how success should be measured.

Obtaining Scale Economies

Scale economies can occur from product standardization. The Ford global footprint, for example, allows product design, tooling, parts production, and product testing to be spread over a much larger sales base. Standardization of the development and execution of a marketing program can also be an important source of scale economies. Consider Coca-Cola, which since the 1950s has employed a marketing strategy—the brand name, concentrate formula, positioning, and advertising theme—that has been virtually the same throughout the world. Only the artificial sweetener and packaging differ across countries.

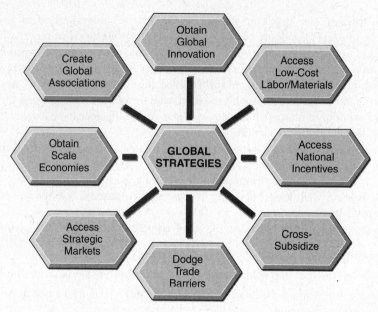

Figure 14.1 Global Strategy Motivations

Scale economies can also occur from standardization of marketing, operations, and manufacturing programs. Brands that share advertising (even when it is adjusted for local markets) spread the production and creative effort over multiple countries and thus a larger sales base. A firm similarly benefits when fixed costs involving IT and production technologies can be distributed over countries.

Global Brand Associations

Being global generates the image of being global, which turns out to be a significant advantage. A study of associations made of global brands involved qualitative interviews with 1,500 consumers over 41 countries, followed up with a quantitative study that included a preference scale of three leading brands in six product categories.[1] The result showed that associations with being global impacted preference. In fact, 44 percent of the variance in preference is caused by the fact that consumers believe that global brands have higher quality in part because they tend to have the latest innovations. Two other associations, the prestige of being global and social responsibility, also influence preference but much less so (12 percent and 8 percent, respectively) than the quality dimensions.

Global Innovation

Being global means that innovation around brand building, new product, and product improvements can be sourced anywhere. At P&G, for example, the successful Pantene positioning ("For hair that shines") came from P&G Taiwan, and the midtier priced feminine protection brand Naturella featuring the herbal ingredient chamomile came from P&G Mexico. The black Coke Zero package came from Australia and the U.K. And collaboration

INDICATORS THAT STRATEGIES SHOULD BE GLOBAL

- Major competitors in important markets are not domestic and have a presence in several countries.
- Standardization of some elements of the product or marketing strategy provides opportunities for scale economies.
- Costs can be reduced and effectiveness increased by locating value-added activities in different countries.
- There is a potential to use the volume and profits from one market to subsidize gaining a position in another.
- Trade barriers inhibit access to worthwhile markets.
- A global name can be an advantage and the name is available worldwide. ·
- A brand position and its supporting advertising will work across countries and has not been preempted.
- Local markets do not require products or service for which a local operation would have an advantage.

from other firms is becoming important for most global companies. P&G has people all over the world coordinating the development efforts of firms that have a collaborative relationship with P&G. As a result, their R&D budget and capability is highly leveraged. IBM and others are creating major R&D centers in India to access talent but also to participate in the intellectual vitality of the region.

The classic global innovation model, trickle down, no longer works.[2] The products of the developed countries, even with some features omitted, are often too high priced for the emerging country world. Local innovation is needed. For example, GE Healthcare, leaders in ultrasound machines, sold very few devices in China and India in the 1990s. However, by 2007, a local business unit developed an ultrasound machine that could be sold for $15,000 as opposed the U.S. price range of $100,000 to $350,000. The sales took off. Significantly, such innovations can be brought to the markets of developing countries. GE's inexpensive ultrasound machine became a major business in the U.S. used by ambulance units and rural hospitals and others. As a result, GE launched an initiative to generate 100 other similar innovations that would service the local market but also create new markets at home.

Access to Low-Cost Labor or Materials

Another motivation for a global strategy is the cost reduction that results from access to the resources of many countries. Substantial cost differences can arise with respect to raw materials, R&D talent, assembly labor, and component supply. Thus, a computer manufacturer may purchase components from South Korea and China, obtain raw materials from South America, and assemble in Mexico and five other countries throughout the world in order to reduce labor and transportation costs. Access to low-cost labor and materials can be an SCA, especially when it is accompanied by the skill and flexibility to change when one supply is threatened or a more attractive alternative emerges.

Access to National Investment Incentives

Another way to obtain a cost advantage is to access national investment incentives that countries use to achieve economic objectives for target industries or depressed areas. Unlike other means to achieve changes in trade, such as tariffs and quotas, incentives are much less visible and objectionable to trading partners. Thus, the British government has offered Japanese car manufacturers a cash bonus to locate a plant in the United Kingdom. The governments of Ireland, Brazil, and a host of other countries offer cash, tax breaks, land, and buildings to entice companies to locate factories there.

Cross-Subsidization

A global presence allows a firm to cross-subsidize, to use the resources accumulated in one part of the world to fight a competitive battle in another.[3] Consider the following: One firm uses the cash flow generated in its home market to attack a domestically oriented competitor. For example, in the early 1970s, Michelin used its European home profit base to attack Goodyear's U.S. market. The defensive competitor (in this case, Goodyear) can reduce prices or increase advertising in the United States to counter, but by doing so, it will sacrifice margins in its largest markets. An alternative is to attack the aggressor in its home market, where it has the most to lose. Thus, Goodyear carried the fight to Europe to put a dent in Michelin's profit base.

The cross-subsidization concept implies that it is useful to maintain a presence in the country of a competitor. The presence should be large enough to make the threat of retaliation meaningful. If the share is only 2 percent or so, the competitor may be willing to ignore it.

Dodge Trade Barriers

Strategic location of component and assembly plants can help gain access to markets by penetrating trade barriers and fostering goodwill. Peugeot, for example, has plants in 26 countries from Argentina to Zimbabwe. Locating final-assembly plants in a host country is a good way to achieve favorable trade treatment and goodwill because it provides a visible presence and generates savings in transportation and storage of the final product. Thus, Caterpillar operates assembly plants in each of its major markets, including Europe, Japan, Brazil, and Australia, in part to bypass trade barriers. An important element of the Toyota strategy is to source a significant portion of its car cost in the United States and Europe to deflect sentiment against foreign domination.

Access to Strategically Important Markets

Markets can be strategically important because of their size and growth. It is hard to be successful be avoid the large growth markets. There is good reason that firms are looking to the emerging markets of China, India, and others in order to participate in growth when home markets are often stagnant. For example, the 2010 growth in the beauty market was only 1.1 percent in the US. and nearly zero in Japan but over 10 percent in the major South American countries.[4] Firms in the industry recognize that leaders need to find to be relevant in these markets.

Other markets may be strategically important because of their role in the industries value chain. And a firm needs to have a presence. It could be because of a raw material supply, labor cost structure, or technology. An electronics firm, for example, may need to have a presence in Mumbai and Silicon Valley because both are sources of engineering innovation. A firm in the fashion industry may benefit from a presence in countries that have historically led the way in fashion.

STANDARDIZATION VS. CUSTOMIZATION

Standardized products and brands gained widespread credence as a strategy because of Ted Levitt's classic 1983 *Harvard Business Review* article, "The Globalization of Markets," which gave three reasons why standardization would be a winning strategy.[5] First, the forces of communication, transport, and travel were breaking down the insulation of markets, leading to a homogeneity of consumer tastes and wants. Second, the economics of simplicity and standardization—especially with respect to products and communication—represented compelling competitive advantages against those who held on to localized strategies. Third, customers would sacrifice preferences in order to obtain high quality at lower prices. The article provided an academic underpinning to the logical premise that standardization should be the goal of a global business.

Pringles, Visa, MTV, Starbucks, Sony, Dove, Vodafone, BP, DeBeers, Heineken, Nike, McDonald's, Pantene, Disney, and IBM are the envy of many because they seem to have generated global businesses with a high degree of similarity in terms of product, brand, position, advertising strategy, personality, packaging, and look and feel. Pringles, for example, stands for "fun," a social setting, freshness, less greasiness, resealability, and the whole-chip product everywhere in the world. Further, the Pringles package, symbols, and advertising are almost the same globally. Disney's brand of magical family entertainment is implemented by theme parks, movies, and characters that are remarkably consistent across countries.

These "standardized" products and brands are often not as identical worldwide as one might assume. McDonald's, once the model of standardization, now has rice burgers in Taiwan, vegetarian entrees in India, tortillas in Mexico, rice cakes in the Philippines, and wine with meals in many European cities. Pringles uses different flavors in different countries, and advertising executions are tailored to local culture. Heineken is the premium beer to enjoy with friends everywhere—except at home in the Netherlands, where it is more of a mainstream beer. Visa even has had different logos in some countries (such as Argentina), and even Coke has a sweeter product in areas such as southern Europe. Regardless of these variations, however, brands that have moved toward the standardized end of the spectrum demonstrate some real advantages.

A standardized offering can achieve significant economies of scale. For example, when IBM decided to exchange some three dozen advertising agencies for one in order to create a single global campaign (even if it needed some adapting from market to market), one motivation was to achieve efficiencies. The task of developing packaging, a Web site, a promotion, or a sponsorship will also be more cost-effective when spread over multiple countries. Economies of scale across countries can be critical for sponsorships with global relevance, such as the World Cup or the Olympics.

Perhaps more important, though, is the enhanced effectiveness that results from better resources. When IBM replaced its roster of agencies with Ogilvy & Mather, it immediately became the proverbial elephant that can sit wherever it wants. As the most important O&M client, it gets the best agency talent from top to bottom. As a result, the chances of a well-executed breakout campaign are markedly improved.

Cross-market exposure produces further efficiencies. Media spillover, where it exists, allows the standardized brand to buy advertising more efficiently. Customers who travel can get exposed to the brand in different countries, again making the campaign work harder. Such exposure is particularly important for travel-related products such as credit cards, airlines, and hotels.

A standardized brand is also inherently easier to manage. The fundamental challenge of brand management is to develop a clear, well-articulated brand identity (what you want your brand to stand for) and to find ways to make that identity a driver of all brand-building activities. The absence of multiple strategies makes this task less formidable with a global brand. In addition, simpler organizational systems and structures can be employed. Visa's "worldwide acceptance" position is much easier to manage than dozens of country-specific strategies.

The key to a standardized brand is to find a position that will work in all markets. Sprite, for example, has the same position globally—honest, no hype, refreshing taste. It is based on the observation that kids everywhere are fed up with hype and empty promises and ready to trust their own instincts. The Sprite advertising tagline ("Image is nothing. Thirst is everything. Obey your thirst.") resonates around the world. In one scene from a Sprite ad, kids are discussing why their basketball hero would drink Sprite.

Several generic positions seem to travel well. One is being the "best," the upscale choice. High-end premium brands such as Mercedes, Montblanc, Heineken, and Tiffany's can cross geographic boundaries because the self-expressive benefits involved apply in most cultures. Another is the country position. For example, the "American" position of brands such as Coke, Levi's, Baskin-Robbins, KFC, and Harley-Davidson will work everywhere (with the possible exception of the United States). A purely functional benefit such as Pampers' dry, happy baby can also be used in multiple markets. Not all brands that are high-end or American or have a strong functional benefit, however, can have a common position globally.

Standardization can come from a centralized decision to create a global product. Canon, for example, developed a copier that had a common design throughout the world in order to maximize production economies. Unfortunately, the copier could not use the standard paper size in Japan, resulting in substantial customer inconvenience. The risk inherent in a truly global standardization objective is that the result will be a compromise. A product and marketing program that almost fits most markets may not be exactly right anywhere; such a result is a recipe for failure or mediocrity.

Another strategy is to identify a lead country, a country whose market is attractive because it is large or growing or because the brand has a natural advantage there. A product is tailored to maximize its chances of success in that country, then exported to other markets (perhaps with minor modification or refinements). A firm may have several lead countries, each with its own product. The result is a stable of global brands, with each brand based in its own home country. Nissan has long taken this approach, developing a corporate fleet car for the United Kingdom, for example, and then offering it to other countries. Lycra, a 35-year-old ingredient brand from DuPont, has lead countries for each of the product's several applications all under the global tagline "Nothing moves like Lycra." Thus, the Brazilian brand manager is also the global lead for swimsuits, the French brand manager does the same for fashion, and so on.

Global Leadership, Not Standardized Brands[6]

The fact is that a standardized global brand is not always optimal or even feasible. Yet, attracted by the apparent success of other brands, many firms are tempted to globalize their own brand. Too often the underlying reason is really executive ego and a perception that a standardized brand is the choice of successful business leaders.

Such decisions are often implemented by a simple edict—that only standardized global programs are to be used. The consolidation of all advertising into one agency and the development of a global advertising theme are typically cornerstones of the effort. Even when having a standardized brand is desirable, though, a blind stampede toward that goal can be the wrong course and even result in significant brand damage. There are three reasons.

First, economies of scale and scope may not actually exist. The promise of media spillover has long been exaggerated, and creating localized communication can sometimes be less costly and more effective than adapting "imported" executions. Further, even an excellent global agency or other communication partner may not be able to execute exceptionally well in all countries.

Second, the brand team may not be able to find a strategy to support a global brand, even assuming one exists. It might lack the people, the information, the creativity, or the executional skills and therefore end up settling for a mediocre approach. Finding a superior strategy in one country is challenging enough without imposing a constraint that the strategy be used throughout the world.

Third, a standardized brand simply may not be optimal or feasible when there are fundamental differences across markets. Consider the following contexts where a standardized global brand would make little sense:

- ***Different market share positions.*** Ford's European introduction of a new van, the Galaxy, into the United Kingdom and Germany was affected by its market share position in each country. In the United Kingdom, as the number-one car brand with a superior quality image, Ford sought to expand the Galaxy's appeal beyond soccer moms to the corporate market. The U.K. Galaxy became the "nonvan," and its roominess was compared to first-class airline travel. In Germany, however, where Volkswagen held the dominant position, the Galaxy became the "clever alternative."

- ***Different government contexts.*** The Galaxy also faced in the United Kingdom (and not in Germany) the fact that because of the tax structure, corporations supplied cars to their employees as a way to provide compensation with less onerous taxes. As a result, a model with the price range of the Galaxy needed to appeal to corporate buyers or it would not be relevant to a major segment of buyers of vehicles in the Galaxy price range. A soccer moms position would not work, but the "first-class" travel provided a rationale for the inclusion of a van among the acceptable vehicles to buy.

- ***Different brand images.*** Honda means quality and reliability in the United States, where it has a legacy of achievement based on the J.D. Powers ratings. In Japan, however, where quality is much less of a differentiator, Honda is a car-race participant with a youthful, energetic personality.

- ***Different customer motivations.*** P&G's Olay found that in India, people wanted lighter-looking skin rather than younger-looking skin, as was the case in the United States and Europe. Campbell Soups found little demand for ready-to-eat soups in soup-loving Russia and China but did better when they introduced "starter soups" and broths. According to a 2008 study, 78 percent of consumers in China cited health benefits are important in food buying compared with 55 percent in the United States. In the United Kingdom and Argentina, the number was less than 50 percent, and in Germany, it was only 34 percent.[7]

- ***Different distribution channels.*** The distribution channel can affect the offering and the marketing strategy. In China, reaching rural areas can involve many levels of distribution, so that it is hard to control the brand using methods that would work in the United States, where the distribution channel tends to be shorter and clearer. In the United States, ice cream is sold in bulk for people to use at home, but in many countries, it is mainly sold on a stick for snacks.

- ***Different stages in customer trends.*** A brand may not be at the same stage in all countries even though a common customer trend exists in each. The appreciation of wine varies from country to country. In China, it exists but is embryonic and affects the go-to-market strategy of a company such as the E. & J. Gallo Winery—it does not use its premium offerings in the Chinese market. Trends toward health and healthier eating are further along in the United States than in many other countries.

- ***Different social economic stage.*** For some markets, such as in rural India or some parts of China and Africa, most products and brands sold in the West are simply irrelevant. When an area lacks electricity or when it is unreliable, the product profile and attribute preferences change dramatically. Or when the household budget is a small fraction of that in developed countries, constraints dictate buying habits.

- ***Strong local heritage.*** Nestlé and Unilever often retain an acquired local brand simply because there is significant customer loyalty based on the brand's heritage and connection to the local community that could not be transferred to a global brand. Relationships with local brands can be powerful, especially in contexts in which the incidence of advertising is low and the historical relationships therefore take on more weight.

- ***Preempted positions.*** A superior position for a chocolate bar is to own the associations with milk and the image of a glass of milk being poured into a bar. The problem is that different brands have preempted this position in different markets—for example, Cadbury in the United Kingdom and Milka in Germany.

- ***Different customer responses to executions and symbols.*** There are tactical concerns as well. A Johnnie Walker ad in which the hero attends the running of the bulls in Pamplona was effective in some markets, including Spain, but seemed reckless in Germany and too Spanish in other countries. The attitude toward diet drinks and food outside the United States is very different and is one reason that *light* instead of *diet* is seen on food products.

A global business strategy is often misdirected. The priority should not be to develop standardized brands (although such brands might result) but global brand *leadership*, strong brands in all markets. Effective, proactive global brand management should be directed at enhancing brands everywhere by allocating brand-building resources globally, creating global synergies, generating common marketing planning processes, enhancing cross-country communication, stimulating common performance measures, and coordinating and leveraging the strategies in individual countries. Chapter 16 elaborates.

A key to a successful global strategy is to understand the local marketplace and customers. Panasonic's experience in China is informative. Starting in the late 1970s, Panasonic entered China to source manufacturing. However, as China became an important market, Panasonic created offerings based on their Japanese products sometimes stripped down. But by 2000, it became clear that they needed products more responsive to Chinese consumers. In 2003, the

Shanghai-based China Lifestyle Research Center was launched, the first serious attempt to develop a deep understanding of the Chinese customer. The center was close to the technology and R&D staffs in Japan and worked together to create China-oriented products.

The resulting products made Panasonic a player against tough local competition. In studying some 3,000 households throughout China, researchers at the center noticed that in Chinese kitchens, the space of a refrigerator is usually 10 centimeters less than the standard width of the Panasonic product. This simple finding that had eluded Panasonic allowed changes that resulted in a 10-fold increase in the sales of Panasonic's refrigerators. Another study uncovered the fact that in more than 90 percent of Chinese homes with washers, consumers were still washing by hand underwear fearing that bacteria from outerwear would be transferred to underwear. The solution was a means to sterilize clothes in the wash using silver ions. Refining and publicizing the new technology in 2007, Panasonic increased their share of the washer market from 3 to 15 percent in China. The technology was imported back to Japan, where it was employed in refrigerators as a way to sterilize food.[8]

The key takeaway is that Panasonic got serious about understanding the Chinese households and provided the Chinese Panasonic operation to have at least an equal role in charting strategy and precipitating innovation.

EXPANDING THE GLOBAL FOOTPRINT

Motivation to be global naturally leads to global initiatives to expand a firm's market footprint, a task that can be messy and difficult. Strategy development gets much harder when the context is a different language, an unfamiliar culture, new competitors and channels, and very different sets of market trends and forces. There are many routes to failure. A study of some 150 international expansion initiatives during a five-year period showed that less than half avoided failure. However, the examination of those that survived suggested that success was usually accompanied by four conditions.[9]

- **A strong core.** A strong home market provides resources and experience that can be leveraged in geographic expansion. It is a rare firm that finds success abroad without a successful home market.

- **A repeatable formula for expansion.** When the same model works in country after country, the risk of entry is reduced. Avon, for example, uses its direct model everywhere and has refined the execution to a science.

- **Customer differentiation that travels.** When the same segments are targeted and the same product and position work across countries, there is no need to research the market and reinvent the offering every time a new country is entered. Nike, Pampers, and Heineken, for example, have been able to differentiate their respective brands the same way everywhere.

- **Industry economics.** It is important to recognize whether global share or local share will drive success. Some industries like razors or computers, for example, provide cost advantages for global scale. Others, like beer, cement, and software, reward high local share. A mistake is to expect global scale in a local scale industry.

To the extent that any of these conditions are missing, the task will be more difficult, but strategic considerations may still make it imperative to find a way to succeed.

What Country to Enter?

Once a firm has decided to become global, deciding what country or countries to enter—and in what sequence—is a key challenge. Entering any new market can be risky and take away resources that could be used to make strategic investments elsewhere. A frequently unforeseen consequence of global expansion is that healthy markets, especially the home market, are put at risk by this diversion of resources. It is thus important to select markets for which the likelihood of success will be high and the resource drain minimized.

Market selection starts with several basic dimensions:

- Is the market attractive in terms of size and growth? Are there favorable market trends? For many companies, China and India often appear attractive because of their sheer size and growth potential.

- Can the firm add value to the market? Will the products and business model provide a point of differentiation that represents a relevant customer benefit? Tesco has developed an Internet-based home delivery system for grocery retailers that adds value in many markets.[10]

- How intense is the competition? Are other firms well entrenched with a loyal following, and are they committed to defending their position? Tesco, a major retailer in the United Kingdom, found that expansion to France was unattractive because of the established competition, whereas eastern European countries had much less formidable competition. As a result, Hungary was the first country in continental Europe that Tesco entered.[11]

- Can the firm implement its business model in the country, or do operational or cultural barriers exist? How feasible is any adaptation that is required? Marks & Spencer, a U.K. retailer spanning food, clothing, and general merchandise, attempted to export its products and the look and feel of its stores to the Continent, only to find that these offerings had little appeal to Europeans.

- Are there political uncertainties that will add risk? In addition to the obvious risks of political instability, there are more subtle issues. Coke and Pepsi got blindsided in India when a nongovernmental entity claimed to have found residue of pesticides in their products. Despite the firms' protestations and evidence that the claims were unfounded, their businesses took a 12 percent dive, and their images suffered. A false claim of contamination similarly hurt P&G's cosmetics effort in China.

- Can a critical mass be achieved? It is usually fatal to enter countries lacking the sales potential needed to support the marketing and distribution effort needed for success.

Wal-Mart's surprising failure in Germany shows the power of the last three dimensions.[12] In 2006, the firm gave up a 10-year effort to get a successful presence in Germany in the wake of several mistakes and misjudgments. For example, the first CEO spoke only English and insisted that his managers do the same. The next CEO tried to manage from the United Kingdom. The short shopping hours in Germany and the fact that Germans did not want assistance in the store were just a few of the conditions to which Wal-Mart had trouble adjusting. Wal-Mart also seemed to underestimate the major German competitors, which did not provide much of an opening for a value offering. Finally, Wal-Mart failed to achieve the economies of scale needed to justify its infrastructure. Wal-Mart's failure in Germany and the fact that it is weak elsewhere in the world

MARKETING IN CHINA

An *Advertising Age* study by Normandy Madden, a student of developing markets, provided some warnings to those Western firms that enter China:[13]

- China is not a single country. Rather, it is more like dozens of countries each with its own points of difference in spending power, motivations, and channels. Looking at China as a single market is like believing Europe is a homogeneous entity.
- Western goods are popular and provide self-expressive benefits, but that does not mean that the Chinese people are not grounded in their Confucian traditions and culture.
- The Chinese consumer is price conscious, demanding, and knowledgeable in part because of the rise of the Internet. Beware of talking down to them.
- Don't underestimate local brands. In many categories, local brands were bystanders at first but rose to be market contenders if not leaders.
- Mass media in China has limitations: the audience will include many who are unable to buy some brands, and the programming is not compelling.
- The more effective route is often more focused marketing using events, sampling, promotions, or digital marketing. In large retail outlets, there are often up to 100 "push girls" in action. They provide energy to the store and influence the ability of a brand to get attention and trial with often loud and aggressive sampling efforts.[14] Shopping in China is, in part because of the push girls, likely to be a considered entertainment to be enjoyed rather than drudgery to be endured.

makes visible the difficulty of exporting even successful business models, especially those based on scale.

A strategy of entering countries sequentially has several advantages. It reduces the initial commitment, allows the product and marketing program to be improved based on experience in preceding countries, and provides for the gradual creation of a regional presence. Other factors, however, argue that global expansion should be done on as wide a front as possible. First, economies of scale, a key element of successful global strategies, will be more quickly realized and will be a more significant factor. Second, the ability of competitors to copy products and brand positions—a very real threat in most industries—will be inhibited because a first-mover advantage will occur in more markets. Third, standardization, is more feasible because it can be planned before local decisions fragment the marketing and branding program.

STRATEGIC ALLIANCES

Strategic alliances play an important role in global strategies because it is common for a firm to lack a key success factor for a market. It may be distribution, a brand name, a sales organization, technology, R&D capability, or manufacturing capability. To remedy this deficiency internally might require excessive time and money. When the uncertainties of operating in other countries are considered, a strategic alliance is a natural alternative for reducing investment and the accompanying inflexibility and risk.

A strategic alliance is a collaboration leveraging the strengths of two or more organizations to achieve strategic goals. There is a long-term commitment involved. It is not simply a tactical device to provide a short-term fix for a problem—to outsource a component for which a temporary manufacturing problem has surfaced, for example. Furthermore, it implies that the participating organizations will contribute and adapt needed assets or competencies to the collaboration and that these assets or competencies will be maintained over time. The results of the collaboration should have strategic value and contribute to a viable venture that can withstand competitive attack and environmental change.

A strategic alliance provides the potential for accomplishing a strategic objective or task—such as obtaining distribution in Italy—quickly, inexpensively, and with a relatively high prospect for success. This is possible because the involved firms can combine existing assets and competencies instead of having to create new assets and competencies internally.

A strategic alliance can take many forms, from a loose informal agreement to a formal joint venture. The most informal arrangement might be simply trying to work together (selling our products through your channel, for example) and allowing systems and organizational forms to emerge as the alliance develops. The more informal the arrangement, the faster it can be implemented and the more flexible it will be. As conditions and people change, the alliance can be adjusted. The problem is usually commitment. With low exit barriers and commitment, there may be a low level of strategic importance and a temptation to back away or to disengage when difficulties arise.

Motivations for Strategic Alliances

Strategic alliances can be motivated by a desire to achieve some of the benefits of a global strategy, as outlined in Figure 14.1. For example, a strategic alliance can:

- **Generate scale economies.** The fixed investment that Toyota made in designing a car and its production systems was spread over more units because of a joint venture with GM in California, which lasted for some 25 years.
- **Gain access to strategic markets.** The Italian auto maker Fiat combined with Chrysler to access the U.S. market.
- **Overcome trade barriers.** Inland Steel and Nippon Steel jointly built an advanced cold-steel mill in Indiana. Nippon supplied the technology, capital, and access to Japanese auto plants in the United States. In return, it gained local knowledge and, more important, the ability to get around import quotas.

Perhaps more commonly, a strategic alliance may be needed to compensate for the absence of or weakness in a needed asset or competency. Thus, a strategic alliance can:

- **Fill out a product line to serve market niches.** Ford, General Motors, and Chrysler have, for example, relied on alliances to provide key components of its product line. Ford's longtime relationship with Mazda has resulted in many Ford models, as well as access to some Far East markets. When Mazda decided not to build a minivan, Ford turned to Nissan for help. One firm simply cannot provide the breadth of models needed in a major market such as the United States.
- **Gain access to a needed technology.** While Fiat gained access to the U.S. market, Chrysler gained economy car designs.

- ***Use excess capacity.*** The GM/Toyota joint venture used an idle GM plant in California.
- ***Gain access to low-cost manufacturing capabilities.*** A host of companies from Wal-Mart to Dell have alliances in China to source products.
- ***Access a name or customer relationship.*** NGK bought an interest in a GE subsidiary whose product line had become obsolete in order to access the GE name and reputation in the U.S. electrical equipment market. A U.S. injection molder joined with Mitsui in order to help access Japanese manufacturing operations in the United States that preferred to do business with Japanese suppliers.
- ***Reduce the investment required.*** In some cases, a firm's contribution to a joint venture can be technology, with no financial resources required.

The Key: Maintaining Strategic Value for Collaborators

A major problem with strategic alliances occurs when the relative contribution of the partners becomes unbalanced over time and one partner no longer has any proprietary assets and competencies to contribute. This has happened in many of the early partnerships involving U.S. and Japanese firms in consumer electronics, heavy machinery, power-generation equipment, factory equipment, and office equipment.

The result, when the U.S. company has become de-skilled or hollowed out and no longer participates fully in the venture, can be traced in part to the motivation of the partners. Offshore firms are motivated to learn skills; they find it embarrassing to lack a technology, and they work to correct deficiencies. U.S. firms are motivated to make money by outsourcing elements of the value chain in order to reduce costs. They start by outsourcing assembly and move on to components, to value-added components, to product design, and finally to core technologies. The U.S. partner is then left with just the distribution function, whereas the offshore firm retains the key business elements, such as product refinement, design, and production.

One approach to protecting assets and competencies is to structure the situation so that operating management is shared. Compare, for example, the joint Toyota/GM manufacturing facility, where GM was involved in the manufacturing process and its refinements, with Chrysler's effort to sell a Mitsubishi car designed and manufactured in Japan. In the latter case, Mitsubishi eventually developed its own name and dealer network and sold its cars directly. When the motivation for an alliance is to avoid investment and achieve attractive short-term returns instead of to develop assets and competencies, the alliance will break down.

Another approach is to protect assets from a partner by controlling access. Many Japanese firms have a coordinated information transfer. Such a position avoids uncoordinated, inappropriate information flow. Other firms put clear conditions on access to a part of the product line or a part of the design. Motorola, for example, releases its microchip technology to its partner, Toshiba, only as Toshiba delivers on its promise to increase Motorola's penetration in the Japanese market. Still others keep improving the assets involved so that the partner's dependence continues. Of course, the problem of protecting assets is most difficult when the asset can be communicated by a drawing. It is somewhat easier when a complex system is involved—when, for example, the asset is manufacturing excellence.

A second set of problems involves execution of the alliance. With strategic alliances, at least two sets of business systems, people, cultures, and structures need to be reconciled. In addition, the culture and environment of each country must be considered. The Japanese, for example, tend to use a consensus-building decision process that relies on small group activity for much of its energy; this approach is very different from that of managers in the United States and Europe. Furthermore, the interests of each partner may not always seem to be in step. Many otherwise well-conceived alliances have failed because the partners simply had styles and objectives that were fundamentally incompatible.

When a joint venture is established as a separate organization, research has shown that the chances of success will be enhanced if:

- The joint venture is allowed to evolve with its own culture and values—the existing cultures of the partners will probably not work even if they are compatible with each other.

- The management and power structure from the two partners is balanced.

- Venture champions are on board to carry the ball during difficult times. Without people committed to making the venture happen, it will not happen.

- Methods are developed to resolve problems and to allow change over time. It is unrealistic to expect any strategy, organization, or implementation to exist without evolving and changing. Partners and the organization thus need to be flexible enough to allow change to occur.

Alliances are a widespread part of business strategy (the top 500 global businesses have an average of 60 major alliances each) but need to be actively managed. One study of some 200 corporations found that the most successful at adding value through alliances employed staff who coordinated all alliance-related activity within the organization.[15] This function would draw on prior experiences to provide guidance to those creating and managing new alliances. One firm, for example, has "thirty-five rules of thumb" to manage alliances from creation to termination. The dedicated alliance staff would also increase external visibility (an alliance announcement has been found to influence stock price), coordinate internal staffing and management of alliances, and help identify the need to change or terminate an alliance.

GLOBAL MARKETING MANAGEMENT

Managing a global marketing program is difficult. The country or regions are often highly autonomous. Each manager tends to think that he or she is different and others, particularly those in "central marketing," cannot understand the culture, customers, distribution, competitors, etc. of their country. As a result there tends to be little leveraging of successful programs from country to country and even little communication about common problems and programs that are successful. Further, the expertise around such areas as Internet communication, sponsorships, market research, etc. tends to be limited because of scale.

The challenge for global marketing teams is to change that—to create cooperation and communication where there have been competition and isolation. In Chapter 16 the problems that silo organizations present to marketing teams are further outlined, and practical ways to make marketing more effective in a silo world are discussed.

KEY LEARNINGS

- A global strategy considers and exploits interdependencies among operations in different countries.

- Among the motivations driving globalization are obtaining scale economies, accessing low-cost labor or materials, taking advantage of national incentives to cross-subsidize, dodging trade barriers, accessing strategic markets, enhancing firm innovation, and creating global associations.

- A standardized brand is not always optimal. Economies of scale may not exist, the discovery of a global strategy (even assuming it exists) may be difficult, or the context (for example, different market share positions or brand images) may make such a brand impractical. However, the management of the business should be common across countries—all using the same planning processes and performance measures.

- Companies successful at expanding their global footprint usually had a strong core market, a repeatable expansion formula, customer differentiation that travels, and an understanding of local vs. global scale. The selection of a country to enter should involve an analysis of the attractiveness of the market and the ability of the firm to succeed in that market.

- Strategic alliances (long-term collaboration leveraging the strengths of two or more organizations to achieve strategic goals) can enable an organization to overcome a lack of a key success factor, such as a brand or distribution. A key to the long-term success of strategic alliances is that each partner contributes assets and competencies over time and obtains strategic advantages.

- Global brand management needs to include moving the silo country business units from competition and isolation to cooperation and communication.

FOR DISCUSSION

1. Assess the motivations for going global. What would be the most important for a bank?

2. What products are likely to be more standardized across countries? Why? What products are least likely?

3. Pick a product like Cadillac or Sara Lee Deli products or service like Mr. Clean Performance Car Wash or a car and home insurance company that is offered in a limited number of countries. Assess the advantages of expanding to a more global presence.

4. For a particular product or service, such as Crest toothpaste or the Toyota Scion, how would you evaluate the countries that would represent the best prospects? Be specific. What information would you need, and how would you obtain it? Prioritize the criteria that would be useful in deciding which countries to enter.

5. For a brand such as Bank of America, Pantene, or Ford, how would you go about creating blockbuster global brand-building programs—for example, sponsorships, promotions, or advertising? How would you leverage those programs?

6. Select a company. How would you advise it to find an alliance partner to gain distribution into China? What advice would you give regarding the management of that alliance?

7. What is the advantage of a global brand team? What are the problems of using a team to devise and run the global strategy?

NOTES

1. Douglas B. Holt, John A. Quelch, and Earl L. Taylor, "How Global Brands Compete," *Harvard Business Review*, September 2004, pp. 68–75.

2. C. K. Prahalad and Hrishi Bhattacharyya, How to be a Truly Global Company," *Strategy & Business*, 64, Autumn, 2011, pp. 54–61.

3. Gary Hamel and C. K. Prahalad, "Do You Really Have a Global Strategy?" *Harvard Business Review*, July–August 1985, pp. 139–148.

4. Geoffrey Jones, " The Growth Opportunity that Lies Next Door," *Harvard Business Review*, July–August 2012, p. 145.

5. Theodore Levitt, "The Globalization of Markets," *Harvard Business Review*, May–June 1983, pp. 92–102.

6. The material in this section draws from Chapter 5 of the book *Spanning Silos* by David Aaker, Boston: Harvard Publishing Company, 2008.

7. Karlene Lukovitz, "Brands Lose Relevance in Food-Buying Decisions," *Marketing Daily*, October 21, 2008.

8. Toshio Wakayama, Junjiro Shintaku, and Tomofumi Amano, "What Panasonic Learned in China," *Harvard Business Review*, December 2012, pp. 109–112.

9. James Root and Josef Ming, "Keys to Foreign Growth: Four Requisites for Expanding Across Borders," *Strategy & Leadership*, Vol. 34, No. 3 (2006), pp. 59–61.

10. Victoria Griffith, "Welcome to Your Global Superstore," *Strategy+Business*, Vol. 26, 2002, p. 95.

11. Ibid.

12. "Heading for the Exit," *Economist*, August 5, 2006, p. 54.

13. Normandy Madden, "Looking to Grow in China? Ad Age Has 10 Surefire Tips," *Advertising Age*, May 4, 2009, pp. 3, 30.

14. Anita Chang Beattie, "Catching the Eye of the Chinese Shopper," *Advertising Age*, December 10, 2012. pp. 20–22.

15. Jeffrey H. Dyer, Prashant Kale, and Harbir Singh, "How to Make Strategic Alliances Work," MIT *Sloan Management Review*, Summer 2001, pp. 37–43.

CHAPTER FIFTEEN

Setting Priorities for Businesses and Brands—The Exit, Milk, and Consolidate Options

There is nothing so useless as doing efficiently that which should not be done at all.
—*Peter Drucker*

If you want to succeed, double your failure rate.
—*Thomas Watson, founder, IBM*

Anyone can hold the helm when the sea is calm.
—*Publilius Syrus*

All firms, from Mercedes to GE to Nestlé to Marriott to Intel, should view their business units as a portfolio. Some should receive investment because they are cash-generating stars in the present and will be into the future. The investment is needed to keep them healthy and to exploit growth opportunities. Others need investment because they are the future stars of the company even though they now have more potential than sales and profits. Identifying the priority business units, the ones that merit financial and managerial resources, is a key to a successful strategy.

Equally important, perhaps more important, is to identify those business units that are not priorities. Some of them should assume the role of generating cash through a milking or harvesting strategy. These units, termed *cash cows*, should no longer absorb investments aimed at growing the business. Still other units should be divested or closed or merged because they lack the potential to become either stars or cash cows—their profit prospects may be unsatisfactory, or they may lack a fit with the strategic thrust going forward. These decisions, which are strategically and organizationally difficult, often are crucial to organizational success and even survival.

A related issue is dealing with too many brands by eliminating or merging them. Brand strategy and business strategy are closely related because a brand will often represent a business. As a result, brand strategy is often a good vehicle to develop and clarify the business strategy. Too many brands, like too many business units, result in confusion and inefficiency. The firm can support only so many brands, and brand proliferation has often grown to the point of paralyzing the organization. In the automobile field there are now over 300 brands, which have resulted in confusion, overlap, inefficiency, and, worse, an inability to fund promising brands. Certainly, one reason behind the restructuring of GM, which resulted in the dropping of Oldsmobile and Saturn, was that there were too many brands with the result that some were underfunded and potential scale economies were unrealized.

We start with an overview of portfolio strategy and then discuss the divest and milk strategy options. We then turn to the problem from the perspective of brand strategy and explore how brand portfolios can be reduced so that more brand focus becomes possible and clarity can be enhanced in both the brand strategy and the accompanying business strategy.

THE BUSINESS PORTFOLIO

Portfolio analysis of business units dates from the mid-1960s with the growth-share matrix, which was pioneered and used extensively by the BCG consulting group. The concept was to position each business within a firm on the two-dimensional matrix shown in Figure 15.1. The market-share dimension (actually the ratio of share to that of the largest competitor) was a summary measure of firm strength and cost advantages resulting from scale economies and manufacturing experience. The growth dimension was defended as the best single indicator of market attractiveness.

The BCG growth-share matrix is associated with a colorful cast of characters representing strategy recommendations. According to the BCG logic, the stars, important to the business and deserving of any needed investment, resided in the high-share, high-growth quadrant while the cash cows, the source of cash, occupied the high-share, low-growth quadrant. In addition, we have the dogs, which are potential cash traps and candidates for liquidation-, in the low-growth, low-share quadrant and problem children with heavy cash needs but the potential to eventually convert into stars-, in the low-share, high-growth quadrant.

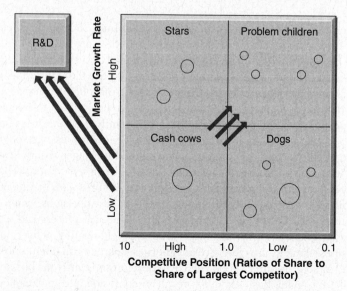

Figure 15.1 The Growth-Share Matrix

The BCG growth-share model, although naive and simplistic in its analysis and recommendations, was very influential in its day. Its lasting contribution was to make visible the issue of allocation across business units, that some businesses should generate cash that supports others. It also introduced the experience curve (discussed in Chapter 11) into strategy and showed that, under some conditions, market share could lead to experience-curve-based advantage.

A more realistic, richer portfolio model associated with GE and McKinsey also evaluates the business on two dimensions—market attractiveness and the business position. Each of these dimensions, as suggested by Figure 15.2, is richer and more robust than those used in the BCG model. The investment decision is again suggested by the position on a matrix. A business that is favorable on both dimensions should usually be a candidate to grow using the tools of the last four chapters.

When both market attractiveness and business position evaluations are unfavorable, the harvest or divest options should be raised. Of course, even in a hostile environment, routes to profitability can be found. Perhaps the business can turn to new markets, growth submarkets, superpremium offerings, new products, new applications, new technologies, or revitalized marketing. When the matrix position is neither unambiguously positive or negative, the investment decision will require more detailed study.

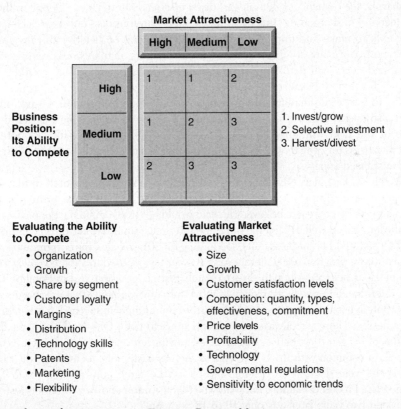

Figure 15.2 The Market Attractiveness/Business Position Matrix

DIVESTMENT OR LIQUIDATION

There are usually three drivers of a divestment decision besides the current and expected profit drain. The first is market demand. Perhaps demand estimates were overly optimistic in the first place or perhaps the demand was there but deteriorated as the market matured and the excitement faded. The second is competitive intensity. New competitors could have emerged or the existing competitors may have been underestimated or could have enhanced their offering. The third is a change in strategic thrust of the organization, a change that affects the fit of the business. The firm may no longer be a synergistic asset or the business may no longer be a link to the future. In fact, the business may be not only a resource drain but a distraction to the internal culture and the external brand image.

These factors all came into play when Home Depot made the painful decision after a 17-year effort to close their 34 Expo Design Centers, stores that carried high-end products embedded in an upscale design service and elaborate aspirational displays.[1] Introduced in the early 1990s as a way to provide a high margin, growth platform, the idea was to introduce chain economies into what is a mom and pop industry buttressed by the buying clout and logistic assets of Home Depot. Even during the housing boom, the concept struggled perhaps because Home Depot's image of functionality and value got in the way of delivering the self-expressive benefits that were the heart of Expo; perhaps because the design culture just did not fit organizationally; and perhaps because the design community turned out to be tougher competitors than envisioned. When new housing construction declined sharply, the demand, such as it was, dried up. In addition, Home Depot, in the midst of a recession, needed to sharpen its strategy to focus on its core business and Expo needed to go.

Being able to make and implement an exit decision can be healthy and invigorating. The opportunity cost of overinvesting in a business and of hanging on to business ventures that are not performing and never will perform can be damaging and even disastrous. Further, this cost is often hidden from view because it is shielded by a nondecision. When a business that is not contributing to future profitability and growth absorbs resources in the firm—not only financial capital but also talent, the firm's most important currency—those businesses that do represent the future of the firm will suffer. Perhaps worse, some businesses with the potential to be important platforms for growth will be left on the sidelines or starved, victims of false hopes and stubborn, misplaced loyalty.

Jack Welch, the legendary GE CEO, believed that identifying the talent of the future was his most important job and equally important was identifying those who did not fit the future plans and letting them seek careers elsewhere. He believed the firm would be stronger and the people involved would benefit in the long run as well. He felt the same about business units. Welch, during his first four years as GE's CEO, divested 117 business units, accounting for 20 percent of the corporation's assets. Such an active divestiture program can generate cash at a fair (as opposed to a forced-sale) price, liberate management talent, help reposition the firm to match its strategic vision, and add vitality. The divested businesses often benefit as well, as many will move into environments that are more supportive in terms of not only assets and competencies but also the commitment to succeed. It is healthy all around to trim businesses. There will always be business units to trim. One study by Bain & Company estimated that of 181 growth initiatives that involved moving into a business adjacent to a core business (having much in common with the core business such as customers, technology, distribution, etc.) only 27 percent were deemed successful, and about the same number were clear failures.[2] In packaged goods, a Procter & Gamble study showed that the number of new products tested that were still on the shelf two years later was only 10 to 15 percent.[3]

Achieving sustained growth is rare, and when it appears, it is often fueled by new businesses. One theory advanced by James Brian Quin, a strategy theorist, and others on how to find and develop successful new businesses is to "let a thousand flowers bloom," tend those that thrive, and let the rest wither. The venture capital industry lives by the mantra that if you fund 10 ventures, two will be home runs, and they will represent overall success. Getting home runs requires funding many ventures. The key to the prescription that it takes many tries to find success is to have a process and the will to terminate business units that are not going to fuel growth in the future. Without that process, a thousand flowers will result in an overgrown garden where none are healthy.

Many firms avoid divestiture decisions until they become obvious or are forced by external forces. In addition to wasted resources, delayed divestiture decisions result in lower prices being obtained for the business. As painful divest decisions are delayed, the forces that create the decline of the business continue to exert pressure and often increase. The result is a declining value often accompanied with more losses. One study showed that organizations that actively manage these decisions by systematically evaluating the strategic fit and future prospects of each business and then regularly make divestiture decisions or placing business units on a probationary status are more profitable.[4]

When any of the following are present, an exit strategy should be considered:

Business Position

- The business position is weak—the assets and competencies are inadequate, the value proposition is losing relevance, or the market share is in third or fourth place and declining in the face of strong competition.
- The business is now losing money, and future prospects are dim.

Market Attractiveness

- Demand within the category is declining at an accelerating rate, and no pockets of enduring demand are accessible to the business. It is unlikely that a resurgence of the category or a subcategory will occur.
- The price pressures are expected to be extreme, caused by determined competitors with high exit barriers and by a lack of brand loyalty and product differentiation.

Strategic Fit

- The firm's strategic direction has changed, and the role of the business has become superfluous or even unwanted.
- Firms' financial and management resources are being absorbed when they could be employed more effectively elsewhere.

Exit Barriers

Even when the decision seems clear, there may be exit barriers that need to be considered. Some involve termination costs. A business may support other businesses within the firm by providing part of a system, by supporting a distribution channel, or by using excess plant capacity. Long-term contracts with suppliers and with labor groups may be expensive to break. The business may have commitments to provide spare parts and service backup to retailers and customers, and it may be difficult to arrange alternative acceptable suppliers.

An exit decision may affect the reputation and operation of other company businesses, especially if that business is visibly tied to the firm. Thus, GE was concerned about the impact its decision to discontinue small appliances would have on its lamp and large-appliance business retailers and consumers. At the extreme, closing a business could affect access to financial markets and influence the opinion of dealers, suppliers, and customers about the firm's other operations.

If there is any reason to believe the market may change, making the business more attractive, the exit decision could be delayed or changed to a milk or hold decision. Remaining in the business may be a contingency play.

Biases Inhibiting the Exit Decision

There are well-documented psychological biases in analyzing a business. One such bias is reluctance to give up. There may be an emotional attachment to a business that has been in the "family" for many years, or that may even be the original business on which the rest of the firm was based. It is difficult to turn your back on such a valued friend, especially if it means laying off good people. Managerial pride also enters in. Professional managers often view themselves as problem solvers and are reluctant to admit defeat. Several anecdotes describe firms that have had to send a series of executives to close down a subsidiary. Too frequently, the executive would become convinced that a turnaround was possible, only to subsequently fail at the effort.

Another obstacle is called confirmation bias.[5] People naturally seek out information that supports their position and discount disconfirming information, whatever the context. The audiences for partisan political observers do not represent a cross-section but involved people who seek out those who support their beliefs. Confirmation bias can be rampant in evaluating a business to which some have emotional and professional ties. Information that confirms that the business can be saved is more likely to be uncovered and valued than disconfirming information. Questions asked in market research may be slanted, perhaps inadvertently, toward providing an optimistic future for the business. When there is uncertainty, the bias can get large. When predicting future sales or projecting costs, for example, extreme numbers may be put forth as plausible. Such a tendency is seen in major governmental decisions, such as funding a fighter plane or building a bridge.

Another bias to deal with is the escalation of commitment. Instead of regarding prior investments as sunk costs, there is a bias toward linking them to the future decisions. Thus, a decision to invest $10 million more is framed as salvaging the prior $100 million investment.

All three biases were in view when Tenneco Oil Company made some decisions that helped lead to its demise.[6] Tenneco Oil was a healthy company, a top 20 in the Fortune 500, but stole defeat from the jaws of victory, so to speak. They had a division, J. I. Case, a manufacturer of agricultural and construction equipment, which was doing badly. Case had weak products, weak distribution, high costs, and a 10 percent market share facing a declining, low-profit industry with excess capacity that was dominated by John Deere. Instead of facing reality, Tenneco doubled down by buying International Harvester, a competitor of Chase, with 20 percent share and on the verge of bankruptcy. The market did not improve, synergies did not materialize in a timely fashion, and the losses of the combined equipment company were substantial, while the profit flow of the energy operations faltered as the price of oil fell. These events coupled with high leverage meant the end of Tenneco Oil; the company was sold off in pieces. A series of bad decisions was driven not by an objective analysis but rather by these biases coupled with the illusion that success and cash flow largely dependent on external events will continue.

Injecting Objectivity into Disinvest Decisions

To deal with these biases, the decision needs to be more objective in terms of both process and people. The process should be transparent and persuasive, thereby encouraging the discussion to be professional, centered on key issues and discouraging emotional gut reactions. It helps if it is applied to a spectrum of business units instead of just the marginal ones. It is well known that the only way to close down a defense plant is to evaluate all of them and let the process identify which ones are no longer needed. When politicians are faced with such objective evidence and required to make an up or down vote, it becomes harder to fight for their "base."

It is also helpful to have people interjected into the analysis without a history that prevents them from being objective. Such people can be from within the firm, but sometimes an outside party from a consulting company or a new hire can be more objective. This can be done vicariously as well. There is the often-repeated story of how Intel made the painful decision to turn its back on the memory business, which represented not only its heritage but also the bulk of its sales. Intel's president Andy Grove at one point looked at CEO Gordon Moore and asked what a new outside CEO would do. The answer was clear—get out of memory. So the two men symbolically walked out the door and walked back in and then made the fateful decision to exit a business that had been destroyed by Asian competitors. Even after making the decision, it was difficult to cut out all R&D and close it down. Two people sent to close the business dragged their heels and continued to invest; finally, Grove himself had to step in. It turns out that the implementation of an exit decision is also difficult.

Peter Drucker recounted a story about a leader firm in a specialized industry that organized a group of people every three months to look critically at one segment of the company's offerings. This group was a cross-section of young managers and changed every quarter. They addressed the Andy Grove question—if we were not in this business now, would we go into it? If the answer was no, an exit strategy would be considered. If the answer was yes, then the next question was whether the existing business strategy would be used. A negative judgment would lead to proposed changes. One key to the firm's success was that this process led to the exit or modification of every single one of its businesses over a five-year period.

THE MILK STRATEGY

A milk or harvest strategy aims to generate cash flow by reducing investment and operating expenses to a minimum even if that causes a reduction in sales and market share. The underlying assumptions are that the firm has better uses for the funds, that the involved business is not crucial to the firm either financially or synergistically, and that milking is feasible because sales will stabilize or decline in an orderly way without supporting investment. The milking strategy creates and supports a cash cow business.

There are variants of milking strategies. A fast milking strategy would be disciplined about minimizing the expenditures toward the brand and maximizing the short-term cash flow, accepting the risk of a fast exit. A slow milking strategy would sharply reduce long-term investment but continue to support operating areas such as marketing and service. A hold strategy would provide enough product development investment to hold a market position, as opposed to investing to grow or strengthen the position.

Conditions Favoring a Milking Strategy

A milking strategy would be selected over a growth strategy when the current market conditions make investments unlikely to improve a rather negative environment caused by competitor aggressiveness, consumer tastes, or other factors. Sometimes it is precipitated by a new entrant that turns a market hostile. Chase & Sanborn was once a leading coffee; the "Chase & Sanborn Hour," starring Edgar Bergen, was one of the most popular radio shows of its time. After World War II, though, Chase & Sanborn decided to retreat to a milking strategy rather than fight an expensive market retention battle against the rising popularity of instant coffee and the appearance of General Foods' heavily advertised Maxwell House brand.

Several conditions support a milking strategy rather than an exit strategy:

- The business position is weak, but there is enough customer loyalty, perhaps in a limited part of the market, to generate sales and profits in a milking mode. The risk of losing relative position with a milking strategy is low.

- The business is not central to the current strategic direction of the firm but has relevance to it and leverages assets and competencies.

- The demand is stable or the decline rate is not excessively steep, and pockets of enduring demand ensure that the decline rate will not suddenly become precipitous.

- The price structure is stable at a level that is profitable for efficient firms.

- A milking strategy can be successfully managed.

One advantage of milking rather than divesting is that a milking strategy can often be reversed if it turns out to be based on incorrect premises regarding market prospects, competitor moves, cost projections, or other relevant factors. A resurgence in product classes that were seemingly dead or in terminal decline gives pause. Oatmeal, for example, has experienced a sharp increase in sales because of its low cost and associations with nutrition and health. In men's apparel, suspenders have shown signs of growth. Fountain pens, invented in 1884, were virtually killed by the appearance in 1939 of the ballpoint. However, the combination of nostalgia and a desire for prestige has provided a major comeback for the luxury fountain pen. As a result, the industry has seen years in which sales doubled.

Implementation Problems

It can be organizationally difficult to assign business units to a cash cow role because in a decentralized organization (and most firms pride themselves on their decentralized structure), it is natural for the managers of cash-generating businesses to control the available cash that funds investment opportunities. The culture is for each business to be required or encouraged to fund its own growth, and of course all business units have investment options with accompanying rationales. As a result, a fast-growing business with enormous potential but relatively low sales volume will often be starved of needed cash. It requires a sometimes disruptive centralized decision to assign a large business unit a cash cow role. The irony is that the largest businesses involving mature products may have inferior investment alternatives, but because cash flow is plentiful, their investments will still be funded. The net effect is that available cash is channeled to areas of low potential and withheld from the most attractive areas. A business portfolio analysis helps force the issue of which businesses should receive the available cash.

Another serious problem is the difficulty of placing and motivating a manager in a milking situation. Most SBU managers do not have the orientation, background, or skills to engage in a successful milking strategy. Adjusting performance measures and rewards appropriately can be difficult for both the organization and the managers involved. It might seem reasonable to use a manager who specializes in milking strategies, but that is often not feasible simply because such specialization is rare. Most firms rotate managers through different types of situations, and career paths simply are not geared to creating milking specialists.

There are also market risks associated with a milking strategy. If employees and customers suspect that a milking strategy is being employed, the resulting lack of trust may upset the whole strategy. As the line between a milking strategy and abandonment is sometimes very thin, customers may lose confidence in the firm's product, and employee morale may suffer. Competitors may attack more vigorously. All these possibilities can create a sharper-than-anticipated decline. To minimize such effects, it is helpful to keep a milking strategy as inconspicuous as possible.

The Hold Strategy

A variant of the milking strategy is the hold strategy, in which growth-motivated investment is avoided, but an adequate level of investment is employed to maintain product quality, production facilities, and customer loyalty. A hold strategy will be superior to a milk strategy when the market prospects and/or the business position is not as grim. There may be more substantial and protected pockets of demand, better margins, a superior market position, a closer link to other business units in the firm, or the possibility of improved market prospects. A hold strategy would be preferable to an invest strategy when an industry lacks growth opportunities and a strategy of increasing share would risk triggering competitive retaliation. The hold strategy can be a long-term strategy to manage a cash cow or an interim strategy employed until the uncertainties of an industry are resolved.

Sometimes a hold strategy can result in a profitable "last survivor" of a market that is declining slower than most assume. A strong survivor may be profitable, in part because there may be little competition and in part because the investment to maintain a leadership position might be relatively low. The cornerstone of this strategy is to encourage competitors to exit. Toward that end, a firm can be visible about its commitment to be the surviving leader in the industry by engaging in increased promotion or even introducing product improvements. It can encourage competitors to leave by pricing aggressively and by reducing their exit barriers by purchasing their assets, by assuming their long-term obligations, or even by buying their business. Kunz, which made passbooks for financial institutions, was able to buy competitor assets so far under book value that the payback period was measured in months. As a result, Kunz had record years in a business area others had written off as all but dead decades earlier.

A problem with the hold strategy is that if conditions change, reluctance or slowness to reinvest may result in lost market share. The two largest can manufacturers, American and Continental, failed to invest in the two-piece can process when it was developed because they were engaged in diversification efforts and were attempting to avoid investments in their cash cow. As a result, they lost substantial market share.

A hold strategy is particularly problematic if a disruptive innovation appears and the strategy prevents a firm from making necessary investments to remain relevant. As a result, firms may be slow to convert from film to digital, to reduce trans fats from packaged goods, or to adapt hybrid technology. The result could be a premature demise of a cash cow business.

PRIORITIZING AND TRIMMING THE BRAND PORTFOLIO

Brands are the face of a business strategy, and getting the brand strategy right is often a route to making the right business strategy decisions. One element of brand strategy is to set priorities within the brand portfolio, identifying the strong strategic brands, other brands playing worthwhile roles, brands that should receive no investment, and brands that should be deleted.[7]

One reason to prioritize brands and trim the brand portfolio is that the exercise provides a good way to prioritize the business portfolio because the brand will usually represent a business. When the brand perspective is used, the business prioritization analysis can sometimes be more objective and the resulting conclusion more transparent and obvious. The brand is usually a key asset of the business and represents its value proposition. Thus, a recognition that the brand has become weak can be a good signal that the business position is weak. Without prioritization of the brand portfolio, strategic brands will lose equity and market position because marginal brands are absorbing brand-building dollars and, worse, managerial talent. Managers simply follow an instinct to solve problems rather than exploiting opportunities, and too many marginal brands create a host of problems.

A second reason is that prioritizing and trimming the brand portfolio can correct the debilitating confusion associated with overbranding. Most firms simply have too many brands, subbrands, and endorsed brands, all part of complex structures. Some brands may reflect product types, others price value, and still others customer types or applications. The branded offerings may even overlap. The totality often simply reflects a mess. Customers have a hard time understanding what is being offered and what to purchase; even employees may be confused. The business strategy therefore operates at a huge disadvantage.

A third reason is to address the strategic paralysis created by an overbranded, confused brand portfolio without priorities. It is all too common for a firm to be immobilized by an inability to commit to how a new offering or new business should be branded. To provide a brand to a new offering or business that will foster success, there needs to be a sense of what brands will be strategic going forward and what their role and image will be. Assigning a brand that lacks a strategic future or whose future is incompatible with that assignment can be a serious handicap to a business strategy.

One partial step to reduce overbranding is to be more disciplined about the introduction of new offerings and new brands, avoiding ad hoc business expansion decisions made without a systematic justification process. In particular, any proposed new brand should represent a business that is substantial enough and has a long enough life to justify brand-building expenses, and it should have a unique ability to represent a business—that is, no other existing brands would work.

Controlling the introduction of new brands is only half the battle. There needs to be an objective process to phase out or redeploy marginal or redundant brands after they have outlived their usefulness. The strategic brand consolidation process, summarized in Figure 15.3, addresses that challenge. It involves five distinct steps: identifying the relevant brand set, assessing the brands, prioritizing brands, creating a revised brand portfolio strategy, and designing a transition strategy.

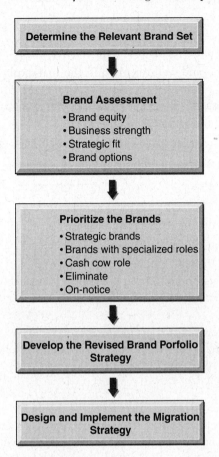

Figure 15.3 The Strategic Brand Consolidation Process

1. Identify the Relevant Brand Set

The brand set will depend on the problem context. It can include all brands or subsets of the portfolio. For example, an analysis for GM might include the brands GMC, Chevrolet, Pontiac, Buick, and Cadillac. Or it might include the brand set within a narrow context such as the Chevrolet Silverado truck brands 1500, Hybrid, 2500HD, 3500HD, and Chassis. When brands are involved that share similar roles, it becomes easier to evaluate the relative strength.

2. Brand Assessment

If brand priorities are to be established, evaluation criteria need to be established. Further, these criteria need to have metrics so that brands can be scaled. A highly structured and quantified assessment provides stimulation and guidance to the discussion and the decision process. There should be no illusion that the decision will default to picking the higher number. The criteria will depend on the context, but in general, there are four areas or dimensions of evaluations:

Brand Equity

- Awareness—Is the brand well known in the marketplace?
- Reputation—Is the brand well regarded in the marketplace? Does it have high perceived quality?
- Differentiation—Does the brand have a point of differentiation? A personality? Does it lack a point of parity along a key dimension?
- Relevance—Is it relevant for today's customers and today's applications?
- Loyalty—How large a segment of loyal customers is there?

Business Prospects

- Sales—Is this brand driving a significant business?
- Share/market position—Does this brand hold a dominant or leading position in the market? What is the trajectory?
- Profit margin—Is this brand a profit contributor and likely to remain so? Or are the market and competitive conditions such that the margin prospects are unfavorable?
- Growth—Are the growth prospects for the brand positive within its existing markets? If the market is in decline, are there pockets of enduring demand that the brand can access?

Strategic Fit

- Extendability—Does the brand have the potential to extend to other products as either a master brand or an endorser? Can it be a platform for growth?
- Business fit—Does the brand drive a business that fits strategically with the direction of the firm? Does it support a product or market that is central to the future business strategy of the firm?

Branding Options

- Brand equity transferability—Could the brand equity be transferred to another brand in the portfolio by reducing the brand to a subbrand or by developing a descriptor?
- Merging with other brands—Could the brand be aggregated with other brands in the portfolio to form one brand?

Brands need to be evaluated with respect to the criteria. The resulting scores can be combined by averaging or by insisting on a minimal score on some key dimensions. For example, a low score on strategic fit may be enough to signal that the brand's role needs to be assessed. Or, if the brand is a significant cash drain, then it might be a candidate for review even if it is otherwise apparently healthy. In any case, the profile will be important and judgment will need to be employed to make final assessments of the brand's current strength.

3. Prioritize Brands

The brands that are to live, be supported, and be actively managed need to be prioritized or tiered in some way. The number of tiers will depend on the context, but the logic is to categorize brands so that precious brand-building budgets are allocated wisely. The top tier will include the strategic power brands—those with existing or potential equity that are supporting a significant business or have the potential to do so in the future. A second tier could be those brands involving a smaller business, perhaps a niche or local business, or brands with a specialized role such as a flanker brand (a price brand that deters competitors from penetrating the market from below). A third tier would be the cash cow brands, which should be dialed down with little or no investment of brand-building resources.

The remaining brands need to be assigned descriptor roles, eliminated, placed on notices, or restructured.

- **Become descriptors.** Those brands that have no equity but serve to describe an offering could be assigned a descriptive role. The Dell Dimension computer, for example, could be judged to have its equity in the Dell brand. The Dimension brand, with no equity, would then be assigned a descriptive role. It could be replaced by the term desktop, but it also could be retained to describe the desktop line of Dell computers.

- **Eliminate.** If a brand is judged to be ill suited for the portfolio because of weak or inappropriate brand equity, business prospects, strategic fit, or redundancy issues, a plan to eliminate the brand from the portfolio is needed. Selling it to another firm or simply killing it become options.

- **On notice.** A brand that is failing to meets its performance goals but has a plan to turn its prospects around might be put on an on-notice list. If the plan fails and prospects continue to look unfavorable, elimination should then be considered.

- **Merged.** If a group of brands can be merged into a branded brand group, the goal of creating fewer, more focused brands will be advanced. Microsoft combined the products Word, PowerPoint, Excel, and Outlook into a single product called Office. The original product brands are now reduced to descriptive subbrands.

- **Transfer equity.** Unilever transferred the equity of Rave hair products to Suave and the Surf detergent products to All.

Nestlé has long had in place a system of brand portfolio prioritization. Twelve global brands are the tier one brands on which they focus. Each of the global brands has a top executive who is designated as its brand champion. These executives make sure that all activities enhance the brand. They have final approval over any brand extensions and major brand-building efforts. Peter Brabeck, who became CEO, has elevated six of these brands—Nescafe for coffee, Nestea for tea, Buitoni for pasta and sauces, Maggi for bouillon cubes, Purina for pet food, and Nestlé for ice cream and candy—as having priority within Nestlé. Nestlé has also identified 83 regional brands that receive management attention from the Swiss headquarters. In addition, there are hundreds of local brands that are either considered strategic, in which the headquarters is involved, or tactical, in which case they are managed by local teams.

4. Develop the Revised Brand Portfolio Strategy

With brand priorities set, the brand portfolio strategy will need to be revised. Toward that end, several brand portfolio structures should be created. They could include a lean structure with a single master brand, such as Sony or HP, or a "house of brands" strategy like P&G, which has over 80 major product brands. The most promising options are likely to be in between. The idea is to create structures around two or three viable options, with perhaps two or three suboptions under each.

The major brand portfolio structure options, together with suboptions, need to be evaluated with respect to whether they:

- Support the business strategy going forward
- Provide suitable roles for the strong brands
- Leverage the strong brands
- Generate clarity both to customers and to the brand team

THE CASE OF CENTURION

A large manufacturing firm, which is here labeled as Centurion Industries, went through a strategic brand consolidation process before selecting its portfolio strategy going forward. The process started when the CEO observed that the brand portfolio in a major division was too diffuse and that future growth and market position were dependent on creating a simpler, more focused portfolio of powerful brands. The division had grown in part by acquisition and now had nine product brands, only three of which were endorsed by the corporate brand, Centurion. The nine brands served a variety of product markets that could be roughly clustered into two logical groupings. One, the green business group, included five brands. The other, the blue business group, involved four brands. Competitors with less brand fragmentation and more natural brand synergy had developed stronger brands and were enjoying share growth.

In the green business group, a brand assessment supported by customer research was conducted on all five brands. One, Larson, represented the largest business, had substantial credibility in that business, and had high awareness levels. Further, it could be stretched to cover the other four areas even though it had no current presence in any of those areas. It did have a visible quality problem, however, that was being addressed. The decision was made to migrate all of the green business brands to Larson and to make the quality issue at Larson a corporate priority. The first migration stage was to endorse three of the brands with Larson and replace the fourth brand, which drove a small business, with the Larson brand. The second stage, to occur within two years, was to convert all of the brands in the green business group to the Larson name and add an endorsement by the corporate brand.

In the blue business group, the brand Pacer emerged from the brand assessment stage as the strongest, especially in terms of awareness, image, and sales. Because Pacer was in a business area closely related to that of the other three brands, using the Pacer brand for the entire blue business group was feasible. However, one of the four brands in the blue group, Cruiser, was an extremely strong niche brand with a dominant position in a relatively small market and delivered significant self-expressive benefits to a hard-core customer base. Thus, it was decided that migrating the Cruiser brand to Pacer would be too risky but that the balance of the blue group would operate under the Pacer brand. Again, both Pacer and Cruiser going forward would be endorsed by the corporate brand.

The end result was a brand architecture involving three brands rather than nine, with all three consistently endorsed by the corporate brand. The critical decision was making the tough call that in the long run, the brand architecture would be stronger if niche brands were migrated into one of two broader brands. There were emotional, political, economic, and strategic forces and arguments against each move. The fact that one exception was allowed made the case more difficult to make and to implement. Critical to organizational acceptance was the use of an objective assessment template, which clearly identified the dimensions of the decision and facilitated the evaluation. It helped that much of each assessment was quantified from hard sales and market research data. Also critical was the strategic vision of the top management because at the end of the day, owners of some of the niche brands were not on board, and without a commitment from the top, it would not have happened.

5. Implement the Strategy

The final step is to implement the portfolio strategy, which usually means a transition for the existing strategy to a target strategy. That transition can be made abruptly or gradually

An abrupt transition can signal a change in the overall business and brand strategy; it becomes a one-time chance to provide visibility and credibility to a change affecting customers. So when Norwest Bank acquired Wells Fargo and changed the name of Norwest to Wells Fargo, it had the opportunity to communicate new capabilities that would enhance the offering for customers. In particular, Norwest customers could be assured that the personal relationships they expected would not change, but they could also expect upgraded electronic banking services because of the competence of Wells Fargo in that area. The name change reinforced the changed organization and the repositioning message. An abrupt transition assumes that the business strategy is in place; if not, the effort will backfire. If, for example, the Wells Fargo technology could not be delivered, the best course would have been to delay the name change until the substance behind the new position could be delivered.

The other option is to migrate customers from one brand to another gradually perhaps with intervening steps where the brand becomes an endorsed brand and then a subbrand before disappearing. Each stage may involve years. This will be preferred when:

- There is no newsworthy reposition that will accompany the change.
- Customers who may not have high involvement in the product class may need time to learn about and understand the change.
- There is a risk of alienating existing customers by disrupting their brand relationship.

KEY LEARNINGS

- The exit decision, even though it is psychologically and professionally painful, can be healthy both for the firm because it releases resources to be used elsewhere but even for the divested business, which might thrive in a different context.
- A milking or harvest strategy (generating cash flow by reducing investment and operation expenses) works when the involved business is not crucial to the firm financially or synergistically. For milking to be feasible, though, sales must decline in an orderly way.

- Prioritizing and trimming the brand portfolio provides another perspective on prioritizing businesses, can clarify brand offerings, and can remove the paralysis of not being able to brand new offerings. A five-step prioritization process involves identifying the relevant brand set, assessing the brands, prioritizing brands, creating a revised brand portfolio strategy, and designing a transition strategy.

FOR DISCUSSION

1. Ford in 2008 sold Jaguar to Tata Motors for $2.3 billion, about half of what it cost Ford in 1989. The sunk costs including investments in quality and product were estimated to be over $12 billion. Ford in 2001 introduced the Jaguar X type (to compete with the BMW 3), which added sales but affected the image. What analyses should be conducted to determine whether Jaguar should be sold? Would that differ if the subject was another Ford brand, Volvo, which was profitable?

2. Consider a divestment strategy. Why is it hard to divest a business? Jack Welch divested hundreds of businesses during his tenure. What are some of the motivations that led to these divestitures?

3. Identify brands that are employing a milking strategy. What are the risks?

4. How would you determine if a firm had too many brands?

5. What, in your judgment, are the key problems or issues in the brand consolidation process?

NOTES

1. Tom Kraeutier, "The Home Depot drops EXPO business," Weblogs, January 27, 2009.
2. Chris Zook, *Beyond the Core*, Boston: HBS Press, 2004, p. 23.
3. Zook, op-cit, p. 24.
4. Lee Dranikoff, Tim Koller, and Antoon Schneider, "Divestiture: Strategy's Missing Link," *Harvard Business Review*, May 2002, pp. 75–83.
5. An excellent article that documents these biases and suggests solutions is John T. Horn, Dan P. Lovallo, and S. Patrick Viguerie, "Learning to Let Go: Making Better Exit Decisions," *McKinsey Quarterly*, 2006, No. 2, pp. 65–76.
6. Dale E. Zand, "Managing Enterprise Risk: Why a Giant Failed," *Strategy & Leadership*, 2009, Vol. 37, No. 1, pp. 12–19.
7. This material draws from David Aaker, *Brand Portfolio Strategy*, New York: The Free Press, 2004, Chapter 10.

CHAPTER SIXTEEN

From Silos to Synergy—Harnessing the Organization[1]

All progress is initiated by challenging current conceptions and executed by supplanting existing institutions.
—*George Bernard Shaw*

Structure follows strategy.
—*Alfred Chandler, Jr.*

Those that implement the plans must make the plans.
—*Patrick Hagerty, Texas Instruments*

*I*n 1922, Alfred Sloan, a legend in management history, instituted a divisional structure at GM with Chevrolet at the low end, Cadillac at the high end, and Pontiac, Oldsmobile, and Buick in between. The divisions had distinct offerings and no price overlap. His admonition at the time was that "The responsibility of the CEOs of each operation should be in no way limited." In no way limited!! Total autonomy. The business world now had a method to deal with the emerging complexity of multiple product lines. Since that time, decentralization has refined and became the dominant organization form. Nearly every organization, from Nestlé to HP to Bank of America to Nissan to Stanford University, prides itself on being decentralized with autonomous organizational groups termed silos, a metaphor for a self-contained entity.

There is good reason why silo units, usually defined by products or countries, are widely used—they have enormous inherent advantages. The managers are close to the market and can therefore understand customer needs. They are also intimate with the product or service and the underlying technology and operations, and thus can make informed offering and operational decisions. Being empowered to act quickly means no delays in making and implementing strategic decisions, an attribute that is vital in dynamic markets. Also, because distinct business units can be held accountable for investments and results, business performance will be known in a timelier and less ambiguous manner. The most impressive feature of decentralization, however, is that it fosters incredible energy and vitality. Managers are empowered and motivated to innovate, to gain competitive advantage by providing superior value propositions to the customers.

SILO-DRIVEN PROBLEMS—THE CASE OF MARKETING

Relying on an unfettered decentralized organization with highly autonomous silo units, even with all its attributes, is no longer competitively feasible. Looking at silos from the marketing perspective, six specific problems or missed opportunities can be associated with the silo structure, as shown in Figure 16.1. They provide a rationale not necessarily for eliminating silos but for finding ways to harness the silo energy so that both business and marketing strategies can emerge and succeed. It is important to understand these problems not only to motivate change but also to provide a change target. The marketing set of problems may be the most severe, but there are serious problems, some virtually identical, that face other functions such as manufacturing, operations, or IT. Further, the potential source of competitive advantage, synergy across silos, is put into jeopardy when the silos cannot be spanned.

Marketing resources are misallocated

The silo structure nearly always leads to the misallocation of resources across product and country silo units, functional teams, brands, and marketing programs with smaller units getting under-funded even when strategically important. Silo teams are organizationally and psychologically unable to make these cross-silo judgments. They only want more for themselves and view other silo units as competitors. Further, such judgments require a hard nosed, objective analysis of the

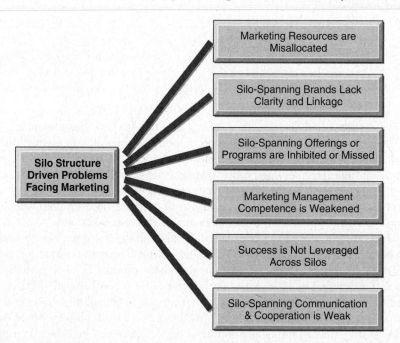

Figure 16.1 Silo Structure Driven Problems Facing Marketing

potential of the business using cross-silo data plus specialized frameworks and methods that will seldom be developed outside of a central marketing unit.

Silo spanning brands lack clarity and linkage

Too often a master brand, perhaps even the corporate brand, is shared by many, sometimes all, silo groups. Each silo is motivated to maximize the power of the brand without any concern with the brand's role in other business units. Especially when there is overlap in markets, inconsistent product and positioning strategies can damage the brand and result in debilitating marketplace confusion. Having a mixed brand message also makes it hard to convince the organization that the brand stands for something, and it is worthwhile to have discipline in being true to that message.

Silo spanning offerings and programs are inhibited or missed

Silo barriers often prevent marketing programs being shared. The result is that the most effective marketing programs that require scale—such as the World Cup sponsorship or even a national advertising campaign—are not feasible. Further, silo barriers can seriously inhibit the development of cross-silo offerings in part because the execution of cross-silo collaboration may not be in the DNA of the silos, and in part because autonomous silo units tend to look at the market with a narrow perspective and can often miss changes in the marketplace that are making their silo's offering less relevant. Yet many customers are drawn to silo-spanning offers. The movement from products to systems solutions has become a tidal wave. Global customers are increasingly demanding global services and offerings.

Marketing management competencies are weakened

The quality of marketing talent, specialized support, and management sophistication tends to be dispersed and weak when silos are running their business autonomously at a time in which specialized capability is needed in multiple areas such as digital marketing, CRM programs, marketing effectiveness modeling, social technology, blog management, sponsorship management, PR in an Internet world, and on and on. Further, redundant marketing staff results in costly inefficiencies and limits opportunities for career opportunities and specialty growth.

Success is not leveraged across silos

With a multi-silo organization, pockets of brilliance may result, but they will tend to be isolated and rarely leveraged. It is not enough to have a success here and there. "Maybe" and "occasionally" are not good enough. The key to moving from good to great is to develop an organization that will identify marketing excellence within the silos and be nimble enough to leverage that excellence.

Cross-silo communication and cooperation is weak or nonexistent

The lack of communication and cooperation between silos is a basic problem that can directly impact organizational performance. When insights into customers, marketing trends, channels, or technologies that could impact strategy are not shared, an opportunity may be lost. When cooperation is not considered or is difficult to implement, successful synergistic programs are unlikely to emerge. Further, communication and cooperation failures are an underlying cause of many of the other silo-driven problems. Fixing them requires not only methods and processes but also changing the culture that inhibits.

ADDRESSING THE SILO MARKETING ISSUES—CHALLENGES AND SOLUTIONS

Simply going to a centralized organizational form by getting rid of silos is not an option. First, managing a large complex multi-silo organization centrally is not feasible. Second, as noted above, silos are there because they provide accountability, vitality, and intimacy with customers, technology, and products, so eliminating them would not generally be wise. The solution rather is to replace competition and isolation with cooperation and communication so that the overall business strategy will succeed and organization synergy will emerge. In the process, it is likely that some selective centralization of some activities and decisions will be useful. This is a tough assignment that is usually given to a new or revitalized CMO (chief marketing officer) slot.

Efforts by a CMO and his or her team to gain credibility, traction, and influence represent a formidable task in the face of silo indifference or, more likely, resistance. Succeeding and even surviving in this effort is at best uncertain. As a result, the tenure of new CMOs is short; it was found to average 23 months.[2] The amazing short window reflects the difficulties of the new CMO's job even when the assignment is labeled as a strategic imperative.

In a study, over 40 CMOs were asked what works in terms of addressing the silo problem.[3] Three headlines:

Realize that nonthreatening roles can be powerful change agents

The CMO can take control of elements of strategy and tactics from silos, and that can be the right course in certain circumstances. However, there are other less threatening roles with reduced risk of failure that can have significant influence on strategy and culture while building credibility and relationships. In particular, the CMO can assume the role of facilitator, consultant, or service provider. In a facilitator role, the CMO team can establish a common planning framework, foster communication, encourage and enable cooperation, create data and knowledge banks, and upgrade the level of marketing talent throughout the organization. In the consultant role, the CMO would become an invited participant in the silo strategy development process. As a service provider, the silo business units would "hire" the CMO team to provide marketing services such as marketing research, segmentation studies, training, or marketing activities such as sponsorships or promotions.

Aim at the silo-driven problems

The all too common instinct of forcing centralization and standardization on the organization can be dysfunctional, even resulting in a flameout of the CMO team. Reducing silo authority, making the organization more centralized, and moving toward more standardized offerings and marketing programs are often warranted and useful. In fact, there is a strong trend in that direction for good reason. However, these changes should not be goals in themselves, but rather one of the routes to a set of goals. The goal rather should be to make progress against the silo-driven problems, improve communication and cooperation, and therefore create stronger offerings and brands and effective synergistic marketing strategies and programs.

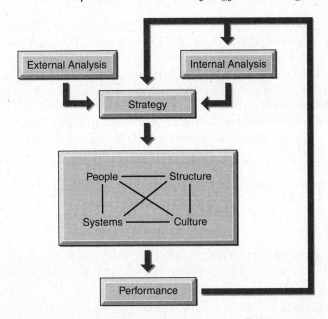

Figure 16.2 A Framework for Analyzing Organizations

Use organizational levers—structure, systems, people, and culture

Each of these involves powerful routes to change an organization. They are not only key to organizational change but also the basis for strategy implementation.

ORGANIZATIONAL LEVERS AND THEIR LINK TO STRATEGY

Organizations can be conceptualized as having four components—structure, systems, people, and culture. Their relationship to strategy and its implementation is summarized in Figure 16.2. The organizational components need to be informed by the strategy. For any business strategy to be successful, the right structure, system, people, and culture need to be in place and functioning. Further, the four components need to be congruent with each other. If one of the components is inconsistent either with the rest or with the strategy, success will be a casualty even if the strategy is brilliant and well-timed.

The Korvette story illustrates. Korvette's started as a luggage and appliance discounter selling name brands at one-third off regular price from a second-floor loft in Manhattan. The firm dramatically expanded both the number of stores and the number of cities served, expanded its product line by adding fashion goods, furniture, and grocery products, and added more store amenities. This was a defensible growth strategy, but one that was not supported by the people, structure, systems, or culture. Korvette's personnel lacked the depth to staff the new stores and the expertise to handle the new product areas. The centralized structure did not adapt well to multiple cities and product lines. The management systems were not sophisticated enough to handle the added complexity. The culture of casual management with low prices as the driving force was not replaced with another strong culture that would be appropriate to the new business areas. Only four years after it had been lauded by a retailing guru, it faced death.

The Korvette story graphically illustrates the importance of making the organization internally congruent and capable of supporting the strategy. The assessment of any strategy should include a careful analysis of organizational risks and a judgment about the nature of any required organizational changes and their associated costs and feasibility.

Each of the four organizational components can be used to address any organizational problem. In the balance of this chapter, we discuss how the organizational structure, systems, people, and culture can be employed to address the silo problem. In doing so, each of the four components will be examined and illustrated. The exercise will also illuminate the levers that an organizational designer can use to address other problems such as silo issues facing the IT group, how to cultivate innovation, or how to make the organization more customer centric. At the close of the chapter, an overview of strategic market management will be presented.

STRUCTURE

The structure of the organization, which includes the lines of authority and the way people and units are grouped, can encourage cooperation, sharing, and communication.

Centralize Selectively

There are a host of marketing modalities and potential tasks facing the CMO, including advertising, promotions, sponsorships, call centers, packaging, PR, digital marketing, brand strategy, visual presentation, market research, and marketing program performance measurement. One issue is: Which of this set should be centralized? Of those that merit centralization, what parts should be centralized? For example, it might be wise to centralize the advertising strategy and not media or creative (those who actually create ads).

In making the judgment as to what, if anything, to centralize, the CMO must carefully balance the needs of the silo units with the program to be centralized. The silos should have the necessary flexibility to succeed in the marketplace. Decisions as to what should be centralized will be based on questions such as:

- What programs or potential programs span markets? To what extent is coordination a key to making them effective? A major sponsorship such as the Olympics or the World Cup can be an ideal vehicle to create an acceptance of cross-business teams because they are so obviously needed and worthwhile in such cases.

- Where is functional expertise best developed? Can redundancy be reduced? It is far better to have one group with a depth of competence in an area such as advertising or sponsorships than many groups with shallow talent and capacity.

- What brands span markets? Does market adaptation compensate for a dilution of the central message? GE Money resisted the "imagination at work" theme at first, and then ultimately came to believe that the value of the corporate effort was worth taking advantage of.

- What truly requires local knowledge and management? Are there positions and programs that work across products and markets? Pringles, for example, requires different flavors in different markets, but most of the social and functional benefits work everywhere.

- What deviations in budgets, reporting lines, and authority can be tolerated? What fights are worth winning? In the case of Visa, the integrity of the brand had the highest priority—the energy to fight battles was devoted to avoiding product offerings (such as charging for converting currency) that would compromise the brand promise.

Use Teams and Networks

The CMO should look toward employing some of the available organizational devices that will advance cross-silo communication and cooperation, such as teams and networks. Teams or councils such as Chevron Global Brand Council, HP's Customer Experience Council, Dow Corning's Global Marketing Excellence Council, IBM's Global Marketing Board, or P&G's Global Marketing Officer's Leadership team are powerful vehicles to create consistency and/or synergy. Perhaps more important, teams also provide vehicles for cross-silo communication and opportunities for relationships to develop.

Formal and informal networks, another key organizational tool, can be based on topics such as customer groups, market trends, customer experience contexts, geographies, or functional areas like sponsorship or digital marketing. The network members are motivated to keep in contact with counterparts in other countries to learn of intelligence around customer strategies and programs that work in their stores. A formal network will have assigned membership, a leadership structure, and a supporting infrastructure such as knowledge banks.

Use Matrix Organizations

A matrix organization allows a person to have two or more reporting links. Several business units could share a sales force by having the salespeople report to a business unit as well as to the central sales manager. A silo advertising manager could also report to a central advertising or marketing group. An R&D group could have a research team that reports to both the business unit and the R&D manager. As a result, the silo salespeople, advertising managers, and research team are each supported by a critical mass of employees and infrastructure that allows them to excel while still being a part of the business unit. The concept of dual reporting requires coordination and communication and often appears to be the ideal solution to a messy situation. However, matrix structures can be unstable and subject to political pressures. Thus, they can create a solution that is worse than the problem.

The Virtual Organization

The virtual organization is a team specifically designed for a particular client or job. The team members can be drawn from a variety of sources and might include contract workers who are hired only for the project at hand. Communication firms have used virtual teams to provide an integrated communication solution involving talent from different modalities. The chances of success are greater when the people are drawn from the same organization such as a full service agency like Dentsu, Y&R, or McCann Erickson. When different companies are involved, success is more elusive.

WPP, the large communication holding company, founded a virtual organization, Enfatico, to handle all the communication needs of Dell. The logic was that the new company would access the best talent throughout the WPP world, which included dozens of top communication and support firms of all modalities. Seemed like an ideal solution to a vexing problem. Just one year later, the entry was folded into Y&R, a major WPP agency. Enfatico had a difficult time delivering top creative work. Getting people from very different backgrounds to work as a team was challenging. Further, it proved difficult to attract a CEO and top talent to a single client firm with the associated risk involved. The Enfatico experience illustrates that asking people to leave a home discipline and firm to go with a new fragile organization without an established culture will be difficult.

SYSTEMS

Several management systems are strategically relevant. Among them are the information, measurement and reward, and planning systems.

Information System

Creating or refining a silo-spanning information system, a system that facilitates communication and stores knowledge, is the most basic and nonthreatening element of the CMO's potential initiatives. The system can share market information regarding customer insights, trends, competitor actions, technology developments, and best practices as well as internal information about processes and methods, new products and technologies, best internal practices, and strategies and programs. Nonthreatening though it may be, such a system can be complex, affected by organizational issues, and difficult to manage so that the participation is widespread. There are a host of ways that communication can be fostered across silos such as:

Knowledge sharing sessions. Formal and informal meetings not only result in information exchange but also create channels of personal communication that can operate after the meetings. Personal links can create a comfort level allowing colleagues to have frank discussions about proposed programs or problems that need to be addressed. Such conversations can stave off a disaster or encourage an initiative. Most companies have in-person meetings that can vary from once a quarter to once every two years. These are often supplemented with telephone meetings. Dell, in fact, has all its global teams (e.g., laptops for business or servers for large businesses) have a conference call every two weeks. Such meetings are a big part of Honda's communication program.

A market university. Frito-Lay sponsors a "market university" about three times a year where 35 or so marketing directors or general managers from around the world come to Dallas for a week. The purpose is to involve the silos in the language and models of the central marketing group, to promote brand concepts, to break down the "I am different" trap, and to seed the company with people who "get brands." During the week, case studies are presented on tests of packaging, advertising, or promotions that were successful in one country or region and then applied successfully in another country. These studies demonstrate that practices can be transferred even in the face of a skeptical local marketing team. At Crotonville, the GE university site, executive programs around case studies of silo units have long been a key to the GE communication system.

Knowledge hub. An organized repository of data, experience, case analyses, and insight can provide a sustainable asset by making useful information readily available to all silos. It has the potential to make information handling and exchange productive, easy-to-use, and efficient. MasterCard, a firm that was early in its appointment of a "knowledge-sharing facilitator" to identify and disseminate best brand practices, credited the program with leveraging the very effective "Priceless" advertising campaign across country silos.

Center of excellence. Within a central marketing team, a group will focus on a particular issue that spans silos such as a customer trend, an emerging product subcategory, or a technology. The center could be staffed by a single person or a group of dozens. The charge would be to gain deep insights into the issue and to stay abreast of developments. The center should actively reach out to the silo teams in order to both receive and disperse information and thus provide a catalyst for communication and information flow. Nestlé USA has several centers of excellence around topics such as mom and kids, the Hispanic market, and major customers such as Tesco and Wal-Mart. In each case, they formed an advisory council with members from the silos for which the topic would be relevant. The council provides silo-based information and participates in insight meetings.

Measurement and Reward System

Measurement can drive behavior and thus directly affect strategy implementation. The key to strategy is often the ability to introduce appropriate performance measures that are linked to the reward structure.

One concern is to motivate employees to cooperate, communicate, and create synergy. The reward system can operate at two levels. At the level of the individual performance review, the ability to be collaborative and to initiate and participate in cross-silo initiatives could be measured. In fact, the central marketing group at IBM evaluates people in silo groups in terms of how collaborative they are. At the organization level, rewards that are based too closely on a business unit's performance can work against this motivational goal. As a result, many companies deliberately base a portion of their bonuses or evaluations on the results of a larger unit. Prophet, a brand strategy consulting firm with seven offices, encourages cross-office support by making its bonuses conditional on firm-wide performance. Another business may focus on divisional performance because synergy across divisions is not realistic.

It is also helpful if the rewards are balanced with a long-term perspective as well as short-term financials. Thus, measures such as customer satisfaction, customer loyalty, quality indicators, new products brought to market, or training program productivity may be useful to gauge the progress of strategic initiatives.

Planning System

A standardized brand and/or marketing program, one that is virtually the same across country or product silos, is rarely optimal. What is optimal is to have both a business and marketing planning process, including templates and frameworks, and a supporting information system that are the same everywhere. Having a common planning process provides the basis for communication by creating a common vocabulary, measures, information, and decision structures. It also leads to an elevated level of professionalism throughout the silo units. Unless there is a clear, accepted planning process with understandable and actionable components, every unit will go its own way and, as a result, some will be mismanaged strategically and tactically.

There should be a process that adapts brands to silo contexts. To avoid having a brand that spans silos becoming confused and inconsistent, a best practice organization will have brands that are adapted to silo contexts while still maintaining consistency of the brand character. ChevronTexaco, for example, has a core brand identity that consists of four values—clean, safe, reliable, and quality. The silo markets are free to interpret the core elements in their marketplace. So what is quality in the context of a convenience store? Or in a lube business? Or in Asia? In addition, the silo business units have the flexibility to add one additional element to the four-element core identity. The lube business could add "performance" and the Asian group "respectfully helpful." The result is more ability to link with the silo customer.

PEOPLE

A key to overcoming silo issues is to have a strong CMO team that is staffed with quality talent. Any visibly weak link can be damaging. One CMO reported that an advertising manager who lacked competence set back the group a full year by interacting with silo organizations and making naive recommendations. Who is added, and even more important, who is asked to leave will be closely observed. Adding people who are respected can give the group a lift, while retaining people who do not fit the role can be debilitating.

The problem is that the qualifications needed by the central marketing group are extraordinary. Collectively, the group needs to be knowledgeable about marketing, branding, markets, products, and their organization. In addition, the group needs to have a strategic perspective and be collaborate, persuasive, a change agent, and, especially for a global firm, multicultural. Thus, people need to be sought who have as many of these characteristics as possible.

Knowledgeable. An effective central marketing management team will collectively need to have a breadth of knowledge. Achieving that breadth can involve a mix of generalists with insight, specialists, and outside resources, but it needs to create competence in the following:

- **Marketing knowledge**—marketing strategy, communication tools including new media, measurement, and marketing programs and their management.
- **Brand knowledge**—brands, brand power, brand equity, brand roles, brand portfolio strategy, and brand building programs.
- **Market knowledge**—markets, country cultures, market trends, competitor dynamics, customer segmentation, and customer motivation.
- **Product knowledge**—product or service attributes and their underlying technology plus the innovation flow that will define future products and services.
- **Organizational knowledge**—the organization, its culture, strategies, values, and formal and informal influence and communication structure.

Strategic perspective. The CMO team needs to be able to strategize, to move beyond being proficient in a set of tactics to being involved in marketing strategy. Because they will be dealing with a dynamic marketplace, they will also need to be comfortable with adapting strategy to reflect those dynamics. Without a strategic flair, the team will not be capable of devising cross-silo marketing strategies that should be a major goal and will not be a candidate to sit at the strategy table.

Change agent. The CMO team will need to be a change agent. That means that there needs to be the capability of generating the feeling and substance of being creative and innovative. There should be a sense of energy and purpose. Life will not go on as before. Change will happen. There is a fine line between being a loose cannon and a positive catalyst for change, however; the change message should be surrounded by professionalism. To be a change agent, at least some team members need to be persuaders with communication and leadership skills. Collaborative skills are also necessary especially when the incentives are silo oriented.

Instigator. In the middle of the first decade of the 2000s, GE upgraded marketing and in doing so identified four characteristics of the marketing staff. One was being an instigator, able to lead innovation by looking at market needs going forward. Such a perspective led GO to develop products that would track patients in their home so that hospitalization would be less frequently needed. The QuietCare home sensing systems was the result.

Innovator. Another was being an innovator, to be an active participant in bringing an offering to fruition and to market. Marketing was instrumental, for example, in championing the concept of "air taxis" that carry four to six passengers to small regional airports. Another initiative was around improving the operational efficiency of aircraft based on "myEngines," software that provides customers with real-time updates as to when repairs are required, how long they will take, and so on. The information is delivered to customer's smartphones or tablets.

Integrator. A third market quality specified by GE was that of integrator, the ability to integrate across silos and functional areas. This can involve being a translator able to speak the language of design engineers and production people as well as that of the customers and those in the marketing disciplines. It involved getting disparate people together. GE Capital has a weekly "war room" in which a wide spectrum of managers sort out current issues and develop meaningful action plans. This process has been copied by other units as well.

Implementer. The final marketing quality was that of an implementer, ensuring that the best marketing tools were available and used by the business units. This involved creating a central source of information about best practices. It also involved introducing metrics and processes that encouraged best practices to be used.[4]

Multicultural. When the global overlay is added, the ability to work with different languages and cultures is added. Particularly, in a culturally homogeneous country like Japan, where few citizens are proficient in other languages, it is necessary to build a team that is culturally sensitive with adequate language skills. One route, used by Schlumberger, the oil field services firm, is to deliberately source the whole firm with nationals from around the world. The result is one of the few companies that can say they are truly multicultural. Another is to rotate people around the globe, as Nestlé and Sony do, creating the absence of country-specific people. Still another is to explicitly train people in cultural knowledge, market insights, etc. so that their limitations can be reduced. But it will remain a challenge for the firm with global aspirations.

Sourcing: Insiders vs. Outsiders

A basic decision is whether the CMO and his or her staff members should be outsiders or insiders. There is usually a sharp trade-off. The insider will be more likely to know the organization, its culture and systems, will have a network of colleagues to tap for help, and will know the actors behind the formal organization chart—who are the real keys to getting things done. The insider will thus be at low risk. However, the insider may also lack the marketing skills and credibility to know what to do and how to do it. He or she may also be unwilling or unable to create the needed organizational change.

An outsider with the needed functional expertise, experience, and credibility can serve as a change agent in part because he or she is less tied to past decisions, relationships, and political pressures. The problem is that he or she will often lack a feel for the culture and an established network throughout the firm to draw on. This is the riskier route, but one that might be more likely to make a difference when the organization is in need of change. The risk goes up when the outsider is changing industries (e.g., from package goods to business-to-business marketing) and facing new and different marketing challenges. Sometimes, team members from outside the firm can be more effective change agents than insiders.

The trade-offs between the inside vs. outside source suggest staffing routes for the CMO slot. An insider with a proven record as a change agent who has or could obtain credibility in marketing and brands may be available. Or an outsider who has demonstrated an ability to adapt to organizations may be a target. Sequencing the marketing manager is possible as well. An insider might get started and gain some momentum, providing an outsider with a platform poised for more rapid change. In other situations, an outsider who shakes up the organization would be followed with an insider to channel and broaden the momentum.

One way to reduce the tensions is to form a blended team of outsiders and insiders, as GE and others have done. An outsider playing a leadership role will be surrounded by insiders, and when an insider is asked to lead change, he or she will be supported by whatever outside talent is needed. Another is to change the culture in order to make a new strategy viable and the task of a change agent more tractable.

Upgrading the Marketing Staffs

For several reasons a strong marketing team is needed throughout the organization, not just in the central marketing group. First, a strong marketing presence in the silos will reduce the need to justify brand and marketing strategy. The conversation can be elevated. Second, whatever level of central control is achieved, silo organizations will still have a design and implementation role that will require talent.

Dow Corning has a Global Marketing Excellence Council that leads in building up the marketing capability of the firm. It detects capability gaps and develops initiatives to fill them by outside hiring, training initiatives, and mentoring programs. They sponsored, for example, a "lunch and learn" program around lunch events. At GE, the CMO has a program of identifying potential marketing talent through the firm and influencing their career paths.

Training and upgrading people is a key part of the equation. They will need to learn general marketing, skills in functional areas of marketing, the process models and information system, and the brand and marketing strategy and the rationale for it. The first step is to understand the gaps of knowledge for each member of the marketing team. One role of a CMO may be to evaluate the marketing talent in the silo organizations and get involved in their career paths, including guiding them into the right training program.

STRATEGY AND PEOPLE DEVELOPMENT AT GE

Jack Welch, the legendary former GE CEO, created a system and culture to develop both strategy and people throughout his twenty-year tenure. Five elements were involved:[5]

- Each January, the top 5,000 GE executives gathered in Boca Raton to share best practices and set major business priorities. (In the past, priorities included e-commerce, globalization, and six-sigma quality.) Webcasts of the event were available to the whole organization.
- Each quarter, top executives met in two-day retreats facilitated by Welch and focused on initiatives related to the agenda set in Boca Raton. This was a key place for future leaders to emerge, earn respect, and demonstrate growth.

- Twice a year, Welch and others focused on personnel needs for each business, such as how to handle each unit's top 20 percent and bottom 10 percent of employees.
- In addition, biannual sessions (one in the spring and one in the fall) looked at each business over a three-year horizon.
- The entire effort was supported by the GE social architecture of informality, candor, substantive dialogue, boundaryless behavior, emphasis on follow-through, and making judgments on qualitative business dimensions.

CULTURE

The organizational culture drives behavior and is the glue that holds everything together. If cooperation and communication between silos are to replace competition and isolation, the culture will usually need to change. As suggested by Figure 16.3, an organizational culture involves three elements: a set of shared values that define priorities, a set of norms of behavior, and symbols and symbolic action. Each has a key role to play in getting people to work together across silos.

Shared Values

Shared values, or dominant beliefs, underlie a culture by specifying what is important. In a strong culture, the values will be widely accepted, and virtually everyone will be able to identify them and describe their rationale.

Shared values can have a variety of foci. They can involve, for example:

- A key asset or competency that is the essence of a firm's competitive advantage: We will be the most creative advertising agency.
- An operational focus: SAS focused on on-time performance.

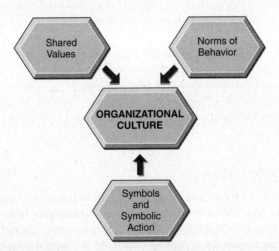

Figure 16.3 Organizational Culture

- An organizational output: We will deliver zero defects, or 100 percent customer satisfaction.
- An emphasis on a functional area: Black & Decker transformed itself from a firm with a manufacturing focus to one with a market-driven approach.
- A management style: This is an informal, flat organization that fosters communication and encourages unconventional thinking.
- A belief in the importance of people as individuals.
- A general objective, such as a belief in being the best or comparable to the best.

For an organization to make progress on silo problems, cooperation and communication will need to become one of the shared values. That means that all employees and partners need to both know about the priority and believe in it.

Norms

To make a real difference, the culture must be strong enough to develop norms of behavior— informal rules that influence decisions and actions throughout an organization by suggesting what is appropriate and what is not. The fact is that strong norms can generate much more effective control over what is actually done or not done in an organization than a very specific set of objectives, measures, and sanctions. People can always get around rules. The concept of norms is that people will not attempt to avoid them because they will be accompanied by a commitment to shared values.

Norms can vary on two dimensions: the intensity or amount of approval/disapproval attached to an expectation and the degree of consensus or consistency with which a norm is shared. It is only when both intensity and consensus exist that strong cultures emerge.

Norms encourage behavior consistent with shared values. Thus, in a quality service culture, an extraordinary effort by an employee, such as renting a helicopter to fix a communication component (a FedEx legend), would not seem out of line and risky; instead, it would be something that most in that culture would do under similar circumstances. Furthermore, sloppy work affecting quality would be informally policed by fellow workers, without reliance on a formal system. One production firm uses no quality-control inspectors or janitors. Each production-line person is responsible for the quality of his or her output and for keeping the work area clean. Such a policy would not work without support from a strong culture.

With a culture around cooperation and communication, people would instinctively reach out and communicate across silos. Teaming would become natural. Those engaging in behavior that was silo centric and detrimental to the organization as a whole would feel uncomfortable or worse.

Symbols and Symbolic Action

Corporate cultures are largely developed and maintained by the use of consistent, visible symbols and symbolic action. In fact, the more obvious methods of affecting behavior, such as changing systems or structure, are often much less effective than seemingly trivial symbolic actions.

A host of symbols and symbolic actions are available. A few of the more useful are discussed next.

The Founder and Original Mission

A corporation's unique roots, including the personal style and experience of its founder, can provide extremely potent symbols. The strong culture of L.L. Bean is due largely to its founder's involvement in the outdoors and his original products for the hunter and fisherman. The concept of entertainment developed by Walt Disney, the customer-oriented philosophy of J. C. Penney, the innovative culture at HP symbolized by the garage used by Don Hewlett and David Packard, the personality of Virgin's Richard Branson, and the product and advertising traditions started by the founders of Procter & Gamble continue to influence the cultures of their firms generations later.

Modern Role Models

Modern heroes and role models help communicate, personalize, and legitimize values and norms. Lou Gerstner became a symbol of the new marketing-focused culture at IBM that replaced a country and product silo centric organization with a customer centric one. Other examples are the managers at 3M who tenaciously pursued ideas despite setbacks until they succeeded in building major divisions such as the Post-it Notes division, and the Frito-Lay workers who maintained customer service in the face of natural disasters.

Rituals

Rituals of work life, from hiring to eating lunch to retirement dinners, help define a culture. One of the early success stories in Silicon Valley was a firm with a culture that was based in part on a requirement that a person commit before knowing his or her salary, and considerable pride in a Friday afternoon beer-bust ritual that served to break down product and functional silo barriers and create communication channels.

The Role of the CEO and Other Executives

The way that a CEO and other executives spend their time can be a symbolic action affecting the culture. An airline executive who spends two weeks a month obtaining a firsthand look at customer service in country silos sends a strong signal to the organization that programs need to be shared. Patterns of consistent reinforcement can represent another important symbolic activity. For example, a firm that regularly recognizes cross-silo activity accomplishments in a meaningful way with the visible support of top management can, over time, affect the culture. When a type of question is continually asked by top executives and made a central part of meeting agendas and report formats, it will eventually influence the shared values of an organization.

Given that the CEO is crucial in culture development, how do you get the CEO on board with respect to enhancing a culture of cross-silo cooperation and communication? Three suggestions from the CMO study:[6]

- The problems need to become visible; too often they are ignored as part of the way it's always been done. If some of the inefficiencies and missed opportunities can be quantified, there will be a worthwhile problem for which cooperation and communication is part of the solution.

REPRESENTING CULTURE AND STRATEGY WITH STORIES, NOT BULLETS

Research has shown that stories are more likely than lists to be read and remembered. Nevertheless, most business strategists rely on bullet points to communicate both culture and strategy. 3M is one firm that has based its culture on classic stories—how initial failures of abrasive products led to product breakthroughs; how masking tape was invented; how a scientist conceived of Post-it Notes when his bookmarks fell out of a hymnal, and how the Post-it-Notes team, instead of giving up in the face of low initial sales, got people hooked on the product by flooding a city with samples. These stories communicate how innovation occurs at 3M and how its entrepreneurial culture operates.

At 3M, business strategy is also communicated via stories rather than the conventional bullets, which tend to be generic (the goal of increased market share applies to any business), skip over critical assumptions about how the business works (will increased market share fund new products, or result from new products?), and leave causal relationships unspecified (if A is done, B becomes effective). A strategic story will involve several phases—setting the stage by describing the current situation, introducing the dramatic conflict in the form of challenges and critical issues, and reaching resolution with convincing stories about how the company can overcome obstacles and win. Presenting a narrative motivates the audience, adds richness and detail, and provides a glimpse into the logic of the strategist.[7]

- The CMO needs to become credible so that there is buy-in as to his or her role. One approach is to align the role of marketing with that of the CEO's priority agenda by focusing growth objectives instead of brand extensions, efficiency and cost objectives instead of marketing synergy or scale, and building assets to support strategic initiatives instead of brand image campaigns.

- Get easy wins. These early successes often involve identifying organizational units that will support (or at least not oppose) change because they need help to address a meaningful problem or opportunity. They can also involve programs that can be implemented "under the radar." For example, at Cigna, a real estate manager who needed artwork for a building was persuaded to use brand visuals. The CEO of a major division saw the result and promptly decided to extend the idea to all buildings.

A RECAP OF STRATEGIC MARKET MANAGEMENT

Figure 16.4 provides a capstone summary of the issues raised in both strategic analysis and strategy development/refinement. It suggests a discussion agenda to help an organization ensure that the external and internal analysis has the necessary depth, breadth, and forward thinking and that the strategy creation and refinement process yields winning, sustainable strategies.

CUSTOMER ANALYSIS

- Who are the major segments?
- What are their motivations and unmet needs?

COMPETITOR ANALYSIS

- Who are the existing and potential competitors? What strategic groups can be identified?
- What are their sales, share, and profits? What are the growth trends?
- What are their strengths, weaknesses, and strategies?

MARKET/SUBMARKET ANALYSIS

- How attractive is the market or industry and its submarkets? What are the forces reducing profitability in the market, entry and exit barriers, growth projections, cost structures, and profitability prospects?
- What are the alternative distribution channels and their relative strengths?
- What industry trends and emerging submarkets are significant to strategy?
- What are the current and future key success factors?
- What are the strategic uncertainties and information need areas?

ENVIRONMENTAL ANALYSIS

- What are the technological, consumer, and governmental/economic forces and trends that will affect strategy?
- What are the major strategic uncertainties and information-need areas?
- What scenarios can be conceived?

INTERNAL ANALYSIS

- What are our strategy, performance, points of differentiation, strengths, weaknesses, strategic problems, and culture?
- What threats and opportunities exist?

STRATEGY DEVELOPMENT

- What are the target segments? What is the product scope?
- What value propositions will be the core of the offering? Among the choices are superior attribute or benefit, appealing design, systems solution, social programs, customer relationship, niche specialist, quality, and value.
- What assets and competencies will provide the basis for an SCA? How can they be developed and maintained? How can they be leveraged?
- What are the alternative functional strategies?
- What strategies best fit our strengths, our objectives, and our organization?
- What alternative growth directions should be considered? How should they be pursued?
- What investment level is most appropriate for each product market—withdrawal, milking, maintaining, or growing?

Figure 16.4   Strategy Development: A Discussion Agenda

KEY LEARNINGS

- Decentralization with powerful silo groups can inhibit synergy and efficiency. For marketing, it leads to misallocation of resources, confused brands, inhibited cross-silo offerings and programs, weak marketing staffs, the failure to leverage success, and inadequate cooperation and communication.

- In dealing with the problem, CMOs should consider nonthreatening roles such as facilitator and service provider consultant, and should not have as an objective to centralize and standardize.

- The organizational levers are structure, systems, people, and culture. Each of these needs to be congruent and support the business strategy.

- The organizational structure lever provides the option to centralize selectivity, use teams and networks, use matrix reporting structures, and employ a virtual organization.

- Management systems involve the information, measurement and reward, and planning systems that can all promote cooperation and communication.

- People on the CMO team, who can be sourced internally or externally, need to be knowledgeable about marketing, brands, markets, products, and the organization in addition to being strategic and serving as change agents.

- Culture involves shared values, norms of behavior, and symbols and symbolic action. The CEO is a key driver of the culture, and it is important to get him or her on board.

FOR DISCUSSION

1. What are the advantages of decentralization? Some people argue that more centralization is needed to develop and implement strategy in these dynamic times. Express your opinion, and illustrate it with examples. When would you recommend that the central team use a facilitative role, rather than impose its advice?

2. The Korvette concept was started and run by one person and his group of friends. How could its failure have been avoided? Was the problem one of strategy (overexpansion), or was it organizational? Why?

3. How would you go about changing the culture of an organization to improve the level of cooperation and communication?

4. If you were assigned to be the new CMO of a firm like General Mills with silo issues, what would you do in the first 100 days?

5. If you were the CMO of HP with dozens of product units in over 100 countries, how would you decide which elements of advertising to centralize—what elements of media, creative, account management, strategy? Of brand strategy?

6. What do you believe would be the best way to get a finance-oriented CEO to support marketing and its efforts to get silos to work together on offerings, brands, and marketing programs?

7. Consider PowerBar, the strategy for which is summarized in the PowerBar case. What implications for the culture, structure, systems, and people would you suggest

given the nature of the product and the company. Would this change when it was purchased by Nestlé?

NOTES

1. This chapter draws on the material in David Aaker, *Spanning Silos: The New CMO Imperative*, Boston: Harvard Business Press, 2008.
2. Greg Welch, "CMO Tenure: Slowing Down the Revolving Door," Spenser Stuart Blue Paper, 2004.
3. Aaker, op cit.
4. Beth Comstock, Ranjay Gulati, and Stephen Liguori, "Unleashing the Power of Marketing," *Harvard Business Review*, October 2010, pp. 90–98.
5. "GE's Ten-Step Talent Plan," *Fortune*, April 17, 2000, p. 232.
6. Aaker, op cit.
7. Gordon Shaw, Robert Brown, and Philip Bromiley, "Strategic Stories: How 3M Is Rewriting Business Planning," *Harvard Business Review*, May–June 1998, pp. 41–50.

Strategic Repositioning

HOBART CORPORATION

While Hobart Corporation, a manufacturer of equipment for the food service (restaurants and institutions) and retail (grocery and convenience stores) sectors for more than a century, had developed a solid reputation for high quality and extremely reliable products, it wasn't necessarily seen as an industry leader. It had credentials, however. In addition to being the largest firm in terms of sales, it also had broad coverage of the industry and its product categories and a respected service network, with some 200 locations and over 1,700 service vans. The better competitors excelled in a particular product category (refrigeration, for instance) or were well known in one of the industry sectors but lacked Hobart's breadth of offerings.

Hobart was concerned with less expensive competing products that were made overseas. Most customers were continuing to buy Hobart products, but the threat was growing. Further, it was hard to create advertising and trade show material that would break out of the clutter. Breakthrough products that would attract attention were not easily generated.

In response to these concerns, Hobart sought to establish a different customer-facing brand that would be the "thought leader" in the industry, not just the product leader. It wanted to be known for the best quality, "plus more." The driving idea was to offer solutions to everyday issues its customers faced in their businesses—things like finding, training, and retaining good workers; keeping food safe; providing enticing dining experiences; eliminating costs; reducing shrinkage; and, for some, enhancing same-sales growth. The firm systematically marshaled a knowledge base in order to address these problems.

This driving idea of solving everyday concerns led to a powerful brand-building program around the tagline, "Sound Equipment, Sound Advice." One element was a customer magazine called *Sage: Seasoned Advice for the Food Industry Professional* (later made available via the Internet at Sage Online). Sage's in-depth, objective treatment of customer problems and issues made it feel more like a newsstand publication than a corporate promotional tool. At industry trade shows, the Hobart company booth had an "Idea Center" where people could approach industry experts for sound advice about the problems they faced in their businesses. Hobart conducted seminars using leading experts; "The State of Collegiate Dining" was one topic. Internally, the leadership message was reinforced at department and company-wide meetings and through internal newsletters.

Hobart also offered useful content about key issues on its Web site, hobartcorp.com. Visitors could find papers, question-and-answer sessions with industry experts, briefing documents, and other material updated on a weekly basis. This program grew to over 100 papers on technology, saving labor, reducing shrinkage, productivity, improving food safety, growing sales, and cost management. The brand lived on the Web and in other places as well, thanks to the strategic placement of Hobart content on many other sites frequented by people in the industry. Select elements of this Web content were converted to printed pieces and disseminated broadly.

Hobart shared more sound advice through speeches at key industry shows, events like the Home Meal Replacement Summit, and articles for trade magazines (for example, "Cold War: Smart Refrigeration Arms Restaurateurs Against Food-Borne Illnesses" in *Hotel Magazine*).

The goal of public relations became idea placement rather than product placement. Hobart also changed its approach to new product releases to emphasize how each product helps the customer deal with key business issues. For instance, rather than emphasize specific features like the recessed nozzles on the Hobart TurboWash, the firm communicated how easy it made the task of scrubbing pots and pans, thereby creating happier restaurant and food service employees.

Print advertising, once the prime brand-building tool, played a lesser but still important role, focusing on key customer issues. For instance, one ad showed a sign at a bathroom sink reading, "Employees Must Wash Hands Before Returning to Work." The text underneath the picture asked, "Need a more comprehensive approach to food safety?" and then described the solutions recommended by Hobart.

The Hobart program was impacted perceptions of the brand and propelled Hobart into a leadership role that lasted well over a decade until they were bought and integrated into a larger firm.

FOR DISCUSSION

1. Why do chefs buy Hobart for their kitchens?
2. What was the value proposition before the "Solid Equipment, Sound Advice" program? How did it change?
3. What functional strategies did Hobart pursue?
4. The new program soaked up resources, thereby reducing the effort to communicate new product innovations. Was that a wise decision? Which approach is more likely to support a quality image?
5. How could competitors position themselves against Hobart's value proposition?

Source: Adapted with the permission of the Free Press, a division of Simon & Schuster Adult Publishing Group from Brand Leadership, by David A. Aaker and Erich Joachimsthaler. Copyright © 2000 by David A. Aaker and Erich Joachimsthaler. All rights reserved.

Leveraging a Brand Asset
DOVE

In 1955, Unilever (then Lever Brothers) introduced Dove, which contained a patented, mild cleansing ingredient, into the soap category. It was positioned—then and now—as a "beauty bar" with one-fourth cleansing cream that moisturizes skin while washing (as opposed to the drying effect of regular soap). Advertisements reinforced the message by showing the cream being poured into the beauty bar. In 1979, the phrase "cleansing cream" was replaced with "moisturizer cream."

Also in 1979, a University of Pennsylvania dermatologist showed that Dove dried and irritated skin significantly less than ordinary soaps. Based on this study, Unilever began aggressively marketing Dove to doctors. Soon about 25 percent of Dove users said they bought the brand because a doctor recommended it, greatly enhancing the bar's credibility as a moisturizer. By the mid-1980s, Dove had become the best-selling soap brand and commanded a price premium.

The first effort to extend the Dove brand occurred in 1965. The extension, into dishwashing detergent, survives but has to be regarded as disappointing. Because the leading competitor at the time, Palmolive, promised to "soften hands while you do dishes," the hope was that the Dove cleansing-cream message would translate into a competitive benefit. Instead, customers felt no reason to change from the well-positioned Palmolive, and since Dove's reputation for moisturizing and beauty did not imply clean dishes, there was simply no perceived benefit. After receiving weak market acceptance for the extension, Dove lowered the price, creating another source of strain on the brand. Fifteen years after its launch, the brand languished at a rather poor seventh in the U.S. market, with a share of around 3 percent. The dishwashing detergent not only failed to enhance the Dove brand, but it also undoubtedly inhibited Dove from extending its franchise further for decades.

In 1990 the Dove soap patent ran out, and arch-competitor P&G was soon testing an Olay beauty bar with moisturizing properties, a product that rolled out in 1993. One year later, Olay body wash appeared and soon garnered over 25 percent of a high-margin product category. Blindsided, the Dove brand team belatedly recognized that theirs was the natural brand to own the moisturizer body wash position. The firm had apparently missed the chance to be a leader in this new subcategory.

In response to Olay, the firm rushed Dove Moisturizing Body Wash into stores. The product did not live up to the Dove promise, however, and a reformulation in 1996 was only a partial improvement. In 1999, though, Dove finally got it right with the innovative Nutrium line, based on a technology that deposited lipids, vitamin E, and other ingredients onto the skin. The advanced skin-nourishing properties provided enough of a lift to allow Dove to charge a 50 percent premium over its regular body wash. Later, Dove introduced a version of Nutrium with antioxidants (which have been linked to reduced signs of aging), which helped Dove to pull even with Olay in the body wash category. By leveraging strong brand equity, pursuing innovative technology, and being persistent, Dove was able to overcome a late entry into the market.

The Dove body wash efforts influenced the brand's soap business, which was flat until the mid-1990s (and, in fact, declined in 1996). The introduction of the body wash corresponded to a 30 percent growth surge in Dove soap from the mid-1990s to 2001, evidence that the energy and exposure of the Dove brand helped even though the product was somewhat waning during much of that period. In addition, the Nutrium subbrand, established in the body wash category, was employed to help the soap business. In 2001, Unilever introduced a Dove Nutrium soap (positioned as replenishing skin nutrients) that was priced about 30 percent higher than regular Dove.

Another battlefield, entered in 2000, was the rather mature category of deodorants—even though dryness, the key benefit, seemed contradictory to the Dove promise of moisturizing, and the target segment was younger than the typical Dove customer. Despite these apparent risks, Dove introduced a deodorant line with uncharacteristically bold advertising (for example, one tag line was "Next stop, armpit heaven"). As it turned out, the deodorants were named as one of the top 10 nonfood new products in 2001, garnering over $70 million in sales with close to 5 percent of the market, making Dove the number-two brand among female deodorants. The "one-quarter moisturizing lotion" positioning, effectively communicated as protecting sensitive underarm skin, generated a Dove spin on dryness that differentiated the product line.

In spite of this win, P&G's Olay again beat Dove to a new market in the summer of 2000, this time with disposable face cloths infused with moisturizers. It took Dove about a year to respond with its Dove Daily Hydrating Cleansing Cloths. With the body wash success behind it, however, the Dove brand was well suited to compete in this category.

The next product extension was Dove Hair Care, whose moisturizing qualities were directly responsive to one of the top two unmet needs in the category. The product's branded differentiator, Weightless Moisturizers, is a set of 15 ingredients designed to make the hair softer, smoother, and more vibrant without adding any extra weight. After achieving top-selling status in Japan and Taiwan, Dove Hair Care entered the U.S. market in early 2003 with a massive introduction campaign, joining a product family used by nearly one-third of American families. Two years later it introduced Dove Body Nourishers Intensive Firming Lotion, formulated with collagen and seaweed, intended to give the user firmer skin after two weeks.

These extensions contributed to a dramatic sales success. The brand's business grew from probably around $200 million in 1990 to over $4 billion by some estimates in 2013 (the bar itself was enjoying substantial growth in sales). Geographic expansion also contributed. Dove's presence increased to nearly 80 countries, far more than in 1990, with particular strength in Europe (where it gained 30 percent of the cosmetics and toiletries market), Asia-Pacific (25 percent), and Latin America (11 percent).

In 2005, with no major geographic expansion or brand extension in sight, Dove looked to another route to add energy. The result was an advertising campaign (first created in the United Kingdom) featuring "real women" with real dress sizes instead of ultra-thin models. Dove branded campaigns to educate and inspire girls to adopt a wider definition of beauty and to achieve a higher self-esteem level supplemented by the advertising. The new direction for the brand was based in part on a global study involving 3,200 interviews that revealed that only 2 percent of women thought themselves beautiful, 50 percent of women thought their weight was too high (60 percent in the United States), and two-thirds of women felt that the media and advertising set an unrealistic standard of beauty. The campaign received enormous exposure in the media with over a thousand stories, most but not all positive (some felt it would be ineffective, others pointed out that Unilever was still using models for its other products, and still others thought Dove was promoting obesity). It generated a 10 percent sales boost.

Another initiative was aimed at girls who are too often held back by low self-esteem and anxiety about their looks. Dove's social mission was to encourage girls to develop a positive relationship with beauty, helping to raise their self-esteem and thereby enabling them to realize their full potential. There are a variety of programs to promote the development of body confidence among girls using support of their families and communities. Over 8.5 million young people in 26 countries have received help from 2005 through 2012.

In addition, Unilever has a men's product named Axe (called Lynx in some countries), which was introduced into the United States in 2002 as a spray deodorant and now covers shampoo, shower gels, aftershave, and other products. The Axe brand was built around the humorous premise that beautiful women would go crazy over a man (or even a male mannequin) if the Axe spray had been used. The advertisements and promotions were widely perceived as sexist and even degrading. Some pointed out that Unilever was hypocritical to claim some kind of feminine champion when they have the Axe brand so blatantly being the opposite of the "real women" concept.

FOR DISCUSSION

1. Why was Dove dormant for so long?

2. What were the keys to the success that Dove achieved in building its brand into a $4 billion business? What were the roles of success momentum and of branded differentiators?

3. What was the role of a vigorous competitor? Would Dove have gotten there without P&G pushing (or, more accurately, pulling) the brand?

4. Why were Dove soap sales affected by the other Dove successes?

5. What does this case tell you about first-mover advantage?

6. What is your opinion of the "Real Beauty" campaign? Does the existence of the Axe brand affect your views?

Source: Adapted with the permission of the Free Press, a division of Simon & Schuster Adult Publishing Group, from *Brand Portfolio Strategy: Creating Relevance, Differentiation, Energy, Leverage, and Clarity*, by David A. Aaker. Copyright © 2004 by David A. Aaker. All rights reserved.

Competing Against the Industry Giant

COMPETING AGAINST WAL-MART

Wal-Mart is the most successful retailer ever. In 2012, at $464 billion in sales, it was by far the world's largest retail company. Its sales represented over 5 percent of the total U.S. retail volume. And its share of the total market in some categories, such as disposable diapers and hair care products, was well over 25 percent. Wal-Mart regularly appears on *Fortune*'s list of the most admired companies in America.

Wal-Mart was founded in Arkansas by Sam Walton in 1962. Six years later, it expanded into neighboring states, and in the 1970s, it ventured beyond the South. Over time it added products such as jewelry and food, as well as pharmacy and automotive departments. By 2009, there were some 900 Wal-Marts, over 2,600 Wal-Mart Supercenters, and 150 neighborhood markets in the United States. Over 90 percent of Americans live within 15 miles of a Wal-Mart store. In 1983, Wal-Mart went into the wholesale club business under the Sam's Club brand name; this concept grew to over 500 stores within two decades and in 2009 had over 600 stores. In 1991, it began its international quest by opening a store in Mexico. In 2009, Wal-Mart had nearly 3,600 stores in 15 markets outside the United States and was the leading retailer in both Mexico and Canada.

For its first 30 years, Sam Walton was the heart and soul of Wal-Mart. An inspirational and visionary influence, he created strategies, policies, and cultural values that fueled the firm's success. He would spend much of his time visiting stores and meeting customers and "associates" (employees). The visits would always result in customer and merchandising insights, pats on the back for workers, and suggestions for improvement. He would summon managers back to the headquarters in Bentonville, Arkansas, for Saturday morning meetings that kept the firm focused and provided a pervasive work ethic. He also enjoyed celebrating successes, once keeping a promise to do the hula on Wall Street if the company achieved an 8 percent pretax profit. For employees and customers alike, Sam Walton *was* Wal-Mart.

In 1962, Walton started his firm with three basic beliefs—respect for the individual employee, exceptional customer service, and a striving for excellence. He developed a host of rules for associates. He challenged them to engage in "aggressive hospitality," to be ready with a smile and assistance to all customers. The "10-foot rule" decreed that whenever an associate was within 10 feet of a customer, the associate was to look that customer in the eye and ask if he or she needed help. His "sundown rule" meant that any task that could be done today would be not put off until tomorrow—especially if the task involved customer service. Exemplifying his belief in empowerment, Walton instituted the Volume Producing Item (VPI) program, in which an associate would pick an item, design a merchandising effort for it, and monitor and communicate the results.

In his 1992 book *Made in America*—a title that reflects Wal-Mart's positioning strategies in the early 1980s, as well as a comment on the founder's career—Sam Walton listed 10 key factors that he felt were key to his success. One was to appreciate your associates and their contribution; a second item was to share your profits with them. A third factor was to talk to the customer and listen to what that customer is saying. Another item was to exceed your customer's expectations ("satisfaction guaranteed" really meant something to Sam Walton). Still another factor was to control your expenses better than your competition; Walton prided himself on having a number-one ranking in the ratio of expenses to sales.

Sam Walton offered strategies as well as charisma. One basic early strategy was to bring discount stores to cities of roughly 50,000 people. While the large discount stores of the day were fighting for prime spots in large cities, Wal-Mart had the smaller metropolitan areas to itself. Second, because of the location of its early stores and its headquarters site, Wal-Mart had an employee cost advantage from top to bottom. Third, by setting up distribution centers, Wal-Mart from the outset gained operational and logistic efficiencies. Over time Wal-Mart relentlessly innovated in warehousing, logistics, information technology, and operations to create more and more savings. In part, this innovation was done in partnership with suppliers like P&G.

Wal-Mart continued to prosper after 1992 when Sam Walton passed away. Although his strategic flair and connection with employees and customers was missed, many of his ideas had become institutionalized. Aggressive merchandising led by empowered associates and the trademark greeters, for example, remained part of the Wal-Mart profile. In addition, there was a focus on energy-adding "Retailtainment," including live concert broadcasts in the home entertainment departments, exclusive promotional events around video releases, and exhibits by local organizations. Equity was built into private-label brands, such as Ol' Roy dog food (which has surpassed Purina as the world's top-selling dog food), White Cloud tissues and diapers, and the Sam's Choice and Great Value product lines.

Low prices and cost containment have continued to be the focus—some say the obsession—of Wal-Mart management. The customer promise of "Low Prices, Always" drives the culture and the strategy. Suppliers are continuously and aggressively challenged to reduce costs. Wal-Mart will set demanding cost reduction goals, on occasion showing suppliers how to achieve them. Operations are continuously made more efficient. The resulting cost savings are passed on to customers, as Wal-Mart does not support suppliers' premium-price brand policies. The firm's private-label lines are often sourced directly from foreign factories, creating significant cost advantages and disrupting price norms in many categories. Wal-Mart views itself, first and foremost, as the customer's purchasing agent, and its goal is to reduce prices. By some estimates, Wal-Mart saves consumers $20 billion a year.

Wal-Mart has significant detractors as well. One set of arguments, summarized in a *Business Week* cover story questioning whether Wal-Mart is too powerful, relates to jobs. Wal-Mart has been accused of hastening the move of jobs abroad, as its focus on costs led the company to buy over $27 billion in goods from China alone in 2006 (some 11 percent of the U.S. trade deficit with China). Some even argue that suppliers, in order to meet Wal-Mart's cost targets, are forced to move jobs to China and elsewhere. In addition, it is estimated that for every supercenter that Wal-Mart opens, two supermarkets will close. When Wal-Mart went into Oklahoma City, for example, 30 supermarkets closed. Because of the loss of local businesses, many communities have resisted Wal-Mart's entry. Even the jobs that Wal-Mart adds are said to be inferior, as the company's antiunion, low-pay policy has been hypothesized to hold down wages in retail America and throughout local regions. On average, a Wal-Mart sales clerk in 2001 made less than $14,000, which was below the poverty line for a family of three. Labor costs have been estimated to be 20 percent less than competing unionized supermarkets because fewer employees receive benefits. Dozens of lawsuits related to overtime pay and sex discrimination have been filed against the firm. Sam Walton's values of "Made in America" and "respect for the individual" seem to some a distant memory. The Wal-Mart green initiatives, described in Chapter 6, are intended in part to counter this negative publicity.

Wal-Mart also faces some more intangible concerns. Because it controls over 15 percent of all nonsubscription magazine and video/DVD sales, some fear that the firm wields an unwelcome and arbitrary influence on culture. Wal-Mart elects to stock some magazines while banning or hiding the covers of others (a nearly naked woman on the cover of *Rolling Stone* is acceptable but not on the front of *Glamour* and *Redbook*), and it sells only videos that meet family-friendly standards. As a result, some movie producers have felt compelled to create a "Wal-Mart version" of their films. Further, Wal-Mart's market power is so high that some people fear it has an inordinate influence on product design (for example, a particular design direction may be deemed by Wal-Mart as too costly for its customers). In a wide variety of product areas, manufacturers cannot afford to deviate from specifications set by Wal-Mart.

Wal-Mart has plans to expand dramatically. The primary vehicle for this growth will be Wal-Mart Supercenters, often located in malls where sites are available at distressed prices, face fewer zoning issues, and precipitate less neighborhood opposition. Another is Neighborhood Markets, its small-format stores that offer perishable food, household supplies, and beauty aids as well as a pharmacy. The obsession with low prices, costs, and efficiency will not change. In fact, suppliers have been given a deadline to attach radio-frequency identification tags to all packages and pallets in order to create a new level of efficiency. There will be an increased emphasis on the growth of private-label goods, such as the great value line. A program to upgrade Sam's Club by adding pharmacy, optical, one-hour photo, fuel, and other services is under way.

FOR DISCUSSION

1. Grocery stores and general merchandise stores must look forward to more intense challenges from Wal-Mart in the future. Such firms need to understand Wal-Mart and how it competes. What Wal-Mart strategies led to success? What was the role of Sam Walton?

2. What is the company's likely future direction beyond its stated intentions? Would it make sense for Wal-Mart to extend its brand into stand-alone grocery stores (such as Safeway) or convenience stores (for example, 7-Eleven)?

3. Is Wal-Mart positive or negative for consumers? For suppliers? For employees? For communities? For the United States?

4. What impact have the Wal-Mart green programs described in Chapter 5, page 80, had on its image?

Consider two competitors, Costco and Wegmans, that must design a strategy that will lead to success in the Wal-Mart environment.

WEGMANS

There are 70 Wegmans Food Markets in New York, Pennsylvania, New Jersey, and Maryland. Wegmans has seen sales (including same-store sales) grow steadily over the years to around $4 billion with very healthy margins and sales per square foot—numbers that are much higher than other supermarkets. The newer stores have an enormous prepared food section, a wide selection of organic foods, some 500 cheeses with a staff knowledgeable about them, a fresh bakery, a bookstore, child play centers, a photo lab, a florist, a wine shop, a pharmacy, and an espresso maker. Shopping becomes an event. Wegmans' passion for food shows. They sponsor classes on cooking, wine selection, and other food topics and have a catering service with an extensive menu. Their Web site has an "Eat Well, Live Well," section and weekly comments on food from their senior vice president for consumer affairs.

The staff is friendly, helpful, and committed. Several times Wegmans has been one of the top five firms in *Fortune*'s list of best companies to work for. They hire only people who share their passion about food and provide wages and benefits much higher than competitors. As a result the employees don't leave and are enthusiastic about their mission to delight customers. Their bakery chef once worked at the French Laundry at Napa, one of the world's top restaurants. Their customer set includes many devoted fans and their influence spills over to new stores. A Dallas store attracted 15,500 shoppers on its first day.

However, Wal-Mart looms. Many of the Wegmans stores are within 20 miles of a Wal-Mart Supercenter.

FOR DISCUSSION

1. What are the strengths and weaknesses of Wal-Mart from the perspective of Wegmans?
2. What strategies should Wegmans avoid?
3. What strategies will allow Wegmans to thrive or at least survive in the face of Wal-Mart's strengths?
4. How should Wegmans exploit the Wal-Mart resentment factor?

COSTCO

Costco started in 1981, just a few years before Sam's Club appeared. In 20011, it had some 600 stores doing around $90 billion in sales, with some 60 million individual members, 5 million business members, and more than $1.5 billion in net profit. Annual growth is in the 6 to 10 percent range, and per-store sales have risen from $77 million in 1996 to $1154 million in 2011—performance far better than Sam's Club, the Wal-Mart entry. Their membership fees represent about 15% of the value of the firm.

Unlike Sam's Club, which focuses on price, Costco offers upscale brands such as Callaway golf clubs, Starbucks coffee, and expensive jewelry, and thus it attracts a different kind of shopper. Costco prides itself on providing "treasure hunt" experience for their clients who can search for that special item among the ever-changing selection. Sam's Club is attempting to attack Costco by adding upscale brands and integrating more closely with Wal-Mart in order to achieve more buying power and logistical efficiencies.

FOR DISCUSSION

1. What are the strengths and weaknesses of Sam's Club from the perspective of Costco?
2. How should Costco react to the Wal-Mart threat?

Sources: Wal-Mart, Costco, and Wegmans company Web sites in 2008; Wal-Mart annual report for 2008; Anthony Bianco and Wendy Zellner, "Is Wal-Mart Too Powerful?" *Business Week*, October 6, 2003, pp. 100–110. "Wal-Mart Celebrates Its Growing Market Share," *Fortune*, June 8, 2009.

Creating a New Brand for a New Business
CONTEMPORARY ART

Contemporary art, often defined as nontraditional art from the 1970s, can sell for incredible amounts. Damien Hirst, currently one of the world's most expensive living artists, commissioned a shark to be killed and preserved floating in formaldehyde in a large glass case. The display is titled "The Physical Impossibility of Death in the Mind of Someone Living." It is now in the Metropolitan Museum of Art and is said to be worth $12 million. Hirst also creates a square array of colored dots that sell for up to $1,500,000. Hundreds of these have been made and sold. While still unknown, Hirst sold a work to Charles Saatchi, the advertising executive and prominent collector, that consisted of flies being hatched and attracted to a decaying cow's head only to be zapped by a bug zapper along the way. It was called "A Thousand Years" and was said to depict life and death. Saatchi, who owns over 3,000 contemporary artworks, is generous about loaning them to museums if they agree to display other pieces (so that they can be said to have been displayed in the museum).

There are dozens of artists who command high prices. Some samples:

- On Kawara paints a date such as Nov 8, 1989 on a canvas. There are some 2,000 in existence, and one was sold for around $500,000 in 2006 at a Christie's auction. Christie's and Sotheby's are the two most prestigious auction houses. It has been estimated that a painting will get 20 percent more if sold at one of these two auction houses in part because of their brand.

- Felix Gonzalez-Torres obtained 355 pounds of individually wrapped blue and white candies, piled them in a rectangular shape, and called the result "Lover Boy." It was sold for $450,000 in 2000.

- Christopher Wool sold a painting of some 15 stenciled letters that spelled Rundogrundogrun for $1.24 million in 2005.

- In 2008, a seven-foot Mark Rothko painting that had been owned by David Rockefeller (who bought it in 1960 for $8,500) sold at Sotheby's for $72.8 million, nearly three times more than the previous high for a Rothko.

- In the late 1950s, Leo Castelli opened a New York gallery and proceeded to sponsor some young artists with personality, including Jasper Johns, Robert Rauschenberg, and Cy Twombly. He bought an early controversial Johns work that consisted of nine wooden boxes in one of which was a green plaster cast of a penis for $1,200. He sold it to the collector David Geffen for $13 million in 1993, and it is now said to be worth over $100 million.

- Jeff Koons, famous for making vacuum cleaners an art object, sold a sculpture of Michael Jackson and his pet monkey for $5.6 million despite the fact that there were two other copies of the piece. The fact that the other copies were owned by the San Francisco MOMA and a prominent collector actually enhanced the value of the third piece.

- Tracey Emin established a brand and the premium prices that go with it by creating a bad girl image. For example, she posed nude for commercials, created a tent embroidered with names of her past lovers, and apparently appeared on television so drunk that she had no memory of it.

Why these prices? One hypothesis is that this art is objectively exceptional, and its high quality merits a premium price. That is demonstratively false. Consider the following.

- A person named Eddie Sanders mounted a shark, framed it, and offered it for only $1 million, one-twelfth of the price of the Hirst piece. There were no takers even though objectively it was aesthetically similar.

- There was a painting of Joseph Stalin, worthless until Damien Hirst painted a red nose on the subject and signed his name—it then sold for $250,000.

- A Jackson Pollock look-alike painting was bought at a flea market. A series of experts could not ascertain if it was an authentic Pollock or not. The same painting was either worth a few thousand or tens of millions depending on whether it was deemed authentic. One Pollock sold for $140 million in 2006, the highest price ever paid for a contemporary art piece.

- An authenticity board attempts to ascertain whether Andy Warhol actually saw and approved a piece of art. If so, the piece goes from worthless to highly valued.

An auction professional once said, "Never underestimate how insecure buyers are about contemporary art, and how much they always need reassurance."

What makes these prices even more puzzling is the fact that several of the top artists do not do their own work. Andy Warhol famously did little of his own artwork. Hirst has a staff of 20 or so who do all of his work, including the colored spots. And Jeff Koons, who keeps a staff of 80 busy, was quoted as saying that he is the idea person and is not physically involved in the production of art because he lacks the necessary abilities.

So the question is why do these artists attract such prices? And more basically, how does a painter create a brand that will command fantastic sums?

These questions are more general than they might seem. There are many businesses for which it is not possible to objectively know the value of the product or service. Most customers lack the information and often the expertise to evaluate service firms. There are also products, such as motor oil, for which it is not possible to judge the quality. Even products such as cars or computers are difficult to evaluate because they are complex and specifications do not tell the whole story. Further, even if a person took the time to pour through *Consumer Reports*, it is not clear that its recommendations will reflect the right decision criteria.

FOR DISCUSSION

1. Why might the demand for contemporary art increase?
2. Why do people buy contemporary art?
3. How does an artist develop a brand? What is the role of an art dealer in brand development?
4. Is Damien Hirst famous because of his work and its shock value, because of Charles Saatchi, or because he is famous?
5. How would you develop a brand if you were a new investment advisory service? Can you use any of the techniques that artists use?

Source: This case draws on material in Don Thompson, *The $12 Million Stuffed Shark: The Curious Economics of Contemporary Art*, London: Aurum Press, 2008.

Barriers to Innovation

SONY VS. iPOD

A vivid example of the silo problem, the failure of autonomous product and functional silos to cooperate, comes from Sony's incredible miss of the iPod. The iPod was a natural for Sony; it was theirs to lose. Sony has long been the leader in portable music from the Walkman to portable CD players to the mini-disc. And Sony, unlike Apple, had a big presence in music. More generally, Sony has excelled at transformational innovation from the Trinitron in 1968 to the BetaMax in 1975 to the camcorder in 1985 to the VAIO in 1997 to the Blu-ray Discs of 2003. Further, it has been the miniaturization company ever since the "transistor radios" of the 1950s, and no firm has been better at creating new categories than Sony.

There are several reasons why Sony missed the iPod opening. Their hope that the analogue world, where Sony had a significant investment and competitive edge, would hang on inhibited their commitment to digital. This despite the pronouncement by Nobuyuki Idei, the new Sony CEO in 1995, that Sony would be the company of Digital Dream Kids—aspirational, having fun, exciting products, and being part of the digital revolution. Another reason was their long-term tendency to avoid industry standards in favor of creating products they could own. This policy was risky—sometimes it did not work, as when Betamax lost the battle for VCR standard. But sometimes Sony won—Blu-ray did become the DVD standard. The main reason Sony missed out on the iPod was that silos paralyzed it at exactly the wrong time. It was not from lack of innovation.

At the huge Las Vegas Comdex trade show in the fall of 1999, Sony introduced two digital music players two years before Apple brought the iPod to the market. One, developed by the Sony Personal Audio Company, was the Memory Stick Walkman, which enabled users to store music files in Sony's memory stick, a device that resembled a large pack of gum. The other, developed by the VAIO Company, was the VAIO Music Clip, which also stored music in memory and resembled a stubby fountain pen. Both were flawed but provided the bases for a new product category. Each had 64 megabytes of memory, which stored only 20 or so songs, and was priced too high for the general market. Both also featured a Sony proprietary compression scheme called ATRAC3. Software to convert MP3 files to the Sony standard was not convenient and, worse, resulted in slow transfers. There is little question that, over time, Sony had the potential to improve the products to address these limitations. However, the fact that Sony promoted two different devices created by two fiercely independent silos confused the market as well as the Sony organization.

There was a third silo involved—Sony Music, an entity that owes its origin to the purchase of CBS records in 1988. Along with Sony Pictures, it is part of a Sony strategy to bring content to digital convergence, the effort to tie together all the digital components delivering entertainment. Firms representing computers, cable networks, telephone networks, electronic games, consumer electronics, and computers were all vying to be the captain of the digital home. Sony believed that having content would be an advantage in that race.

Sony Music in 1999 turned out to be a handicap instead of an advantage for the Sony digital music players because it was preoccupied with avoiding piracy and freeloading. The success of the new digital products was not a priority. As a result, it inhibited the products' ability to provide access to a broad array of music and led to the use of the cumbersome uploading process, which turned out to be a burden.

Sony's three silos thwarted the efforts by Sony to create a new category and preempt Apple's iPod, which sold around 200 million units in its first nine years. It is likely that a product that combined the energies, resources, and customer insights of the three silos and was improved over time would have been successful and that the iPod opening would not have materialized.

Sony has begun the process of changing the silo culture so that cooperation and communication replaces competition and isolation and Sony can return to its innovation heritage, avoid other iPod misses, and liberate synergy potential. Ironically, Mr. Idei in 1995 also called on all employees to "collaborate with team spirit." The task is not easy, however, because silo issues are embedded in entrenched organizational structures and cultures. These are difficult but not impossible obstacles to overcome. Chapter 16 elaborates on silo issues and how to address them.

FOR DISCUSSION

1. What are the advantages of proprietary products like Sony and Apple employ vs. open source products like IBM or Dell advocate? How and under what conditions do proprietary products pay off? Consider two consulting companies. One publishes all its intellectual property in books and articles, and the other has a set of back boxes. Which model is better?

2. Why was Sony slower at going digital than its stated strategy and aspirations would suggest?

3. The holy grail of consumer electronics is digital convergence, to own the digital command center. Do you agree that owning content, movies, music, and TV shows is a big advantage in that race?

4. Why did two competing Sony products get into the market at the same time? How could that happen? How could it be prevented? Would it happen in another company?

5. What should Sony have done to correct the silo problem? How could Sony Music have been motivated to be a helpful member of the team?

Sources: Sea-Jin Chang, *Sony vs. Samsung*, New York: John Wiley & Sons, 2008, and from the Sony History section of the Sony Web site, 2009. For more on silo problems and how to address them, see David A. Aaker, *Spanning Silos: The New CMO Imperative*, Boston: Harvard Business School Press, 2008.

APPENDIX

Planning Forms

A set of standard forms can be helpful in presenting strategy recommendations and supporting analyses. The forms can encourage the useful consistency of the presentation over time and across businesses within an organization. They can also provide a checklist of areas to consider in strategy development and make communication easier. The following sample forms are intended to provide a point of departure in designing forms for a specific context. The external analysis in the example is drawn from the pet food industry. The forms are for illustration purposes only.

Planning forms need to be adapted to the context involved: the industry, the firm, and the planning context. They may well be different and shorter or longer given a particular context. Forms for use with other product types—an industrial product, for example—could be modified to include information such as current and potential applications or key existing or potential customers.

THE PET FOOD INDUSTRY

Section 1. Customer Analysis

A. Segments

Segments	Market (Billions)	Comments
Dog—dry	7.1	Largest segment, segmented nutritional offerings, growing
Dog—canned;	1.8	Made from real meat and by-products, etc.
Cat—dry	3.1	Second largest segment, nutritional offerings, accelerating growth
Cat—canned	2.1	Made from real meat, high levels of flavor and textural variety, etc.
Dog treats	1.6	Del Monte dominates with Milk-Bone
Pet specialty (including pet shops, veterinarians, farm and feed)	5.6	Large players—Science Diet and Iams, uses vets and pet stores, about 70% dog food, mostly dry, growing at 5%

B. Customer Motivations

Segment	Motivations
Dog—dry	Nutrition, convenience, teeth cleaning, often better value than canned pet food in grocery and mass channels
Dog—canned	For finicky dogs, taste and nutrition, variety
Cat—dry	Nutrition, convenience, complement to meal, teeth cleaning
Cat—canned	Taste, convenient sizes, easy to serve, for finicky cats, variety of textures and flavors
Treats	Complement to meal, reward, animal likes it, functional nutritional benefits (e.g., tartar control)
Pet specialty	Health concern, scientific nutrition, perceived superior ingredients

C. Unmet Needs

Information on pets
Further subneeds of segments (as defined by human nutrition, e.g., allergies)

Section 2. Competitor Analysis

A. Competitor Identification

Most directly competitive: Nestlé Purina Petcare, Iams (P&G), Del Monte, Mars
Less directly competitive: Hill Petfood (Colgate Palmolive), Blue Buffalo

B. Strategic Groups

Strategic Group	Major Competitors	Dollar Share
(1) Mainstream brands from large consumer firms	Nestlé Purina Petcare	44.2%
	Mars	11.7%
	Del Monte	13.7%
	Iams (P&G)	5.7%
(2) High-end specialty brands	Hill's (Colgate-Palmolive)	3.5%
	All other	8.1%
(3) Private-label brands	Other	13.1%

Strategic Group	Characteristics/ Strategies	Strengths	Weaknesses
(1) Mainstream brands from large consumer firms	*Mainstream products* • *Large portfolio of products* • *Wide range of price points to meet the needs of many* • *Sell to multiple channels* • *Heavy use of advertising* • *Emphasis on nutrition and variety*	• *Production-scale economies* • *Significant presence in supermarkets and mass merchandisers, where ~70% of industry volume is sold* • *Deep global financial resources and expertise (e.g., dedicated R&D)* • *Long-term commitment to industry*	• *High fixed cost commitment to capacity increases competitive pressure on all players to defend share through promotions, etc.* • *Perception as less nutritious than specialty brands* • *Private label share at Wal-Mart and elsewhere is increasing*
(2) High-end specialty pet food brands	• *Narrowly focused, super premium–priced product lines* • *High presence in nonsupermarket channels, such as veterinary offices, pet breeders, and pet specialty stores(e.g., Petsmart)*	• *Product line focus on health, natural ingredients, and nutrition, resulting in increasing consumer demand; high-margin business* • *First-in advantage to high-end specialty segment, resulting in a perceptual edge that mainstream brands find difficult to overcome* • *Sell through alternative channels, which are growing faster and are less competitive and offer limited access to other brands, a barrier to entry* • *High volume and low unit costs*	• *Higher ingredient and production costs* • *Lack economies of scale* • *Ultra premium price points limit appeal*

Strategic Group	Characteristics/ Strategies	Strengths	Weaknesses
(3) Private-label pet foods	• *Sell through multiple supermarkets and mass merchandisers under house brand designation*	• *Profit margins are attractive to retailers* • *Power of Wal-Mart as number-one retailer* • *Good-quality offerings with high perceived consumer value*	• *Little brand differentiation* • *Weak brand equity*

C. Major Competitors

Competitor	Characteristics/ Strategies	Strengths	Weaknesses
Nestlé Purina Petcare	• *Overall market leader, product line is broad and deep* • *Increasing move toward "premiumization" with niche product lines and upgrade of products to premium status* • *Large, powerful brand names with high consumer loyalty* • *Heavy emphasis on innovative first-to-market new products* • *Massive advertising and promotional spending to grow share* • *High commitment to category* • *Deep financial resources* • *Company takes long-term view on brand-building efforts; high level of commitment to brands* • *Global commitment to building brands*	• *Economies of scale, low costs* • *Supply-chain efficiencies* • *Strong retailer relationships* • *Global expertise and R&D support*	• *Weak presence in specialty segment* • *Need to support multiple brands across multiple categories with finite resources*

Competitor	Characteristics/ Strategies	Strengths	Weaknesses
Del Monte	• *Emphasis on cat food and dog treats but competes in all segments of market* • *Low-cost producer strategy* • *Migrating to a more consumer-centric model with recent acquisitions*	• *Focused on few brands and categories* • *Acquired strong brands in Milk-Bone and Meow Mix*	• *Relatively weak in brand building* • *Milking brands, such as 9-Lives* • *Lack of product innovation in cat and dog food*
Mars	• *Leadership position outside of the U.S.* • *Commitment to building brands* • *Upgrading supermarket brands for premium appeal*	• *Dog food expertise* • *Economies of scale, low costs with acquisition of the private-label supplier Doane* • *Deep financial resources* • *Private firm gives freedom from short-term pressures*	• *Lack of cat food expertise and market share in U.S.*
Hill's Petfood	• *Strong player in specialty and vet markets* • *Entry barriers in vet business for Science Diet brand*	• *Leading recipient of veterinary recommendation* • *Best niche-market product positioning in the industry*	• *No presence in supermarkets or mass outlets, where 60%+ of industry volume is sold* • *Under pressure from new high-end specialty Brand (e.g., Blue Buffalo)*
Iams (P&G)	• *Traditionally a specialty market brand, with emphasis on specialty-store sales and referrals from pet breeders* • *Moved to grocery and mass merchandise channels, which stimulated growth*	• *Deep financial recourses* • *Strong brand equity*	• *Economies of scale* • *Limited market penetration and share* • *Limited portfolio variety*

D. Competitor Strength Grid

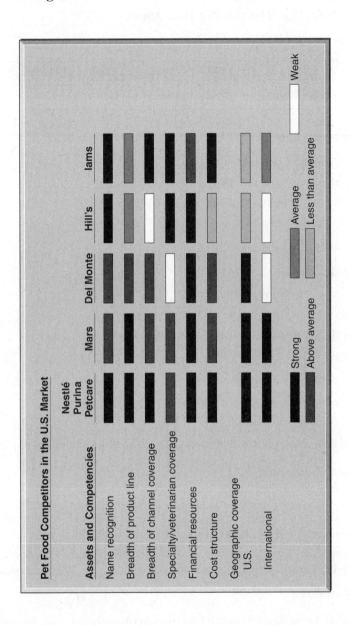

Pet Food Competitors in the U.S. Market

Assets and Competencies	Nestlé Purina Petcare	Mars	Del Monte	Hill's	Iams
Name recognition					
Breadth of product line					
Breadth of channel coverage					
Specialty/veterinarian coverage					
Financial resources					
Cost structure					
Geographic coverage U.S.					
International					

Strong · Above average · Average · Less than average · Weak

Section 3. Market Analysis

A. Market Identification: The U.S. Pet Food Market

B. Market Size

	1990	1995	2000	2005	2008	2013
U.S. industry sales ($ in billions)	7.7	9.1	11.1	13.9	16.1	21.3

Emerging Submarkets

- Special diet-based products
- Wal-Mart and other private-label products
- Wellness-focused items (e.g., Naturals)
- Product "humanization"

Market Growth (in Dollars vs. 2011)

- Overall pet—growing at 5 percent
- Supermarket—growing at 3 percent
- Specialty store—growing at 3 percent annually
- Mass merchandisers—growing at 7 percent annually
- Drug—growing at 5 percent

Factors Affecting Sales Levels

- Growth of pet population
- Growth of higher-value products
- General economic consumer pressure, especially at low end of the market

C. Market Profitability Analysis

Barriers to Entry

- Brand awareness, budget for marketing programs, access to distribution channels, large investment required for manufacturing, science, and technology.
- For pet specialty segment—loyalty to Hill's Science Diet and other entrenched specialty brands; difficulty of getting recommendations of vets and other influentials

Potential Entrants

- The probability of new entrants is quite low because the pet food industry is already very competitive, with lots of incumbents, and barriers to entry are high.

Threats of Substitutes

- Human food leftovers
- Food cooked especially for pets

Bargaining Power of Suppliers

- Growing.
- Raw materials shared with human food markets.
- Consolidation of suppliers.
- Quality of raw ingredients requirements growing.

Bargaining Power of Customers

- Grocery stores and warehouse clubs have strong bargaining power over pet food suppliers.
- Specialty stores and veterinarians might have moderate bargaining power.
- Mass merchandisers (especially Wal-Mart, with around 24 percent of the volume in this category) have very strong bargaining power.

D. Cost Structure

- Diversified firms have lower cost because of economies in advertising, manufacturing, promotion, and distribution.
- Specialized firms have higher costs and often are required to co-manufacture their products.

E. Distribution System
Major Channels

- Supermarkets are dominant in terms of quantity they deal with (35 percent).
- Mass merchandisers handle about 29 percent of market and are growing.
- Pet foods are effective traffic builders in supermarkets and mass merchandisers.
- Farm-supply stores are generally located in suburbs
- Pet stores handle most premium brands and many "mainstream" national brands.
- Veterinarians handle only superpremium brands.

Observations/Major Trends

- Vets' sales are flat and have very high margins both for producers and for themselves.
- Specialty stores' sales are growing at approximately 6 percent.
- These two channels have captured high-involvement customers' needs to feed their pets healthier foods.
- Warehouses have gained footholds in market-leader brands.
- Innovations in packaging are begging to address unmet needs around convenience
- Product innovations are creating subcategories.

F. Market Trends and Developments

- Premium and superpremium brands have grown, and most producers are introducing new products in this area.
- Large manufacturers are introducing new products continuously.

G. Key Success Factors

Present

- Brand recognition
- Product quality
- Access to major channels
- Gain market share in premium brands
- Introduction of new products
- Breadth of product line
- Marketing program
- Cost reduction
- Awareness or recommendation by specialists
- Packaging
- Capitalizing on relevant human trends (naturals; shift to healthier, higher-quality ingredients)

Future

- Continue to capture the trends of consumers
- Packaging
- Follow the trends of distributors Ability to demonstrate corporate responsibility (e.g., environmental sustainability)

Section 4. Environmental Analysis

A. *Trends and Potential Events*

Source	Description	Strategic Implication	Time Frame	Importance
Technological	New product forms	Limited		Low
Regulatory	Impose standards of content	Limited		Low
Economic	Insensitive to economic changes	Very limited		Low
Cultural	Think of pets as members of families Demand for new, healthy products Users' needs have diversified	Growth of superpremium brands Introduction of healthy products Multiple specialized segments	Since the mid-1980s	High
Demographic	Household formation is slowing The number of cats is increasing more than dogs The baby boomer is aging	Continued innovation of product and communications to keep brands relevant	Since the 1980s	Medium–high
Threats	High dependence on animal proteins	Risk of animal-borne diseases (e.g., BSE) could severely impact ingredient	Current	Medium
Opportunities	Growing market for premium brands Expanding market for private labels	There is still room for growth in specialized segments	Since the mid-1980s	High

B. Scenario Analysis

Two most likely are:

1. Little growth in specialty-store and superpremium segments
2. High growth in both specialty-store and superpremium segments

C. Key Strategic Uncertainties

- Will growth in demand for superpremium specialty products continue?
- What new subcategories will emerge as significant markets?

Section 5. Internal Analysis

A. Performance Analysis

Objective Area	Objective	Status and Comment
1. Sales		
2. Profits		
3. Quality/service		
4. Cost		
5. New products		
6. Customer satisfaction		
7. People		
8. Other		

B. Summary of Past Strategy

C. Strategic Problems

Problem   Possible Action

D. Characteristics of Internal Organization

Component*   Description—Fit with Current/Proposed Strategy

* Structure, systems, culture, and people.

E. Portfolio Analysis

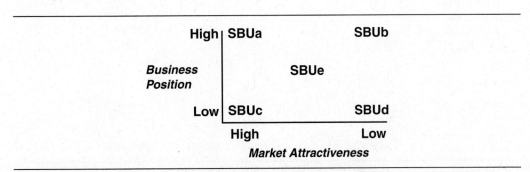

Note: An SBU (strategic business unit) can be defined by product or by segment.

F. Analysis of Strengths and Weaknesses

Reference Strategic Group	Competencies/Competency Deficiencies, Assets/Liabilities, Strengths/Weaknesses with Respect to Strategic Groups

G. Financial Projections Based on Existing Strategy

	Past	Present	Projected
Operating Statement			
Market share			
Sales			
Cost of goods sold			
Gross margin			
R&D			
Selling/advertising			
Product G&A			
Div. & corp. G&A			
Operating profit			
Balance Sheet			
Cash/AR/inventory			
AP			
Net current assets			
Fixed assets at cost			
Accumulated depreciation			
Net fixed assets			
Total assets—book value			
Estimated market value of assets			
ROA (base—book value)			
ROA (base—market value)			
Uses of Funds			
Net current assets			
Fixed asset			
Operating profit			
Depreciation			
Other			
Resources Required			
_____			
_____			
_____			
_____			

Note: Resources required could be workers with particular skills or backgrounds or certain physical facilities. A negative use of funds (i.e., profit) is a source of funds. Projected numbers could be for several relevant years.

Section 6. Summary of Proposed Strategy

A. *Business Scope—Product-Market Served*

B. *Strategy Description*

- Investment Objective   Product Market
  Withdraw   ☐
  Milk   ☐
  Maintain   ☐
  Grow in market share   ☐
  Market expansion   ☐
  Product expansion   ☐
  Vertical integration   ☐

- Value Proposition   Product Market
  Quality   ☐
  Value   ☐
  Focus   ☐
  Innovation   ☐
  Global   ☐
  Other   ☐

- Assets and Competencies Providing SCAs

- Functional Strategies

C. *Key Strategy Initiatives*

D. Financial Projections Based on Proposed Strategy

	Past	Present	Projected

Operating Statement
  Market share
  Sales
  Cost of goods sold
  Gross margin
  R&D
  Selling/advertising
  Product G&A
  Div. & corp. G&A
Operating profit
Balance Sheet
  Cash/AR/inventory
  AP
  Net current assets
  Fixed assets at cost
  Accumulated depreciation
  Net fixed assets
  Total assets—book value
  Estimated market value of assets
  ROA (base—book value)
  ROA (base—market value)
Uses of Funds
  Net current assets
  Fixed assets
  Operating profit
  Depreciation
  Other
Resources Required
  _____
  _____
  _____
  _____

INDEX

A

Aaker, Jennifer, 142, 143
acquisitions for leveraging a
    business, 200
Acura, 147
Adidas, 26, 191
advantages
    cost advantage, 96–98, 114, 144, 147,
        148, 231, 234, 239, 248, 288
    innovator's advantage, 217–219
    overview, 113, 114
    synergistic advantage, 120
    See also leveraging the business;
        sustainable competitive
        advantage
advertising, 43, 49, 50, 69, 70, 219,
    235–239
aesthetic design, 140
affinity charts, 29, 30
affordability and perceived value, 147
Aflac, 193
aggregate impact, 28
aging and aged (elderly), 78, 81
airline industry, 26, 30, 32, 40, 50, 57,
    63, 69
Ajax brand identity, 162
alliance partners, 120, 241–244, 245
alternative value propositions (AVPs),
    130–149
    appealing design, 134, 135
    business strategy challenges,
        131, 132
    corporate social programs, 135–137
    cost advantage, 145–149
    experience curve, 146, 147
    niche specialist, 137, 138
    overview, 130–133
    superior attribute or benefit,
        133, 134
    superior quality, 138–143, 147
    systems solutions, 135
    value positions, 143–148
    See also scale economies
Amazon
    alliances creating synergy, 120
    as benchmark standard, 100

early positioning, 156
failure to brand customer reviews,
    183–184
leveraged assets and competencies,
    118, 119
niche marketing, 59
ordering process as value added
    component, 48
scale economy of, 147
scope of, 4, 5
as top service company, 140
value proposition of, 6, 156, 157
American Can Company, 255
American Express, 140, 161
Ampex video recorders, 218
analyses, common goal of, 91
analysis outputs
    competitive strength grid, 50–52,
        53
    creating strategy from, 101
    overview, 9, 10
    scenario analysis, 21, 22, 87–89,
        306
    See also external analysis; internal
        analysis; opportunities;
        strengths and weaknesses
Annie Chun, 205, 223
annual strategic plan, 1, 12–13, 22,
    23. *See also* business strategies
anthropological research, 34, 35, 222
AOL, 100, 127
Apple Computer
    continuous innovations, 225
    design as AVP, 134, 135
    green rating, 79
    Internet users groups, 78
    iPhone, 134, 217
    iPod, 130, 183, 184, 223
    iPod versus Sony, 294, 295
    key customer motivation strategy,
        48
    Macintosh, 224
    Newton's failure, 69
application segment for customer
    analysis, 27, 28
Ariat, 31

Arm & Hammer, 27, 196, 204
Armstrong Rubber, 137
art price premiums, 176, 292, 293
Asahi Dry Beer, 215, 218
aspirational associations, 154, 160, 164
aspirational brand positions, 164
asset leverage, 219
assets and competencies
    of competitors, 47, 48, 301
    export of, 42
    identifying for leveraging, 200, 201
    and innovation evaluation, 224, 225
    key success factors, 66, 67
    marketing involvement in
        strategizing, 14, 15
    overview, 6, 7, 102
    protecting during strategic
        alliances, 243, 244
    and SCAs, 115–117
    and strategic imperative, 162, 163
    and strategic opportunism or drift,
        123, 124, 127, 128
    and strengths and weaknesses
        analysis, 57, 99
    as synergistic advantage, 120, 121
    See also brand assets; relevant
        assets and competencies
assets and liabilities, 150. *See also*
    brand
asset turnover and return on assets,
    92–94
associations, 159, 160. *See also* brand
    associations
Atkins Advantage, 105
automobile industry
    4-wheel drive offerings, 184, 185
    Korean perception liability, 99
    luxury car market competitor
        strength grid, 50–52
    managing visible price points, 148
    as powerful customer for tire
        companies, 64
    product and service quality
        measures, 94, 95
    relevance concept, 57, 58, 147
    transformational innovations in, 74